Leeds and its Jewish community

Leeds and its Jewish community
A history

Edited by
DEREK FRASER

Manchester University Press

Copyright © Manchester University Press 2019

While copyright in the volume as a whole is vested in Manchester University Press, copyright in individual chapters belongs to their respective authors, and no chapter may be reproduced wholly or in part without the express permission in writing of both author and publisher.

Published by Manchester University Press
Altrincham Street, Manchester M1 7JA

www.manchesteruniversitypress.co.uk

British Library Cataloguing-in-Publication Data
A catalogue record for this book is available from the British Library

ISBN 978 1 5261 2308 4 hardback
ISBN 978 1 5261 2310 7 paperback

First published 2019

The publisher has no responsibility for the persistence or accuracy of URLs for any external or third-party internet websites referred to in this book, and does not guarantee that any content on such websites is, or will remain, accurate or appropriate.

Typeset by
Servis Filmsetting Ltd, Stockport, Cheshire

The publication of this book has been made possible by the support of Phil, Jane, Amelia and Rebecca Fraser.

Selig Brodetsky by Jacob Kramer, c. 1943.
A portrait of the leader of Leeds Zionism by the most famous Leeds Jewish artist.

Contents

List of figures	*page* ix
List of tables	xii
Notes on contributors	xiii
Preface	xvi
List of abbreviations	xviii
List of Hebrew/Yiddish terms used in the text	xix
Introduction	1

Part I The context

1	National: Jews in Britain – a historical overview *Geoffrey Alderman*	9
2	Local: Leeds in the age of great cities *Derek Fraser*	23
3	Demographic: The Jewish population of Leeds – how many Jews? *Nigel Grizzard*	35

Part II The chronology

4	Jews as Yorkshiremen: Jewish identity in late Victorian Leeds *James Appell*	49
5	Britishness and Jewishness: integration *and* separation *Aaron Kent*	63

6	Pragmatism or politics: Leeds Jewish tailors and Leeds Jewish tailoring trade unions, 1876–1915 *Anne J. Kershen*	83
7	The Edwardian Jewish community and the First World War *Nigel Grizzard*	100
8	Zionism in Leeds 1892–1939 *Janet Douglas*	113
9	The unwalled ghetto: mobility and anti-Semitism in the interwar period *Amanda Bergen*	125
10	The Second World War *Ian Vellins*	149

Part III The contours of the Leeds Jewish community

11	Jewish heritage in Leeds *Sharman Kadish*	175
12	Fellowship and philanthropy *Derek Fraser*	215
13	At rest and play: leisure and sporting activities *Phil Goldstone*	235
14	The influence of personalities *Michael Meadowcroft*	267
15	Spaces of Jewish belonging *Irina Kudenko*	294
16	The community today and its recent history *Derek Fraser*	311

Index — 333

List of figures

	Selig Brodetsky by Jacob Kramer, c. 1943. A portrait of the leader of Leeds Zionism by the most famous Leeds Jewish artist. Estate of John David Roberts. By permission of the Treasury Solicitor	*page* vi
2.1	Plan re lawsuit rights, Thoresby Society, X (1899); redrawn in D. Fraser (ed.), *A History of Modern Leeds* (Manchester University Press, 1980), p. 9	31
2.2	Cossins' map of Leeds, 1726. Courtesy of Leeds City Library	32
2.3	Ordinance Survey map of Leeds, 1847. Courtesy of Leeds City Library	33
5.1	Samuel Goodman family. Courtesy of Gene Gold	78
5.2	Sam and Belle 'Gold', 1931. Courtesy of Gene Gold	79
7.1	War memorial at UHC Shadwell Lane. Courtesy of Nigel Grizzard	109
7.2	War memorial at Street Lane. Courtesy of Malcolm Sender	110
9.1	North Street premises of David and Annie Segal, c. 1913. The little girls outside are their daughters Ida and Esta. Courtesy of Amanda Bergen	140
9.2	June 1939: Mizrachi card afternoon at the home of David and Annie Segal, 1 Moorland Garth, Moortown. The small child is Bernice Pearlman (née Olsburgh). Courtesy of Amanda Bergen	141

9.3	Harold Brostoff. Early 1930s. Courtesy of Amanda Bergen	142
9.4	Wedding of Jenny Tagger to Benjamin Gothelf, c. 1926. Courtesy of Amanda Bergen	143
9.5	Minnie Marks and Harry Tagger, c. 1938. Courtesy of Amanda Bergen	144
9.6	A crowd of friends from Leeds on a walking trip, c. 1938. Minnie Marks and Harry Tagger are pictured on the right of the photo, which also shows their dear friend Ida Poyser. Courtesy of Amanda Bergen	145
9.7	Minnie Marks seated bottom right on holiday with Leeds Jewish friends, c. 1935. Courtesy of Amanda Bergen	146
10.1	War memorial at Street Lane. Courtesy of Malcolm Sender	168
10.2	Sol Myers of Leeds. Killed in action, 1942. Courtesy of Leeds Makor	169
11.1	Belgrave Street Synagogue, undated. Courtesy of Manchester Jewish Museum	199
11.2	Belgrave Street Synagogue, the Ark, undated. Courtesy of Manchester Jewish Museum	200
11.3	The Ark in the *Beth Medrash* at Leeds United Hebrew Congregation in Shadwell Lane. The pulpit came from Belgrave Street. Courtesy of Historic England. Photo by Keith Buck	201
11.4	Albert Grove *mikveh*. Photograph on the front cover of *City of Leeds, Jewish Baths, Opening by the Right Hon. The Lord Mayor, Wednesday 25th October, 1905*. Courtesy of Leeds Library and Information Service	202
11.5	Leeds Jewish Tailors' Building, inscription. Courtesy of Historic England. Photo by Bob Skingle	203
11.6	The former Leeds New Synagogue, Chapeltown Road. Courtesy of Historic England. Photo by Bob Skingle	204
11.7	Leeds United Hebrew Congregation, Shadwell Lane, the ceiling. Courtesy of Historic England. Photo by Keith Buck	205
12.1	First President of the Leeds Jewish Board of Guardians. Courtesy of Leeds Jewish Welfare Board	229

List of figures xi

12.2	Board of Guardians Offices in Chapeltown. Courtesy of Leeds Jewish Welfare Board	230
12.3	Victor Lightman. Courtesy of Leeds Jewish Welfare Board	231
12.4	Sir Keith Joseph visiting the Community Centre. Courtesy of Leeds Jewish Welfare Board	232
12.5	Leeds Jewish Housing Association, Queenshill Estate, 1962. The Community Centre with its parobalic roof is at the top of the picture. Courtesy of Leeds Jewish Housing Association	233
13.1	Wilf Rosenberg	260
13.2	Wilf Rosenberg scoring for Leeds RL	261
13.3	Bernard Shooman receiving his award. Courtesy of Bernard Shooman	262
13.4	Alan Alster with Larry Holmes. Courtesy of Alan Alster	263
13.5	Alan Alster with Mohamed Ali. Courtesy of Alan Alster	264
13.6	Alan Alster with Antony Joshua. Courtesy of Alan Alster	265
14.1	Hyman Morris with his wife	288
14.2	Alderman Morris as Mayor. Courtesy of Leeds City Library	289
14.3	Sketch of Jacob Kramer, 1918. Courtesy of Leeds City Library	290
16.1	Map of main Jewish area, 2011. Census 2011	328
16.2	Sketch of Rev. M. Abrahams, 1909. Courtesy of Leeds City Library	329
16.3	Waldenberg poster, 1949. Courtesy of Steve Waldenberg	330
16.4	Malcolm Shedlow at work in North Street, 1953. Courtesy of Malcolm Shedlow	331

List of tables

2.1	The population of Leeds Borough	*page* 25
3.1	Jewish population of Leeds together with figures on marriages and deaths	38
3.2	Children born in Leeds with the name Cohen	39
3.3	Religious minorities in Leeds from the 2001 and 2011 censuses	44
3.4	Leeds Jewish population estimates, *Jewish Year Book* 1990–2014	45
7.1	Yorkshire Regiments that included Leeds, Bradford and Sheffield with numbers of Jewish soldiers serving (1914–18)	107
15.1	Ranking of Jewish identity attributes by different groups of community members	301

Notes on contributors

Derek Fraser is Emeritus Professor of History at the University of Teesside where he served as Vice-Chancellor for eleven years. He has published books and articles on British social and urban history, including *A History of Modern Leeds* (1980) which he edited. He is best known for his book *The Evolution of the British Welfare State*, the 5th edition of which was published in 2017.

Geoffrey Alderman is the Michael Gross Professor of Politics and Contemporary History at the University of Buckingham, formerly Professor of Politics and Contemporary History and Pro-Vice-Chancellor at the University of London. He has published extensively and is the acknowledged authority on the history of Jews in Modern Britain.

Nigel Grizzard is a historian and researcher who has written extensively on Jewish affairs in Yorkshire and takes Jewish heritage tours. He was awarded a Social Science Council Research Grant to survey the remaining Jews in Chapeltown, Leeds in the 1980s. He managed a Heritage Lottery Project – 'Making their Mark' – on the contribution of the Jews to the building of Bradford from 2011–13.

James Appell has studied both history and Russian and Eastern European Studies at Oxford. His MPhil thesis was on Jews in the Kovno region. He has spent time as a journalist and has published an article on the differences between the Jewish communities of Leeds and London.

Aaron M. Kent has taught history at Austin Community College, the University of Phoenix and California State University. He is currently an instructor for the University of Maryland (Europe). His Leeds doctoral research has been published in his book, *Identity, Migration and Belonging. The Jewish Community of Leeds 1890–1920* (2015).

Anne Kershen was Barnet Shine Senior Research Fellow at Queen Mary University of London 1990–2012 and founder and Director of the Centre for the Study of Migration from 1994–2012. Her area of specialisation is migration – with particular focus on London – and she has acted as a consultant for radio and television. Her publications include: *Uniting the Tailors: Trade Unionism amongst the Tailoring Workers of London and Leeds 1870–1939* (1995); *Tradition and Change: A History of Reform Judaism in Britain 1840–1995* (1995); *Strangers, Aliens and Asians: Huguenots, Jews and Bangladeshis in Spitalfields 1660–2000* (2005); and *London the Promised Land Revisited* (2015). Her latest book, jointly edited with Colin Holmes, is *An East End Legacy. Essays in Memory of William J Fishman* (2018). She is currently an Honorary Senior Research Fellow at Queen Mary and an Honorary Senior Research Associate at the Bartlett School of Architecture, University College London, and is a FRHS and a FRSA.

Janet Douglas was formerly Principal Lecturer in Politics at Leeds Beckett University in the Cultural Studies Department. Since her retirement, her research has largely focused on the history of her adopted home town of Leeds. She has lectured widely on a variety of subjects relating to the nineteenth- and twentieth-century city, and is the author of a number of publications, many concerned with Leeds architecture. Currently she is researching 'Women and the Leeds Library' for a volume which celebrates the 250th anniversary of the Library in 2018.

Amanda Bergen originally qualified as a solicitor. She completed her history masters degree at Leeds University. Her thesis on anti-Semitism and the Leeds Jewish community in the 1930s won the Marion Sharples Prize and was published by the Thoresby Society. She has since completed a PhD on Victorian social policy.

Ian Vellins studied at Oxford and graduated with a degree in Jurisprudence. He is a retired solicitor and immigration judge, who has done masters research degrees in Jewish history at both Manchester and Leeds. He has researched the impact of Kindertransport in Yorkshire and lectures frequently on Jewish history, particularly with reference to Jewish art treasures stolen by the Nazis.

Sharman Kadish was born in London and educated at University College London and St Antony's College Oxford and at the Hebrew University of Jerusalem. She has taught at the universities of London and Manchester and is the author of a number of books on Anglo-Jewish history and heritage, including companion architectural guides *Jewish Heritage in England* (first edition 2006) and *Jewish Heritage in Gibraltar* (2007). Her monograph, *The Synagogues of Britain and Ireland: An Architectural and Social History* (Yale University Press 2011), was short-listed for the American Society of Historians of British Art Prize in 2013. A new edition of her guidebook *Jewish Heritage in Britain and Ireland* was published in 2015 by Historic England. Having been active in Jewish Built Heritage Conservation for 30 years, she is currently a member of the Northern Buildings Committee of the Victorian Society, a Fellow of the Society of Antiquaries of London as well as a Fellow of the Royal Historical Society.

Phil Goldstone has had a successful business career in international sales and is active in interfaith initiatives in Leeds. He has a masters degree from De Montford University in Sport and Society and is registered for a PhD in the history of sport in England.

Michael Meadowcroft is the former Liberal MP for Leeds West and is a frequent lecturer on the political history of Leeds. He was for many years the Chairman of the Leeds Library, whose holdings include important Leeds historical sources. Among his publications is an article on the political leadership in Leeds during the interwar years.

Irina Kudenko works as a Research and Evaluation Lead in the National STEM Learning Network at the University of York. She did her PhD in the geography department at Leeds University on the subject of Jewish identity within the Leeds Jewish community.

Preface

Anybody embarking on a history of the Leeds Jewish community is indebted to those enthusiasts who laid the groundwork for future enquiries. In particular, I and my fellow authors have learned a great deal from the writings of Louis Saipe and Murray Freeman, who have been frequently cited in these pages. We also build on the valuable compilation of words and images produced by Diane Saunders and Philippa Lester in *From the Leylands to Leeds 17*.[1] This book attempts something different but would not have been possible without the valiant efforts of those who went before us.

I have been much encouraged by the wide-ranging support the book's gestation has attracted. During the early stages, it was most helpful to have the endorsement of the Leeds Jewish Representative Council, the Leeds Jewish Historical Society, the Thoresby Society and the Leeds Civic Trust. Members of the community came forward in large numbers to produce family archives, photographs, reminiscences and documents. We place on record our warmest thanks to Sue Appleson, Cliff Barnett, Brenda Baskind, Tracy Bickler, Lee Bloomfield, Liz Bradbury, Neville Bush, Ruth Bush, Brian Daniels, James Denton, Helen Frais, Jill Franklin, Tim Friedman, Philip Glynn, Harvey Kleiman, Antony Ramm, Laurence Saffer, Victoria Sandler, Malcolm Sender, Malcolm Shedlow, Craig Simons, Steve Waldenberg, Alwyn Ziff and Suzanne Ziff. My apologies if lapses of memory have left anyone out.

I am most grateful for access to, and permission to quote from, the archives of the Leeds Jewish Welfare Board and the Leeds Jewish Housing Association. The staff at Leeds City Library have been unfailingly helpful and facilitated the use of their holdings. I am grateful to the University of Leeds and Mishcon de Rea for permission to use Jacob Kramer's portrait of Selig Brodetsky. Our editors at MUP have been a source of encouragement and advice and I thank Tom Dark and Rob Byron most warmly for seeing the book through to publication.

Preface

An edited book is by definition the work of many hands and I wish to place on record my thanks to my team of authors for their support and cooperation throughout. They treated my frequent requests with stoicism and good humour. I hope they now feel proud, as I do, to have been part of such a worthwhile and fruitful project.

I trust that readers will agree that we have collectively produced a unique and valuable addition to the historiography of both Leeds and its Jewish Community. However, our writing would not be in the public domain, nor our book published, if it had not been for the generous subvention of our benefactor. I, the authors and Manchester University Press are most grateful for this financial support, without which publication would not have been possible. I am pleased that it turned out to be a family affair!

Note

1 Leeds 17 is the postal district of the main Jewish residential area from the 1950s and 1960s onwards (now LS17). Several of the contributors to this volume, including me, refer to Jewish social progress being matched by a geographical progress northwards up the A61; that is, from the original settlement in the Leylands, to Chapeltown, then to Moortown and Alwoodley (LS17).

Derek Fraser
Leeds, May 2018

List of abbreviations

AJEX	Association of Jewish ex-Servicemen
AJR	Association of Jewish Refugees
AJTMP	Amalgamated Jewish Tailors', Machiners' and Pressers' Trade Union
AST	Amalgamated Society of Tailors
AUCO	Amalgamated Union of Clothing Operatives
BHH	Beth Hamedrash Hagadol Synagogue
BJB	British Jewish Book of Honour
COS	Charity Organisation Society
DPs	Displaced Persons
GGLU	Gasworkers' and General Labourers' Union
IZO	Jewish Territorial Society
JLB	Jewish Lads Brigade
JNF	Jewish National Fund
JP	Justice of the Peace
LJHA	Leeds Jewish Housing Association Limited
LJRC	Leeds Jewish Representative Council
PAC	Public Assistance Committee
UHC	United Hebrew Congregation
ULTTU	United Ladies' Tailors' Trade Union
WIZO	Women's International Zionist Organization

Glossary of Hebrew/Yiddish terms used in the text

Aliyah	Emigration to Israel
Ashkenazi, pl. **Ashkenazim**	Jews originating in Central and Eastern Europe.
Barmitzvah	Coming of age ceremony for boys aged 13
Beth HaMedrash	Religious study hall often attached to a synagogue
Beth Din	Religious court
Bimah	Reading platform, traditionally centrally placed in Ashkenazi synagogues
Charedi	Ultra-Orthodox Jews
Cheder (heder)	Part-time religious school
Chevroth	Small self-administered religious congregation
Frumkeit	Religious observance, piety. See also *Yiddishkeit*
Habonim	Zionist youth group
Hazan (chazan)	Cantor
Hevrah kadisha	Burial society; voluntary society which prepares the dead for burial
Kashrus/t	Keeping the dietary laws
Kibbutzim	Collective farms in Israel
Kolel	Joint enterprise association of rabbis
Landsman/landsmanshaft	A person hailing from the same town of origin
Litvak	Jews originally from the Lithuanian and Baltic region
Luhot	Tablets of the Law, dual stone bearing the Ten Commandments

Magen David	(lit.) Shield of David. Star of David emblem
Menorah	Seven-branched candelabrum. Popularly used to refer to the nine-branched candelabrum lit on the festival of Hanukah
Mikveh	Women's ritual bath. Sometimes found in the basement of a synagogue
Minyan	Quorum of 10 males, over the age of 13, required for collective worship
Ohel pl. *Ohelim*	Prayer hall at a cemetery
Polak	Jews originally from Polish regions
Schmatter	Rags, as in 'the rag trade', i.e. textiles and clothing industry
Sefer Torah, pl. *Sifrei*	Scrolls of the Law containing the Pentateuch, stored in the synagogue Ark
Sephardi, pl. **Sephardim**	Jews originating from the Iberian Peninsula
Shechita (Board of)	Organisation ensuring the provision of kosher meat for the community
Shechitah	Jewish ritual slaughter of animals for kosher food
Shool/shul	Synagogue
Shtiebl	Small, sometimes domestic, prayer meeting place
Succah	Temporary booth open to the sky erected to celebrate the festival of *Succot*
Succot	Festival of 'Tabernacles' or 'Booths'
Talmud Torah	Religious primary school for children
Treife	Description of food not permitted for consumption by Jews
Yeshiva	Rabbinical religious seminary for young men
Yiddishkeit	Traditional Judaism

Introduction

Long before the mass migration of Jews to Leeds in the last quarter of the nineteenth century, the city had already become a major commercial and industrial metropolis during what Victorians called 'the age of great cities'. Benefiting from its location at the boundary of a manufacturing region to the west and south, and an agricultural region to the north and east, by the early eighteenth century Leeds had become a thriving mercantile town as a place of exchange and commerce. The Industrial Revolution transformed Leeds, which became by the mid-nineteenth century a hive of factory-based manufacturing in wool and flax, in chemicals and engineering, as its population grew dramatically. Its fast rate of growth was due to the fertility factors which affected England as a whole, together with short-distance migration from neighbouring areas and long-distance migration predominantly from Ireland. When Jews began to arrive to add further to this growing population, they were crammed into inner city districts. Whatever their previous rural occupations in the enforced village communities of Poland, Russia or Lithuania, the uprooted Jewish migrants became classic new city dwellers. It was almost inevitable that this would be so, since Jews needed a concentration of people to provide the sustaining social and religious environment necessary for community survival.

Like migrants before and since, the Jews co-located with earlier arrivals which in turn created a form of ghetto community, created not by state fiat but by the need for social security and protection in a city where they were patently 'strangers in our midst'. Jews had particular needs beyond the characteristic immigrant comfort of the extended family network. Dietary laws required specially prepared foods which spawned retail outlets for this growing but specialised market. Jewish communities have always been characterised by both informal and formal mutual aid activity, which could only be sustained in a concentrated urban environment. Above all, Jews looked to their synagogues to provide spiritual cohesion, whatever their degree of religious observance. With synagogues came Sabbath and festival celebrations and the vital lifeblood of religious education which ensured the transmission of the culture between the generations.

In exploring the fascinating story of this migrant community, this book seeks to elucidate what the Jewish community contributed to the social, economic and cultural life of Leeds. Of equal importance (and sometimes ignored in such studies), the book also examines how Leeds, with its distinctive economic and cultural make up, affected the development of the Jewish community itself. It was a story of changing interactions between host and migrant communities in a mutually influencing environment. In terms of both urban and Jewish historiography, this book is both timely and fills a perceived gap. There has been a rich flowering of Jewish historical studies in recent decades, particularly associated with the scholars working under the leadership of the late David Cesarani (who spent some time as a lecturer in Leeds). However, this work has almost exclusively concentrated on London, perhaps justified by the fact that over two thirds of the UK's Jewish population is located there. This book tilts the balance back towards what Londoners, in a somewhat patronising way, always refer to as 'the provinces'. Moreover, Leeds was and is an important Jewish community in its own right, the third largest in the country, and in the mid-twentieth century was the city with the highest Jewish percentage (always said to be 5%). Developments in urban history have moved the subject away from a narrow emphasis on physical development and urban social problems (slums and suburbs) to encompass a broader cultural approach which makes this book particularly relevant. Urban historians have long contended that the study of cities brings into sharp focus wider developments that can be analysed within an individual city context, and the contents of this book exemplify that view.

There is an understandable current political interest in immigration, which has spawned studies in historical migration experiences. The story of the Leeds Jewish community provides a micro case study of the wider patterns of international migration in recent European history. When geographers study migration, they seek to explain the relative importance of the 'push' factors which cause migrants to leave their country of origin, as against the 'pull' factors which attract them to their country of destination. Migration specialists prefer to think in terms of 'voluntary' and 'forced' migration, where the former is motivated by the pull of the destination, while the latter is prompted by the push engendered in the home country. In current terminology, forced migrants tend to be referred to (sometimes incorrectly) as refugees, while those leaving to seek a better life elsewhere are described as economic migrants. In Leeds, the small early and mid-nineteenth-century

Jewish population grew as a result of the commercial attraction of the city, as mainly central European Jews arrived to develop business opportunities, many German families moving on to Bradford. In the late nineteenth century, by contrast, the rapid increase in numbers arriving was almost wholly caused by religious persecution within the Russian Empire. Anecdotally, many of those reaching Leeds were actually en route to Liverpool from their east coast port of arrival in the hope of reaching America. Indeed, in some Leeds families there are (probably apocryphal) stories that their ancestors were led to believe they had reached America when they got to Leeds, for there were then as now unscrupulous people exploiting the ignorance and desperation of the migrants. On the other hand, our historical study reveals a concentration of location of origin for Leeds arrivals which suggests a logistical and communications network that identified Leeds as the planned destination point.

Similar push factors explain the second wave of Jewish migration in the 1930s; nothing like as big, but clearly identifiable, as German Jews fled the Nazi persecution – including the dramatic stories of the Kindertransport and the later arrival of holocaust survivors. The hostile political environment also spawned smaller scale Jewish immigration from Egypt in the 1950s and Iran in the 1960s and 1970s. Migration is actually not just about transnational incomers, and as Leeds developed further as a vibrant commercial and industrial centre in the twentieth century, so it attracted many Jewish citizens from elsewhere in Britain who were motivated by career and job opportunities. These were perhaps more than balanced by those Leeds Jews choosing to leave the city, not returning to the original home country (as is common with certain ethnic groups) but often to London, following their children, or to Israel after 1948. It is said that families whose origins lie elsewhere are more likely to be willing to up sticks a second time, and there is a sizeable Leeds Jewish diaspora both elsewhere in the UK and in Israel and beyond.

What happened to these alien incomers over two or three generations is a remarkable story of social mobility. In political rhetoric, much is made of the 'challenge' of large-scale immigration and the social problems engendered – and the Leeds host community was certainly concerned about this obviously un-English invasion. Yet, migration experts point out that migrants are often characterised by hard work and entrepreneurial talent, highly motivated to make a success in their new country. The Leeds Jewish community is largely a success story of social and economic progress. Beginning, like immigrants elsewhere, in cheap and overcrowded tenements and working in what were termed 'sweat shops', the new arrivals had to pursue an economy of makeshifts, supplementing meagre wages with domestic activity involving their wives and children. Many brought highly developed skills which were often diluted under the harsh demands of the Leeds industrial environment. Most became absorbed into the industrial working class and were involved in trade union and radical (usually socialist) political activity. The expansion of the ready-made clothing industry (notably Burtons), which gave much employment to Jewish male and female workers in the interwar years, reinforced the character of the Jewish working population as proletarian. Yet, by the second half of the twentieth century, there had been an almost total embourgeoisement of the Leeds Jewish working class.

This was partly a generational issue. The second generation, the children of the immigrants, had known the poverty of their parents and were motivated to improve the family lot. Some worked in skilled and semi-skilled trades and established businesses in footwear, furniture, printing or engineering. Their children and grandchildren were Leeds born and benefited from an English education, going to college and university. This generation was able to penetrate the higher levels of law, medicine, education, accountancy and other professions, which was a tribute to the application and industry of the Leeds Jews themselves as well as to the essentially meritocratic and relatively open social and economic structure of the city. There were periods of vitriolic anti-Semitism and there were insidious forms of prejudice in alleged social and educational bans or quotas, which for example led the embryonic Leeds Jewish middle class to establish Moor Allerton as a Jewish golf club. Yet Leeds Jews apparently suffered little of the so-called 'ethnic penalty' which has held back some other more visibly ethnic minority communities. As the twenty-first century economy has changed dramatically, so a new generation is exploiting the opportunities by establishing media- and internet-based businesses. This book's sponsor (third generation maternally and fifth generation paternally) is a good example of the new economy and of the distance travelled since the original emigration from Eastern Europe.

The social mobility described has been accompanied by a degree of spacial concentration and development, which though common is not universal among urban Jewish communities. Leeds is often compared to Manchester and the Jewish community's northerly progress up the Chapeltown Road is paralleled by a similar journey up Cheetham Hill Road, though Leeds has no equivalent of Manchester's southern outpost development in Didsbury. The Leeds Jewish community's social and economic progress has been exemplified in a steady physical mobility from the Leylands, to Chapeltown, through Chapel Allerton to Moortown and thence to Alwoodley and beyond. Leeds Jews have chosen to live no more than a mile either side of the A61 over the last 100 years. However, not all cities have followed the same pattern. In Birmingham, for example, the similar central city concentration was fragmented as the Jews moved in at least three different suburban directions, which has left the magisterial (and listed) Singers Hill Synagogue now in splendid isolation from its dispersed community. Modern urban historians stress the importance of citizens collectively making their town's history in

Introduction 5

the decisions they take, and this is vividly illustrated in the residential choices Leeds Jews have made both individually and collectively. Once freed from the poverty of the Leylands, many Jews moved into the North Street area and then to the southern end of Chapeltown Road. There they occupied the solidly built terraces of a previous generation of Leeds merchants who had moved up the hill to be literally above the smoke of the city. By the 1950s, many had moved on to Moortown and in the 1960s and after to Alwoodley.

This physical concentration reinforced community cohesion, as a Jewish social infrastructure was developed alongside the geographic progress. Food shops, butchers and poulterers, wine merchants and small retailers meeting every family need abounded in Chapeltown Road, along with synagogues and charitable institutions. Three splendid buildings – the Rakusen food factory, the Jewish Institute and the New Synagogue – neatly reflected the economic, social and spiritual progress. Yet even as this comforting physical environment was being created, it was fast being superseded by the residential choices being increasingly made by this now socially mobile community. The splendid New Synagogue opened in 1932 well illustrates the point. Designed to express both the successful transition from immigrant origins and a confidence in the permanence of the future, the building was a clear outward statement that 'we have arrived and are here to stay'. However, the further movement northwards to Moortown following the tram to Street Lane rapidly reduced the local Jewish population it was intended to serve. In fact, the New Synagogue was a viable entity for barely three decades and is now a dance studio. In turn, the newly developed Moortown community appropriated existing buildings for its use and both a Methodist Church and cinema were converted to synagogues.

Modern urban history is increasingly concerned with culture and one of the themes being explored is identity. How did the host community view this segment of urban society and how did they regard themselves? It is important to distinguish here between assimilation and integration. Between, say, 1880 and 1914, it would have been obvious to Leeds citizens that these newly arrived strangers were outsiders. Their mode of dress, physical appearance and language will have marked them out. From the end of the First World War, as Jewish citizens became absorbed into the commercial and social life of the city, they were less visibly identifiable – even allowing for their geographical concentration. Given the social mobility already discussed and the penetration into the upper echelons of Leeds business and professional activity, Jews became integrated, but not necessarily assimilated, into British society. Communal and religious leaders now bemoan the behavioural patterns which appear to dilute the Jewish identity, where many marry out of the faith – often depriving their children of a Jewish upbringing and education – or move away both physically and spiritually. Such people are probably best described as having been assimilated, where they have a Jewish ancestry but currently feel little current Jewish identity. By contrast, despite varying degrees of religious observance, most Leeds Jews retain a clear culturally Jewish identity.

Of course, self-identity is not a single entity and most people can comfortably accommodate two or more descriptors. Hence, many Jews would describe themselves as British Jews rather than Jewish Britons. The leading civic, professional and business roles occupied by Leeds Jewish citizens, such as councillor, Lord Mayor, MP, judge, captain of industry, head teacher or Vice-Chancellor, demonstrate that the Jewish community is integrated into the multicultural mix which Leeds has become. This book suggests that the number of Jews in Leeds has fallen to about 6,000–7,000 from a peak of probably 25,000 in the second quarter of the twentieth century. The difficulty of precisely quantifying the size and character of the community may be reduced in the future by the digitisation of census material and the use of new methodologies. Despite this decline in numbers, the Leeds community is characterised by vibrant and clearly identifiably Jewish institutions. Giving the lie to the sometimes expressed public perception that all Jews are wealthy, there are strong and active Jewish charities meeting welfare, housing and elderly care needs within the community. There is a successful social centre and a variety of sporting and cultural organisations. The active members and leaders of synagogues and other Jewish institutions are often the same people who have made a mark in their business or professional life and are thus integrated into Leeds society, while retaining a clear Jewish cultural identity.

The authors have been encouraged to use a wide range of analytical and historiographical methodologies. The historical research has encompassed a rich variety of source material, including newspapers and other printed records, official reports, institutional records and publications, yearbooks and business directories, manuscript collections where available, political archives and propaganda and census data. Visual records have been researched and use has been made of oral testimony, including the archive of interviews recorded in recent years. Building on previous work on Leeds Jewish history, this book now stands as the definitive fully researched history of the Leeds Jewish community.

Part I
The context

1

National: Jews in Britain – a historical overview

Geoffrey Alderman

Although it is possible that Jews – merchants, perhaps, purchasing Cornish tin – visited the British Isles before the eleventh century, there was no settled Jewish community in Britain until after the Norman Conquest. Following his victory at Hastings in 1066, Duke William of Normandy, anxious to establish strong financial and economic ties between his existing French territories and his newly-acquired English domains, invited and encouraged Jewish businessmen and their families then living in Rouen to cross the Channel and relocate themselves in England.

These were indeed 'the king's Jews'. That is to say, as the only residents of Norman England legally entitled to lend money upon interest, they enjoyed the full protection of the Crown, to which they could appeal if a debtor defaulted on her or his loan repayment. Repayment of the debts owed to them was in fact guaranteed by the Crown, which levied a fee per loan. A special department of government – the Exchequer of the Jews – was established for this purpose. In practice, it acted as a Ministry of Jewish Affairs.

But this royal protection was both a blessing and a curse. As the Jews of York were to discover in 1190, in troubled economic times those in debt to them did not take kindly to having the debts enforced by the king's officers: extensive rioting, encouraged by a number of such individuals, resulted in virtually all of York's 150 or so Jews being massacred 'without [so recorded the chronicler William of Newburgh] any scruple of Christian conscientiousness'.

Although the Jews of medieval England (never numbering more than 5,000 souls) had originally settled in London, within a century they had established communities in most of England's large towns, including York, Lincoln, Northampton, Winchester, Gloucester, Bristol, Norwich and Oxford. There were certainly periods of relative tranquillity when the Jews prospered and even enjoyed cordial relations with their Christian hosts. The reign of Henry II

(1133–89) is in this respect regarded as a 'golden age'. But with the spread of the Blood Libel (which originated in Norwich in 1144), and the deterioration of law and order during the reigns of Richard I (1189–99) and his brother John (1199–1216), the position of the Jews became ever more precarious. During the reign of Henry III (1216–72), the impoverished crown engaged in systematic spoliation of Jewish wealth, a policy which was enforced with even greater rigour by his son and successor Edward I. In desperation, some Jews undoubtedly engaged in coin-clipping: hundreds of Jews were consequently hanged. In 1290, in return for a parliamentary grant of £100,000, Edward bowed to popular demand and expelled England's remaining Jews to Northern France.

Jews were not permitted to re-enter England until some 360 years later. But it is certain that early modern England was never entirely 'Jew-free'. To begin with, Jews who agreed (however insincerely) to convert to Catholicism were spared the 1290 decree. Following the expulsion of Jews from Spain (1492), and the increasing hostility between Catholic Spain and Protestant England in the late sixteenth century, individual Jews travelled to and settled in England, often presenting themselves simply as refugees from Spanish and/or Catholic persecution. In 1581, a Bohemian mining engineer then living in Bristol, Joachim Ganz, admitted in public that he was Jewish. In the 1630s, there was certainly a small community of mainly Portuguese Jews living quite openly in that great port city; although nominally Christian they appear to have been leading a way of life that was recognisably Jewish. And by mid-century, a community of Jews was living quietly, but again relatively openly, in London.

The rise of Puritanism had certainly acted as a catalyst in this process of toleration. Puritans were not necessarily friendly to Jews. But the Puritan ethic was marked by a desire to understand – and even imitate – the ways of the Hebrews. In the 1650s, following the execution of King Charles I and the installation of a military dictatorship led by the Puritan commander Oliver Cromwell, the political climate became distinctly philosemitic. The Puritans who had abolished the monarchy had a great deal of sympathy with all things Jewish. Puritan divines read the 'Old Testament' in Hebrew. Some even circumcised themselves.

Cromwell agreed to consider a petition from the Amsterdam Rabbi Manasseh ben Israel that Jews be permitted to dwell once more in England. The precise circumstances surrounding this petition are unclear. Manasseh played on the Puritan conviction that the appearance or reappearance of the Messiah was at hand, but that this would not happen until Jews lived in England once more. But in the event, it was not Manasseh's petition that was granted in 1656, but that of seven Marranos [crypto-Jews who had secretly practised their religion in post-expulsion Spain and Portugal, but who had later relocated in the Spanish Netherlands] already living in London. Furious with Manasseh for having poked his unwelcome nose into their business, they argued simply for the right of private worship for Jews already settled here, and for permission to purchase land for a cemetery outside the limits of the City of London. The last thing they wanted was the right of Jews to enter the country as they pleased. And they certainly did not relish the unwelcome publicity to which Manasseh's melodramatic initiative had given rise.

In the debates that ensued within and beyond the Council of State a great deal was said about the role that Jews might play in the economic development of the country. But the truth probably was that Cromwell and his Puritan allies hoped that by inviting the Jews to live in England they might be all the more easily converted to Christianity. There were clearly sharp differences of opinion within the Council of State. The actual page which – it is said – recorded the decision to readmit the Jews was torn out of the Minute Book and does not survive. Perhaps there was no such decision. There was certainly no Act of Parliament, or even a public proclamation.

The community of the Cromwellian Resettlement was a Sephardic community. Many of the Jews who took advantage of Cromwell's generosity were Marranos and were, on the whole, well-to-do merchants and tradesmen. They lived in a very small area of the City of London, establishing a synagogue which was rebuilt in 1701 in a courtyard in the City known as Bevis Marks. This synagogue, a replica of the Great Synagogue in Amsterdam, is still standing and in regular use – the oldest surviving synagogue in Britain.

Cromwell died in 1658. Two years later the English monarchy was restored. For a moment it was unclear whether the Jews of the Resettlement would be permitted to remain in the country. But the tolerant outlook of Charles II seems to have protected them from the ambitions of those who hoped to expel them once more. The famous Restoration diarist and gossip Samuel Pepys recorded a visit to Bevis Marks on *Simchat Torah* ['Rejoicing of the Law']: he compared the noisy service to a mad-house. Clearly the Jews practised their religion openly and without hindrance.

In time, the Sephardim were joined by Ashkenazic, Yiddish-speaking Jews from Germany – wealthy merchants, jewellers and craftsmen. Soon, Ashkenazim outnumbered Sephardim, a situation which intensified during the early Hanoverian years. Several large and imposing Ashkenazic synagogues were built in the City of London, which by the mid-eighteenth century also boasted a number of smaller houses of worship – *shtiebls* – established by less wealthy Jews of German and, significantly, Polish origin.

During the course of the century, large numbers of Polish Jews settled in England – small tradesmen and itinerant peddlers. Jewish communities began to thrive in the large provincial towns, such as Birmingham, Manchester and Leeds, as well as in Scotland (Glasgow and Edinburgh) and Wales (Cardiff and Swansea). Most of these congregations were too small to afford to appoint a full-time rabbi. Instead, they looked to the rabbi of the oldest Ashkenazic synagogue in England, the Great Synagogue (also in the City of London), as their religious leader. And successive rabbis of the Great Synagogue came to be regarded as the 'chief rabbis' of the German and Polish Jews of Britain.

The community of Spanish and Portuguese Jews languished. At the beginning of the eighteenth century there were some 2,000 Spanish and Portuguese Jews in England. The number had not grown significantly by the end of the century. The major reasons for this state of affairs were inter-marriage and assimilation. One the one hand this demonstrates how well these Jews socialised with the host society. Wealthy Sephardim seem to have mingled easily with the social and political elites of Hanoverian England; a good number married their daughters into the English landed aristocracy. Several Sephardi converts to Christianity became Members of Parliament.

On the other hand, we should not underestimate the intensity of populist Judeophobia or the ease with which it could be exploited by unscrupulous politicians of the period. In 1753, the government of George II agreed to sponsor legislation to make it easier for foreign-born Jews to become naturalised British citizens. This concession was a sort of 'thank you' for the financial support which Jews had given to the government a few years earlier, during the attempt by the Jacobite pretender to the throne – 'Bonnie Prince Charlie' – to invade England and oust the Hanoverians (1745). No sooner had the legislation been passed than a vicious agitation was whipped up against it by opposition politicians. In 1754, following these 'Jew Bill' riots, the Act was quickly repealed.

The need for concerted action on occasions such as these led the two communities, or 'nations' as they called themselves – the Spanish and Portuguese Jews and the German and Polish congregations – to consider ways in which they might cooperate, even though on a day-to-day basis they had little to do with each other. In 1760, their leaders agreed to form a 'London Committee of Deputies of British Jews', so called because each participating congregation elected representatives ('Deputies') to it. Meeting infrequently at first, the Board of Deputies (as it was subsequently known) had by the early nineteenth century come to be regarded as the official representative body of British Jewry, and its President as the acknowledged lay leader of the Jewish communities of the British Isles.

The period of the French Revolution and the Napoleonic Wars marked a watershed in the history of British Jewry. Further immigration of foreign-born Jews to Britain all but ceased. In the turmoil of war – and in the midst of the Industrial Revolution – there was a great deal of popular xenophobia. At the same time Jewish financiers entered into lucrative partnerships with the government, being especially helpful in financing the war effort. When the army of the Duke of Wellington needed to be paid in gold, in Spain, the only banking house in London that could guarantee to facilitate such payments was the English branch of the House of Rothschild. At the other end of the social scale, we find that Jews served in the navy of Admiral Lord Nelson and fought under him at the Battle of Trafalgar (1805). Jews became – and came to be regarded as – patriotic Englishmen and women.

Britain itself became a more tolerant society. In the post-1815 period, which was characterised by a reforming zeal in all facets of life, liberal-minded politicians began to sweep away discriminatory legislation dating from earlier centuries. In 1835, Jews received the right to vote in parliamentary elections (a right which they had in practice been exercising freely, though illegally, for some considerable time hitherto). A decade later they were permitted to play a full part in local government. In 1836, the Board of Deputies received statutory recognition in an Act of Parliament passed that year to reform the civil registration of marriages.

The prize that eluded British Jewry was full political emancipation – meaning the right of professing Jews to stand as candidates for, and be elected to, the House of Commons. Jews were not the only religious group to be denied this right. Catholics had only won the right in 1829. Unitarians did not then enjoy the right, nor did atheists.

The truth was that most British Jews did not consider this subject of much, if any, importance. It was not until 1911 that Members of Parliament received any kind of salary. In the nineteenth century one needed to have a considerable private income in order to pursue a parliamentary career. For this reason, most British Jews had not the slightest interest in being elected to Parliament or in agitating for this right to be conferred. The campaign for political emancipation was in practice conducted by a few very wealthy Jews, pre-eminently Lionel de Rothschild and his fellow financier (and communal rival) David Salomons.

The religious leadership of British Jewry, in the shape of successive (Ashkenazic) Chief Rabbis (Solomon Hirschell, 1802–42 and Nathan Adler, 1845–90), was ambivalent on this issue. While neither Hirschell nor Adler opposed political emancipation, neither was enthusiastic about a process which it was feared would encourage assimilation. The two issues which preoccupied these rabbis were the religious laxity of British Jewry overall and the establishment of a Reform synagogue in London in the early 1840s. Hirschell issued a 'Ban' on the Reform congregation, while Adler formed a strong alliance against it with the acknowledged lay leader of British Jewry – the banker and born-again ultra-Orthodox Moses Montefiore – who as President of the Board of Deputies ensured that no 'Reformer' could be elected as a Deputy. The part played by the Deputies in the campaign for political emancipation was – not surprisingly therefore – minimal.

A further worry for these leaders was the evident connection between those who campaigned for political emancipation and the Reform movement. While neither Rothschild nor Salomons were Reformers, many of their supporters were, including the financier and social reformer Isaac Lyon Goldsmid (one of the founders of the University of London). As early as 1830, as Montefiore noted in his diary, Isaac Goldsmid had warned the Board of Deputies that if it did not support his campaign for political emancipation, he would 'establish a new Synagogue ... [and] ... would alter the present form of prayer to that in use in the [Reform] Synagogue in Hamburg'. And so it was.

The foundation of a Reform synagogue was in part, therefore, a deliberate act of communal disobedience – a breaking of ranks that gave at least some of the emancipationists a quite separate platform from which to launch their campaign, in which Isaac Goldsmid played a critical role. In 1838, he broke with the Deputies and in 1845 took the extreme step of leading a deputation to Sir Robert Peel, the Prime Minister, in opposition to one led by Moses Montefiore; Goldsmid claimed to speak in the name of British Jewry, and argued that it was precisely because they had reformed their ritual that the Jews – that is, the Reformers – had proved that they were worthy of emancipation.

Emancipation came in 1858, when a minority Conservative government led in the House of Commons by the baptised Jew Benjamin Disraeli persuaded Parliament that professing Jews who were elected to the Commons need not take a Christian oath before they could take their seats. Within a few years there was a distinct Jewish 'lobby' in Parliament. The issue then ceased to be of any political importance.

As the late Dr Vivian Lipman observed, British Jewry in 1850 – numbering in all no more than around 60,000 persons – resembled a pyramid, but one whose base was much broader and flatter at the bottom relative to its midriff. At the top were members of the so-called 'Cousinhood' – a small group of exceedingly wealthy, interrelated families that funded most of the community's ecclesiastical and philanthropic endeavours. Beneath them were the Anglo-Jewish gentry – comfortably-off middle-class families engaged, for the most part, in business and the professions, who also provided the day-to-day management of communal institutions. At the pyramid's base were the poor, many of whom were very poor indeed.

In 1855, the *St. James's Medley* estimated that about five-twelfths of London Jewry were of the 'lower classes', barely making a living.[1] The problem of the poor obsessed mid-Victorian Jewry. The communal leadership did not want this pauper class to become a burden on local non-Jewish ratepayers who maintained parish workhouses. It also wished to break the link between poverty and criminality among the Anglo-Jewish pauper classes. In 1859, the major synagogues of London established a 'Board of Guardians & Trustees for the Relief of the Jewish Poor' in the capital. The Board did not regard poverty as necessarily a crime, or as self-evident proof of idleness. Accordingly, loans and apprenticeships were financed side by side with schemes of cash and medical relief. Cases on the books for more than six months were freshly investigated. Jews wishing to emigrate (generally to the USA or the colonies), or to return to their country of origin, were given assistance. It was a condition of relief by the Board that children attended school; certificates of attendance were accordingly required. Relief was not available at all during the first six months' residence. What were termed 'confirmed paupers' were despatched to the mercies of the Poor Law.

The overriding aim, however, was to put the poor in a position where they might fend for themselves. Poverty caused by seasonal unemployment, or simply by a depression of trade or industry, was to be met by a policy of diversification, of schemes of training for a wider variety of occupations. In time, however, the Board of Guardians came to concern itself with the wider issues of housing and sanitation with which the poor had to contend.

The Board of Guardians model pioneered in London was adopted and developed in south Lancashire and other provincial localities. In Birmingham, a Board of Guardians was set up in 1870, awkwardly co-existing with the much older Hebrew Philanthropic Society. In Glasgow, the Board of Guardians itself emerged out of the earlier Philanthropic Society; the Board of Guardians at Leeds dated from 1878. Whether all these efforts would have succeeded in actually eradicating Jewish poverty in Britain is of course problematic. The approach adopted by these organisations was, however, predicated upon a dangerous assumption, namely that what was being confronted was finite in size. By the late 1870s, it was becoming clear that emigration of Jews from Eastern Europe was accelerating and that, moreover, its fundamental characteristics were changing.

The assassination of Tsar Alexander II (1881) and the subsequent persecution of Jews in the Russian Empire wrought a profound and fundamental change in the size and social composition of British Jewry. In the mid-Victorian period there were perhaps as many as 60,000 Jews living in the British Isles. Between 1882 and 1906 this 'native' community was swamped by at least twice that number of Jewish refugees from Russia and Russian-Poland. Poor (for the most part), Yiddish-speaking, Orthodox, socialist and Zionist, these new arrivals (the bulk of whom came in the period 1882–1906) posed a number of major challenges for the existing community.

To begin with, their arrival in Britain marked out British Jewry as 'foreign' rather than as British. A serious anti-Jewish agitation arose, culminating in the Aliens Act of 1905, the first modern restriction on the right of aliens to freely enter the UK. Partly as a result, the communal grandees took steps to encourage the dispersal of immigrant Jews from slum-ridden inner-city centres and relocate them to relatively anonymous suburbs. But if the demographic impact of the immigrants was dramatic in London, it was spectacular in the provinces: between 1881 and 1911 the size of provincial Jewry more than quadrupled, from 20,000 to nearly 100,000. Existing provincial communities were revitalised by the immigrants; others were virtually immigrant creations. Towns such as Birmingham (the Jewish population of which numbered 5,500 by 1911), Liverpool and Glasgow (7,000 each), Leeds (25,000) and pre-eminently Manchester (30,000) became major centres of Anglo-Jewry, with their own independent communal structures. By 1911, Jews constituted 2% of the population of London but 5.8% of the population of Leeds and 5.5% in Manchester. Provincial Jewry as a whole possessed, for the first time, an existence of its own; it was no longer a mere adjunct of the capital.[2]

Meanwhile, the passionate orthodoxy of the immigrants led them to reject the then existing religious structure in Anglo-Jewry – principally the idea of a Chief Rabbinate. When, on the death of Nathan Adler (1890), his son Hermann succeeded him as Ashkenazic Chief Rabbi, a veritable *kulturkampf* erupted: Hermann refused to recognise the rabbinic status of the rabbis whom the immigrants had brought with them from Eastern Europe, and these gentlemen in turn refused to recognise his status or authority, and indeed openly flouted it. We find that in Leeds immigrants kept away from the *Englische Shool* – the Great Synagogue erected in Belgrave Street – and founded instead, in the early 1870s, the *Beth Hamedrash Hagadol* ['Great House of Study'], the Central Synagogue and *Beth Hamedrash* in Templar Street (1885), the *Mariempoler Chevra* in Hope Street (1885) and the *Polnische Shool* ['Polish Synagogue'] in Byron Street (1893). A similar pattern emerged in other provincial centres, and – naturally – in London.

On Hermann Adler's death (1911), there was a serious communal debate as to whether a Chief Rabbinate was any longer wanted or needed. But wealthy supporters of the institution, who saw in the office an indispensable instrument of social control, appear to have won the argument: Dr J. H. Hertz was appointed to the office in 1913, serving until his death in 1946. But Hertz of all people knew that he walked a tightrope. Foreign-born himself, he was forced to concede a status and a standing to fellow immigrant rabbis, especially those serving in synagogal bodies not under his direct control (principally the Federation of Synagogues in London) and in major provincial centres. But the independent Orthodox community in Gateshead was never reconciled to him and succeeded (in spite of Hertz's best efforts) in establishing a *yeshiva* on Tyneside that easily rivalled Jews' College, the London-based training centre for dog-collared 'Reverends' that Nathan Adler had set up.

The immigrants also brought with them a vibrant proletarian culture. Prominent within this was a history of militant collective bargaining. The only substantially Jewish industrial employment to be found in Great Britain before 1880 was the cigar- and cigarette-making activities of the small community of London-based Dutch Jews; the first recorded strike of Jewish workers in Britain involved this community, in 1858. But by the end of the 1880s an authentic Yiddish-speaking Jewish trade-union movement had come into existence in England, covering various branches of the clothing trades, the boot and shoe industries, cabinet making, the tobacco trades and a miscellany of smaller occupations.

In some cases, where Jewish workers joined existing unions, specifically Jewish branches were formed, usually to cope with language difficulties. Thus, there existed in London and Manchester Jewish branches of the National Amalgamated Furnishings Trades' Association, complete with Yiddish rule-books. A special Jewish branch of the National Union of Boot and Shoe Operatives was established in 1890. But, certainly in the clothing trades, the preference at this time was for separate Jewish unions: the Manchester Jewish Tailors', Machinists' & Pressers' Trade Union (formed at the end of 1889), which by 1903 could claim to have recruited 60% of Jewish tailors in the city; the Leeds Jewish Working Tailors' Trade Society, which had some 3,000 members on its books by 1888; in London the Jewish Boot Finishers' Society (formed early in 1886), the Hebrew Cabinet Makers' Union (founded 1887), the London Tailors' & Machinists' Society (1886), the United Ladies' Tailors and Mantle-makers (1889) and the Independent Tailors Machinists & Pressers.

The immigrants also provided fertile ground for the propagation and growth of socialist dogma. Early attempts to establish specifically 'Jewish' socialist parties in England all ended in failure. In 1907, the Marxist Jacob Lestschinsky opined that the number of Jewish socialists in London amounted to no more than about 200, in a community – he claimed – of some 130,000 persons.[3] To some extent the weaknesses apparent in the Jewish labour movement in Britain at the end of the nineteenth century and the beginning of the twentieth constituted no more than an extreme case of the general experience of trade unionism and socialism in Britain at this time: only a minority of British workers were unionised; hostility to socialism was very strong – especially within the Trades Union Congress; socialism itself was hardly a growth industry. Nonetheless, it was pre-eminently in and through the world of trade unions that British Jewry found a place for itself within the British Labour movement.

There were, however, a number of factors which affected the Anglo-Jewish working classes in a uniquely adverse manner. The first was that their outlook differed fundamentally from the British craft tradition; they saw themselves, as we have already observed, as potentially upwardly mobile, not as perpetual members of the proletariat. In the second place, they had to contend with a special blend of lay and ecclesiastical opposition, at one and the same time brutal and subtle; had Hermann Adler championed the London Jewish tailors as Cardinal Manning had the London Gentile dockers, the course of Anglo-Jewish labour history might have been very different.

The third factor, so obvious that it can be easily overlooked, was that the continued influx of fresh waves of immigrant labour created, as Lestschinsky observed, a 'reserve army' of Jewish workers, all seeking work in a very narrow range of employments. Fourthly, some of the most energetic and talented leaders of Jewish trade unions in Britain were attracted to the United States. Under the secretaryship of David Policoff, the Manchester Jewish Tailors' Machinists' and Pressers' Union grew to embrace about three-quarters of all the Jewish tailors in that city. In 1905, Policoff emigrated to the USA. For the first time in a decade his union was not represented at the TUC, and it collapsed shortly afterwards. Finally, we need to remember that the mass of Jewry was concentrated in London; London, certainly until the First World War, was an area of trade union weakness. If we examine the development of Jewish trade unionism in Leeds, the picture that emerges is far less depressing.

The story of Jewish trade unionism in the Leeds ghetto exemplifies the points which have just been made. The Jewish Working Tailors' Trade Society had been formed as long ago as 1876, but was unable to take effective action to force the Jewish masters to comply with the Factory Acts until the immigrant influx. Both Orthodox and socialist Jewish workers supported its campaign. In 1885, it conducted a successful two-week strike for a one-hour reduction in the length of the working day, without loss of pay. Three years later, however, another strike – to achieve the closed shop – was defeated by the masters and the Society – then numbering around 3,000 members – collapsed.

This outcome might have spelt the end of Jewish trade unionism in the Leeds clothing industry, more particularly as the employers drew up a blacklist to isolate potential troublemakers. Prominent members of William Morris's Socialist League made it their business to involve themselves in Jewish labour problems in Leeds, and to make friends with the Jewish socialists, such as Lewis Frank and Morris Kemmelhor, who were now to be found dominating the organisation of the Leeds Jewish tailors. In February 1890, a most remarkable alliance was formed between the Jewish tailors in the city and the English gas workers, united to fight for shorter hours; in August the tailors struck, and by the end of that month had won a uniform twelve-hour day.

The union of Jewish tailors and English gas workers in Leeds came to an end in 1891. But, in 1893, the entire Jewish branch of the Leeds tailoring trade was reorganised as the Leeds Jewish Tailors' Machinists' & Pressers' Union, with (from 1895) a full-time paid General Secretary, Sam Freedman. The Union was regularly represented at the Trades Union Congress and became an early affiliate of the Labour Representation Committee – which became the Labour Party in 1906. Membership rose from 1,180 in 1902 to 4,465 in 1913. With its social clubs and schemes of sickness and unemployment benefit, the union became, in effect, the premier Jewish representative communal body in the city.

It would be an exaggeration to say that this political dynamic would never have happened but for the great immigration. The decline and fall of the old Liberal Party in the first quarter of the twentieth century would have affected Anglo-Jewish politics irrespective of other circumstances. There were, however, matters of peculiar interest to the Jews that impinged upon the Jewish view of Liberalism, as of Conservatism, at this time. Pre-eminent among these was the support given by the early twentieth-century Conservative Party to state aid for faith schools, an issue which bitterly divided the Liberals in the decades immediately preceding the First World War. Another was the fondness of David Lloyd George, when Chancellor of the Exchequer, for indulging in crude anti-Semitic rhetoric aimed at Lord Rothschild, the premier Jewish peer and still, in many ways – not least as President of the United Synagogue – the premier British Jew.

The United Synagogue had been established by a private Act of Parliament in 1870. This legislation amalgamated the three largest Ashkenazi synagogues in London, and placed at their ecclesiastical head 'a Chief Rabbi' – first Nathan Adler, then his son Hermann, then Dr Hertz, to be followed (1948–65) by Israel Brodie, and after him by Immanuel Jakobovits (1967–91). The United Synagogue was – and has remained – Orthodox in its religious leadership while catering – in the main – for congregants who were and are not Orthodox in practice.

In its early decades, there was little to distinguish the service at a United Synagogue constituent congregation from that to be found at the West London Reform Synagogue, which opened its doors in 1842: an organ; a mixed choir; a disdain for the Talmud and the multifarious minutiae of Orthodox practice. The contrast was certainly much greater with respect to the Liberal Jewish Synagogue, which dated from 1911 and which boasted services mainly in English and mixed-gender seating. To the religious right of the United Synagogue was the Federation of Synagogues, founded in 1887 as a loose and quarrelsome alliance of 'minor' synagogues established by strictly Orthodox immigrants from Eastern Europe, and to the right of the Federation was – and is – the Union of Orthodox Hebrew Congregations, which dates from 1926 and is an umbrella body serving the interests of over a hundred so-called 'ultra-Orthodox' communities in London and the provinces.

However, by virtue of the wealth it represented and the social status of its leading members, by the end of the Great War the United Synagogue had acquired a centrality in the affairs of London – and therefore of British – Jewry which it could not honestly have claimed twenty years before. Its historic focus continued to be located in the City of London, but the membership was fast on the way to removing itself thence, and the destruction of its founding synagogues by enemy bombing during the Second World War marked in dramatic fashion the end of an era. The United Synagogue had become, in the nicest sense of the word, a business enterprise; it could be run, Israel Zangwill had declared in *Children of the Ghetto*, 'as a joint-stock company ... [and] ... there wouldn't be an atom of difference in the discussions ... Long after Judaism has ceased to exist, excellent gentlemen will be found regulating its finances.'[4] 'Head Office' – located from 1932 until 1996 at Woburn House, Euston – handled every aspect of property building, acquisition and management; maintained and operated burial grounds and burial facilities; superintended a variety of bequests and trusts for charitable purposes; helped fund, through the Jewish Religious Education Board, a network of religion classes; centralised the payment of Ministers, Readers and other synagogue officials; and contributed very heavily to many metropolitan and national Jewish bodies, including, of course, the Chief Rabbinate.

This pattern was to be found repeated – albeit on a much smaller scale – in many provincial cities. The aptly named *minhag Anglia* [English service] which the United Synagogue celebrated and exemplified, embraced pomp and ceremony and was characterised by a fusion of tradition with moderation. Ironically, by the mid-twentieth century its most enthusiastic adherents were to be found among the sons and daughters of the immigrants of half a century before. Suburbanisation was a key catalyst in this process.

Even before 1914, Jews were moving away from their original areas of settlement – such as the slums of London's East End, the Gorbals in Glasgow and the Leylands in Leeds – and into middle-class suburbs. Jews who settled in the suburbs were not seeking to escape from Judaism and certainly not from their identity as Jews. Rather, they were seeking to escape from a particular form and intensity of Judaism and of Jewish life, which had suited their grandparents and parents, but which did not suit them. The world of the immigrant Jew was introspective; the popular abuse to which the immigrant was subject made it more so. In the suburbs, the Jew could face his Gentile neighbour on more equal terms:

> Whatever the strength of his Judaism [a writer in *The Times* observed in 1924] the middle-class Jew who settles outside the largely Jewish areas is bound to see more of the Gentile, and I think it would be rather an exception to find a Jewish family established for more than a few years in London outside the Jewish areas of East London and a few smaller settlements who had not Gentile friends as well as acquaintances.[5]

This movement, well under way in the interwar period, was accelerated by wartime bombing and destruction of homes. Jews moved out of the declining industrial towns of Victorian England, where self-sufficient communities could no longer be sustained. Today, most British Jews live in the affluent suburbs of Greater London (and adjacent parts of the Home Counties) and Manchester, and the south-coast 'dormitory' towns of Southend, Brighton and Bournemouth.[6] They work for the most part in professional occupations, and on average they are about a third wealthier than their non-Jewish counterparts.

At the end of the Second World War, it was said commonly that around 'half a million' Jews lived in the UK. Post-1945, British Jewry has become pluralised and polarised as it has slowly contracted in size to around 330,000 at the beginning of the twenty-first century. The religious extremes of left and right do not talk to each other. And Zionism, which was in the immediate aftermath of the Holocaust a unifying force, has now itself become a divisive factor.

It is undeniable that Zionism, which once united the Jews of Britain and, indeed, provided them with an alternative ethnic identity, now divides them. Or rather, what they are divided over is what 'Zionism' actually means. We can dismiss as a tangential oddity the few dozen or so British adherents of *Neturei Karta* – the Charedi sect that regards the creation of a Jewish state as blasphemous (as Hermann Adler did more than a century ago). There is, however, a genuine debate, among British Jews, as to the essential characteristics of the polity called Israel – the Jewish State.

A wide-ranging survey of Anglo-Jewish attitudes to Israel, carried out by Jewish Policy Research in 2010, revealed that 95% of respondents had visited Israel, 90% believed that Israel is the 'ancestral homeland' of the Jewish people and 82% confessed that Israel played a 'central' or an 'important but not central' part in what they took to mean their Jewish identity; 72% categorised themselves as 'Zionists'. While two-thirds favoured giving up land for peace with the Palestinians, 87% agreed that Jews are responsible for ensuring Israel's survival. But, asked whether 'Because of events in Israel I feel uncomfortable as a Jewish person living in Britain', 71% disagreed – that is, they felt comfortable.[7] This particular response validates data collected a decade earlier: that a substantial proportion of British Jews feel secure in British society, and certainly do not think of themselves as living in exile.[8]

This reflects a success story: Jews have been free to integrate themselves – as far as they wish – into British society, while retaining – as far as they wish – a distinct ethnic and/or religious identity. How many of them will in fact want to retain any such distinctiveness as the twenty-first century progresses is, of course, beyond the competence or business of any historian to address.

Notes

1 *St. James's Medley*, November 1855, pp. 235–6.
2 These figures are taken from the *Jewish Year Book* for 1911.
3 J. Lestchinsky, *Der Idisher Arbayter (in London)* [Yiddish: 'The Jewish Worker (in London)'] (Vilna, 1907), pp. 31–2.

4   I. Zangwill, *Children of the Ghetto* (London: White Lion Edition, 1972), pp. 241–2.
5   *The Times*, 8 December 1924, p. 15.
6   Gateshead is a unique exception to this pattern.
7   D. Graham and J. Boyd, *Committed, Concerned & Conciliatory: The Attitudes of Jews in Britain towards Israel* (London: Institute for Jewish Policy Research, 2010), p. 32.
8   S. Miller, M. Schmool and A. Lerman, *Social and Political Attitudes of British Jews* (London: Institute for Jewish Policy Research, 1996), p. 3.

Further reading

1066–1290

R. Huscroft, *Expulsion: England's Jewish Solution* (Stroud: History Press, 2006).
R. R. Mundill, *The King's Jews* (London: Bloomsbury Publishing, 2010).

1290–1656

A. Bale, *The Jew in the Medieval Book: English Antisemitisms, 1350–1500* (Cambridge: Cambridge University Press, 2006).
A. Hessayon, 'From Expulsion (1290) to Readmission (1656): Jews in England': www.jewishgen.org/jcr-uk/england_articles/1290_to_1656.htm (accessed 11 September 2016).

1656–1850

T. M. Endelmann, *The Jews of Georgian England* (Michigan: University of Michigan Press, 1999).
D. S. Katz, *Jews in the History of England, 1485–1850* (Oxford: Oxford University Press, 1997).

1850–2014

G. Alderman, *The Jewish Community in British Politics* (Oxford: Oxford University Press, 1983).
G. Alderman, *British Jewry Since Emancipation* (Buckingham: University of Buckingham Press, 2014).
T. M. Endelmann, *The Jews of Britain, 1656 to 2000* (California: University of California Press, 2002).
V. D. Lipman, *Social History of the Jews in England 1850 – 1950* (London: Watts & Co., 1954).

2

Local: Leeds in the age of great cities

Derek Fraser

Leeds was one of the 'shock cities' of the nineteenth century, always cited along with Manchester and Birmingham as among the earliest examples of the modern industrial city, in the first country to have an industrial revolution. Yet Leeds was not an 'instant city' like, for example, Middlesbrough, which grew from a small hamlet to an industrial town in one generation. Leeds in fact had a long history and its medieval field patterns are still identifiable in the yards and alleys off the main street of Briggate. Leeds is mentioned in the Domesday Book and its famous Cistercian monastery, Kirkstall Abbey, was founded in 1152. The town received its borough charter in 1207, from which date the history of Leeds as a separate identifiable community may be traced. Leeds was historically a combination of the in-township central area together with ten out-townships, some of which – like Armley, Holbeck or Hunslet – were woollen manufacturing villages and others, such as Potter Newton, agricultural. The earliest plan of Leeds was a simple sketch map produced in 1560 for a water rights dispute and this shows the still recognisable central street arrangement, which has changed little despite major redevelopment outside this area (Figure 2.1).

By the seventeenth century, Leeds had a population of some 6,000–7,000 and was known as a centre of woollen manufacturing, but with an extra dimension which distinguished it from neighbouring West Riding wool towns. Its geographic location, with an agricultural hinterland to the north and east and manufacturing towns and villages to the south and west, made it an ideal location as a place of exchange. Hence, one of the continuities of Leeds history is that it has always been a centre of commerce as well as manufacturing, exemplified today in the important industries of financial and legal services. The dominance of merchants was reflected in the municipal charter granted in 1626 which established the Leeds Corporation as a self-elected, self-perpetuating oligarchy, dominated by leading merchants and clothiers who wished to impose stronger regulations on the woollen cloth trade.

Georgian Leeds, a gentleman merchant town, was described by Defoe as 'large wealthy and populous', and its bustling Tuesday cloth market in Briggate was, he believed, 'a prodigy of its kind'. The first proper map, Cossins' of 1726, shows the medieval street pattern, the orchards and tenter fields and the expansion to Hightown, with its surviving St John's Church. The still rural area of Ley Lands, which is to be so important in this book, is clearly identified (Figure 2.2).

The dominance of Leeds over the marketing and sale of woollen cloth and its determination to preserve that status were reflected in the impressive Cloth Hall buildings of the eighteenth century. The White Cloth Halls were built in Kirkgate in 1710, in Meadow Lane in 1755 and in the Calls in 1793. The most impressive was the Coloured Cloth Hall, erected at a cost of £5,000 in 1755 at Quebec (now City Square), which accommodated 1,770 stalls.

From the late eighteenth century, dramatic economic and social change engulfed the town, which between about 1790 and 1830 became a modern industrial metropolis. Water transport improvements through the Aire and Calder Navigation, which linked Leeds to Hull, and later the Leeds and Liverpool Canal, effectively made both the continent and America accessible to Leeds commercial activity. Increasingly, the domestic system of cloth making was being superseded by mechanisation, powered first by water and soon after by steam. Only a few eighteenth-century workshops housed between 25 and 50 workers, yet by the early nineteenth century Leeds could boast two mills (gradually being dubbed 'factories') with over 1,000 employees. Benjamin Gott's massive Armley Mills, said to be the world's first mechanised wool factory, employed 1,200 people at its peak, many of them women and children. Meanwhile, John Marshall established the Leeds flax spinning industry in Holbeck, which by 1803 employed 1,000. His famous 1840 Temple Mill, with its Egyptian motif and sheep grazing on the roof, was hailed as one of the wonders of the modern world. Completing the trio of founding Leeds industrial entrepreneurs was Matthew Murray, who pioneered the engineering industry – also in Holbeck. His foundry manufactured textile machinery and steam engines, which in turn led him to steam locomotives. It was his locomotive which pulled coal from Middleton Colliery to Leeds Bridge for shipment beyond.

Gott, Marshall and Murray were exceptional individuals and the scale of their operations was atypical, yet their enterprising spirit was echoed in countless smaller ventures which developed these key industries of wool, flax and engineering and extended the range of Leeds industrial activity. The town developed a thriving chemical industry, based on the original textile needs of

Table 2.1 The population of Leeds Borough

Year	Population
1801	53,276
1811	62,665
1821	83,943
1831	123,548
1841	152,054
1851	172,270
1861	207,270
1871	259,212
1881	309,119

bleaching and dyeing, and then spreading out to serve the needs of a range of other industries. As the town grew, more animals and horses were slaughtered, and this led to leather and tanning industries – the tanning works dating from the 1820s are still standing in Scott Hall Road. Woodworking and wrought iron developed to make the tools and parts needed for a variety of trades, while printing became and remains a key Leeds industry. Carpetmaking and the glass trade complemented an industrial economy which was firmly based on textiles and engineering, but which diversified as the Industrial Revolution developed pace. Leeds had some natural advantages in the availability of coal and water, together with acquired benefits through good transport links and commercial and financial services.

There were two obvious and visible consequences of all this economic development: more people and more smoke. Leeds had grown steadily in the eighteenth century and its population had reached around 30,000 by the 1770s. The first census was in 1801 and thereafter the decennial census surveys show a dramatic rise in the population, fuelled by short and long distance (mainly Irish) migration and natural increase (Table 2.1).

The town doubled in size in one generation and then doubled again in the next. Remarkably, the population grew by almost 50% during the 1820s, two thirds of the growth coming from in-migration. Such rapid growth put an inevitable strain on the town's infrastructure and environmental services lagged well behind, which made early industrial Leeds an insanitary and unhealthy place to live. The pioneering Leeds doctor, Robert Baker, was one of the first to demonstrate the link between ill health and the physical environment, and his map of the spread of cholera in Leeds in 1832 visibly tracked the epidemic, spawned by poor housing and infected water supply. The lower growth rate in the 1840s reflected the economic, social and sanitary problems of what was probably the worst decade of the Victorian era, popularly described as 'the hungry forties'.

At least until the mid-eighteenth century, Leeds merchants and clothiers lived in the central area, often building large impressive houses which were both domestic and business premises. As the lower lying east end of the town near the parish church became more crowded, there were moves to create a more salubrious environment in the west. The Park Estate was described in 1806 as having 'a very elegant range of buildings ... built in a very superior style principally inhabited by affluent merchants or gentleman who have retired from business'.[1] This east–west axis was shattered by the smoke of the Industrial Revolution. Whereas visitors to Georgian Leeds described a pleasant market town, early nineteenth-century observers noticed the smoke as the principal characteristic. In 1824, the poet William Hazlitt bemoaned, 'O smoky city, dull and dirty Leeds', while four years later a German visitor commented:

> A transparent cloud of smoke was diffused over the whole space which it occupies, on and between several hills, a hundred red fires shot upward into the sky and as many towering chimneys poured forth columns of black smoke. The huge manufactories, five stories high, in which every window was illuminated, had a grand striking effect.[2]

The smoke of industrial Leeds and the prevailing winds ruined the desire to create an affluent west end and so the whole axis of Leeds change from east–west to north–south. The new industrial middle class moved up the hills, literally to get above the smoke. Woodhouse, Headingley and Potter Newton became the fashionable suburbs with fine stone-built houses and mansions.

Most of the new economic elite were dissenters, Protestant Nonconformists outside the established Church of England. Unable to parallel their economic dominance by political authority because of the closed corporation and the lack of Parliamentary representation, these men turned their attention to the minor offices of Leeds to express their political influence. The parish vestry, the office of churchwarden, the Improvement Commission and the Poor Law became highly politicised, as the new whig-liberal elite created an alternative political focus to rival the existing tory-Anglican establishment entrenched in the unreformed Leeds Corporation. These new social classes had their own press mouthpiece in the *Leeds Mercury* which promoted the interests of the new society. The *Mercury* had a great journalistic coup in exposing the use of government *agents provocateurs* at the time of Peterloo. Denounced by the radical, William Cobbett, as 'the Great Liar of the North', the *Mercury*, through its owners and editors – Edward Baines, father and son – nevertheless achieved the status in Victorian England which the *Manchester Guardian* was to exemplify a century later, as the voice of provincial middle-class liberalism. The old elite also had a promoter in the rival *Leeds Intelligencer*, which particularly gave a platform to the tory-radical, Richard Oastler, to attack the new middle class which supported the abolition of slavery abroad, but ignored what Oastler called the 'White Slavery' of child labour.

One of the main objectives of the *Mercury* and its readership was to secure Parliamentary reform and the proper representation of Leeds in the House of Commons. Nothing illustrates more clearly the dissonance between the old traditional political system and the reality of the new industrial society than the lack of Parliamentary representation for Leeds, with over 100,000 citizens. The 1832 Great Reform Act began to address the anomaly by wiping out many 'pocket and rotten boroughs' and giving Leeds and other new industrial cities seats their own two MPs. When the first election campaign in Leeds took place, there was an unexpected piece of evidence as to the existence of a small but identifiable Jewish community. Baines and the *Mercury* decreed that Leeds liberals should have one local MP and one national figure. The local was John Marshall junior, an obvious choice given the importance of the family flax-spinning business. The national figure was Thomas Babington Macaulay, an intellectual promotor of the new free-market economics favoured by industrial middle classes and later the most famous historian of the Victorian era. The tories also had a natural choice in Michael Sadler, a linen merchant and member of the Leeds Corporation and already an MP for a seat disappearing under the Reform Bill.

It was Sadler's electioneering style which revealed the Jewish presence in Leeds. The liberal side favoured public meetings and argument to persuade the voters, but Sadler adopted a personal canvass, meeting groups of voters personally. It was in this context that it was reported that Sadler had visited Jewish voters and had grown a beard for the occasion. An anonymous pamphleteer asked sarcastically what other rites of the Jewish religion Sadler was prepared to undergo in order to capture the Jewish vote. At the time this produced a high-principled response, condemning the 'filthy and obscene' reference 'to a certain part of the human body to which it has hitherto been thought in a civilised society indecent to allude'.[3] For present purposes, the key inference is that an identifiable community existed of a size which would make it worthwhile to visit and of an economic status which would earn a vote as £10 householders. Local historians have found references to the occasional Jewish name in Georgian records and there are early nineteenth-century comments on itinerant Jewish pedlars visiting Leeds. From the Sadler controversy it may be inferred that there was a visible (not hidden) Jewish presence which was known locally and at a location suitable for a meeting with an aspiring candidate. Murray Freedman identified Phineas Abrahams, a silversmith, Wolf Abrahams, a confectioner, and Barnett Joseph, an outfitter, as trading in Leeds city centre about this time and they would have been the members of this early community.

The year 1840 is conventionally taken as the start of a viable community, as in that year the first Jewish cemetery was opened and a *minyan* was meeting in a loft in Bridge Street. In 1842, the first Jewish marriage took place of the daughter of Gabriel Davis, truly the father of the Leeds Jewish community. It was Davis – who had arrived as German migrant to Leeds about 1815 and was an optical instrument maker – who purchased a house in Back Rockingham Street which became the first official synagogue in Leeds in 1846. (In 1996, The United Hebrew Congregation celebrated the 150th anniversary of the founding of the first synagogue, thus marking 1846 as the beginning of continuous synagogue existence in Leeds.) The synagogue is clearly identified in the 1847 Ordnance Survey map of Leeds (Figure 2.3). At that time the community numbered about 100, rising to 144 at the 1851 census, below the numbers recorded in Manchester, Liverpool and Birmingham.

By the time Davis died in 1851, buried in the cemetery which he had established, Leeds was emerging from the traumas, both political and economic, which marked the 1840s and entering a period of prosperity and improvement. The local economy diversified even further, with specialised branches of engineering expanding rapidly, such that engineering overtook textiles as the leading industry, the town being noted particularly for boilers and steam locomotives. The leather, printing and chemical industries developed further, and by the late nineteenth century spawned further activities in dyeware and explosives, to be joined by trades relevant to the new immigrants: footware and clothing. In common with its commercial tradition and history, Leeds had well-developed legal, financial and business services, including the only provincial stock exchange. Transport links were improved still further with the coming of the railways and Leeds was served by three stations: Leeds New, Central and Wellington Street. The railways altered the fabric of the city centre, not only through the building of stations but also through embankments and viaducts which altered the skyline. In terms of the growth of the Jewish community, the building of the Leeds–Selby–Hull railway in 1840 was to be of critical importance, while the westward route to Manchester and Liverpool was improved with the building of the New (now the only) Leeds station, erected on the 'Dark Arches' over the Aire – a major civil engineering achievement.

The population prior to the main mass Jewish immigration had already reached 300,000, and the teeming mass of people were mostly accommodated in the classic Leeds housing model of back-to-backs. These were sturdily built of brick and slate, but lacked basic amenities of light, water and sewerage. Sanitary problems accompanied this massive and unplanned expansion for which the civic authorities were ill-prepared. The Leeds Corporation was reformed in 1835 and became an elected Council – but with few powers to address the city's environmental and health problems. This was gradually addressed by the passage of the Leeds Improvement Acts of 1842 and

1866 and the acquisition of the waterworks in 1852 and the two gas companies. Slowly the Council acquired powers to regulate building, improve environmental services and to demolish insanitary houses. The first demolition scheme in 1871 included removing the very first back-to-backs which had been built in the 1780s.

Both the Council and Leeds itself received a great accolade in 1858 when Queen Victoria visited Leeds to open the splendid and impressive Town Hall, designed by Cuthbert Brodrick. The occasion of the Queen's visit was accompanied by an exhibition of local industry and a music festival. The exhibition illustrated the great diversity of the Leeds economy which protected the town from the worst effects of the trade cycle. The Town Hall was an expression of both pride and confidence and its tower, added only after much debate and controversy, dominated the urban vista. The Town Hall was and remains the most potent symbol of what was described at the time as 'a stirring and thriving seat of English industry', in a city in all but name (the city title was eventually awarded in 1893). The Queen's visit meant that for a couple of days 'this old and busy seat of industry becomes in a sense the seat of Empire'.[4]

Such an important and attractive place acted a magnet to migrants from near and far and its diverse economy provided ready opportunity for employment. In the mid-Victorian years, Leeds was attracting Jewish migrants mainly from Germany, normally to work in the wool industry, and already in the 1860s and 1870s there were reports of growing numbers leaving the Russian Empire to avoid conscription. When the mass Jewish migration began in the 1880s, the push of persecution was balanced by the pull of Leeds as a well-known destination. It is sometimes said that most of those who finished up in Leeds did so by accident and the growth of a large Jewish community was the result of a random process. It is true that for many migrants from the east, America was the preferred destination. Victor Lightman was but one of many who had intended to move westward again, viewing Leeds as temporary location, but who then established himself in Leeds as a successful entrepreneur and civic leader. Yet far more migrants knew that Leeds was their destination through the personal, trading and communication links between the town and a specific and limited area of the Russian Empire. The *'landsman'* nexus acted a centrifugal force which made Leeds a 'Litvak' community, which in turn meant that large numbers were bound for Leeds – not the USA or another British city. As often in the history of migration, the link with Leeds was reinforced by marriage, either between a migrant and a Leeds bride or a marriage partner summoned from the home country. As one of the earliest Russian migrants recalled late in his life:

> I came to Leeds from Russia in 1852 and was a fugitive from Russian militia men. I was on my way to America, via Hull and Liverpool, when someone

persuaded me to go to Leeds. I took my chance here and have never regretted it ... We had a place of worship in Back Rockingham Street and I was married there. All of those I remember in my early days came here as single men ... the early ones were single who either made wives of Jewesses in this country or sent to Russia for them. In my own case I had a friend who sent to Russia for her sister and I married her. It was the usual thing for young fellows when they had settled here to send for Russia for their parents and brothers and sisters and that is how the Jewish people made a home in Leeds.[5]

It was the economy of Leeds which made it so appropriate a destination for the Jewish migrants. The diversity of industry meant that a variety of trades were open to the skills the migrants brought with them. But it was also important and timely that manufacturing changes in the clothing industry provided the opportunities in tailoring which were to be so vital in securing the economic wellbeing of the migrants, particularly women, in their new home. John Barran developed the use of the band knife for cutting multiple pieces of cloth which, combined with sewing machines, permitted the subdivision of the manufacturing process with countless opportunities for outsourcing and subcontracting in a long supply chain. The Jewish migrants brought with them key skills needed for the clothing industry just when rising standards of living led to increased demand for ready-made clothing. Economists have noted that the capital requirements for establishing small businesses in the clothing supply chain were modest and small workshops and even domestic annexes sprang up to support the major players. The firm of John Barran and his Jewish partner Herman Friend employed up to 2,000 workers, whose functions were reliant on hundreds of outworkers. It was this and other trades in which Jewish migrants had skills – such as the making of caps, slippers, boots and wooden items – which allowed the newcomers initially to survive and later to prosper.

Hence, Leeds was no random recipient of Jewish migrants. Its employment opportunities were particularly well tuned to the skills of the incomers and the city was growing. It had fine public buildings, such as the Town Hall and the Corn Exchange, good communications by road, rail and water, publicly owned utilities such as tramways, a wonderful seat of recreation in Roundhay Park – said at the time to be the biggest in Europe, and music halls and theatres. The 1870 Education Act led to a significant increase in the provision of accessible primary schools for the mass population and the 1875 Public Health Act strengthened the powers of the local authority to deal with the known health problems associated with deficient housing and poor sanitary facilities. In an often-quoted survey, *The Lancet* confirmed in 1888 the start and end of the migrants' journey:

> The greater part came from the province of Kovno; and at starting they are often acquainted with but one word of English, and that word is Leeds

Leeds in the age of great cities

... It seems evident that, as a whole, they readily earned their living at Leeds and to the Russian jew, in dread of obligatory military service and suffering from religious persecution, the name of Leeds was but a modern term for an El Dorado.[6]

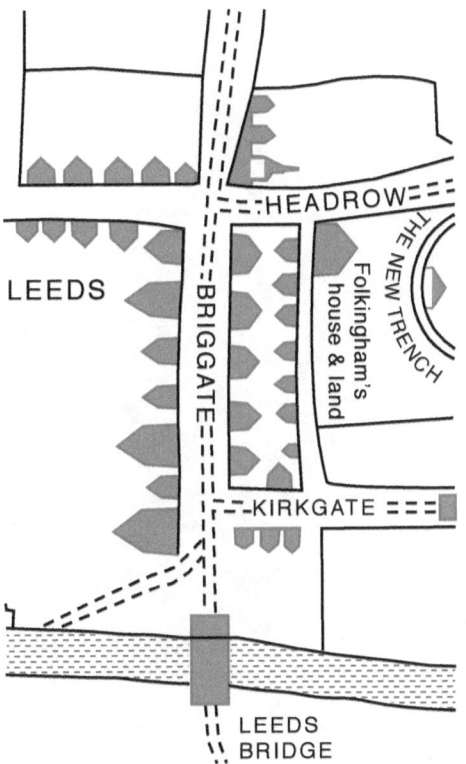

2.1 Plan re lawsuit rights, Thoresby Society, X (1899)

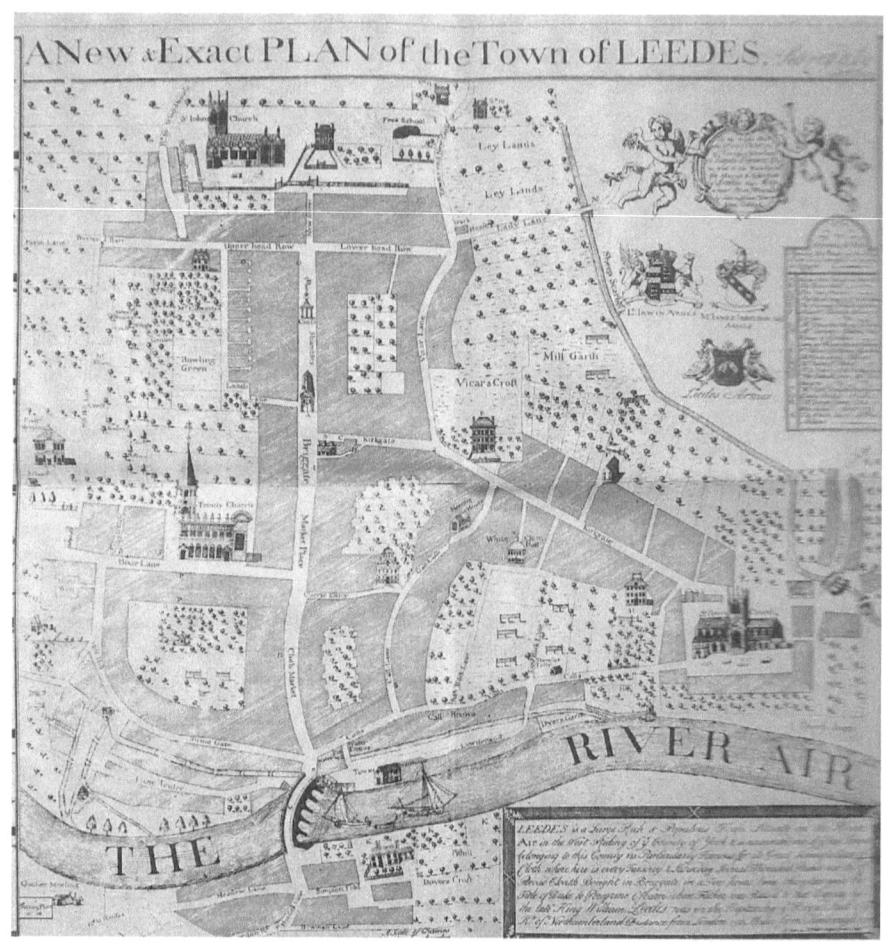

2.2 Cossins' map of Leeds, 1726

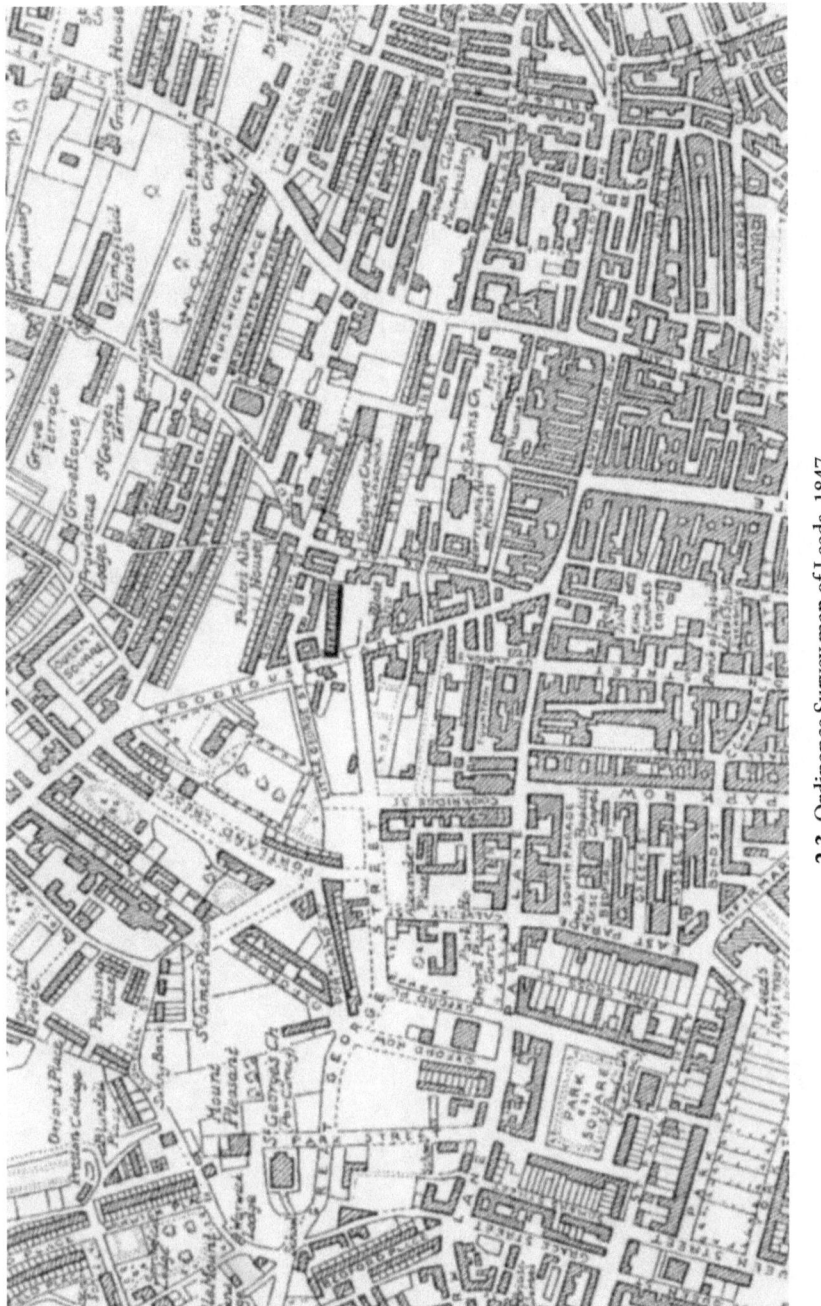

2.3 Ordinance Survey map of Leeds, 1847

Notes

1. K. Grady, 'From Medieval Borough to Great Victorian City' in C. Webster (ed.), *Building a Great Victorian City. Leeds Architects and Architecture* (Huddersfield: Jeremy Mills Publishing, 2011), p. 14.
2. Quoted in Grady, 'From Medieval Borough to Great Victorian City', p. 15.
3. Quoted by D. Fraser, 'Politics and Society' in D. Fraser (ed.), *A History of Modern Leeds* (Manchester: Manchester University Press, 1980), p. 277.
4. A. Briggs, *Victorian Cities* (London: Penguin, 1963), p. 177.
5. M. Freedman, 'The 150th anniversary of the first Leeds Synagogue' in *United Hebrew Congregation Leeds: The First 150 Years 1846–1996* (1996), p. 13.
6. Quoted by C. J. Morgan, 'Demographic change 1777–1911' in Fraser, *A History of Modern Leeds*, p. 62.

3

Demogaphic: The Jewish population of Leeds – how many Jews?

Nigel Grizzard

This is a question that has been asked not just in Leeds but in Jewish communities worldwide. Is the Jewish community growing, declining or staying numerically static and what are the future projections? Will there still be a Jewish community in ten, twenty or fifty years' time?

Counting Jews

Counting Jews in the United Kingdom has always been difficult. The figures obtained are often regarded as 'best estimates'.

Over time, researchers have used techniques such as the Frequency of Distinctive Jews Names, where the frequency of names such as Cohen and Levy are used as estimators of the Jewish population. The 1891, 1901 and 1911 census figures on the number of Jews were based on households where at least one member was born in Russia and Poland as an estimate for the Jewish population. Other researchers have looked at the number of Jewish deaths and then, using age-specific death rates, estimated the Jewish population. Similarly, a count of the number of boys circumcised has been used as an estimator of the number of Jewish births. Synagogue records have also provided data on the location and number of members, as well as marriages, and have therefore been used as a basis for population estimates.

All these methods have been fraught with difficulty and there are many arguments about their validity. However, they can often be regarded as providing 'the best estimates' of the time. Contemporaries were just as perplexed as modern historians. For example, the Select Committee on Immigration in 1889 consulted two leading Leeds citizens, one of whom estimated the Jewish population at 15,000 and the other at 30,000. The actual figure at the time was probably around 6,000.

In 2001, the England and Wales Census included a question on religion for the first time.[1] This was the first opportunity in England and Wales to enumerate the Jewish population. When the results were published the question then was: 'Did all Jews complete the religious question?' The 2011 Census figures gave a total of 6,847 Jews in Leeds – in other words, 0.9% of the Leeds Metropolitan District's population of 751,500 was Jewish.

Leeds Jews: an introduction

To gain an understanding of the Leeds Jewish population, it needs to be examined in relation to the forces acting both on the Jewish world and the general economic position of the city of Leeds.

In writing this chapter, there are eight key periods that can be defined.

1 The period from 1840–80 until the Russian influx that began in 1881.
2 The period of Russian migration – which lasted from 1881 to 1914.
3 The interwar period, which includes the influx of German, Austrian and Czech Jewish refugees who start slowly coming in the 1930s but become a much larger number post-*Kristalnacht* – the anti-Jewish pogrom perpetrated by the Nazis on 11 November 1938.
4 The Second World War 1939–45.
5 The immediate postwar period when more refugees arrived and the State of Israel was created.
6 The 1950s and 1960s when many left Leeds in search of a new life.
7 The 1970s and 1980s when Leeds benefited from the decline of many smaller regional Jewish communities.
8 The 1990s to the present; the city of Leeds is an economic powerhouse attracting new people to join its growing economic base.

The period up to the Russian immigration 1840–80

When the huge Russian influx began in 1881, the Jewish population in Leeds was estimated to be 1,000. Who were these Jews and where did they come from? A clue to their origins can be found in research carried out in the Leeds Jewish cemeteries and in historical studies about individual Jewish residents.

We know that they were not all Russian born;[2] there were Jews from Germany, from the Netherlands[3] and from other parts of the UK. Jews at that time were also mobile. Jacob Unna, who was born in Hamburg in 1800 and came to Manchester in 1820, was in Leeds by the time of the 1841 Census – married with children to Sarine Salomon, a Danish Jewish lady – and by 1851 was living in Bradford. Martin Hertz, another German Jewish merchant, moved to Bradford at the same time because Bradford was growing with the coming of the railway and the expansion of the wool trade. Gabriel Davis, one of the early leaders of the Leeds community, had a son who went to Shrewsbury – an unlikely move. However, there was a Leeds–Shrewsbury connection as one of Leeds' major mill owners, John Marshall – who owned Marshall's Mill – was a joint owner of Ditherington flax mill in Shrewsbury. Maximillian Zossenheim, who came from Germany to Huddersfield as a textile merchant, relocated to Leeds and became Italian Consul. In the same way as today's Jews are mobile, so in the nineteenth century members of the Leeds Jewish community were moving.

The opening of Belgrave Street Synagogue in 1861 shows the growth of the community in a growing industrial city. It was a community containing the poor, who included travelling salesmen making their living going from town to town and village in Yorkshire,[4] through to shopkeepers and opticians in Leeds. The community grew slowly; but in 1881 there was a sea change in Leeds Jewry.

The period of Russian migration 1881–1914

The assassination of Tzar Alexander II on 13 March 1881 and the anti-Semitic May Laws of 1882 drove two million Jews to leave Russia in the period 1881–1914.

Those living in villages and small towns realised there was no future for them, for they were at the mercy of the Russian State and the anti-Semitic peasantry, and they knew they had to leave Russia for a new life. (The film and the play *Fiddler on the Roof* are a recreation of the Jewish dilemma in Eastern Europe.)

The Jews moving West were looking for new homes in the Americas, in the United States, in Canada, in Argentina – all countries of opportunity. Others were going to South Africa – a developing economy because of the mining opportunities – and still others left for Palestine, then a rundown province in the Turkish Empire. Many people who were involved in this migration came through the ports of Hull[5] and Grimsby.[6] Moving west to Liverpool to catch a boat to their final destination they came to Leeds, the first industrial centre in the English-speaking world and an industrial centre based on an industry suited to Jewish skills – tailoring. Many chose to stay in Leeds and the influx changed the Leeds Jewish community out of all recognition.

A community that had become relatively well established and anglicised was now confronted with newcomers who spoke Yiddish rather English, were more religious than the traditional Anglo-Jew and were 'a foreign element' in the city. There are many myths about the Russian migration that may well have been regarded as truth, but the immigration process took place in the main between 1881 and 1905 when the Aliens Act introduced immigration controls – though people were still arriving up to 1914.

Table 3.1 Jewish population of Leeds together with figures on marriages and deaths

Year	Jewish Population	Marriages	Deaths
1896/7	10,000	102	130
1897/8	10,000	111	137
1898/1900	12,000	100	163
1901/2	12,000*		
1902/3	15,000	103	179
1903/4	15,000	109	105
1904/5	15,000	98	149
1914	25,000		

*2.78% of the population of Leeds

Over this thirty-year period, an unorganised migration became more organised; shipping companies took Jewish migrants as part of their regular passenger cargo and Jewish communities at the ports ensured immigrants were greeted and fed before travelling onwards. Relatives came to Leeds to join their families, while those who were subsequently born in Leeds were English speaking and UK nationals. Some of the Leeds-born were able to use this advantage to emigrate to the United States, and when they arrived at US Immigration at Ellis Island they were English speaking and not Russian. It put them in a different category to those who could only speak Yiddish.

Population estimates

To try and estimate the Jewish population in hindsight is a near impossible task – it can only be a guesstimate. However, from 1896 the *Jewish Year Book* appears. Published by the *Jewish Chronicle*, it includes statistics on the Jewish population of cities and towns across the UK.

For the period 1896 to 1914 the figures are in Table 3.1.

The data from the *Jewish Year Book* do not say how they were estimated, but they show the following figures:

1 Rapid growth from the figure of 1,000 in 1880 to a figure of 10,000 in 1896/7. A tenfold increase in the community – which involved the creation of a Jewish district: the Leylands adjacent to the city centre.
2 Continued growth from 10,000 to 12,000 in the 1898/1900 *Year Book*, further growth to 15,000 in 1902/3 and then, by 1914, a figure of 25,000 Jews in the city.
3 Jewish marriage and death figures are also given for the periods 1896/7 to 1904/5.

The Jewish population of Leeds

Table 3.2 Children born in Leeds with the name Cohen

Period	Births
1845–50	2
1851–60	22
1861–70	31
1871–80	99
1881–90	173
1891–1900	367
1901–10	329
1911–20	237
1921–30	133
1931–40	93
1941–50	91
1951–60	64
1961–70	54
1971–79	23

How correct are these numbers?

First, the population estimates: they show a rapidly rising Jewish population, an increase from 10,000 in 1896/7 to 25,000 by 1914. Looking back over the period, the community was growing and if it increased by 1,000 a year from 1896 onwards then a figure of 25,000 Jews would be feasible. In 1901/2, it was estimated that the Jews comprised 2.78% of the Leeds population, or 1 in every 36 citizens of Leeds was Jewish. Demographic studies show that immigrant populations generally tend to be younger than the norm and more fertile, and Russian Jews coming to Leeds would have been in this category. In a relatively safe environment, even though living conditions were poor, they would have had children.

An estimator of Jewish population that researchers such as Kosmin and Waterman[7] have used is 'the Cohen Count'. The name Cohen is used as it was by far the most frequently appearing Jewish surname.[8] Looking at Leeds in the period 1845 to 1910, the number of births of children with the name Cohen increases dramatically with a high of 367 in the period 1891–1900, the figure then declines to 23 in the period 1971–79, the latest data available (Table 3.2). Many families called Cohen changed their name to variants, so the frequency of Jewish families with the name declines over the period.[9]

Figures are also available for infant deaths, and in the same period as there were 367 births there were also 52 deaths of infants with the name Cohen aged 0 and 1 years. So, in a ten-year cohort there are 315 Jewish children named Cohen born in Leeds who survived until their second birthday. If the Cohen name was found in 1 in 20 Jews at the beginning of the twentieth century, then there would have been 6,300 Jewish children under 10 in Leeds. Here we go into the realms of speculation, but the Cohen birth figures show a young and growing community. Recent demographic research has used new methodologies to analyse census data based on the original census forms, which permits a more detailed picture of Jewish migration and occupation.

The figures for 1901–10 show a decline, and this was at a time when families were not changing their names as this was a later phenomenon. The decline may have been due to the start of integration and the use of contraception to limit family size. By 1910, families who had arrived in 1890 had been in Leeds twenty years, and those who had come in 1880 some thirty years, so they had had time to become integrated. Like many migrants, their migration was not only from country to country but also from rural to urban. Hence, primarily rural migrants became urban workers, and it may be estimated that in the early twentieth century the Jewish community occupational structure was 80% tailoring, 7% boot and shoe, 7% furniture, 2% masters and 4% others.

The figures for deaths and marriages reveal someone within the Anglo-Jewish world with an interest in statistics; and likewise that there must have been someone in Leeds knowledgeable enough about the records to send the information to the *Jewish Year Book*. For these reasons the Jewish population figures for Leeds are likely to be accurate.

The interwar period 1919–39

Throughout this period, the *Jewish Year Book* gives a static figure of 25,000 Jews in Leeds. In 1937, it adds a rider that the Jewish population comprises 5.49% of the total population of the city of Leeds which is 458,320.

Nationally, Leeds was known as the city with the highest proportion of Jews to the general population. In 1936, the statistician Kantorowitsch[10] is quoted in the *Jewish Year Book* claiming that Manchester and Salford have 37,500 Jews out of a total population of 989,775. This equated to 3.85% of the population. Figures for Greater London were given as 233,991 Jews out of a total population of 8,281,118, or 2.82% of the population.[11]

There seems to be little evidence to justify the static Leeds figure of 25,000. In retrospect, was that the correct number of Jews in the city? Looking at the community, it would have benefited from a trickle of immigration from Eastern Europe, but at the same time how many of the Leeds-born Jews had left for other cities in Britain or new lives in the United States?

Leeds Jews lived together in the northern districts of the city, starting with the Leylands, moving to Chapeltown in the first decades of the twentieth century, then onto Moortown and to Alwoodley. This segment of the city looked Jewish with shops and Jewish institutions. The Nazis' rise to power in Germany in 1933, the Anschluss in Austria in 1938 and the annexation of Sudetenland in Czechoslovakia brought a flood of Jewish refugees to Britain. Figures for the number of entrants nationally are given as 70,000.

Again, was this an exact figure or an underestimate? Refugees fleeing found any way possible to enter Britain; they may not all have come legally. We know that some had tenuous links with the British Jewish community, some moved on at the first opportunity to the United States, while the majority stayed and made new lives and homes in the United Kingdom. Leeds did not receive a large number of refugees, at the highest estimate perhaps 500 Jews came to settle in the city.

Interestingly, for 1939 the *Jewish Year Book* gives the Jewish population of Leeds as 30,000 – the highest figure it ever reaches – but this seems to have been over-optimistic, for in 1940 it returns to the figure of 25,000.

Second World War 1939–45

The six-year period of the Second World War saw vast changes in British Jewish life. Thousands of young men and women from the Leeds Jewish community join HM forces and served out of Leeds for the war years. Leeds, as a city, was spared the heavy bombing experienced in London, Coventry, Hull and Sheffield and was consequently seen as a safe haven. Many families from London who were 'bombed out' moved north to make new lives in Leeds. Again, there are no figures but perhaps 1,000 Jews moved north to Leeds to get away from wartime bombing.

The end of the war and demobilisation brought troops back to their homes in Leeds, and there was a continuing residential move from the inner city to the suburbs.

Among the servicemen were Polish Jews who served in the Polish army in the UK and had no homes or family left in Poland. Some of these Jews – again, very small numbers – found their way to Leeds; at most 100 people.

The immediate postwar period

Two key developments took place in the postwar years. First, the troubled period of the last years of the British Mandate in Palestine, which saw a rise in anti-Semitism in Britain and in Leeds and then, when the Mandate ended in 1948, the establishment of the State of Israel. A number of Jewish ex Servicemen volunteered from Leeds to fight in the new Israeli military and on the demographic front; there was now the opportunity to build a new life in the Jewish homeland. Jews left Leeds for Israel, not in any surge, but as a constant trickle which continues today.

The 1950s and 1960s

There were also opportunities for Britons to make new lives in Australia, through the Assisted Package Migration Scheme. Leeds, as a community, had a large proportion of working-class Jews and some saw the advantages of making new and better lives in Australia.

The *Jewish Year Book* sticks to its constant figure of 25,000 Jews in Leeds – it was a convenient figure and it was good for the Jewish community because it showed Leeds to be Anglo-Jewry's third largest Jewish community after London and Manchester.

1965 Krausz's estimate

Sociologist Ernst Krausz, an Orthodox Jew – son of *Dayan* Dr M. Krausz [a *Dayan* is a Jewish religious judge], a well-known Jewish scholar – carried out field research in 1958 and 1959 for a research degree. His conclusions, which are a detailed study of the Leeds Jewish community, are published in his book *Leeds Jewry*.[12]

In the first chapter, Krausz looks at population figures. He argues that Leeds received comparatively few immigrants from the pre- and postwar refugee influx: he puts the figure as low as 200. He then states that the influx of Hungarian and Egyptian Jewish refugees who came to Britain brought very few Jews to Leeds. He then calculates the Leeds Jewish population by using the average number of Jewish deaths per year and applying the death rate for residents of Leeds. The figures showed there were on average 206 deaths annually in the Leeds Jewish community. Using the Leeds death rate of 11.4 deaths per thousand inhabitants gave a Jewish population estimate of 18,070. Krausz's figure went against the conventional view that the Jewish population of Leeds was 25,000. He wrote 'the most we can say is that the Jewish population of Leeds is somewhere in the region of 18,000 to 20,000'.

After his book's publication in 1964, this figure of 20,000 – the top-end estimate – was used in the *Jewish Year Book* for 1965. This marked an acceptance by the community that the figure of 25,000 which had been consistently used – and which was a convenient figure as Leeds' total population was around 500,000 – was too high. At 20,000, it meant Jews comprised 4% of the city's population.[13]

The 1970s and 1980s economic and structural change in the north

Until the end of the 1960s, life in the north of England was comparatively stable. Towns and cities existed on their main industries and the Jewish communities that lived alongside them also experienced comparative stability. Jewish communities in these centres had functioning synagogues and an organised communal life. Leeds was a clothing centre and the Jewish community was involved at all levels in the industry, from capitalists who ran major UK clothing chains to those who worked as tailors and pressers in the factories.

Then came industrial change. In Leeds, the clothing industry, which had been a locally-based manufacturing industry, started closing factories and moving production abroad. Other clothing businesses closed down completely. In other northern industrial centres there was also great change. In Sunderland, the ship building industry was decimated; in Grimsby and Hull, the fishing industry – which was the main industry – was hit; in Bradford the textile industry saw huge redundancies.

The other change was the expansion of further education and the generations born in the 1950s and 1960s going to university. In many of the smaller centres, Jewish communities started to collapse. As children left for university and did not return, and economic prospects declined, so Jews moved. Many left smaller centres for Leeds – which was a positive move both economically and in terms of reinforcing Jewish identity. In Leeds, the community saw its economic base changing, moving away from the clothing industry which had provided jobs and wealth and into the city's growing service sector.

At the same time, there was an outflow of young people from Leeds; those who went to university and did not return to their home city – many making their lives in London. The net effect was a demographic decline in the Jewish population. The *Jewish Year Book* reduces the figure to 18,000 in 1966 and then to 15,000 in 1982. This figure reduces again to 12,000 in 1987 and 10,000 in 1992. It's clear that Leeds Jewry was declining; the key questions were by how much and when was the decline likely to stop?

The 1990s to the present

As Leeds Jewry declined numerically, other minorities in the city the city grew their communities. Whereas in the first part of the twentieth century Jews had been the city's main minority, now it was one minority among many in Leeds.

The 2001 Census was the first in which a question about religious affiliation was asked (Table 3.3).[14]

Leeds Jewry, through its communal leadership from the 1960s onwards, has never been happy to portray the community as declining in numbers. Krausz, who was published in 1964, received criticism for suggesting the community was less than the accepted 25,000 and was only around 18,000. Murray Freedman,[15] in numerous press releases from 1988 onwards in the *Leeds Jewish Telegraph*, charted the further numerical decline of Leeds Jewry and became embroiled in numerous arguments with the Leeds Jewish Communal Leadership over the size of the community.

Table 3.3 Religious minorities in Leeds from the 2001 and 2011 Censuses

Year	2001	2011
Jews	**8,267**	**6,847**
Muslims	21,394	40,772
Sikhs	7,586	8,914
Hindus	4,183	7,048
Total Population	715,600	751,500*

* In 1974 the Leeds Metropolitan District was created that included both the city of Leeds and outlying areas which increased the population from around 500,000 to over 700,000.

At the time of writing this chapter, in 2017, it has been six years since the last census was taken; according to ONS, the Office for National Statistics, there is likely to be a census again 2021. What will the 2021 Census show for Leeds Jewry? To try and answer this, we have to look at the current forces acting on Leeds Jewry.

The reservoirs of small Jewish communities in the north that sent families to Leeds in the 1970s and 1980s are now empty. Leeds is a still a city of opportunity, an economic powerhouse with jobs in both the service and university sectors that make it attractive to Jews. The housing costs are moderate when compared to London, and this might influence younger people when making decisions on where to live. Leeds also has a Jewish High School[16] established in 2014, which makes the community attractive to Jewish in-migrants.

Economics seems to be the main force. If young Leeds Jews stay in Leeds, have families and are joined by other Jews coming from other centres, then the community has a future. If the out-migration continues, then a community that once numbered 25,000 and reduced to around 7,000 may find it has reduced further by 2021. This will be psychologically bad news as no one wants to live in what is perceived as a 'declining community' (Table 3.4).

In the 2011 Census, nationally Anglo-Jewry had grown by 3,000 – from 267,000 to 270,000 – a trend of growth unlike those in most diaspora communities where decline is the order of the day. This was seen as a great positive for Anglo-Jewry, that the downward spiral had been stopped. For Leeds Jewry, the question is whether the decline can be arrested and the community can grow.

The Jewish population of Leeds

Table 3.4 Leeds Jewish population estimates, *Jewish Year Book* 1990–2014

Year	Population
1990	12,000
1991	12,000
1992	10,000
1993	10,000
1994	12,000
1995	9,000
1996	9,000
1997	9,000
1998	8,250
1999	10,000
2000	8,000
2001	8,000
2002	9,000
2003	9,000
2004	8,267
2005	8,267
2006	8,267
2007	8,267
2009	8,267
2010	8,000+
2011*	8,000+
2012	8,000+
2013	8,000+
2014	8,000+

*The figures from 2011 onwards are communal estimates and are at variance with the 2011 Census figure of 6,847.

Notes

1 The Northern Ireland Census has included a religious question since 1926.
2 Russian here is used for all Jews in the Russian Empire and includes Jews from Poland.
3 In the United Hebrew Congregation, one of the memorial stained-glass windows is to Keetje Hertzveld, born in Arnhem.
4 Research in both Huddersfield and Bradford finds talk about a class of travelling Jewish salesmen, often in the jewellery or gifts trade, who worked across Yorkshire.
5 In Hull Paragon Station there is an Emigrants Platform and a plaque jointly unveiled by Hull City Council and Howard Golden, the President of the Borough of Brooklyn, New York, USA, to remember the two million people – a vast number of whom were Jews – who passed through the station on their way to America.

6 In Grimsby, it has been estimated by the authors of *The Story of the Grimsby Jewish Community* (Daphne and Leon Gerlis, Hull: Humberside Leisure Services, 1986), that 200,000 Jews came through the port in the period 1881–1914.
7 B. Kosmin and S. Waterman, 'The Use and Misuse of Distinctive Jewish Names in Research on Jewish Populations', Avraham Harman Institute of Contemporary Jewry, Hebrew University of Jerusalem, 1985.
8 The method used was to calculate the frequency with which the name Cohen appeared in a particular Jewish community and then use it as a multiplier against, for example, Cohens in synagogue membership lists to act as an estimator of population.
9 The figures were obtained using the Free BMD: website www.freebmd.org.uk (accessed 3 May 2017).
10 Miron Kantorowitsch, 'Estimate of the Jewish Population of London in 1929–1933', Royal Statistical Society, 1936.
11 These figures were calculated before the Holocaust. In Poland, Lodz, an industrial city with a population of 665,000 – slightly larger than Leeds – had a Jewish population of 233,000.
12 E. Krausz, *Leeds Jewry* (Cambridge: W. Heffer & Sons Limited for the Jewish Historical Society of England, 1964).
13 In Bradford, the adjoining Local Authority to Leeds, in 2016 the Metropolitan District's population was estimated at 531,000, of whom 131,000 – just under 25% – were estimated to be Muslim. www.bradford.gov.uk/open-data/our-datasets/population (accessed 3 May 2017).
14 There were debates about whether all Jews answered the religious question.
15 Murray Freedman, 1928–2011, was a retired dentist who for many years kept meticulous records on the demography of Leeds Jewry. He was a great researcher of the community, helping many discover their ancestors.
16 LJFS – the Leeds Jewish Free School.

Part II
The chronology

4

Jews as Yorkshiremen:
Jewish identity in late-Victorian Leeds

James Appell

In June 1888, *The Lancet* medical journal published a report by its Special Sanitary Commission which gave an eye-witness account of life in Leeds' predominantly Jewish quarter, the Leylands. For several years *The Lancet* had reported on the risks to the health of the general population posed by unsanitary conditions in the tailoring industry, particularly in the many hundreds of small, reeking, unventilated workshops, where 'Jew sweaters' toiled for 16 hours or more and, in the breaks between, snacked on bread and weak tea or simply curled up on a bed, pulling the clothes they were making over themselves into a makeshift blanket, to rest for a while.[1] Dispatched to Leeds, Britain's tailoring heartland, in the wake of several significant outbreaks of smallpox and typhoid, *The Lancet*'s correspondents bravely took to their task of describing, in often lurid detail, the strange liquids, noxious odours and foul conditions they encountered in the streets, workshops and lavatories of the Leylands.

> Close by, we ascended a dark dirty staircase, where a fetid odour prevailed, and reached a large barn-like garret in which some forty people were at work. The heat from the coke fire was intense; and this and the sulphur fumes, when mingling with the damp (caused by the water coming through the roof), did not improve the quality of the air we had to breathe. There were two good closets with flush working well, but the boards wanted scrubbing, and there was no separate room for meals. Tea was taken while at work, and dinner anywhere outside.[2]

Even a century and a quarter hence, *The Lancet*'s account possesses a vividness that resonates with modern readers. Few other contemporary sources have so successfully brought the Leylands to life and given the report's brevity – it stretches over barely five pages of the journal – even fewer have been so richly detailed. For that reason, time and again, those who seek to tell the story of the Leeds Jewish community have returned to the report of the Special Sanitary Commission for inspiration.

The Lancet's report stuck largely to its stated task of investigating links between conditions in the workshops and poor health, but here and there it offered up tantalising detail on the thoughts, feelings and opinions of the local Jewish population. Included in the report's preamble was the brief observation that many of the Jewish immigrants to Leeds, of which by 1888 there were as many as 8,000 making up around 2% of the city's population, 'boast that they are Yorkshire men, but they rarely qualify themselves as Englishmen'.[3] It is a statement which, though frustratingly unsubstantiated, nevertheless strikes a chord today. To this Leeds Jewish boy, writing in the twenty-first century, the existence of a distinct Leeds Jewish identity, infused with Yorkshire pride – I note with particular satisfaction *The Lancet*'s deployment of the verb 'boast' – feels incontestable, even as, paradoxically, research has repeatedly challenged the idea of a monolithic communal identity common to all members.[4] Irina Kudenko's 'typical Jewish Loiners', 'a uniform Jewish group in terms of its immigrant origin, adherence to traditional Orthodoxy, working class status and affiliation with tailoring businesses', are not simply pastiche.[5] Add in the socio-cultural reference points, identified by Anthony Clavane, that tie Leeds Jews to their non-Jewish neighbours as much as to one another – from a love of Leeds United Football Club to a defiantly 'Northern' working-class spirit found in the poetry of Tony Harrison or the novels of David Peace – and a quite evocative picture of modern Leeds Jewish identity emerges.[6]

It is reaffirming to glimpse in the anecdotes of a nineteenth century observer the roots of that identity. And there is good reason to explore the historical record further, to understand more deeply what constituted the identity of the nascent Leeds Jewish community in the years of mass immigration and population growth, from 1880 to 1920. To what extent was this community idiosyncratic, specifically conditioned by its location in Leeds? How were the Leylands Jews united with and divided from their non-Jewish neighbours, and from their co-religionists in other parts of Great Britain? The answers to these questions are relevant to today's Jewish communities, where debates over the nature of Jewish identity are commonplace at the family dinner table and at the synagogue pulpit, as much as on the pages of Jewish historiography.[7] More broadly, with migration and its discontents once again on the political agenda, understanding the way in which Jewish immigrants to Leeds defined themselves, both within and against the society around them, can be valuable to academics, policymakers and ordinary members of the public. And for anyone who calls themselves a Leeds Jew, looking at how the community took shape in the late nineteenth century can simply enrich one's own sense of self.

The Jews who had established themselves in Leeds in 1880 were almost all first-generation immigrants to Britain. Leeds had a population of fewer than thirty Jewish families throughout the first half of the nineteenth century, and such was the city's status as a relative backwater in this period that the early community sourced its kosher meat from Sheffield and only opened a dedicated synagogue in 1846.[8] The nearly 3,000 Jewish men, women and children registered in the city in 1881 were thus the product of the migratory trend from Eastern Europe which took off in the 1860s. In several significant respects, these Leeds Jews shared aspects in common which helped to shape an idiosyncratic communal identity, distinct from London and other provincial cities.

First, the mass of Jewish migrants did not arrive in Leeds to find an Anglo-Jewish community already in situ. In the urban centres of London and Manchester – but also in provincial market towns, resorts and ports across the country – a pre-existing Jewish community largely made up of Spanish, Portuguese, German or Dutch emigres was on hand to greet them. For these Jews who had worked hard to establish their position in British society, the mass influx of immigrants from the East represented a challenge. 'As long as there is a section of Jews in England who proclaim themselves alien by their mode of life, by their very looks, by every word they utter, so long will the community be an object of distrust to Englishmen', a *Jewish Chronicle* editorial thundered in 1891.[9] There ensued attempts of various kinds to sand off the immigrants' rough edges, whether in promoting Anglo-Jewish religious doctrine, through English-style schooling, or – in the case of the London Board of Guardians – sending volunteers into new arrivals' homes to offer advice on childrearing and hygiene. In Leeds, pre-existing institutional structures were conspicuous by their absence. The local Jewish Board of Guardians was founded only in 1878, to be joined by at least ten other charitable organisations which sprang up by the end of the century, as did the Leeds Jewish Workers' Burial and Trading Society, a cooperative to enable members to afford the cost of burial and of kosher meat (and whose sign above the shop window, reputed to have read 'Leeds Jewish Workers Burial Society – Fresh Supplies Daily', has become the community's oldest-running joke).[10] The initiatives to support new arrivals and speed their process of adaptation into the Leylands were thus spearheaded by the immigrants themselves, and Anglo-Jewish influence on the community's identity was comparatively restricted.

Augmenting the specifically Eastern European Ashkenazi flavour of the community was the fact that it appears to have been largely drawn from the Northern Pale of Settlement, rather than a 'cosmopolitan' mix of Jews from across the Pale. Across Britain's immigrant Jewish communities, social groupings formed based on solidarity among *landsmen*. *Chevroth*, small, self-administered religious congregations established by groups of immigrants, were named for the towns and villages from which their members emigrated. In London, the Kalisch, Kovno and Kiev *chevroth* which formed during the period denote a wide area of provenance, from modern-day Poland, Lithuania and Ukraine respectively – and by extension, a diverse set of regional identities within the immigrant population. Northern Pale Litvaks and Southern Polaks, for instance, were both represented in the capital and in other provincial towns. *The Lancet*, however, stated that 'the greater part [of the Leeds community] come from the province of Kovno', and further research has centred on an area 75 miles in radius around the modern Lithuanian city of Kaunas.[11]

The pattern of formation of *chevroth* in Leeds somewhat complicates this picture: the Lithuanian town of Marijampole, which gave its name to the city's Mariempoler Synagogue, is a mere 40 miles from Kaunas – and Vilnius, home to the founders of the Vilna Synagogue, is 65 miles away – but the Lokever *chevrah*, named for the modern-day village of Laukuva, is more than 90 miles away, and the accounts of individual immigrants suggest many came to Leeds from even further afield.[12] Certainly, though, there was a greater affinity for Northern Pale Litvak identity in Leeds. In 1889, presenting evidence to the Select Committee on the Sweating System, Reverend Moses Abrahams noted that 'there are not more than 35 Polish Jews in the whole of Leeds, the majority come from Russia'; while Murray Freedman reports that David Shiffer, who moved to Leeds in 1913, was forced to change his Yiddish pronunciation from his native Polak to Litvak to ease his way into the community.[13] This brief detail hints at the narrower form of immigrant identity deemed permissible in Leeds at the time.

Indeed, this relatively narrow cultural identity manifested in religious identity too. Observers noted the relative unanimity with which Leeds Jews of all *chevroth* dealt with matters of faith and religious practice, in contrast to 'the bickersome congeries of bethels in every larger community'.[14] At least in part, this came down to the early community's apparent ambivalence towards synagogue attendance, with A. S. Diamond estimating that as many as two-thirds had no synagogue membership at all in the period.[15] Nevertheless, the degree of unity around the figure of Rabbi Israel Daiches, who arrived in Leeds from the Lithuanian village of Darsunskis (25 miles from Kovno, incidentally) in 1901, suggests a community of limited heterodoxies. Daiches became, in the words of Lloyd Gartner, 'the communal rabbi of the immigrants', despite officially serving as the Rabbi of Beth Hamedrash Hagadol synagogue, and successfully united the community around matters of *shechita* and a unified *Beth Din* [religious court] for the city by the early 1910s.[16] Out of this, perhaps, sprung the system of 'traditional' religious practice apparent across the Leeds community a century later.[17]

Outside of synagogue, the workplace also served to underscore relative homogeneity in the community. Leeds was neither a capital city nor a port of entry, which meant that anyone migrating there did so with specific purpose. Family members or *landsmen* were one natural pull factor in bringing others to the city – men sending for wives from the Old Country, or inviting their friends and relatives to join them. But the main engine of migration was the city's burgeoning textile industry, and this too left its mark on the Leeds Jewish community. Quite simply, tailoring dominated the lives of Leeds Jews to an extent unmatched in any other city. Records show that in 1891, 72% of working adults (male *and* female) were participating in the tailoring trade, and the link between the industry and Leeds community remained so close that as late as the 1920s, 62% of men who married in local synagogues were tailors or connected in some other way to the clothing trade.[18] Contrast this with Londoners, who could engage in shoe- and boot-making, cabinet-making, slipper-making, cap-making, fur work, cigarette-making and artificial flower work, all of which were relatively large employers of immigrant Jewish labour in the capital (leaving aside the livelihoods of the more esteemed Anglo-Jewish aristocracy).[19] In Leeds, tailoring was in the blood. The mechanisms of the tailoring trade also hint at Leeds's connection to the Kovno region – a Kovno master tailor, Moyshe (Morris) Goodman – recognised the opportunity for enrichment in the industry on his arrival in Leeds in 1866, and made numerous trips back to his home city to recruit *landsmen* for his workshops.[20] Aspects of Leeds Jewish identity thus neatly overlapped.

Unquestionably, too, this was a poor community. The general standard of living in the Leylands paints a picture of stark poverty. In 1881, 15.5% of Jewish families settling in the Leylands shared a home with at least one other family.[21] Piled cheek-by-jowl in meagre accommodation, with unhygienic lavatories and stinking 'middens' into which rubbish was poured, the immigrants scratched out a tough existence. As one writer put it, 'bread, finding work, clothing the children, keeping alive, the day to day struggle, these were the problems they went to bed with and which each morning light greeted them'.[22] The response from the community was to largely self-support through the charitable organisations mentioned above, but also informally – sometimes providing food for the needy, at other times raising money to buy back the possessions of indebted neighbours from bailiffs.[23]

Was this solidarity evidence of the formation of a Jewish working class in Leeds? In the sense described by Todd Endelman, 'meant to convey the occupational structure, poverty, working conditions, labour struggles', certainly.[24] Jewish tailors were not part of the 'aristocracy' of skilled master tailors in Leeds. The development across the nineteenth century of a sub-divisional system of garment manufacture, in which the process of making an item of clothing was broken down into individual tasks to be divided among a number of workers, was a boon for lower-paid and lower-skilled workers. By the 1880s, Leeds' factories were struggling to keep up with demand, and workshops sprang up to provide ancillary labour. These workshops were the domain of the Jewish tailors and, unlike the atomised homeworkers of London's East End, were often large enough to be considered factories in their own right. Anne Kershen finds that an average Leeds workshop employed twenty-five to thirty-five hands, while a more typical figure for London would be eight to twelve.[25] Life was tough in the workshops, where, for upwards of 14 hours a day, workers toiled, sharing the dangers and stresses of their environment with their fellow Jews.[26] The insanitary conditions noted by *The Lancet* were bad enough but, depending on levels of seniority or skill, the work itself could be perilous:

> The cloth, said a cutter to me, is made of anything and everything except cast iron. It is sized with manure, so that when we put the iron to it we get choked with stinking gas. The cutter added that string, cork, feathers, wire and stones are found in quantities in this kind of cloth … and when the knives come into contact with a hard stone or wire there is a danger of breaking. And when one of those endless band knives does break, as happens very often, you never know where it's going to fly to.[27]

To suggest this was a conscious, organised working class, however, would be stretching the point. Shared economic experience did not automatically lead to a shift towards organised politics. Unlike in London, where groups of radical intellectuals constituted part of the formation of a uniquely Jewish political identity ('a conduit through which Jewish immigrant workers found their way into the mainstream British labour movement'),[28] in Leeds ideology failed to resonate. London was the home of radical newspapers such as *Arbeter Fraynd* and *Der Poylisher Yidl* which played an instrumental role in the political education of the Jewish East End; it also attracted leading figures in the socialist movement such as Morris Winchevsky and Elijah Wolf Rabbinowitz, whose leadership helped to organise politically the capital's Jewish workers.[29] In Leeds there was little working-class political theory being discussed.

This has led to the suggestion among some observers that the Leeds Jewish community of this period was, in the delicate words of Murray Freedman, 'culturally undistinguished'.[30] The London-based *Poylisher Yidl* newspaper, founded by Morris Winchevsky in 1884, used its inaugural edition to berate Leeds Jews' preference for gambling over more constructive political or educational pursuits:

> Leeds workers and small masters, as soon as they are paid run straight to the pubs and bet on horses. The main centre for these pursuits is Swan Street, the Leeds workers' main rendezvous. Here 6 to 1 is offered for 'Tsadik' which Charles Ward will ride; 3 to 1 elsewhere, while another shouts and makes hand

signals. Cries of 'Little Dog!' and 'Cleopatra!' for the winners. Everyone has a Sporting Chronicle in his hand to learn whether he can retrieve from the horse the week's wages he has laid out in bets, counts with his fingers and questions, talking English like a born Russian. In short, the Jewish workers hand over the money and the bookmakers take it gladly.[31]

Aside from what this fanaticism for horseracing might tell us about the culture of the Leeds Jews (the roots of the community's later love affair with football, perhaps?), Winchesvky missed an important fact of life for the Jews of Leeds – the demands of working in the tailoring industry meant there was precious little time for politics during the working week. Moreover, the poverty of the community pressured families to remove children from education and put them in the workplace, even to the extent of deliberately misrepresenting their ages to remove them from the school system.[32] In such circumstances, is it any wonder that Moses Sclare, a prominent Leeds trade unionist, said of the first generation of Jewish settlers in the city that 'few can read an English newspaper, they know no English nor do they want to read or write in Yiddish' – never mind muster up the energy for political debate.[33]

That said, one mode of political expression which did take root in Leeds in the period was trade unionism. The foregoing story of community solidarity undoubtedly played a role in the Jewish tailors' strikes of 1885 and 1888 in Leeds, which constituted possibly the earliest and largest cases of Jewish trade union action in Great Britain. In early summer 1885, Jewish workers won a reduction of one hour from their working day through a week-long strike involving 600 strikers. The strike three years later similarly campaigned 'that hours should be 58 per week, and that any overtime should be paid at the rate of time and a half', this time attracting 3,000 Jewish workers to the pickets.[34] By 1915, Leeds boasted a single union – the Amalgamated Jewish Tailors', Machiners' and Pressers' Trade Union (AJTMP) – with a membership of 4,500 representing around 23% of the Jewish tailoring workforce. London, meanwhile, did not have such coherent unions or such a high membership, with around fifty unions in an atomised structure containing 5,634 Jewish members between them out of a total working population of 65,000, or 8.6%.[35]

The success of trade unionism suggests fractures in the apparent unity of the Leeds Jewish community, with Jewish tailors organising against their Jewish masters. That said, the masters' position was a tenuous one, caught between his workshop hands and the factories or middlemen who fed them often irregular work orders. The Jewish tailor rapidly moved between employee work and bossing others depending on financial circumstances, and strikers in 1885 who deserted their masters' workshops could be the very same people who three years later were on the other end of a walkout. It is important to look at the entire system of subdivisional garment production, rather than focusing simply on the relationship between Jewish workshop hands and masters, to identify the source of industrial strife.[36]

Another lesson to take from Leeds Jewish trade unionism is the way in which Jews and non-Jews began to come together in the period. The Jewish strikers of 1888 were aided by local non-Jewish political organisers, such as James Sweeney and Tom Maguire.[37] As early as 1889, the Jewish tailors' union in Leeds affiliated to the non-denominational local branch of the Gasworkers' and General Labourers' Union, and although that marriage soon fell apart, the amalgamation of the various tailoring unions forming the United Garment Workers' Trade Union in 1915 had Leeds Jewish tailors at the forefront, making up a quarter of the national membership. As head of the Leeds Jewish tailors' union in the early twentieth century, Moses Sclare had built links to the Labour Party and the TUC which furthered rapprochement with non-Jewish institutions. This cooperation between workers across the ethnic divide distinguishes Leeds from other English communities and gives some credence to the idea of Leeds' working-class Jews, as *The Lancet* suggested, being ready to identify as Yorkshiremen.

One serious mitigating factor, however, was the anti-Semitism experienced by the Leylands Jews. Unquestionably, Jews in all parts of Britain experienced anti-Semitism of some kind, so pervasive was the phenomenon across geographies and social strata. The dislocations caused by mass migration inflamed tensions in the period, which were in turn fanned by political developments such as the Aliens' Act of 1905, organisations such as the British Brothers' League or the Londoners League, and notably individuals such as Arnold White.[38] Hence, common to many areas in which immigrant Jews settled in Britain is the kind of account related by E. E. Burgess, writing for the *Yorkshire Post* about the Leylands 'ghetto', of the unfortunate coincidence between the Jewish Sabbath and pay-day for the Gentile working class:

> Then was it that the poor aged immigrant, garbed in his Sabbath best – in those days usually a frock-coat and tall silk hat – became the gibe and sport of the mob. As he wended his way to the Synagogue, he would be jostled, spat and jeered at; delirious and drink-sodden women would hiccough foul suggestions, and sober but perverted Amazons think it a huge joke to tug at his flowing beard and earlocks. The boys and girls, encouraged by their demoralised parents, would contribute their quota to the 'carnival' by making the helpless poor immigrant a target for mud and stone-flinging.[39]

However, while Leeds remains part of this general experience of Jewish immigrants in Britain, the city provided exceptional circumstances in the fact that its inhabitants noted an especially sharp anti-Semitic feeling. As E. E. Burgess put it, 'Leeds had the notorious distinction of being the most anti-Semitic city in the kingdom'.[40] Louis Teeman and Burgess recalled the fear among the Jews of marauding gangs of Irish youths who would cross the Lady Beck armed with rocks and sticks. As late as 1915, Louis Wigoder recalled being refused a job at the Leeds Dental Hospital because of his Judaism, the hospital preferring to appoint a non-Jewish student 'in spite of the fact he was not qualified'.[41] Even in 1920, half a century since the start of the influx of Jews from Eastern Europe, Leeds was often an unwelcoming place for them, as Selig Brodetsky testified:

> We stopped at a restaurant for coffee. No waitress came to our table. I spoke to one of the waitresses about it. She looked embarrassed and said I should speak to the manager. The manager asked me: 'Are you of the Jewish persuasion?' 'Yes,' I said, 'but what has that got to do with coffee?' 'We don't serve Jews here,' he replied.[42]

If Leeds Jews encountered a daily undercurrent of hostility, the events of June 1917 – the largest and most prominent anti-Semitic riot in Britain since the return of the Jews in the seventeenth century – represented an explosive incident of intercommunal strife. A 1911 riot in the Welsh town of Tredegar, and various incidents throughout the period in London's East End, underlined the precarious security of Britain's Jews. Still, reading accounts of what occurred in Leeds over three days beginning Sunday 3 June, in the middle of the First World War, one is struck by the vociferousness of the attack. Police reports suggest that rumours surfaced in the non-Jewish quarters of the city that a gang of Jews had attacked a wounded soldier returned from the front in Northern France. Soon, a large mob, estimated at around one thousand, and mainly comprised of young men not yet old enough for conscription, had assembled and begun breaking windows in the Leylands and looting from the shop fronts – watched by an apparently impassive crowd of 3,000 onlookers. It was clear that only Jewish shops were targeted. The police were called but failed to deal adequately with the situation as unrest resumed the morning after, with further mobs armed with sticks and stones marauding through the Leylands. It was only by the Tuesday that the police had begun to restore order, as a motorcade arrived and dispersed the crowd. No Jews were killed, but the experience must have been traumatic, particularly for those Jews who may have felt that they had long left behind the violence of Tsarist pogroms.[43]

Undoubtedly wartime conditions exacerbated pre-existing tensions. One of the arguments put forward as to why the events of 3–5 June 1917 occurred was the perception that Jewish males of fighting age were avoiding military service. Before the war, Jews had largely avoided voluntary service – only two men signed up for the Leeds Rifles for any significant length of time, with just one, Solly Hernberg, sent to fight in the Boer War.[44] When conscription began, anecdotal evidence exists of Jews emigrating to the United States to avoid service.⁴⁵ Quite clearly, having left Tsarist Russia at least in part to avoid the cantonment – a mandatory six-year period of military service for adolescent Jewish males, used in part to aggressively strip them of their Jewish culture – there was little appetite to join up, much less so on the same side as the Russian Imperial forces.⁴⁶ Perceptions carried over into wartime. As early as the summer of 1915, there had been unease at the presence of Jews who were of fighting age on the streets of Leeds and local newspapers reported that only around 350 Jews of a population of nearly 20,000 had enlisted in the army since the start of the war. As the local chief constable conveyed to the Home Office on 18 June that year, 'the large number of alien Russian Jews of military age that we have in this city … can be constantly seen promenading about our principal streets and the various, pleasure resorts … and members of the Christian population have been heard to ask why these men are not serving in the Army'.⁴⁷

Those perceptions did not, however, always correspond to reality. As many of the Leeds Jewish community were not yet naturalised British citizens, they were classed as friendly aliens and so would not serve in the British Army until the Anglo-Russian Military Service Agreement was concluded in July 1917. For those that did qualify, health problems resulting from the conditions they worked in – the reason, after all, for the investigation by government and *The Lancet* in 1888 – were particularly acute in Leeds. One in five military recruits in the city was rejected, diagnosed primarily with myopia, a dropout rate three times higher than the population at large.⁴⁸ Moreover, the importance of Leeds as a tailoring centre again became apparent, this time in the production of khaki for the troops serving abroad. Jews who were deemed important skilled workers in the trade were provided with war badges exempting them from conscription on the basis that they remained in the textile trade for the duration of the war. Finally, and most significantly, the *British Jewry Book of Honour*, a commemorative register of Jews serving in the First World War, counted 3,040 single and 610 married Jews who had joined the Armed Forces in the years 1914–18, out of a total population of 20,000. The complaint that Jews were not pulling their weight was wide of the mark.⁴⁹

The wartime discord prompted some soul-searching within the community, which began questioning whether the economic and social bonds between Jew and non-Jew, forged in Leeds by the conditions of the tailoring trade, were really as strong as the trade unions and socialist movements might have portrayed. The *Jewish Chronicle* offered its own analysis just a few weeks after the Leeds riot concluded:

> There has been a very large and sudden increase in the Jewish population of Leeds during the last few years, and that there has in consequence been considerable inconvenience in many directions to the indigenous inhabitants … Towns, like countries, can assimilate only a certain Jewish element in a certain

time, and the Jewish addition to the population of Leeds has been too much and too fast.[50]

The rapid entry of nearly 20,000 Jews into Leeds within the space of two generations clearly exerted pressures on the local population. In this respect Leeds may have differed from London and other provincial cities, where Jewish immigration from Eastern Europe was of a longer duration, where an Anglo-Jewish community already existed and where tensions were less marked than in Leeds. Poverty and mode of employment may have united the two groups, but ultimately religious difference divided them. In such circumstances, therefore, Leeds Jews' identity as Yorkshiremen was only ever going to be fragile.

This combination of formative influences – the absence of an elite 'guiding hand', the relatively concentrated area of out-migration to Leeds, the further unifying role played by the tailoring industry and trade unionism, the curbs on assimilation posed by anti-Semitism – were the seeds of a Leeds Jewish identity born and raised between 1880 and 1920. The single line in *The Lancet*'s 1888 report stands up to scrutiny, to a limited degree. Leeds Jews may have boasted they were Yorkshiremen, when contrasting themselves to other Jews in London, Manchester and elsewhere. Leeds Jews shared much in common with one another, notably their place of birth and their place of work, and they succeeded where other communities failed in finding common cause with the city's working class of non-Jews. But in another way *The Lancet* erred entirely – the Jews could never truly be Yorkshiremen because of the racial barriers placed on membership in that group.[51] Anti-Semitism served as a brake on integration, though it did act to unite the inhabitants of the Leylands together in a further kind of shared experience.

Considering quite how homogeneous the Leeds community was, when compared to other cities, it would perhaps be easy to assume that everyone in the community signed up to these core ideas, and that discord or disagreements were consequently more muted. To do so would be to oversimplify the complexity of identity formation, and to obscure individual or collective acts of dissent. Reading the verbatim accounts of life in the period from Louis Saipe's 1956 study of the Leeds Jews, one gets the impression of a community riven with disagreements and infighting.[52] The *Jewish Chronicle* reported in 1906 that '[t]he casual investigator into the conditions of the Leeds Jewish community cannot fail to be struck by the lamentable lack of co-operation that exists among the various sections'.[53] That was a view seconded by A. S. Diamond, who concluded that 'rather than regarding Leeds Jews as forming one community, it seems more appropriate to see them as making up a number of more or less closely linked groups, or sections'.[54]

There are two ways to interpret this phenomenon. One is that it serves to highlight the limitations of any attempt to ascribe a collective identity to groups even as apparently homogeneous as the Leeds immigrant community. The work of this chapter has been to try and build up a picture of shared values, ideas and symbols among the Jews of Leeds. That picture is at best fragmentary. The other, by contrast, is that perhaps this very disharmony among the Leeds Jews of the period is itself indicative of a quintessential element of Leeds Jewish identity, a kind of shared unwillingness to conform and a distaste for authority. Those sentiments at times focused inwards – but arguably became a unifying force when focused outwards. From a 1910 editorial in the (sadly) short-lived, Leeds-based *Anglo-Jewry* magazine, a very Yorkshire defiance seemed to be emerging within the community:

> It [the *Jewish Chronicle*] lives in a little conceited superstructure of its own. It imagines, that as far as English-speaking Jews are concerned, all the wisdom, all the brilliance, all the genius has been drawn from all over the world over into the one great vortex, London; and thence, the remaining quintessence, within the four walls of the Jewish Chronicle offices. But the Chronicle had better disillusion itself. For Jews exist, and in large numbers too, outside London, who are not altogether dumb asses, nor aping mules, and who possess at least a spark of the sense of honour and fair play.[55]

Leeds Jews thumbing their noses at the London elites and complaining about the snootiness of the *Jewish Chronicle*? That's a trait which many modern Leeds Jews would identify with.

Notes

1 'Workmen on the Sweating System', *Lancet*, 109:2806 (9 June 1877), p. 854.
2 'Report of the Lancet Special Sanitary Commission on the Sweating System in Leeds', *Lancet*, 131:3380 (9 June 1888), p. 1147.
3 Ibid., p. 1146; M. Freedman, *Leeds Jewry: The First Hundred Years* (Leeds: Jewish Historical Society of England, 1992), pp. 23–30.
4 A review of the literature on analysing identity within minority groups can be found in I. Kudenko, 'Negotiating Jewishness: Identity and Citizenship in the Leeds Jewish Community' (PhD Dissertation, University of Leeds, 2007), pp. 13–43.
5 Ibid., p. 172.
6 A. Clavane, *Promised Land: A Northern Love Story* (London: Yellow Jersey Press, 2011).
7 'The Jewish identity obsession', *Haaretz*, 10 July 2013; E. Ben-Rafael, Y. Gorny and Y. Ro'I, *Contemporary Jewries: Convergence and Divergence* (Leiden: Brill, 2003).
8 E. Krausz, *Leeds Jewry* (Cambridge: W. Heffer & Sons Limited for the Jewish Historical Society of England, 1964), p. 2; Freedman, *Leeds Jewry*, p. 5.
9 *Jewish Chronicle*, 7 August 1891.
10 D. Francis, *Will You Still Need Me, Will You Still Feed Me, When I'm 84?* (Bloomington: Indiana University Press, 1984), p. 33.

11 'Lancet Special Sanitary Commission on the Sweating System in Leeds', p. 1146; A. Kershen, 'Trade Unionism in London and Leeds, 1872–1915' in D. Cesarani (ed.), *The Making of Modern Anglo-Jewry* (Oxford: Wiley-Blackwell, 1990), p. 51.
12 Betsy Brown's family migrated to Leeds from the Belorussian town of Babruysk in the 1890s, 250 miles from Kaunas. Interview with Betsy Brown, Brown family private collection.
13 Select Committee of House of Lords on Sweating System Fourth Report, 1889 (331), q. 30868; Freedman, *Leeds Jewry*, p. 6.
14 L. Gartner, *The Jewish Immigrant in England 1870–1914* (London: Vallentine Mitchell, 1960), p. 215.
15 A. S. Diamond, 'A Sketch of Leeds Jewry in the 19th Century', paper for JHSE conference *Provincial Jewry in Victorian England* (University College London, 6 July 1975).
16 Gartner, *The Jewish Immigrant*, p. 216.
17 Kudenko, 'Negotiating Jewishness'.
18 Freedman, *Leeds Jewry*, pp. 28–9; T. Endelman, *The Jews of Britain 1656–2000* (Berkley and Los Angeles: University of California Press, 2002), p. 132.
19 Endelman, *The Jews of Britain*, pp. 131–4; Gartner, *The Jewish Immigrant*, pp. 93–4.
20 A. Kershen, *Uniting the Tailors: Trade Unionism amongst the Tailors of London and Leeds 1870–1939* (Abingdon: Routledge, 1996), p. 36.
21 L. Vaughan and A. Penn, 'Jewish immigrant settlement patterns in Manchester and Leeds 1881', *Urban Studies*, 43:3 (March 2006), pp. 653–71.
22 L. Teeman, *Footprints in the Sand* (Leeds: privately printed, 1995), p. 171.
23 Ibid., p. 33; G. Raisman, *The Undark Sky: A Story of Four Poor Brothers* (Newport Pagnell: Harehills Press, 2002), pp. 87–8.
24 Endelman, *The Jews of Britain*, p. 142.
25 Kershen, *Uniting the Tailors*, pp. 41–2.
26 Gartner, *The Jewish Immigrant*, p. 118 mentions 'the usual 13–14 hour day'. The Lords' Select Committee uncovered evidence of work being carried out from 8am 'up until 2 or 3 o'clock in the morning'. Select Committee of House of Lords on Sweating System Fourth Report, q. 30026.
27 R. H. Sherard, 'The slipper-makers and tailors of Leeds', *Pearsons Magazine* (1896), p. 265.
28 G. Alderman, *Modern British Jewry* (Oxford: Clarendon Press, 1992), p. 179.
29 Ibid., pp. 167–79; Endelman, *The Jews of Britain*, pp. 137–42.
30 Freedman, *Leeds Jewry*, p. 10.
31 *Poylisher Yidl*, 25 July 1884, quoted in W. Fishman, *Morris Winchevsky's London Yiddish Newspaper: One Hundred Years in Retrospect* (Oxford: Oxford Centre for Post-Graduate Hebrew Studies, 1985).
32 Interview with Betsy Brown.
33 Kershen, *Uniting the Tailors*, p. 11.
34 C. Holmes, 'Leeds Jewish tailors' strikes of 1885 and 1888', *Yorkshire Archaeological Journal*, 45 (1973), pp. 160–4.

35 Kershen, *Uniting the Tailors*, pp. 1–2; Kershen, 'Trade Unionism in London and Leeds', pp. 35–6.
36 J. Buckman, *Immigrants and the Class Struggle: The Jewish Immigrant in Leeds 1880–1914* (Manchester: Manchester University Press, 1983).
37 Kershen, *Uniting the Tailors*, pp. 64–8.
38 C. Holmes, *Anti-Semitism in British Society* (London: Edward Arnold, 1979) pp. 89–140.
39 E. E. Burgess, 'Soul of the Leeds Ghetto', *Yorkshire Evening News*, 19 January–16 February 1925, p. 6, Leeds Central Library Archives, LQ 296 B912.
40 Ibid., p. 3.
41 Ibid., pp. 7–8; Teeman, *Footprints in the Sand*, pp. 8–9; L. Wigoder and P. Ruby, 'Ruby and Louis: Memoirs', p. 40, West Yorkshire Archives, WYL1978 10/5/1.
42 S. Brodetsky, *Memoirs: From Ghetto to Israel* (London: Weidenfeld and Nicholson, 1960), p. 93.
43 For primary reports on the riot, see *Leeds Mercury*, 4 June 1917; *Yorkshire Evening Post*, 4 June 1917; *Yorkshire Post* 4 and 5 June; *Jewish Chronicle*, 8, 15 and 22 June. Analysis of the events is offered in Holmes, *Anti-Semitism*, pp. 130–4; A. Gilam, 'The Leeds Anti-Jewish riots 1917' *Jewish Quarterly*, 29:1 (1981), pp. 34–8; N. Grizzard, *Leeds Jewry and the Great War* (Leeds: Leeds Jewish Historical Society, 1981) pp. 8–9.
44 P. M. Morris, 'Leeds and the Amateur Military Tradition', PhD thesis, University of Leeds (September 1983), pp. 70–3.
45 Interview with Betsy Brown.
46 On cantonment, see B. Nathans, *Beyond the Pale: The Jewish Encounter with Late Imperial Russia* (California: University of California Press, 2004), pp. 27–30.
47 Home Office record 45 10810/311932/40, cited in Holmes, *Anti-Semitism*, p. 131.
48 Endelman, *The Jews of Britain*, p. 136.
49 M. Adler (ed.), *British Jewry Book of Honour* (London: Caxton, 1922). Of those who served, 98 died, while two Leeds Jews won the Distinguished Conduct Medal and eight the Military Medal.
50 *Jewish Chronicle*, 22 June 1917, p. 8.
51 These racial barriers arguably exist to this day, as evidenced in Fletcher, T., '"Aye, but it were wasted on thee": Cricket, British Asians, ethnic identities, and the "magical recovery of community"', *Sociological Research Online*, 16:4 (November 2011), p. 5.
52 L. Saipe, *A History of the Jews of Leeds* (Leeds: Tercentenary Committee, 1956).
53 *Jewish Chronicle*, 29 June 1906, quoted in Diamond, 'A Sketch of Leeds Jewry in the 19th Century'.
54 Diamond, 'A Sketch of Leeds Jewry in the 19th Century'.
55 *Anglo-Jewry*, 1:2 (15 April 1910), pp. 8–9.

5

Britishness and Jewishness: integration *and* separation

Aaron Kent

In the nineteenth century, the city of Leeds stood out as a beacon to many who sought refuge from oppression and an opportunity to thrive. Conveniently located in the north of England, Leeds was well equipped in the late-Victorian era to act as shelter and catalyst for expanding Jewish and Gentile communities alike. A growing city in terms of population, industry and infrastructure, Leeds naturally benefited as political, economic and religious migrants looked westward. The story of Leeds was one of economic, cultural and religious growth. But for its Jewish community it was also one of evolution. Bernard Silver noted that 'thousands of ... Jewish immigrants ... all came with the purpose of commencing a new life – free from the perils, hardships and persecution of Eastern Europe'. He went on to say that it was also 'a period of terror for Jews'.[1] Any Jew's experiences there were largely dependent on what drove them to the city and how they were embraced. There were varying levels of integration and separation within the Leeds Jewish community and the city at large. An exploration of personal and shared experiences within the rapidly growing Jewish community highlights the challenges of migrant communities; what defines them, who defines them and why we define them.

Understanding the Jewish experience in Leeds enhances the vision and makes for more honest assessments of other communities. Ours is an era of displaced peoples and migrating cultures. With this greater clarity, societies can better serve such groups. However, with that noted, it has been appropriately written that the term Jewish community 'is extremely problematic and its careless usage promotes a false impression of homogeneity and shared values'.[2] Additionally, as noted by Tony Kushner, 'heritage tells us who we are and who we are not'.[3] The story of the Leeds Jews and the level of integration experienced by them reflect the 'heritage' they embraced or observed as vital in their sense of self.

This chapter will explore some experiences of new and young members of the community at the end of the nineteenth century. Their experiences in schools, clubs and with the existing community reveal much. In his study of the Jewish schools of Leeds, Murray Freedman keenly noted that classrooms were often a crucible for change (and not always the changes expected by either side).[4] Community efforts were both national and local, but as noted by John Doyle Klier, many that came from the East struggled with attempts to categorise and classify them. Even members within the existing community balanced ever so carefully between what it meant to be Jewish, Russian and any other number of titles.[5] At the very least they were Eastern as opposed to Western.[6] Or, as discussed by Geoffrey Alderman, Jewry was less than a singular and distinct sense of Jewishness but a number of Jewries.[7]

The existing Jewish community of Leeds offered incoming co-religionists much, but in many instances also expected great adjustments or acclimation. Through exploring this interaction, it becomes clear that both sides had expectations, but in many ways what developed was a third unexpected option or identity. As noted by Todd Endelman, some 'English Jews ... faced challenges to their inherited identities, made decisions to embrace, transform or reject non-Jewish values ... and enter[ed] new spheres of activity'.[8] Or as Rosalind O'Brien suggested, 'total assimilation ... [was] rare, and it depended upon both the majority ceasing to regard the minority as different, and upon the minority ceasing to wish to keep separate from the majority'.[9] This Leeds Jewishness adopted or developed by migrants was in many ways unique.

The exploration of developing identities within religious and ethnic communities serves as a valuable reflection of the greater society. The expectations on a national and local scale send a clear message to migrants on what is acceptable and what is not. Much of the West is currently consumed in multiple conversations about migrants and culture clashes. One cannot avoid the private and public impact these attitudes and actions have on minority groups and the public at large. O'Brien suggested that 'Ethnic identity implies a series of constraints on the kinds of roles an individual is allowed to play, and the partners he may choose for different kinds of transactions'.[10] Many families consulted while preparing this chapter made similar suggestions. There were levels of distinctness carefully managed depending on the situation.

Migration and community are not faceless or nameless experiences. It serves the observer well to look for the personalities impacted by this great upheaval of Eastern Jewry. Not only the individuals impacted, but also the second and third generation in some instances – for it is they who reflect choices made by their ancestors. Reception in Leeds varied greatly, and money, residence, religious devotion and community connections are but a few of the factors that enabled migrants to make a home, or in some cases pushed them on further to the United States. In a valuable discussion of

Integration and *separation*

'otherness' among the Jewish community, David Feldman quoted a popular opinion found in the *Jewish Chronicle* that most of the immigrants heralded from 'Russia and Poland, and whatever they are we are thought to be'. There was a serious concern that the immigrants 'inhabited this "other" Judaism'. There was disdain for their language, attitudes and the ghettos they inhabited. 'Un-English habits and thoughts were nurtured even in London by the institutional and associational life created by the immigrants ... where Pole meets Pole and becomes more Polish than ever.'[11] Ben-Zion Dinur suggested that the periods in which Jews exercised the most influence were periods in which they best assimilated into their various communities. Willingness to adapt and give up some of their distinctive individuality provided stability and led to greater influence among the communities.[12] Similarly, O'Brien argued:

> Because their whole position in society [Eastern Europe] derived from the fact that they were Jewish, so they had had a Jewish identity strongly forced upon them by the majority – and this identity was largely expressed in terms of religion. When they came to England and found themselves no longer living in Jewish enclaves ... and their Jewishness was no longer of prime relevance to every social contact, so the 'Jewishness' of their way of life dropped markedly.[13]

The question facing the community of Leeds was how best to move forward, in public or in the shadows?

Erich Rosenthal suggested that 'in central and western Europe assimilation was the price demanded from the Jews for their legal and social emancipation'.[14] The flight from Eastern Europe was not one made simply as an individual Jew but also one made as a community. Arrival in Leeds and other cities throughout Britain did not rob migrants of identity; rather, it afforded them an opportunity to assess in their own minds what was Jewish and what it meant to be Jewish in Leeds. However, at the same time, those who already resided there and jealously guarded hard won positions in society expressed great concern at how much help should be offered if it meant drawing unwanted attention to the community at large. For as O'Brien noted, 'Variations in dress, dialect, food preparation, form of synagogue service, and social customs in general were enough to be the basis of sharp divisions amongst the Jewish settlers in Leeds'.[15]

Children as a focus

Rich in tradition and history, members of the Jewish community of Leeds sought to instil in their rising generation a real sense of who they were and of belonging. Arnold Burton, a son of Montague Burton, was born in Leeds but later removed to Harrogate. He recalled the thorough study of religious text most evenings. He and the other boys would have often preferred being outside with their schoolmates.[16] Through education, clubs and religious instruction, the community conscientiously worked to ensure there was a level of Jewishness ingrained and retained. It was not enough that the existing community reach out and offer safe harbour for troubled co-religionists; it was also imperative (in their minds) that incoming migrants cast off obvious 'negative' behaviours and traditions while embracing the sense of approved Britishness they offered.

One of the problems faced when assessing emerging identities within Leeds and the development of a communal outlook was the evolving sense of 'home'. At the end of the nineteenth century, the idea of home for the working classes and migrants was less fixed than that of the middle class. Home was where you lived at any given time or it was who was living with you.[17] Migration and shifting work patterns developed breaks in traditional family ties, even among the most religious. There were a wide variety of experiences for children across religion, class and region, but in a general sense one can get a reliable idea of successful integration and evolving identities through the lens of childhood experiences. To community organisers and religious leaders, the children needed a group culture and identity above what their class gave them.[18] And more specifically with the Jewish community, groups such as the Jewish Lads' Brigade helped preserve British public-school/middle-class mentality and encourage a respect of authority.[19]

British Jewry collectively worked to raise a generation of Jews that continued a millennia-old and rich tradition of devotion but also reflected a degree of Britishness that they collectively felt was appropriate and 'safe'. For example, a letter from Gladys Montagu to an unnamed northern member of the Jewish Lads' Brigade read in part:

> Dear Lad, In sending you the photograph of my father, I should like to tell you that it was his hope to be with you in Camp this August, and, the day before his death, he spoke of you, 'his Northern boys,' and said he wanted so much to help you this summer. I am sure you will try and realise how much he cared for all the division of the Brigade of which he was Commandant, and how much he wanted each of you to live up to your highest ideal of a good citizen and a good Jew.[20]

This is the pathway they had to tread carefully. What was a good citizen and what was a good Jew? Did it mean the same as it did in the East? And if not, what was expected? The language of assimilation is not uniform. There were a variety of 'dialects' spoken across Britain. Navigating this delicate course proved to be challenging for many of the rising generation as well as recent immigrants. When interviewing grandchildren of migrants that arrived in the 1890s, O'Brien found a mixed view of the divided community of Jewish Leeds. She noted that 'newcomers looked at them [existing Leeds Jewry] as un Jewish

Integration and separation

or eccentric because of their drift from tradition. Yet they were also looked up to as elite for their time in the community and forward-looking ideas and actions.'[21] Freedman wrote that 'most of the immigrants were very poor and, of those who came to Leeds, few were intellectuals – in any sense'.[22] It was these generations that Leeds Jewry sought to steer towards integration.

Family experiences

Samuel Goodman left Leeds in the early years of the twentieth century. In an attempt to 'make it' in America, he rapidly left behind many of the outward appearances or habits of what was obviously Jewish in the city. Yet his children, and their children, were in many ways framed by his time spent in the city and among his co-religionists. His time in Leeds was largely transitory in nature, but it left an indelible mark which formed an identity that stands today in England and America. His son, Gene Gold, recalled a sense of disillusionment with the Jewish Community of Leeds which is father had always borne.[23] There was a feeling that the community could have done more to unite families but put community first when presented with a choice. Sam briefly enjoyed the safety of the streets of the Leylands. But he quickly realised that merely transporting himself and his brothers from one Jewish community in Eastern Europe to one in Britain was not the life he envisioned for them. He was one of many that sought to find a different place in the community at large rather than stay concealed within Anglo-Jewry, as he saw it. As O'Brien found, many within the existing and migrating communities held derogatory opinions of each other. In the early years they avoided intermarriage and worshipping together. Until the turn of the century, national origin could determine the street you lived on, the synagogue attended, the spouse and people one mixed with.[24] Sam was not ashamed of his Jewishness, but in many ways did not like what that meant for his family on a day-to-day basis. He saw hard work, cramped living conditions, limited food and broken families.

His memories faded with time and much of what he felt he needed to escape was perhaps retouched with a less appealing colour, but experiences remained vividly etched in his mind. His family (Figure 5.1) left Riga and travelled Westward in the hope of security – and followed family who had blazed a trail to Yorkshire. The dark apartment that many generations of the Goodman family shared in the Leylands was cramped. What he found largely matched Freedman's description of the Leylands during this period.

> It was a very poor district with mostly back-to-back houses in cobbled streets with many tumbledown yards. Built mainly at the beginning of the nineteenth century most of the Leylands dwellings had deteriorated to unsanitary slums, but it was here that the immigrant Jews first made their homes.[25]

Sam recalled that most nights three to four children would sleep to a bed. When not in school the children were left to themselves. His grandfather seemed to spend much time in the synagogue and his mother and father were either working in a shop or finishing items at home in the evenings after supper. Sam's memory of his hard-working mother is one of sadness. She walked out of a second-storey window at the age of 42 and he firmly blamed her early death on too much work and too many children. (Both symbols of Eastern Judaism to him.)

His father was ill-prepared to care for the boys or the girls. He quickly remarried but his new wife had very little time for the children. Sam recalled regular beatings and being offered protection by his grandfather and a local Catholic priest. Shoes were provided for the boys and work opportunities offered. Eventually the family was broken up. Some sisters went to live in a Jewish orphanage in London, one sister was adopted by an aunt and some of the boys ventured off to the United States. When Sam travelled to the United States his English was still not good. He covered his face on boats and trains with English newspapers to suggest he belonged there. He chose the name Gold upon arrival when it was explained that certain surnames would never get a callback for work opportunities (Figure 5.2).[26] The sense of Jewishness Sam's children developed in the United States was less focused on embracing religion and culture publicly, but rather more geared towards blending into the surroundings. Early years of desperate financial conditions in Leeds and the perceived lack of support by co-religionists fed into his mentality that the Jewish community came second and family should come first. His efforts then became focused on rearing a family and adopting a lifestyle that was American, financially stable, accepted and, if possible, Jewish.

In many of her case studies, O'Brien found that the successful Jews were the ones primarily involved in the synagogue and Board of Guardians.[27] Community leadership was associated with wealth rather than religious piety and wisdom. In the case of the Goodman family, her findings appear to have merit. Theirs was a story of cramped living conditions and segregation. There is no surprise that most sought eventual refuge in London and the United States. However, while Freedman did find truth in the complaints of those like Sam Goodman, he also came to the defence of those in the city. He wrote:

> There also developed a very evident socio-economic divide between the members of the Englisher Shul and the rest of the community, as the former were generally more affluent than the more recently arrived immigrants. Although these founding families of the community considered themselves to be a cut above their Yiddish speaking co-religionists with their foreign ways … to their credit they did not neglect their religious duty to help the many amongst them who were very poor.[28]

Integration and separation

It is clear that not everyone could be helped and some perhaps did not want the help offered or the strings attached to community support. Failing to find satisfaction in any option afforded them in Leeds, looking elsewhere became the most appealing choice for some.

Conversely, the family of Pamela Mason was an example of migrants finding safety and success within the Leeds Jewish community. Pam is a descendant of immigrants in the latter half the nineteenth century. Looking at all the Jewish immigrants to Leeds as Russians can be the first mistake in attempting to understand culture and identity. In doing this we have already labelled the individuals as a group, one that they may not have felt a part of. Also, while the idea that the majority were fleeing the East was certainly the case for many, there were some simply looking for better economic status and still others drawn to Leeds by family.[29] Fleeing similar problems in the East, Pamela comes from both the Zacklin and Hulman families who made their homes in the Leylands. The Zacklins settled on Van Dyk Street among Poles and Russians. They felt comfortable there for some years until financial success brought them out to Exmouth Street. The Hulmans, similarly, settled among Russians in Queens Place.[30] The desire of this family was to live in surroundings that brought comfort and reminders of community from the East. In housing, then, whom you knew and family relations played an important role. Drawing strength from one's 'neighbours' made the adjustment easier but seemed to prevent community unity. In London, unified religious leadership was able to rein in such varied traditions. Without similar cohesion in Leeds there was absent a common defence and plan for the community and its future. The longer such organisation was missing, the longer the settlement process was to take. The longer the community remained fractured, the more difficult it was to provide coordinated answers to the anglicising effects of school and social activities in the city.

The association of crime and poverty with the 'strange and unknown' immigrants not only created labels for the individuals and community but also the places in which they resided. As time passed and residents became aware of their surroundings and reputation, moving onward toward respectability became a paramount effort.[31] Some have even suggested that the truly religious Jews made their journey to America, while the less motivated remained in Leeds.[32]

The experiences of the Zacklin, Sumrie and Hulman families reveal problems involving class and separation within the Jewish community of Leeds. Their experiences contain elements of both integration and retention of tradition. Abraham Hulman married Esther Sumrie in 1917 in a Leeds synagogue. She was born in Leeds in 1893 and he had arrived with his parents from Russia just prior. While both sets of parents mainly spoke Yiddish, Esther and Abraham spoke English, as did their siblings.[33] Neither was educated much past the age of 10. Their education was basic and a mix of religious education through the synagogue and the teachings of the board school. Abraham followed his father into tailoring and spent many years at Burtons. After his marriage to Esther he moved to work for the competitor, Sumrie. Both grew up in very religious homes yet for some reason did not convey that same earnestness to their children. Abraham had sisters who married rabbis and parents who were firm in their instruction of the faith. Esther was surrounded by brothers keen to continue family traditions, whether they were religious, financial or social. The early married life of these two suggests adherence to Judaism, but their children were quick to point out that the years dulled this sense of commitment. When one son, Cyril, returned from the Second World War, he noted that strict dietary laws were no longer observed. At this point, he was aware that the household would no longer be as kosher as it had once been. Striking perhaps one last blow to his religious heritage, Cyril later dropped the 'u' from Hulman, creating the name Halman – which was much 'less Jewish'.[34] Just as the generation that arrived with the Zacklins, Hulmans and Burtons was greeted by successfully adjusted Jewish immigrants from the previous wave, so too had many of this generation achieved some measure of comfort. This is not to suggest that they had all risen to the level of the Burton family, but twenty years in the country had provided time to adjust, find one's bearings and move forward.

Lest one get the idea that peace reigned in the Hulman home, it is important to note the great divide (financially and socially) between the Hulman and Sumrie families. The latter were well established in tailoring with a respected regional reputation and hundreds of employees.[35] The Hulmans were hard-working immigrants who never travelled in the same circles. Somehow, however, the two met and intended to be married. Esther's family insisted that this would not be the case. They were well aware of the position they had risen to in the community. Here we see the continued 'classifying' of the Jewish community in Leeds and the surrounding areas. This was not just a local issue, but also one that manifested itself nationwide. The Sumrie family was keen to maintain the social superiority they had obtained. Marrying down would signal a slip in success and perhaps mar the family reputation in the Gentile (and Jewish) community. Esther's brothers fought the marriage with zeal but were in the end unsuccessful. They married and enjoyed a short but joyous union only ended by Abraham's early death.

The divides within the Jewish community were often as destructive as the efforts of outsiders to assimilate the children to British ways. Rather than seek strength from one another in a land where they were by far the minority, and an often-unpopular one at that, they instead assimilated local notions of class and used them to differentiate between the groups of immigrants. Worshipping together was no longer enough, the Leeds Jews often found

Integration and *separation*

themselves at odds simply because of the time they arrived in the country or due to the original country of departure.[36] As noted by Alderman, these Jews moving away from the confines of the Leylands and each other were not moving out because they were irreligious. They were leaving because their developing religious outlook was more 'easy going'. They were not escaping Judaism, but the intensity of Judaism found in the city centre.[37]

Jewish Lads' Brigade in Leeds

The issues facing the youth of Britain and Leeds in the latter years of the nineteenth century were often dependent on region, religion, education and employability. These themes permeated through the harshness of daily life that the majority of British youth faced. Education and health reform provided for more control over the bodies and minds of potentially wayward youth.[38] Various youth clubs and wealthy philanthropists sought out this generation in attempts to right the future direction of the Empire. One such group that had particularly good success in moulding the minds and bodies of its wards was the Jewish Lads Brigade (JLB). Separated from their Christian counterparts by religion, the Jewish leaders worked hard to assure fellow Britons that they were British. As noted at the time by H. A. Henry, there was a need to respect the Queen and the laws of the land. He wrote that 'it is the duty of every Israelite to defend his nation from its enemies'.[39]

From the earliest of days in Britain, the Jewish community recognised the value of fitting in. There was a sense that anglicising and blending in with the masses would best protect the people from harassment and provide for more secure futures. The ghetto Jews of the East End posed a serious risk to the respectable reputations well-established Jews had developed.[40] In fact, conscientious efforts were made by Jewish leaders to reduce the flow of immigration that would unsettle the hard-won status quo.[41] For Jews to be readily accepted within society, it was assumed that they must become more British. If Jewish traditions and identities were kept within the synagogues, while Christian ideals were espoused in the school and marketplace, there was a real sense that full integration into society would result.

Many of the problems faced by British youth in general applied to Jewish children as well. They were not immune to society's pressures and the concerns of health associated with urban living.[42] When the JLB joined the movement to guide the youth, the *Jewish Chronicle* welcomed teachings that gave working-class Jews 'the English tone'.[43] The programmes developed to assist in such blending were well established by the early part of Victoria's reign, promoted and assisted by traditional and established Jewish families. However, the community was ill prepared for the influx of new immigrants from the East.

The Jewish Board of Guardians was a powerful force for change and control within London's Jewish community. It imposed strict guidelines and order into the lives of those who would seek its help. Immigrant families were encouraged to move further away from the cities to speed up anglicisation, and families were interviewed in their homes during regular visits in order to assess their true needs.[44] Such invasive behaviour provided for greater control of parents and children. However, this level of influence was not felt or managed in the city of Leeds. Its relative youthfulness as a Jewish community meant that community leaders were still relatively new in the city and were fewer in number than in London. This created a situation wherein the goals of the elite were not always communicated effectively to the rapidly arriving masses of immigrants during this period.

In Sharman Kadish's exploration of the early leaders of the JLB, she found that the primary source for officers was the middle class. Solicitors, doctors, military officers and dentists were but a few of the respectable professions that provided eager leadership within the Brigade.[45] This is the image leaders were attempting to portray as successful and British to members of the community hungering for a sense of belonging. Just like the other youth movements of the era, the well-to-do made their way into the streets to lift the poor up. With fairly unified religious worship and well-organised upper- and middle-class leadership, the Jews of Britain were well prepared and keenly focused on what they must do to provide for secure futures of their people. But, as noted by Freedman, the divisions within the old and new synagogues of Leeds meant there were limits to the integrating efforts of the community leaders.[46]

The JLB in Leeds was expected to play a major role in developing young Jewish boys. However, its existence was brief, unsteady and also produced results unanticipated by the leaders of the Jewish community. Arnold Burton is a good example. As the child of a noted community member, it could be assumed that his father would encourage active participation in the JLB as a means of identity preservation. But in his personal reflections he noted that the Boy Scouts was the preferred after-school activity in his home. Despite hours spent in Jewish studies, his time under canvas was with the Scouts.[47] When queried as to why not the JLB, Arnold's quick response (as if it were obvious) was along the lines of he was British so of course he would join the British movement. This attitude is echoed in the *Jewish Chronicle*:

> What institutions there are [in Leeds], chiefly emanated from the English (anglicised) section, or rather the old Hebrew congregation, upon who a considerable responsibility is laid ... The casual investigator into the conditions of the Leeds Jewish community cannot fail to be struck by the lamentable lack of cooperation that exists among the various sections.[48]

And another grandchild of an early Leeds immigrant also exclaimed: 'I am very proud of being Jewish – But I am also British, and I say when in Rome do as the Romans do.'[49]

It is important to note that the community was much smaller in Leeds. Not only that, it was newer too. The existing Anglo-Jewry of Leeds, for example, did not have its grip fully on the city and community as it did in London. Freedman suggested one reason for its failure was that Leeds did not have the established Anglo-Jewish populace that other cities did. Despite the number of Jews in Leeds, the majority of them were relative newcomers.[50] In 1891, over 60% of Leeds Jewry were born outside Britain. This opens up further possible questions on how the make-up of the Jewish community in Leeds evolved differently because of its relative newness.

Before the JLB arrived in Leeds there was no real national Jewish alternative for young men, as all organisations were geared towards Christians with like ideals. Colonel Albert E. W. Goldsmid's efforts to imitate existing activities in the aid of young Jewish boys were novel and generally well received in the community. Less than ten years later, however, Baden-Powell arrived with the Boy Scouts and a very real competition developed for the hearts and minds of the young Jew in many quarters.[51] For despite the general successes of the JLB, the Scouting movement appeared to capture more of the attention of England's maturing population of young boys.

A report from the JLB's first summer camp clearly defined some goals:

> The chief aim is to instil into the lads the feelings of manliness and honour from an early age, and to keep in touch with them during the critical period between boyhood and manhood ... The co-operation of the community is invited in establishing healthy minds in healthy bodies in our rising generation, so that the lads may become a source of legitimate pride to us.[52]

The JLB in Leeds found it difficult to achieve such goals. The city seems to be an anomaly among the northern companies, particularly surprising given its place as Anglo-Jewry's third city. This problem did not go unnoticed by the staff at the head office and the press. The *Jewish World* commented on the problems in Leeds and suggested there was plenty of material to work with there. There were many interested boys, as past participation in drills and camps had shown. However, the writer suggested that there was very little support from within the community. There were hundreds of young Jews at each of the main board schools in the Leylands. A reasonable percentage was male and so offered a large pool from which youth movements could be drawn. The author wrote,

> For it certainly was a plain act of duty on the part of local Jewry to support the movement, as the lads for the most part were drawn from the poorer classes, and, in addition to the splendid training they received, they looked forward with

keenest anticipation to what was their only chance of enjoying an outing in the country … Surely the large Jewish community here should not be content to treat this matter with indifference.[53]

From its founding years under Goldsmid through the proving ground of First World War, Leeds JLB managed only seven years of activity. A problem that would present itself throughout the twentieth century appeared early on: there was almost no community support.[54]

In March 1900, the JLB headquarters received its first letter of request from Leeds for the establishment of a company in the city.[55] The Reverend M. Abrahams developed an optimistic plan to lead this young group of boys and had assistance from young men who had arrived in the city a generation earlier. One early leader, for example, was Jack Lubelski who was no child but a man who the boys could look up to. He was part of a successful tailoring family, the first captain of the company and later went on to be elected to Leeds City Council in 1904. He was also a founder of the Jewish Young Men's Association in 1897, one of many organisations established for the building of character and strengthening of community ties with Leeds.[56] Leeds was not unique in this aspect of JLB organisation. In most communities, the companies were based in working-class areas of the city, while the staff and officers came from outlying areas and respectable employers. Their existence showed new immigrants that social mobility, even if by small degrees, was possible in Britain. For example, in 1899 Hull JLB listed editors, solicitors and dental students among its leadership and Newcastle had furniture managers and a surgeon.[57] And of course Leeds was no different, with a respected religious leader organising the group, a surgeon volunteering his time along with others like Lubelski.[58] In fact, Leeds was still a generation away from a time when the Jewish community boasted solicitors, doctors and other upwardly mobile individuals; and it was the generation that would become those successes who avoided membership of the JLB at the turn of the century. The original enrolment was forty boys and this proved to be a high point for the movement.[59]

One might quite rightly suggest that the community lack of interest in Brigade activities did not suggest lack of interest in patriotism or Britain and her empire. After all, at the time the company collapsed in Leeds, Baden-Powell's Scouts arrived to a warm reception by the city at large. Even members of the Jewish community were supportive of the organisation. Some parents chose to send their boys to join up as a means of helping them fit in with other young boys in the city.[60] Such attitudes could suggest that the Jewish youth were more integrated than previously thought and were involved in non-Jewish movements. If they were, this would certainly show a generation quickly integrating and in effect fulfilling the dreams of Anglo-Jewry's leadership. However, it appears that in the first two decades of Scouting within Leeds,

Integration and *separation*

there was an almost xenophobic approach to the movement by its leaders. Officers of the Scouts seemed only interested in working with white Christian movements and were even averse to doing anything with their sister group the Girl Guides.[61] With such attitudes, it is fair to assume that it would have been very difficult for Jewish boys to actively participate in the movement.

The struggle of the JLB in Leeds was a part of the unique identity emerging in the city. The numbers were there, as were the templates for making it a success. Anxious support was offered from London and Provincial headquarters, all of which was refused. Over the next century there were four other attempts to restart the Brigade, none of which succeeding until 1972.[62] Rabbi Douglas Charing reasoned that there was simply no interest in the organisation in the Leeds Jewish community. Further, it was his assertion that lack of interest did not equate with community problems and differences when compared to other Jewish areas.[63] However, along with the positive answers the JLB offered Leeds, it also promised an avenue for the young much different than one of crime. The very fact that there was no real interest in the JLB (and what participation there was in the Boy Scouts was so small) tells us that the community did not look to these groups as helpful or meaningful in their integration into the Leeds community. The developing identity of Leeds Jewry was one that did not include uniformed movements. This was a proactive choice. The city was not ignored by national groups or Anglo-Jewry, but rather was made the subject of much effort. These efforts were largely ignored by a community whose priorities were elsewhere.

The failure of the JLB in Leeds reveals something of Leeds Jewry's distinctive character. Free time for young Jewish boys in Leeds was not filled marching in uniform through the streets of the Leylands. What impact did this have? Just a few short years later, at the dawn of the First World War, there were lingering questions in the minds of native Britons about Jewish patriotism and their commitment to their new homeland. These concerns were further enhanced when some young men elected to flee the country rather than serve. Lack of community leadership may be the greatest cause of such a failure.[64] The Anglo-Jewish hierarchy took the lead, even in growing communities like Manchester – and with this lead the JLB grew with its integrating efforts in place. This form of instruction helped the boys develop along lines that did not happen in Leeds: the first generation of boys in the city took British instruction in schools but not under canvas.

Conclusions

The story of Judaism developed in Leeds was a delicate balance of integration and separation, with a small portion of 'other'. The community did not fit the mould of others in England during this period. While its size was impressive, it was newer and less established. Because of this, what existed as an Anglo-Jewry in Leeds towards the end of the nineteenth century was small and impotent when it came to dictating a unified message. London and Manchester experienced much more success in that regard. The varied experiences of families and individuals were such that a singular identity did not emerge (if it were advisable at all to seek one). Rather, instead of a 'Jewish experience' in Leeds, what developed were numerous experiences that were in some cases Jewish, family, financial, social and so much more.

Many in Leeds *chose* to integrate or separate, as the experiences of the Goodmans and Zacklins showed. Others were *forced* to integrate and still some found a mixture of the two that worked best for them. And this should not be a surprise; as O'Brien noted, 'variations in the structures of the societies in which these minorities settle' made a distinct impact on the way in which the community adjusted and was identified.[65] Leeds was not Manchester, London or even Glasgow. Judaism, despite being a common link across millennia, became only one of many options for immigrants to Leeds rather than the only one. As one descendant remarked:

> When I arrived at college I ceased being an Orthodox Jew about as quickly as it took me to unpack, but I picked up another off-the-rack Jewish identity, becoming a social Jew. I was a Jew because on Friday nights I sometimes went to the Hillel, because I understood why the word 'pheh' was funny, because all the other former Jewish Day School students knew me. I could do absolutely nothing Jewish for months at a time and still be a peripheral part of the Jewish 'scene'.[66]

Judaism in Leeds wasn't cast off; it was embraced and retained at different levels, and in some cases transformed.

The Jewish community in Leeds was largely working class, and this created unique problems. The physical closeness of the community in Leeds compounded by the diverse backgrounds and origins all worked together to establish a Jewish community that was not actually a community. Rather, what Leeds Jewry was, was a number of small groups, loyal to one another but not united as a whole. Living in the Leylands, in close quarters with fellow *landsmen,* many Jews felt inclined to maintain communal ties developed in the Old World. This distance from other Jews (especially those who had arrived earlier in the century) led to misconceptions and contention. O'Brien notes, 'the old-timers formed a kind of elite and defended their way of doing things against the newcomers, who seemed to them to old-fashioned, naïve, and (many of them) fanatically orthodox in their religious observance'.[67] Life for the newcomers was often cramped and uncomfortable.

When the depressing circumstances of the home and monotonous employment grew overwhelming, the Jew in Leeds could turn to the synagogue for spiritual strength and camaraderie among fellow Jews. However, religious worship in Leeds developed in such a way that worship was not only divided, but also at times confrontational. There was a great rivalry and distrust between synagogues during this period. Federations of synagogues were not accomplished until many years later.[68] Not until some time after the First World War was the Shechita Board of Leeds established, and prior to that there was much contention and dispute between the congregations about the *shohet* [kosher butchers]. Different synagogues for different languages, lands of origin and class were a dividing factor in Jewish Leeds.

England was a land of opportunity in contrast to the harshness of Russia. However, immigrants were quickly given an education on the reality of intra-religious relationships in Leeds. One could not assume blood or religion provided for mercy.[69] Each was forced to look inward to one's fellow 'grinners' for support and forced to make an important choice, one that would have repercussions for generations of Leeds Jewry: do I retain my orthodox and traditional beliefs and customs or do I reinvent myself in the model of my successful co-religionists? Once answered, the resulting changes brought about an evolution in what it meant to be a Jew in Leeds. The constant drift from tradition, while chasing a British dream, opened an even wider chasm between Orthodox and Anglo-Jew. These changes did not mean that being a good Jew was no longer important; rather, they meant that what being a good Jew in Leeds meant had evolved. Rather than look at Leeds as any type of failure in integrating migrants into the mass of British Jewry, one must recognise that the identities which emerged embraced aspects of many sources. In fact, both integration and separation played pivotal roles in harnessing the natural desire and determination of the growing Jewish community and produced in partnership a sense of self that was both unique and shared.

5.1 Samuel Goodman family

5.2 Sam and Belle 'Gold', 1931

Notes

1. B. Silver, *Three Jewish Giants of Leeds: Selig Brodetsky, Montague Burton and Jacob Kramer* (Leeds: Jewish Historical Society of England, 2000), p. 1.
2. D. Cesarani (ed.), *The Making of Modern Anglo-Jewry* (Oxford: Basil Blackwell, 1990), p. 4.
3. T. Kushner, *The Jewish Heritage in British History* (London: Routledge, 1992), p. 4.
4. M. Freedman, *The 'Jewish' Schools of Leeds 1880–1930* (Leeds: privately published, 2001).
5. John Doyle Klier, *Imperial Russia's Jewish Question 1855–1881* (Cambridge: CUP, 2005), p. 27–9.
6. Ibid., p. 44.
7. G. Alderman, *Modern British Jewry* (Oxford: Clarendon Press, 1998), p. 151.
8. T. Endelman, *The Jews of Britain 1656–2000* (Los Angeles: UC Press, 2002), p. 10.
9. R. O'Brien, 'Establishment of the Jewish Minority in Leeds' (PhD, University of Bristol, 1975), p. 9.
10. Ibid., p. 24.
11. D. Feldman, *Englishmen and Jews* (Guildford: Yale UP, 1994), p. 293.
12. B. Dinur, *Israel and the Diaspora* (Philadelphia: Jewish Publications Society of America, 1969), p. 55.
13. O'Brien, 'Establishment of the Jewish Minority in Leeds', p. 30.
14. E. Rosenthal, 'Acculturation without assimilation? The Jewish community of Chicago Illinois', *The American Journal of Sociology*, 66:3 (November 1960), pp. 275–88.
15. O'Brien, 'Establishment of the Jewish Minority in Leeds', p. 63.
16. Interview with Arnold Burton, 15 June 2007.
17. A. Davin, *Growing up Poor* (London: Rivers Oram Press, 1995), p. 42.
18. M. Blanch, 'Imperialism, Nationalism and Organised Youth' in J. Clarke, C. Critcher and R. Johnson (eds), *Working Class Culture* (London: Routledge, 2006) pp. 103–20 (105).
19. S. Kadish, *A Good Jew and a Good Englishman* (London: Vallentine Mitchell, 1995), p. 38.
20. Jewish Lads' Brigade Annual Report. AR-V. Hartley Library: University of Southampton.
21. O'Brien, 'Establishment of the Jewish Minority in Leeds', p. 46.
22. M. Freedman, *Further Essays on Leeds & Anglo-Jewish History & Demography* (Leeds: privately published, 2005), p. 11.
23. Interview with Gene Gold, 15 May 2009.
24. O'Brien, 'Establishment of the Jewish Minority in Leeds', pp. 64–5.
25. M. Freedman, *1901 Census* (Leeds: privately published, 2002).
26. Interview with Gene Gold, 15 May 2009.
27. O'Brien, 'Establishment of the Jewish Minority in Leeds', p. 151.
28. M. Freedman, *Leeds Jewry a History of its Synagogues* (Leeds: privately published, 1995), p. 4.

29 Feldman, *Englishmen and Jews*, pp. 147–8; and interviews with Pamela Mason, 2 December 2006 and Cynthia Dante, 27 September 2007.
30 Interview with Pamela Mason, 6 December 2006.
31 Interviews with Pamela Mason, 2 December 2006 and Cynthia Dante, 27 September 2007.
32 Interview with Pamela Mason, 2 December 2006.
33 Interview with Pamela Mason, 2 December 2006 and Cynthia Dante, November 2008.
34 Interview with Pamela Mason, 17 November 2006.
35 K. Honeyman, *Well Suited: A History of the Leeds Clothing Industry 1850–1990* (Oxford: Oxford University Press, 2000), p. 78.
36 L. Saipe, *A History of the Jews of Leeds* (Leeds: Tercentenary Committee, 1956), p. 17.
37 Alderman, *Modern British Jewry*, p. 215.
38 Harry Hendrick, *Children, Childhood and English Society 1880–1990* (Cambridge: MacMillan, 1997) pp. 37, 41–9.
39 H. A. Henry (Rv.), *Class Book for Jewish Youth of Both Sexes* (London; Nabu Press, 1901), p. 13.
40 Kadish, *A Good Jew and a Good Englishman*, p. 38.
41 Eugene C. Black, *The Social Politics of Anglo-Jewry 1880–1920* (Oxford: Blackwell, 1988), p. 7.
42 Ibid., pp. 133–5.
43 Kadish, *A Good Jew and a Good Englishman*, p. 39.
44 Black, *The Social Politics of Anglo-Jewry 1880–1920*, pp. 71–5.
45 Kadish, *A Good Jew and a Good Englishman*, p. 38.
46 M. Freedman, *History of Leeds Synagogues* (Leeds: privately published, 1991), pp. 3–5.
47 Interview with Arnold Burton, 15 June 2007.
48 *Jewish Chronicle*, 6 June 1906.
49 O'Brien, 'Establishment of the Jewish Minority in Leeds', p. 272.
50 The 1891 census shows 1404 Jewish families in Leeds, with 1,213 of them having both parents born abroad. The same census records a city population of 367,505 and the Jewish segment is only 2.1% of that at 7,856. M. Freedman, *Leeds Jewry The First Hundred Years* (Leeds: privately published, 1992), pp. 23, 30.
51 15 April 1909, Minutes of JLB Officers University of Southampton MS244 GEN84.
52 Jewish Lads' Brigade Annual Report. 1895–1905. University of Southampton, AR-I. Report One. Inception through 31 March 1898.
53 Ibid.
54 After the first collapse it was written, 'It has come as an unpleasant surprise to many that Leeds has not this year been represented in the camps of the Jewish Lads' Brigade ... owing to lack of interest and support the Leeds Company of the Jewish Lads' Brigade had to be disbanded.' *Jewish World*, 7 August 1908.
55 7 March 1900, Jewish Lads' Brigade, University of Southampton MS244 Gen 80.
56 Jewish Lads' Brigade, University of Southampton MS244 Gen 48. See also Saipe, *Jews of Leeds*, p. 33.

57 JLB minutes, 5 April 1899.
58 Jewish Lads' Brigade, University of Southampton MS244 Gen 48.
59 Jewish Lads' Brigade, University of Southampton, POF.
60 Interviews with Cynthia Dante 7 February 2008, Leonard Fineberg 25 October 2007 and Malcolm Sender 3 March 2008.
61 Officers Minutes, Boy Scouts of Leeds. WYL-808.
62 Jewish Lads' Brigade, University of Southampton, POF.
63 Interview with Rabbi Douglas Charing of the Jewish Education Board, 13 June 2006.
64 N. Grizzard, *Leeds Jewry and the Great War* (Leeds: Leeds Jewish Historical Society, 1981), pp. 11–13.
65 O'Brien, 'Establishment of the Jewish Minority in Leeds', p. 7.
66 Yael Goldstein, 'When God Is Your Favorite Writer' in *Who We Are: On Being (and Not Being) a Jewish American Writer* (New York: Shocken Books 2005).
67 O'Brien, 'Establishment of the Jewish Minority in Leeds', p. 154.
68 E. Krausz, *Leeds Jewry* (Cambridge: W. Heffer & Sons Limited for the Jewish Historical Society of England, 1964), pp. 9–10.
69 Conversation between Nathan, Gilbert and Gwen Pearlman (recorded by Gene Gold, unknown date).

6

Pragmatism or politics: Leeds Jewish tailors and Leeds Jewish tailoring trade unions, 1876–1915

Anne J. Kershen

In July 1915, the United Garment Workers Trade Union (UGWTU) was established following the amalgamation of six clothing workers' unions. The largest of these was the Amalgamated Union of Clothing Operatives (AUCO) whose 12,000 members had voted to become part of a national union.[1] The second largest was the Leeds-based Amalgamated Jewish Tailors', Machiners' and Pressers' Trade Union (AJTMP), which had a membership of 4,500. The significance of a provincial Jewish union representing more than a third of the new union's membership should not be overlooked. Though the new clothing workers' union was a minnow in a pool of much larger fish,[2] the fact that a 22-year-old Jewish tailoring workers' organisation had reached the point at which it was the second largest in the amalgamation and its Secretary, Moses Sclare, was appointed Financial Secretary was impressive. The Leeds Jewish union was founded in 1893 after a number of earlier Jewish unions had failed. This in a city with a range of skilled and unskilled clothing workers employed in tailoring workshops and clothing factories; in the former were to be found Eastern European male tailors, machiners and pressers together with a small number of English females – the latter carrying out unskilled tasks;[3] the factories employed both genders, though few, if any, Jewish workers. In Leeds it was a system of separation yet interdependence between English factory and Jewish workshop.

This chapter will follow the progress of the Jewish section of the Leeds wholesale clothing industry from its earliest beginnings to the point at which workers in Jewish workshops and English factories came together in 1915 to provide an example of unity in an interdenominational national union. It was a template not emulated by the majority of Jewish tailoring workers in London, where only the members of the London Jewish Tailors' and Tailoresses' Union affiliated to the new clothing workers' union. The chapter will seek to determine whether the trade unionism manifested by the Leeds Jewish tailoring workers was borne out of ideological conviction or economic pragmatism. Finally, it will evaluate the factors that led to the successful organisation of the Leeds Jewish tailoring workforce as opposed to the ephemeral nature of the unions created by their London counterparts.

Jewish tailors in the Leeds wholesale clothing industry

The foundations of the Leeds wholesale clothing industry can be traced back to the mid-nineteenth century and the arrival in that city of two migrants: John Barran from Surrey and Herman Friend from Germany. From the 1840s onwards, excellent railway and canal links facilitated the supply of raw materials and the despatching of manufactured and finished goods to and from Leeds; a structure which acted as a magnet for 'men of business'.[4] The city rapidly became a vibrant industrial centre, one which encouraged men such as Barran and Friend to 'set up shop' in Leeds. Barran arrived in the city in 1842 and, after running a small tailor's and outfitter's shop for eleven years, in 1856 made the transition to ready-to-wear manufacturer and opened a wholesale clothing factory in Albert Street. It was the expansion of his business together with his invention of the band knife – a development of the band saw – which enabled the cutting out of a number of garments at one time, that led to the incorporation of the city's Jewish tailoring workshops into his system of production. Within a few years the expansion of his business forced Barran to review his manufacturing methods. There were two alternatives: either increase the capacity of his factory by investing in more machinery and labour or subcontract out the production of coats and jackets. He chose the latter.

Initially, Barran approached some local English journeymen tailors to see if they would make up coats and jackets on an 'outdoor' basis, a process he considered 'too heavy for women' in the factories to undertake.[5] The English craft workers refused, explaining that to agree would mean sacrificing their image as 'aristocrats' of the trade. He then asked Herman Friend, who ran a small tailoring workshop in Templar Street close to Barran's factory and was a member of the Leeds Jewish community, if he would subcontract the production of coats and jackets using subdivisional methods of production. Friend's agreement to work with Barran initiated what would become a pattern that subsequent wholesale clothiers in the city would emulate: Jewish tailoring workshops and English-owned clothing factories working apart and yet together. Among those working in Friend's workshop were future master tailors including David Lubelski, Jacob Frais and Solomon Camrass. The method of production put in place in those early years disproves the theory that Jewish workers introduced the system of subdivisional production into the English tailoring trade. In fact, it was following the paradigm of a process that had been used by tailors decades before the large-scale immigration of Jews from Eastern Europe.[6] It was the introduction of this system of manufacture into the Leeds wholesale clothing industry which set in motion the recruitment of young men from Russia and Russia-Poland to work in the Jewish tailoring workshops of Leeds.

In 1866, a Jewish master tailor from Kovno, Moyshe (Morris) Goodman, settled in Leeds. Doubtless Goodman had learnt of the economic opportunities the city offered via the 'grapevine' that operated between Jews in Eastern Europe and those that had migrated West. Goodman, later to prove himself a successful entrepreneur, identified the potential and need for subdivisional tailoring workers in the expanding wholesale clothing industry. In the following few years, he undertook several journeys to Kovno and Warsaw in order to recruit young men for the subdivisional tailoring trade in Leeds. Following Goodman's expeditions, young Jewish Eastern European immigrants began arriving in the ports of Hull and London, unable to speak English but often clasping a piece of paper upon which was written the legend LEEDS. By the end of the 1870s, recruitment was no longer necessary as there was a widening pool of eager young immigrants seeking work in the wholesale clothing industry. Alongside them were a growing number of workshop masters, some of whom would ruthlessly exploit their 'greener' co-religionists and, by so doing, sow the seeds of labour discontent for the next half century.

Not all workshop masters were cruel exploiters. Some men, such as David Lubelski – who arrived in Leeds from Warsaw the same year as Goodman – were strong believers in the rights of the working man and in the beneficial role of trade unions.[7] By 1887, Lubelski employed between sixty and seventy workers in his workshop, and two years later he entered the ranks of wholesale clothiers when he opened a factory in Park Cross Street.[8] Lubelski and those other early workshop masters reinforced the wholesale clothing industry in Leeds, providing the indirect plant, machinery and labour which facilitated its expansion. Not all were as benevolent employers as Lubelski. As the number of workshops and workers grew, so did the hardships of the trade and the conditions which for many fulfilled the definition of sweating; working the longest hours, for the lowest wages in the worst conditions. The increase in the number of Jewish male tailoring workers in Leeds is reflected in Decennial Census records: in 1881 there were a recorded 1,588, by 1911 that number had risen to over 7,000.[9]

Life was indeed *schwer und bitter* [heavy and bitter] for those working under sweated conditions. Some workers resorted to drinking and gambling to ease their pain. While many of their co-religionists were critical, the Polish Jewish socialist writer Morris Winchevsky[10] took a more sympathetic view. Writing in the Yiddish pamphlet *Zi Aur* [Let There be Light] he argued that the Jewish worker was driven to drink and gambling out of desperation at the plight of his family: 'When there is no work and a child at home is sick from the lack of food ... and the other children cry "father, bread" ... a man can be forgiven for drinking whisky and gambling.'[11] Though based on what he had seen in London, Winchevsky's words were equally applicable to those working in Leeds. As the demand for ready-to-wear men's tailored garments increased, so did the number of Jewish tailoring hands taking the plunge and setting up on their own as masters, seizing the opportunity of acquiring cheap sewing machines and paying low rents; however, there was little security and the master one year frequently returned to being tailoring hand the next. By 1884 there were a number of large-scale workshops, a plethora of medium to small workshops and intensified competition over price and delivery. The size of the Jewish subdivisional tailoring trade in Leeds was now sufficient for Joseph Finn[12] to publish a graphic article in the first edition of the (short-lived) Yiddish newspaper, *Polishe Yidel*. Finn explained that:

> There are many Jewish workers in Leeds. Almost all of them belong to the tailoring trade. Many are machiners, under-machiners, pressers, under-pressers, second (or plain) tailors and tailors who work with needle and thread. I do not know the exact number of workers, I can only say there are a lot ... Most of the workers have not been in England long. Some less than a year, some several years. Mostly greeners learning a part of the tailoring trade. Each worker has a learner living with him. Templar Street in Leeds is a ghetto as existed in the old days in Rome, Prague and Frankfurt on Main.[13]

Numbers did not prevent exploitation or create good working conditions. In 1888, in reaction to the revelations of the appalling working conditions in the Jewish subdivisional tailoring workshops in London's East End, a House of Lords Select Commission on the Sweating System was established. Though London was at the heart of the inquiry, the Leeds sector of the industry was drawn into the net following an outbreak of smallpox in and around the Leylands district of the city in 1888. The Leylands was home to the Jewish tailoring trade and was also where the majority of the Eastern European Jewish immigrants settled on arrival. One of those who gave evidence to the Commission was David Lubelski. He confirmed that the hands were forced to live and work in 'wretched conditions'.[14] Other witnesses described the long hours, low pay and filthy workshops that the immigrant workers were forced to endure. A reporter from *The Lancet* who had visited the city in 1888, in order to see for himself the conditions that prevailed in the Jewish workshops, recorded that 'floors were rarely if ever cleaned [and] the revolting state of the water closets resulted in an appalling stench'.[15] It seemed to matter little that some of the high-class English tailoring workshops were little better. One of the worst aspects of the insanitary nature of the workshops was the dual role of the 'bedroom' workshops; by day a place to make tailored garments and by night a place to sleep, with clothes in the process of manufacture used as bed-covers. The workers were often incubating diseases such as smallpox and scarlet fever, which were passed onto the clothes during the night and then onto the purchaser after sale. In 1912, Moses Sclare laid down a resolution at the TUC General Conference for the practice to be made illegal. The resolution was passed but legislation was delayed by the outbreak of the First World War and workshop masters were able to continue with their insanitary practices.

The process of production in the workshops was graphically described by James Sweeney, a non-Jewish bootmaker and one of the founders of the Socialist League,[16] when giving evidence to the Sweating Commission. Sweeney's conviction that it was imperative for the exploited Jewish tailors to be organised resulted in his being for some time Secretary of the Leeds Jewish Tailors' Society. Sweeney's description provides a means of understanding why there was such a broad wage range in subdivisional tailoring.

> From the fitter-up he hands them [the bundles of cut out cloth collected from the wholesaler] to the machiner; from the machiner ... it goes to the under-presser; other parts of the garment go to the tailor, what they call a tailor is a baster out [basting being tacking], then there is the lining maker that pieces linings before they are put into the garment; to be stitched together and made up ready for the presser. The presser then presses the garments off ... and they have to go through the finishers, feller hands and button-hole hands and then they come to the brusher off, then the garments are ready to go to the warehouse or back to the wholesaler.[17]

The exact division of labour in the workshop was determined by the size of the workforce within it; the larger the unit the more extreme the subdivision. Workshop status determined both the length of the working day and rate of pay, the latter based on either day or piece rates. Payment by piece often resulted in extremes of exploitation. If the worker wanted to earn enough to survive he had to work on as many 'pieces' as he could. Writing in 1943, Joseph Finn recalled his experiences as a machiner in a workshop in Leeds. He worked a twelve-hour day and earned between 6s.0d and 7s.0d. The presser worked a thirteen-hour day for anything between 5s.6d and 6s.0d; lower down the scale came the tailor who took home no more than 6s.0d for his fourteen-hour day. But it was the 'poor devil underpresser who was forced to rise at 5 am to light the oven in which the irons were heated and then work till 9 pm' who suffered worst, and was totally dependent on the presser for his income.[18] It is important to remember that in addition to the inequity of low wages, work in the tailoring trade was irregular and for workers on a daily rate, as opposed to piece work wages, the master often squeezed all the work into the last three days of the week. In addition, there was the busy and the slack, the busy lasting from March until July and the slack from October until late December. In the slack a hand was fortunate to find one day or half a day's work. Despite this, according to Finn, the workers 'held their masters as God', believing their rarely kept promises of overtime. Writing in 1884, Finn believed that the flames of anti-alienism[19] were fanned because the majority of the Leeds Jewish tailoring workers tolerated the harsh treatment meted out by their masters and would 'bend down for the masters to sit on them', rather than join trade unions.[20] Their English counterparts saw this as a betrayal of the brotherhood of labour. Seven years later, the London-based radical Yiddish newspaper *Arbeiter Fraint* warned all Jewish tailors that they could not succeed alone, 'they must unite internationally and with the Christian workers fight the general enemy'.[21] It was a warning that took several decades to be accepted, but it was the Leeds Jewish tailors rather than their London brothers that heeded the message.

Organising the Jewish tailoring workers of Leeds

It was the Jewish subdivisional tailors in Leeds who, in 1876, established the city's first union for workers in the wholesale clothing trade. It certainly did not manifest all the characteristics associated with the craft societies which, according to Sidney and Beatrice Webb, set out to 'protect the interests of craftsmen, seek peaceful negotiation and employ full time officials'.[22] Though conceived at the time of craft 'new model' unionism, the Jewish union was born out of a need for self-defence rather than as a means of preserving skill superiority. It was the conditions the sweated workers were forced to endure, working up to eighteen hours a day and suffering violent physical attacks by their employers, that led to the foundation of a Jewish working tailors' society with an initial membership of 'between forty and fifty men'.[23] The new Jewish Working Tailors' Trade Society was one of only three Leeds unions that appear in the Report of the Chief Registrar for Friendly Societies for 1876, the other two being those for pattern makers and tanners.[24] All three, and the Leeds branch of the national Amalgamated Society of Tailors (AST), were within half a mile radius of each other, and Jewish and English paths must have crossed – if not when buying needles and threads, then when 'putting money on the horses'. And while the AST would not open its doors to alien (Jewish) working tailors, it was keen to encourage them to take steps to prevent exploitation and wage undercutting, practices which weakened the trade as a whole.

The onset of the great depression at the end of the 1870s made it very difficult for small embryonic unions to survive. The Jewish union managed to hold on and even persuade employers to reduce the length of the working day. However, it was not the recession in the wholesale clothing industry which led to the union's demise, but rather the upward mobility of its membership that encouraged them to shed the proletarian image and take on a more middle-class mantle. In 1880, a group of its members converted the 'trade society' into a 'Sick and Burial Society for the Strictly Orthodox'. Three years later, they bid farewell to the 'Orthodox' and affiliated to the Ancient Order of Foresters – the second largest friendly society in the world – and adopted the title of Court of Hope of Israel. A year later, acknowledging the transition, the *Leeds Express* described the new society as 'English in concept'.[25]

However, protection for the Jewish working tailor was not dead. In 1883, the Jewish Working Tailors' Society was resurrected and the following year, in acknowledgement of the subdivisional nature of the trade, the machiners and pressers founded their own separate unions. In truth, the three unions represented only 10% of the city's alien tailoring work force.[26] But this was better than nothing and the foundation of the three societies was welcomed by the Liberal-dominated Leeds Trades Council, relieved to see moves which might reduce the threat posed by unorganised, sweated, alien labour. Respect and sympathy for the, albeit small, number of trade unionists was voiced by the *Leeds Express* in an editorial which appeared in July 1884:

> I know of no class of worker in Leeds who needs protection more than the Jews. A great number come to Leeds with no knowledge of customs and wages and work the hours and accept the wages they have been accustomed to on the continent ... it is a sign of the times that the people are willing to organise to get rid of the evil.[27]

The association with the Liberal Trades Council was short lived. Socialism had arrived in Leeds and one of its advocates was a Jewish tailor's machiner by the name of Joseph Finn, a founder member of the Leeds branch of the Socialist League.[28] Finn, bilingual in Yiddish and English, rapidly created a bridge between himself and the city's exploited Jewish tailoring workforce, keeping them regularly informed of national events such as the Reform Bill of 1884. Unlike their London counterparts, the immigrant tailors of Leeds showed little interest, more concerned to see an amelioration of their working conditions than debates about enlargement of the franchise. In November 1884, the Jewish tailors, machiners and pressers of Leeds downed tools in protest at their increasingly harsh working conditions. Writing of it sixty years later, Finn referred to it as 'the first Jewish strike by the first Jewish trade union in the modern world'.[29] In reality, the timing of the strike was responsible for its failure. November was close to the slack period in the trade and the workers could ill afford to lose income as the period of little employment approached. The masters stood firm, refusing any concessions, and the strikers were forced to give in.

Even if licence is given to Finn's fond reminiscences and the strike's failure taken into account, the tailors' stoppage of work has to be recognised as a landmark in Jewish and English labour history of the 1880s. It also proved to be a learning tool for future protests, one of which followed within six months. Finn's involvement with the Socialist League had put him in touch with non-Jewish labour activist and dedicated socialist James Sweeney, who provided support and guidance for a further assault on the exploitative tailoring masters. On this occasion, timing proved of the essence. At the beginning of May 1885, following a refusal by employers to reduce the length of the working day, a strike was called. This coincided with the start of the busy period of production. A small number of workers called for caution, while others were concerned that the strike be 'kept within the confines of the law',[30] which by and large it was. This time Finn and his colleagues were ready, and when the would-be blacklegs from the capital arrived at Leeds railway station, Finn recalled how they were given 'a brotherly talk and handed pre-paid return tickets to London'.[31] With orders piling up, the masters had no option but to concede to *most* of the workers' demands and working hours were reduced with no accompanying reduction in wages. However, this still left the under-pressers subjected to a sixty-five-hour working week, with no payment for the time they spent lighting the stoves. They were, and remained for many years, the underdogs of the industry. Victory was short-lived and conditions soon reverted back to what they had been before the strike as the onset of the economic recession enabled the employers to renege on their 1885 agreement. Before long, workshop conditions had returned to those that had prevailed before the strike. In addition, the strike's leaders were subjected to harsh victimisation and, as a result, Joseph Finn was forced to leave the city. He travelled to America and settled in Boston where he found work in the city's nascent garment trade.

It took a further three years for the Leeds tailors to mount another attack on their employers. By 1888 there were three Jewish tailoring unions operating in Leeds, these now led by men of strong socialist convictions, under the guidance of a trio of Socialist Leaguers: James Sweeney, Tom Paylor and Tom Maguire – the latter a legend in Leeds Labour history.[32] The strike was precipitated by the employers importing non-union labour from London and other provincial cities in an attempt to increase their profits by shortening the length of the busy season. The Leeds workers responded by calling for a closed shop, a fifty-eight-hour working week and overtime payment at time and a half. Not surprisingly, their demands were refused. On 5 May, 3,000 Leeds Jewish tailors downed tools and called for a general strike of all those employed in subdivisional workshops. Four days later, at a rally held in Victoria Square attended by over 5,000 people, Sweeney, Paylor and Maguire spoke out powerfully and persuasively in support of the tailors' cause. There was just one lone voice of support from the side of the employers, that of David Lubelski who made an emotional appeal on behalf of the workers.

His outspoken support for the exploited drew forth a written notice of censure from the city's Jewish Master Tailors' Association, which he publicly destroyed, an action widely reported in both the Yiddish and Leeds Press.[33] In the excitement of those early days of the strike, membership of the three unions doubled. Within a short time, the atmosphere between employers and workers had developed into one of accusation and counter-accusation, with James Sweeney accusing the middlemen and masters of obtaining orders from the wholesalers through bribery. Not only were workshop hands treated to poor conditions and low pay, they were 'forced to pay for corruption as well as making garments',[34] something that Lubelski confirmed in his evidence to the 1889 Select Committee on Sweating.[35] In spite of support from the city's socialist activists, and demands from wholesalers such as James Rhodes and Hepworths that the employers settle, the masters remained obdurate, aided by the presence of 'a number of unscrupulous blacklegs'.[36]

It was lack of strike funds that brought the strike to an end. Without money for food the men gradually returned to work and the strike collapsed. The victory left the workers and their societies weak and divided. Union membership plummeted as the masters yet again issued a black list. A cooperative workshop set up in Briggate to help those worst affected started with 125 orders, but after a few weeks ceased to exist.[37] The failure of the strike exposed the divisions within the Jewish tailoring workforce. Socialist ideology was all very well, but it didn't put food on the table, and it would seem that while the strike leaders had organised the protests and demands for amelioration of conditions, they had overlooked the needs of the basics of quotidian life. Gradually, membership of the three unions dwindled to zero. There had been no victors among the men, only among the masters.

Attempts were made by Jewish socialist tailors to reconstitute a Jewish tailors' union which was open to all tailoring workers in the manner of 'new unionism' which was emerging in London.[38] Though the new union was open to all workers, the machiners, considering themselves of a higher level skill, retained their independence. It was not only the skill divide which separated the Jewish workforce, there was also a dichotomy between religiosity and new political theory. In the eyes of some non-politicised Jewish tailors, socialism was analogous with atheism. In response, a small clique of observant tailors formed an Orthodox Union; not surprisingly, this was short lived. At the same time, events in London were travelling north and a branch of the Gasworkers' and General Labourers' Union (GGLU) was opened in Leeds, largely due to the pioneering work of Maguire, Paylor and Sweeney. Urged on by the trio of Socialist Leaguers, the Jewish tailors' union (which now also included pressers though still not machiners) affiliated to the local GGLU. A year later the machiners 'threw in their lot' with the GGLU and became part of the phenomenon of new unionism.

For the Jewish tailoring trade unionists of Leeds, as with so many members of the new unions born in the passionate months of 1888 and 1889, the five years that followed were traumatic. The honeymoon of the Jewish tailors' branch with the GGLU was one of goodwill and growth: the branch expanded from 900 members to 2000, the latter representing almost 50% of the Leeds alien tailoring workforce. However, the marriage was short lived, as the alien workers missed no opportunity to take advantage of the support and (physical) strength of the gasworkers. One tailoring worker went as far as to ask for 200 pickets for three weeks to support his claim against a workshop master; elsewhere workers went on strike after their employer refused to provide money for gambling.[39] Criticism came not only from the local press but also from Moses Sclare, who recalled with shame that 'no matter what breach was perpetrated by a member ... he expected to be personally protected right or wrong'.[40] Bad feeling soon developed between the GGLU and its Jewish tailor members. The Jewish tailors were criticised for the irrationality of their behaviour, while they in turn censured the executive for their drinking and bureaucracy. But a wider political rift was emerging between the anarchists and the parliamentarians; and the Socialist Leaguers were the latter. Eventually the anarchist element of the tailors broke away, leaving just forty members of the GGLU Jewish tailors' branch. By 1892 there were only twelve members of the GGLU Jewish tailors' branch left. This was not just a Jewish phenomenon, a number of other local GGLU branches had collapsed, all victims of the national rise in unemployment and the reactionary fall in union membership. In this somewhat chaotic environment a very short lived, anarchist inspired, Leeds Independent Jewish Tailors', Machiners' and Pressers' Trade Union was founded. Though the Union collapsed, its failure as much a part of the economic climate as political philosophy, anarchism in Leeds survived – albeit unwelcomed by the conservative element of the city. Within a few months – despite the depressed economy and high levels of unemployment – at the end of 1893 the AJTMP was founded, with an initial membership of 100. In spite of the early hiccoughs and short-lived breakaway, the union survived to take on the best of both the 'new' and the 'new model' varieties of trade unionism and followed a course which led to the amalgamation of 1915.

The years between 1893 and 1915 were ones of national economic recession and progression, the second Forward March of Labour and – as the numbers of Eastern European Jewish immigrants arrived in increasing numbers – the growth of anti-alien sentiment which resulted in the passage of the Aliens Act of 1905.[41] In London during this period, the peripheral Jewish tailoring unions came and went – there were twenty-nine different Jewish tailoring unions active in the capital between 1892 and 1915. In Leeds there was just one, the Leeds AJTMP.[42] The main reason behind the survival of the AJTMP and the respect it gained from non-Jewish organisations in the city, including other unions and the Trades Council, can be attributed to the pragmatism and foresight of its two full-time secretaries during this period: Sam Freedman and Moses Sclare. Their work ethic, political beliefs and personalities proved central to the growth and development of the AJTMP.

Sam Freedman was an unskilled immigrant from Kovno who arrived in Leeds in 1883 and worked his way up the skills ladder to become a tailors' machiner. As a young socialist he experienced, supported and learnt from the strikes of 1885 and 1888. Following his appointment as Union Secretary in 1895, notwithstanding his socialist leanings, Freedman determined to follow a moderate and productive path, one which would enable a harmonious and supportive association with the City's Trades Council and AUCO, the English clothing workers' union. Regardless of the anti-alien stance of the Trades Union Congress, which put down resolutions demanding the strict control or prohibition of the entry of pauper aliens regularly between 1890 and 1895, Freedman attended every TUC Conference during his period of office; in comparison, 1895 marked the only year that a representative of a London Jewish union attended the Conference. Freedman worked tirelessly for the benefit of his membership and, though not scared of standing up to the employers whenever necessary, followed a moderate path, working to expand his union and secure the status of its members. By the early 1900s, Sam Freedman was on a trajectory to build an impressive and respected union. Sadly, during the severe depression of 1903–4, the man who had devoted himself tirelessly to the wellbeing and advancement of the union himself experienced extreme financial difficulty. When discrepancies in the AJTMP's accounts were investigated, it was discovered that Sam had 'borrowed' from its meagre financial resources. He was forced to resign and despite attempts made to help him pay back the missing funds, in 1905 he fled to New York, unable either to correct the financial misdemeanour or face his former members. After eighteen months his wife agreed to repay his debts, and the leadership of the Union agreed not to pursue charges of theft on condition that Sam Freedman never rejoin the union he had worked so hard to advance. He returned to the city in 1907 and 'opened a business in the clothing trade'.[43]

Sam's mismanagement of funds and his own desperate need could have brought down the Union, something not uncommon in the capital, but the AJTMP survived and appointed Moses Sclare in his place. Moses Sclare was a very different kind of Leeds Jewish tailors' union leader to those of the past. Born in the Ukraine, Sclare trained as an engineer and migrated to Scotland in 1889, within a short while becoming Secretary and President of his branch of the Amalgamated Society of Engineers. His dedicated socialism led to his meeting a broad range of socialists, including the future Labour MP James Keir Hardie, the anarchist Peter Kropotkin and the revolutionary Sergius Stepniak.[44] While Keir Hardie may have influenced Sclare's management of the Union, it is clear that the politics of Kropotkin and Stepniak did not. For a union looking for a stable and erudite general secretary, Moses Sclare's curriculum vitae was not to be overlooked. Fluent in Yiddish, English and Russian, with trade union branch leadership experience and an advocate of labour/socialist politics, he was the ideal man to succeed Sam Freedman and put the AJTMP back on course. Sclare took up his appointment in May 1906, an event noted with approval by Leeds Trades Council, though Councillor Alderman Buckle, an anti-alienist, was reported as advising the Jewish tailors to 'conduct their business in English [not Yiddish]'. [45] By 1907, the membership of the AJTMP had risen from 490 to 900 and, as the *Yorkshire Factory Times* commented, 'there was definitely an improved union spirit under Mr. Sclare's secretary-ship'.[46] Indeed, it was significant that in a demonstration of unity between Jewish and English unions, Moses Sclare and Joseph Young – General Secretary of the AUCO – visited factories and workshops together in recruitment drives, underlining the harmony between the two trade unions.

Moses Sclare was indeed the man who would lead his union into the national amalgamation and a more secure future. It was a journey peppered by improved trade union facilities – including the opening in 1911 of the Union's own custom-built Labour Hall –worker and employer harmony and disharmony and the ongoing fight to end to the despised piecework system – one which benefited the speedy and dexterous rather than the diligent and skilled. In both Freedman's time and then in Sclare's, strikes were held to achieve the abolition of piecework. In 1908, a bitter dispute caused severe disruption. An agreement was reached, but it forced the employer to move to smaller premises and dismiss a number of his workers. Sclare recognised that this was not the way forward – where was the benefit of payment by time if the workshop master could not maintain his business? Recognition of this encouraged worker/employer harmony but was short-lived, and in 1911, just two months after the opening of the Union's Labour Hall, the Jewish tailors of Leeds called a strike. What started out as a small-scale protest gradually grew to large-scale proportions which embraced fifty-six tailoring workshops, 705 men and 402 women.[47] Yet again, timing was of the essence. It was the end of February and the wholesale clothiers were looking to expand production at a time when the slack period was ending and the 'busy' on its way in. Their optimism was enhanced by the lifting of the economic depression and a renewed surge in consumerism. For once, pragmatism by the Leeds Jewish Master Tailors Association won the day. An application was made to the Board of Trade for an independent arbitrator. An award by Alderman Smith of Leeds marked the most significant amelioration in wages, hours and conditions since the formation of the first Jewish tailoring union in Leeds in 1876.

However, 'all that glisters is not gold'. The workers may have been awarded a shorter working week without accompanying wage reductions, but this made inroads into the masters' profits, some of whom were brought to their financial knees. Appeals to the wholesalers for increased manufacturing prices fell on deaf ears, and by the end of 1911 a number of workshops had been forced to close and more than 300 workers made redundant.[48] In this instance, the fault lay neither with the employers nor with the workers but with the system which failed to link minimum rates of pay to prices paid by the wholesaler to the workshop master or middleman. Without coordinated agreement which flowed from the top of the chain of production downwards, strike action only brought about redundancy for the worker and bankruptcy for the small employer. It would seem that this harsh lesson was learnt, as no more reports of strikes by the Leeds Jewish tailors was recorded in either the English or Yiddish press or in government reports. This is not to suggest there were no minor skirmishes, but at a time when thousands of English and alien workers were once again 'marching forward', little is heard from the clothing workers of Leeds. One is left to determine whether this was because of the calm and pragmatic leadership of Moses Sclare, or the workers' fear of job and income loss. The answer is a combination of both.

By 1915, the AJTMP trade union in Leeds and its English counterpart AUCO had come of age, born of new unionism and spawned as the shock waves reverberated. While the Socialist Leaguers of the 1880s had played their part in the initial stages of organising those considered unorganisable, it was Freedman (before his tragic aberration) and Sclare who had withstood the pressures of mounting anti-alienism, periods of economic depression and recession and by 1914 the threat and eventual outbreak of war. Though Freedman and Sclare were ideological trade unionists who believed in the values of combination as much for its reflection of brotherhood (and sisterhood) within the workforce, many of the AMJTMP's members were trade unionists because it brought them amelioration irrespective of politics. The history of the 1915 United Garment Workers' Trade Union demonstrates that regional, ethnic and skill divisions could be overcome in order to benefit the common good. However, not all clothing workers' unions participated in that first amalgamation. While the Leeds Jewish and English clothing workers showed the way, it took another twenty-four years and a further three amalgamations for the creation of a National Union of Tailors and Garment Workers which would fully represent the tailoring workers of Britain, regardless of their religious persuasion, level of skill and/or gender.

A London and Leeds comparative

At the start of this chapter, reference is made to the differences between the London and Leeds Jewish tailoring unions and the fact that the Leeds Jewish union was one of the progenitors of the amalgamation of 1915, while its numerous London counterparts played little or no part in the final fusion. The explanations for this relate to the size and structure of the tailoring workshops in both cities, the deficiencies in trade union leadership and the desire of the London Jewish tailors to retain their ethnic ways.

London tailoring workshops tended to be small scale, holding between five and ten workers, while in Leeds the average size was between twenty-five and thirty-five hands. What was considered large in London – eight to twelve employees – was considered small in Leeds.[49] In this instance size mattered. Larger units led to a distancing between employer and employee, whereas in small workshops where master and hand worked in close proximity – often at the same work bench – relationships developed which extended socially, acting as a deterrent to long-term hostility. Though strikes did occur from time to time it was harder to maintain hostilities when the object of the protest was attending your son's barmitzvah or daughter's wedding. However, this was not the chief reason for the ephemeral nature of the London Jewish unions. The major weakness in trade union durability and effectiveness was the flaws in organisational leadership.

In London, the name of Lewis Lyons runs like a thread through the history of Jewish tailoring unions. He was at times lauded and at others criticised. All too often Lyons mismanaged the unions he led, the outcome being disintegration rather than consolidation. His failing was a talent to create internal disquiet and conflict and an inability to manage trade union finances; not just a one-off tragic aberration as had brought Sam Freedman down – Lyons mismanaged on a regular basis. Between 1895 and 1912 he led, or was involved in the running of, nine different tailoring trade unions, and though his charismatic character led to his being called back again and again, his inability to steer a steady course eventually led to his departure from trade union organisation. In 1912, by then a sick man, Lyons retired completely from the East End Jewish labour scene.[50] Sadly, London had no Moses Sclare to bring the diverse London Jewish tailoring unions to unity and success.

However, there was one Jewish tailors' union which exemplified longevity, though not a desire to operate within a national body. In 1892, in response to the growth in the production of women's tailored outer garments and their manufacture in Jewish subdivisional workshops in the East End, the United Ladies' Tailors' Trade Union (ULTTU) was established. Between 1895 and 1900 the union was led initially by Joseph Finn and then by John Dyche[51] – Finn having returned to America. Both men were proficient organisers and dedicated socialists who steered the union into the twentieth century with a growing membership that, at the time of the 1915 amalgamation, exceeded 3,000. The ULTTU would have seemed a likely candidate to take the lead for Jewish tailoring unionists in the amalgamation discussions, and initially they did attend meetings. However, at the last minute they withdrew, the largely immigrant membership fearing that the new union would not understand their Jewish ways; as one commentator put it, they chose to cling to their 'stetl origins'.[52] Were the Leeds Jewish tailors more assimilated than their London counterparts, had they developed a more interactive life both at work and at play, or was it that the leadership was able to steer the members of the Leeds AJTMP on a firm pathway to amalgamation? Clearly it was a combination of all these factors. Whatever their politics, the members of the AJTMP sought organisational security, and if this came through a national body then so be it.

In 1939, the final amalgamation took place when the ULTTU gave up its independence to become part of the National Union of Tailors and Garment Workers. This union survived until 1992, when it sacrificed its trade and cultural identities to become part of the GMB – a general union which covers a spectrum of trades and professions and, at the time of writing, has some 630,000 members.

Notes

1 The AUCO originated in Leeds as an all male clothing workers union; by the time of the amalgamation it had become a nationwide organisation which gave entry to both men and women.
2 In 1913, the National Union of Railway Workers had been established with a membership of 180,000.
3 Unmarried Jewish females were rarely found at work in tailoring workshops in either London or Leeds, though some masters' wives oversaw work in the workshops, see Beatrice Webb in *The Diary of Beatrice Webb Vol. 1 1873–1892* (London: Virago, 1982), pp. 241–9.
4 T. H. Fentiman & Co., 'An Historical Guide to Leeds and its Environs' (1858), in D. Fraser, *A History of Modern Leeds* (Manchester: Manchester University Press, 1980), p. 143.
5 Report of the Truck Committee 1906, PP 1908, LIX, q. 706.
6 The subdivisional system began years earlier when processes were broken down by tailors who gave tasks such as buttonhole-making to female relatives at home.
7 House of Lords Select Committee on the Sweating System; 4th Report, PP 1889, XIV, Vol.1, q. 31709.
8 Ibid., q. 31654.
9 A. J. Kershen, *Uniting The Tailors: Trade Unionism Amongst the Tailors of London and Leeds, 1870–1939* (Ilford: Frank Cass, 1995), p. 49.
10 For the background of the radical Jewish socialist, Lithuanian-born Morris Winchevsky, see William J. Fishman, *East End Jewish Radicals 1875–1914* (Duckworth: London, 1975), pp. 138–45.
11 Morris Winchevsky, *Zi Aur*, 1885, Papers of Aaron Rapport Rollin, Modern Record Centre, University of Warwick. This quotation and all further quotations from Yiddish sources have been translated by the author.

12 Finn was bilingual in Yiddish and English and believed in socialist ideals. While in Leeds, and later in London, he worked to improve conditions and income for the tailoring hands, while at the same time attempting to build bridges with English workers and their unions. However, after leaving the ULTTU at the beginning of the twentieth century, he eschewed his radical views.
13 *Polishe Yidel*, 25 July 1884.
14 Select Committee on the Sweating System, 4th Report, q. 31709.
15 *The Lancet*, 16 June 1888, p. 1147.
16 Kershen, *Uniting*, pp. 40, 50, 64–71.
17 Select Committee on Sweating System, 4th Report, q. 3029.
18 Letter from Joseph Finn to A. R. Rollin, dated 27 October 1943, Papers of A. R. Rollin.
19 Anti-alienism was the term used to describe the antipathy to Eastern European Jewish immigrants. It was arguably a euphemism for anti-Jewishness or anti-Semitism. The latter was a descriptive which originated in Germany in 1873, coined by a journalist Wilhelm Marr, to describe Jew hatred. It was rarely used in Britain until after the First World War. It was anti-alienism that prevailed in the late nineteenth and early twentieth centuries and which resulted in the Aliens Act of 1905.
20 *Polishe Yidel*, 31 October 1884.
21 *Arbeiter Fraint*, 11 December 1891.
22 S. and B. Webb, *The History of British Trade Unionism* 1666–1920 (London: privately printed for the WEA 1920), p. 204.
23 *Trade Unionist*, July 1899, p. 449.
24 See Report of the Chief Registrar of Friendly Societies 1876, PP 1877, LXXII.
25 *Leeds Express* 2 April 1884.
26 Kershen, *Uniting*, p. 62.
27 *Leeds Express*, 5 July 1884.
28 Socialist League Foundation certificate, February 1885, Leeds City Archives.
29 Finn letter to A. R. Rollin, 27 October 1943.
30 *Yorkshire Post*, 4 May 1885.
31 Finn letter to Rollin, 27 October 1943.
32 For details of Tom Maguire, see E. P. Thompson, 'A Homage to Tom Maguire', in A. Briggs and J. Saville, *Essays in Labour History*, Vol. 2 (London: Macmillan, 1971), pp. 276–316.
33 See *Arbeiter Fraint*, 11 May 1888 and *Leeds Evening Express*, 23 May 1888.
34 *Leeds Evening News*, 7 May 1888.
35 Select Committee on Sweating System 1889, 4th Report q. 31785.
36 *Arbeiter Fraint*, 18 May 1888.
37 Ibid., 29 June 1888.
38 New unionism was a phenomenon of the late 1880s. The unions rejected exclusivity, sought to keep their membership and entrance fees low, were open to the semi-skilled and unskilled and tended towards a socialist bias and industrial action. The London Dock Workers Union and the Gas Workers and General Labourers were among the earliest examples of new unionism.

39 *Yorkshire Factory Times*, 24 October 1890.
40 Aaron Rapaport Rollin Papers, University of Warwick.
41 For an in-depth study of anti-alienism and its political consequences, B. Gainer, *The Alien Invasion: The Origins of the Aliens Act 1905* (London: Heinmann, 1972) and C. Holmes, *Anti-Semitism in British Society 1876–1939* (London: Edward Arnold, 1979) still provide the best accounts.
42 For a list of all the London Jewish tailoring unions, including those of the mantle makers, see Kershen, *Uniting*, pp. 202–3, 209.
43 *Yorkshire Factory Times*, 24 April 1907.
44 *Leeds Weekly Citizen*, 28 March 1941.
45 *Yorkshire Factory Times*, 18 May 1906.
46 Ibid., 1 March 1907.
47 Kershen, *Uniting*, p. 90
48 *Yorkshire Factory Times*, 13 January 1912.
49 Kershen, *Uniting*, p. 42.
50 For details of Lewis Lyons trade union activity in London from the 1880s to 1912, see Kershen, *Uniting*, pp. 132–42.
51 John Dyche subsequently went to America and became General Secretary of International Garment Workers' Union in New York.
52 For the history of the London Jewish tailoring unions, see Kershen, *Uniting*, Chs 3 and 4.

7

The Edwardian Jewish community and the First World War

Nigel Grizzard

Introduction

This period saw the transformation of Leeds Jewry from a migrant community to a community of Englishmen of the Jewish persuasion. The impact of the Aliens Act of 1905 on the community, the slowdown of immigration and the rising proportion of English-born children all changed the face of the community.

The outbreak of the First World War put the Jewish community in the political firing line, with discussions about Jewish loyalty in the local press. The period 1914–18 was one of great tension for Leeds Jews; the low point came in June 1917 with the Leeds Anti-Jewish Riots when, with most of the fit men away in the army, a non-Jewish mob burst into the Leylands Jewish area and attacked women, children and the elderly.

The war had a huge effect on the community as it moved young male Jews into the army and the non-Jewish world; it lost at least 160 of its best young men on the battlefield.

The First World War memorials

In the grounds of the United Hebrew Congregation (UHC) on Shadwell Lane, on the left-hand side of the drive, stands a memorial plaque erected after the First World War by the families of twenty soldiers who died on the battlefields (Figure 7.1). For many years this memorial languished in the Ohel – the Prayer Hall at the Gildersome Cemetery of the UHC. It was perched precariously against the wall and certainly did not have pride of place as war memorials should. In the grounds of the Beth Hamedrash Hagodol in Street Lane is Leeds Jewry's Garden of Rest complete with war memorial (Figure 7.2). It stood as an unnamed memorial for the individuals in the Jewish community who gave their lives in two world wars.

Due to the efforts of three key individuals these war memorials were transformed. In the late 1980s, Joe Manning set about raising the money to create two plaques to be filled with the names of those who made the supreme sacrifice. Joe raised the £5,000, not from the moneyed classes within the Jewish community, but from the workers and their families. They wanted to remember fathers, brothers and uncles who had died and whose sacrifice had been forgotten by the Jewish community at large in Leeds. In the early 2010s, the Glynn family took responsibility for funding the movement of the memorial plaque from a forgotten place in the Gildersome Cemetery to the grounds of the UHC synagogue, where it was placed in a prominent position and can be seen by the many thousands of worshippers and visitors who come to the synagogue.

So why are these two events important? The First World War was a very difficult time for Leeds Jewry and it was an era that the communal leaderships wanted to forget. The First World War was full of bad memories not just on the battlefield but more particularly on the home front. Here actions went from bad to worse, culminating in the full-scale attack on the Jewish community in June 1917 which, however, was expunged from the communal Jewish memory. The great historian of Leeds Jewry, Murray Freedman, related that even though he had been born in Leeds in the 1920s, the first he knew about the riots was when he saw an article by Abraham Gilan published in the 1981 edition of the *Jewish Quarterly*.[1] So what were the events that affected the Leeds Jewish community in the first two decades of the twentieth century?

When Queen Victoria died in 1901 and Edward VII became king, it was twenty years since the start of the great flood of Jewish immigrants into the city of Leeds from Russia and Poland. Twenty years was sufficient time for many to establish themselves, to open shops, businesses and small factories, to make the move from being a 'greenhorn', from being regarded as 'off the boat' and working class towards joining the lower middle classes. The immigrants' children were born in England, they had a 'British education' and were native English speakers, and in an English school system they had the traces of being a 'foreigner' removed. The aim was to make the children of Yiddish-speaking immigrants into young British men and women and this was a view with which the Anglo-Jewish establishment concurred.

The Leylands was Leeds Jewry's ghetto par excellence, an area bounded by North Street, Regent Street, Skinner Lane and the city centre. It was small, claustrophobic, full of back-to-back houses and an area unfit for habitation. Today, very few traces of the Jewishness of the area remain for anyone to see; it is an industrial area and Jewish life has moved on to the northern suburbs.[2] In the Edwardian era, Jews lived in the Leylands, but as the community expanded – due to continued immigration from Russia and Poland and natural growth – Jewish families moved out and into better areas.

The Camp Road area, which was demolished with the building of the Sheepscar interchange in the 1960s, was a secondary area of Jewish settlement, while other families moved out of the Leylands northwards to Roseville Road and Harehills. Here the housing was better; some were back-to-backs, others were through terraces but much better homes than the middens of the Leylands. More prosperous families had moved into the new Chapeltown neighbourhood, which included fine detached houses and large terraces and was a world away from the Leylands, even though geographically it was less than a mile from one area to the other.

Murray Freedman[3] analysed the 1901 Census and found nine families in Chapeltown comprising fifty-eight individuals. He states that 'all were comfortably off and most were prominent members of the community'. By 1910, using Kelly's Directory, Freedman was able to identify fifty-one Jewish households in the area, and by 1917 this number had grown to 113. The movement of Jewish institutions lagged behind the actual residential movement of the Jewish community and the first synagogue to be opened in Chapeltown – the Chapeltown Hebrew Congregation, better known as the Francis Street Synagogue – took place in 1921 after the First World War.[4] Chapeltown underwent many changes after the racial disturbances of 1981, with wholesale demolition and rebuilding, but along the main streets – including Spencer Place and Chapeltown Road – many fine homes still stand.

Leeds Jewry was estimated at 12,000 in 1901 and 25,000 by the start of the First World War.[5] Immigration from abroad had slowed with the Aliens Act of 1905 that stopped unrestricted immigration, but Jews who were joining families and had funds were able to come and settle. No figures exist for how many Jews were moving to Leeds annually; not all were coming from abroad, some came from other Jewish centres in the UK. Throughout the twentieth century Jews moved to and from Leeds. They came as marriage partners and they also came for work opportunities. As a thriving commercial centre Leeds was very attractive to Jewish in-migrants.

The lay leadership of the community was provided in the main by the older and more-established patrician families who belonged to the Belgrave Street Synagogue in the city centre. They were the wealthier anglicised families who had to cope with a community composed of, as they saw it, 'foreigners and their children'. It was not an issue unique to Leeds, a similar problem was faced by Jewish communities in London, Liverpool, Manchester and Glasgow, where established Jewish communities saw themselves numerically increasing, but with people whose way of life differed greatly from their own.

Religious life in Jewish Leeds

Throughout the period 1901 to 1914, Anglo-Jewry saw a conflict between the views of the Eastern Europe rabbis who came from the old world and those of the Anglo-Jewish reverends who came from the new.[6] Questions over interpretation of religious law, the strictness of supervision of kosher food provision, and the closing of shops on Friday afternoons before the Sabbath came in during the winter, were all areas of conflict. In London, the communal lay leadership of the United Synagogue that represented middle-of-the-road Anglo-Jewish Orthodoxy wanted to move forward, whereas the East European rabbis of the masses in the East End of London looked to the past.

In 1901, the Beth Hamedrash Hagodol Synagogue[7] in Leeds brought a new rabbi over from Lithuania: Israel Hayim Daiches (1851–1937). This was a first step in having a strong strictly Orthodox rabbi run a major synagogue in the city. Daiches came to be regarded as the leading East European rabbi outside London in the UK and he published a periodical in Hebrew *Bet Va'ad la Hakhamin* [Meeting House of the Wise]. There were eleven editions between 1902 and 1904 and it was the only Anglo-Jewish religious journal of the period that discussed Halachic issues.[8]

Two of Rabbi Daiches' sons went on to become UK Jewish religious leaders. Samuel Daiches (1878–1949) was rabbi in Sunderland and then moved to Jews College – the main institution for the training of Anglo-Jewish ministers – in London as a lecturer in 1908. Salis Daiches[9] (1880–1945) became rabbi in Edinburgh and spokesman for Scottish Jewry.[10] In 1910, thirty East European rabbis gathered in Leeds to look at issues of concern and insisted that native ministers were excluded from the meeting.[11] The meeting debated religious issues and passed resolutions urging married women to shave their heads and wear a *sheitel* [wig] and for Jews to stay away from dance halls and theatres.

In retrospect, the resolutions passed by the rabbis were not surprising; they show more that among the Jewish community the old practices of Eastern Europe were being discarded. Young Jews were taking to enjoy themselves in social and leisure pursuits provided by the wider community. Leeds Jews were moving 'out of the ghetto' both physically and emotionally. The great mass migration of East European Jews West had started in 1880 and thirty years had passed by 1910. Year on year a growing proportion of Leeds Jews were UK born and Eastern Europe was a world they had never known.[12]

As well as there being a divide between the immigrants and the settled Jews, there was also a class divide in Leeds between the workers and factory owners. In 1899, after the death of a young tailor named Benjamin who was not a member of a burial society – and with the possibility of a Jew receiving a pauper's funeral – the established Jewish authorities allowed his burial in a Jewish cemetery. It forced the workers to band together to form a Leeds Jewish Workers Burial and Trading Society to provide free funerals, with members paying a 1d a week subscription. The Society also provided a kosher butcher's shop and carried out its own *shechita*. In 1911, Rabbi Yehuda Leib Astrinsky was appointed rabbi of the Society, which had over 1,000 members and was also by this time providing synagogue services.[13]

The first decade of the twentieth century also saw the opening of cinemas in Leeds and Jews were prominent in this industry. Adjacent to the Leylands, the Newtown Picture Palace opened on 11 January 1913 in Cross Stamford Street, Sheepscar.[14] The building still stands and as it was located next to the Jewish quarter there would have been a large Jewish clientele.

The workers and socialism

In his work *Immigrants and the Class Struggle*,[15] Joseph Buckman looks at the treatment of Jewish immigrant workers in Leeds by the masters of the enterprises that employed them and the role of socialism in the community. Three industries employed most Jewish workers: the overwhelming majority in the tailoring industry,[16] followed by smaller numbers in cabinet making and slipper making.[17]

The tailoring industry was subject to booms and slumps and the *Jewish Chronicle* noted in 1910 that a considerable number of skilled Jewish tailors had left Leeds for opportunities in the USA and Canada.[18] The start of the First World War in 1914 saw a huge demand for military uniforms which brought work to Leeds factories.

Buckman[19] quotes from the anarchist Yiddish newspaper *Der Arbeiter Freund* – the Worker's Friend – about a socialist meeting that was proceeding quietly at the Leylands Board School on Saturday, the Sabbath.

> A gang of fanatical Jews had broken into the hall and were trying to grab a collection of money. The gang were armed with sticks, knives and meat cleavers with which they attempted to attack our comrades. For us the affair is not ended. Apart from the arrest of Comrades Kurz, Sharefsky and Velinsky we will devote all our strength to defending ourselves against the brutal intolerance of these fanatical bandits.[20]

The event was then followed by an inter-racial meeting of protest at North Street Park.[21]

> To express public disgust at the ignorant and brutal intolerance of the orthodox Jewry of Leeds. The meeting was attended by countless people and English and Jewish anarchists, socialists and freethinkers energetically defended the right of free speech and branded the cowardly attack of the black, dark gang who had sought to emulate the bandits of London.[22]

The Jewish community and the First World War 105

Over 100 years later, what can be learnt from the reporting of the meeting? It shows that there was conflict within the immigrant Jewish community over strongly held principles – especially when it came to public desecration of the Sabbath. There was also the use of violence – which is not unusual in immigrant communities.[23]

The actions in the 1904 meeting were about power and control and the flexing of muscles by different sections of the Jewish community. In this case, the politically left and the religious.

A snapshot of Leeds Jewish life

In 1910, there appeared a journal published in Leeds entitled *Anglo-Jewry* – a monthly magazine devoted to Jewish interests. Printed by William Kristall of Lovell Place, Leeds, and running to twenty pages it gives a snapshot of some of the issues facing Leeds Jewry.

First and foremost was a national issue – the involvement of Jews in white slaving, both as instigators and Jewish women as victims. In 1910, the Jewish Association for the Protection of Girls and Women (JAPGW) called a conference in London to discuss the issue. It was attended by representatives from all over the world and focused on Jewish women from Russia and Romania leaving Europe and becoming involved in prostitution in South America. The editors of *Anglo-Jewry* were concerned that white slaving was seen as a Jewish issue and that more than just Jews were involved in the trafficking of women. At a Yorkshire level, the Hull Jewish community were sufficiently concerned that they monitored all single Jewish girls who came through the port as lone travellers and checked that they safely reached their destination.[24]

Second, at a Leeds level there is mention of new regulations imposed on potential teachers by the Leeds Education Committee. Aspiring teachers were informed that during their second year they must board in at the Training College. For Jewish students who did not want to eat *treife*, that is non-kosher food, it posed a problem. The magazine's writers hoped that it would be possible for the Education Committee to amend their decision, so it did not disadvantage potential Jewish applicants to the teaching profession.

There is an article on the Leeds Jewish Cycling Club, which had been in existence for seven years. It was affiliated to the Leeds District League, which showed that this part of the community was integrated into general Leeds life. The secretary, Mr D. Levy, lived at 8 Crimbles Street, an address in what was known as the 'Camp Road' area, outside of the Leylands.[25]

The Friendly Society movement, which helped members out in difficult times where money was short due to illness or unemployment, was a key part of the communal scene. The Hull Grand Order of Israel made a visit to the Leeds Jewish Institute. Whereas Leeds possessed a building, in Hull this was lacking. In the discussions, the Leeds members pointed out that the Leeds Jewish Institute was set up through their own members' efforts and not through the communal leadership – who were indifferent to such a project. If Hull was to achieve an institute, the members of the Grand Order of Israel had to set it up themselves rather than worry about what their communal leadership did or said.

The First World War

When the First World War broke out in 1914, it caused Leeds Jewry to reflect on and face a number of very difficult questions.

The Leeds branch of the Jewish Historical Society of England produced three booklets[26] on Leeds Jewry and the First World War as a first task on formation in the 1980s. At the time, some of the soldiers were still alive and there was living testimony; equally interesting was the information gleaned from local Leeds papers. As soon as the war started, Ludwig Ash, a German Jew living in Headingley, posed the question: 'What are the Jews of Leeds going to do in the War?'[27] For the duration of the war the Jews of Leeds were in the firing line on the home front. Should they join the Forces? Are they allowed to join the Forces? Are they welcome in the Forces? Are they playing their part?

Jews were often foreign nationals. Those born in Leeds were British, but the young men born abroad had Russian nationality. Without going into all the answers, certainly, by 1916, many Jews had joined the Forces. Specific Jewish battalions – the 38th, 39th and 40th of the Royal Fusiliers, known as the Judeans – had been set up and many Leeds Jews joined as this was an opportunity to join a specifically Jewish regiment.

In 1922, as a national tribute to those Jews who had joined the Forces, Reverend Michael Adler, Chaplain to the Jewish Forces, produced the *British Jewish Book of Honour*[28] (BJB), naming over 50,000 Jews who served in the British and Empire Forces. The book has many photographs and more importantly lists the names and addresses of over 2,000 Jews who died in the conflict.

For Leeds, the BJB lists ninety-one Jews who died in the conflict, one was an officer[29] and the other ninety were enlisted men. The figures demonstrate that in class terms the men who enlisted were overwhelmingly working class – they were not of the calibre of officers. Research carried out using the information from the BJB showed that nationally Jews who were officers in the First World War were from the older established families who had attended public schools where there was a cadet core. The Jewish boys at Bradford Grammar School were in this group, and Bradford's Jews, even though many of them were of German origin, produced an officer class.[30]

The BJB[31] records a Mr L. Rosenberg who was very active as a recruiting officer for the Leeds Jewish community. As well as the recruitment of soldiers,

The Jewish community and the First World War

Table 7.1 Yorkshire Regiments that included Leeds, Bradford and Sheffield with numbers of Jewish soldiers serving (1914–18)

	Officers	Men
West Riding Regiment	13	148
West Yorkshire Regiment	14	516
Yorkshire Light Infantry	16	137
Yorkshire Regiment	8	104
Total	51	905

he was concerned for the care of soldiers and their dependants. He received a certificate from 500 Leeds Jewish soldiers in recognition of his work. It was estimated that he recruited over 3,000 men from the Leeds area.

The BJB lists by regiment the names of Jews who served. Most of the Jewish Officers in these regiments were not from Yorkshire – but the vast majority of the Jewish men had Yorkshire addresses.[32] From the list of casualties in the BJB half of the men listed were in Yorkshire regiments, the others were in a wide variety including the Argyll and Sutherland Highlanders, the London Regiment, the Norfolk Regiment, the Cameron Highlanders and the Essex Regiment. Using the casualties as a proxy, there would have been at least 1,800 Jewish men with Yorkshire addresses. The true number of how many served was most probably nearer 3,000 men recruited through Rosenberg's efforts.

The Anti-Jewish riots

On the home front, the Leeds Jewish Community had to endure a difficult time during the First World War. Their loyalty as British subjects was questioned, and, in June 1917, there was an attack upon the Jewish quarter in the Leylands. The evenings of 3 and 4 June 1917 saw gangs of young men smash Jewish shop windows, loot premises and cause disorder. The rioting on the second night was greater than that of the first. By the evening of 5 June there was a sufficiently strong police presence to deter any potential rioters.

Those arrested were predominantly in the age group 14–20. The reasons behind the riots included a long-running feud between Jewish and non-Jewish gangs who lived side by side in the Leylands and the other suburban areas adjacent to Leeds city enctre. Feelings had been whipped against the Jews, who it was claimed were not doing their bit by serving in the armed forces. However, precisely because at the time of the riots the Jewish young men had joined the forces and were not in Leeds, there were few present to act as a self-defence force to repel the rioters in the Leylands. (The riots are also discussed in Chapter 4.)

Why was so little attention paid to the Anti-Jewish riots in Leeds? Perhaps the reason can be found in events on the battlefield. On 7 June, the British Commander in Chief, Lord Haig, launched the first phase of an offensive to break out of the Ypres salient and the Battle of Messines (7–14 June 1917) resulted in thousands of casualties. The news coming back from the front, with endless columns of names of dead Yorkshire men, made the story of a two-day anti-Jewish riot in a district of Leeds pale into insignificance. Leeds Jewry recovered from the riots and with everything else happening – the vast casualties on the battlefield suffered by communities across Leeds – the Jewish community erased the riots from communal memory.

One important result of the riots was the creation of a key cross-communal body – The Leeds Jewish Representative Council.[33] The community realised there was a need for such a body that could speak for the Leeds Jewish community, rather than a series of disparate voices.

The legacy of the First World War on Leeds Jewry

Despite the popular view that Jews had not supported the war effort, they bore significant losses and, although the BJB list is not complete, it is likely that 160 Jewish soldiers made the supreme sacrifice on the battlefield.[34] It was the first time that many young men in the Leeds Jewish community had lived outside the Jewish world. Their lives until then had been in a Jewish milieu, living in a Jewish neighbourhood, working with other Jews and not coming into the same level of contact with non-Jews as they experienced in the forces. Their service in the forces gave them a chance to become more British and more integrated into British life. The First World War forced Anglo-Jewry and, by inference, Leeds Jewry to grapple with issues which they had previously not faced.

Jews had a long history of serving in the British Military, but as regular servicemen and in small numbers[35] – the First World War, with conscription, brought the Jewish masses into the Army, with over 50,000 Jews serving in the British and Empire Forces. It led to the creation of a chaplaincy to Jewish Soldiers which, as well as bringing Jewish chaplains to Jewish soldiers, took Anglo-Jewish ministers away from their communities and into the battlefields.

The first decades of the twentieth century were decades of transition for Leeds Jewry – moving from an immigrant community toward becoming an accepted part of the city of Leeds. The service in the military and the common bond that all ex-servicemen feel obviously helped. The community on the home front had been through difficult times – not just the rioting but the barrage of questions in the local press about where the Jewish community stood on war issues. Leeds Jewry needed to learn how to defend itself not just physically, but also in combating written attacks in the press. The fact that thousands of Jewish men had joined the Armed Forces meant the 'loyalty question' became defunct.

As Britain recovered from the First World War and moved into the 1920s, Leeds Jewry were becoming more established, less foreign and were moving out into suburbia. This was the start of the growth of a burgeoning middle class in the Jewish community – a process that had taken place decades earlier in other more settled communities such as Bradford, Manchester and north-west London but had now come to Leeds.

The Edwardian Age and the First World War were not the 'immigrant years', they were a period of Jewish history where Leeds Jewry grappled with living in Britain, starting the transformation from a migrant to a more settled community. These years were not years of good memories and, for that reason, until recently the community had forgotten them in the move from the Leylands to Leeds 17.

7.1 War memorial at UHC Shadwell Lane

1914 – 1918

S. ABRAHAMS	L. DANCYGER	A. JACOBS	A. ROSENBAUM
S. ANNENBERG	I. DAVIES	A. JACOBSON	B. ROSENBERG
I. AVERBACK	M. DAVIES	I. JAFFE	F. ROSENBERG
N. BAKER	B. FEARN	J. JAFFE	H. ROSENBERG
G. BARNETT	M. FREEDMAN	M. JOSEPHS	H. ROSENBERG
H. BENJAMIN	H. GALINSKY	L. KAUFMAN	H. ROSENTHAL
K. BENJAMIN	D. GAMPLE	S. LABOR	S. RUDSTEIN
S. BERNSTEIN	A. GANTFORD	S. LANDY	M. SACOFSKY
D. BERSON	M. GETZELLS	P. LEIZABRAM	A. SAMUELS
W. BERSON	A. GILLMAN	H. LEVENSON	J. SANOFSKI
L. BLACK	S. GINSBERG	B. LEVI	L. SAPERIA
H. BLOOM	H. GOLDBERG	E. LEVI	J. SAUNDERS
C. BOAM	S. GOLDING	L. LEVI	S. SHERMAN
M. BRODIE	S. GOLDMAN	B. LEWIS	M. SILBERG
W. BROSGILL	M. GOODMAN	H. LEWIS	B. SIMON
M. CAPLAN	S. GOODMAN	N. LEWIS	S. SOLK
A. COHEN	P. GREENBERG	S. LIPCHINSKY	A. STEINBERG
A. COHEN	M. GREYMAN	M. LIPMAN	I. STEINBERG
A. COHEN	L. HARRIS	P. MAKALINSKY	J. STEINBERG
A. COHEN	M. HARRIS	H. NYMAN	M. STEINBERG
H. COHEN	M. HARRIS	J. PHILLIPS	J. STODEL
I. COHEN	M. HARRISON	L. PRICE	D. STROSS
J. COHEN	M. HESSELBERG	A. QUAITE	M. TOMPOFSKI
M. COHEN	L. HOLLAND	H. RAKUSEN	J. YAFFIN
H. COLLINS	J. HOLMES	M. REUBEN	J. YAMOVSKY
S. COTSON	M. HUROVITCH	P. RIGGLE	J. FREEDMAN
J. COUPLAN	J. HYMAN	M. ROSEMAN	H. GOLDSTEIN
M. COUPLAN	H. JACKSON	M. ROOMS	A. FISHER
		N. G. YAFFA	J. LEVI

7.2 War memorial at Street Lane

Notes

1. A. Gilam, 'The Leeds anti-Jewish riots 1917', *Jewish Quarterly*, 29:1 (1981), pp. 34–7.
2. Jews in Leeds moved in a northern direction along a route comprising the Chapeltown Road and Harrogate Road.
3. Murray Freedman, *Chapeltown and its Jews* (Leeds: privately published 2003), p. 4.
4. The author of this chapter visited the building in the late 1970s, by which time it had become known as 'The Roots Club'. It was at that time still possible to see the building's original use. It has now been demolished.
5. Figures from the 1901/2 and 1914 *Jewish Year Books*.
6. Bernard Homa describes some of the conflicts in his book, *Orthodoxy in Anglo-Jewry 1880–1940* (London: Jewish Historical Society of England, 1969).
7. This community still exists with its large synagogue on Street Lane in Moortown, Leeds 17. The Hebrew means the 'Great House of Learning'.
8. See L. Gartner, *The Jewish Immigrant in England 1870–1914* (London: Simon Publications, 1973), pp. 215–16.
9. See www.jewishvirtuallibrary.org/daiches-family (accessed 3 May 1917).
10. A third son, Eli, went to Chicago; he was an advertising industry executive who was gunned down in an assassination in 1934. See www.jta.org/1934/03/07/archive/daiches-leaves-widow-the-bulk-of-his-estate (accessed 3 May 2017).
11. Gartner, *The Jewish Immigrant in England*, pp. 217–18.
12. Some visible reminders of Eastern Europe remained late into the twentieth century. The New Central Vilna Synagogue housed in the former Kingsway Cinema on Harrogate Road in Moortown, Leeds 17, was in use from 1958 to 1991.
13. For a more detailed history see http://www.etzchaim.co.uk/history.php (accessed 6 June 2017).
14. It closed as a cinema in 1953.
15. J. Buckman, *Immigrants and the Class Struggle: The Jewish Immigrant in Leeds 1880–1914* (Manchester: Manchester University Press, 1983).
16. Today, the tailoring industry has all but disappeared from Leeds Jewish life. The late 1970s and 1980s saw the decline of the many Jewish-owned tailoring businesses. This was mirrored in Bradford, where a number of Jewish-owned large textile companies also disappeared.
17. The decline of this industry was due to two main postwar factors: the introduction of fitted carpets and the fitting of inside toilets to terraced houses and back-to-backs that had been built without these facilities.
18. *Jewish Chronicle*, 5 August 1910.
19. Buckman, *Immigrants and the Class Struggle*, p. 163.
20. *Arbeiter Freund*, 30 September 1904.
21. This park still exists and was colloquially known as 'Sheeny Park' up to the 1930s, where Sheeny was used as a derogatory word for Jews.
22. *Arbeiter Freund*, 14 October 1904.
23. In 2015, at the Bangladeshi Community Centre – on the Roundhay Road, Leeds,

under a mile from the Leylands Board School – a mass brawl broke out between different factions over control of the Centre. www.yorkshireeveningpost.co.uk/news/34-men-charged-over-violent-brawl-at-leeds-council-run-bangladeshi-centre-1-7774472 (accessed 6 June 2017).
24 In the Hull History Centre, in the Jewish Archives collection, there exists a register for single Jewish girls arriving at the port – some of whom were heading for Leeds.
25 The Camp Road area was 'cleared' in the 1960s to make way for the Sheepscar interchange.
26 The three booklets were on Leeds Jewry and the Great War, the Home Front and Mrs Sheinblum's Kitchen.
27 There is a memorial window originally from Belgrave Street Synagogue, but now in the Shadwell Lane Synagogue, to Ash's wife Keetje who was a Dutch Jewess who lived in Leeds.
28 *British Jewry Book of Honour* (BJB) (London: Caxton, 1922).
29 David Stross was an RAF officer who is buried at the UHC Cemetery at Gildersome, Leeds. His tombstone has a biplane inscribed on it.
30 Lieutenant Jack Halle, son of Moritz von Halle, was a former Bradford Grammar School boy who died on the Somme in 1916.
31 BJB, p. 17.
32 For a fuller discussion on Jewish Officers in the First World War, see Martin Sugarman in www.jewsfww.london (accessed 6 June 2017).
33 See http://ljrc.org/about-us-2/history-of-the-ljrc (accessed 6 June 2017).
34 Discussions with Jewish researcher Harold Pollins, who carried out a great deal of work on First World War Jewish casualties, suggests that the BJB under enumerated the Jewish casualties by at least 25%.
35 There were about 1,000 Jews in the British Forces at the start of the First World War according to the BJB.

8

Zionism in Leeds 1892–1939

Janet Douglas

Introduction: genesis of Zionism

The term 'Zionism' was first coined in 1885 by Nathan Birnbaum (1864–1937), a Viennese Jewish activist and writer, but as is often the case the invention of the name actually post-dated the phenomenon it sought to describe. From the 1870s, small Jewish agricultural settlements had been established in Palestine, then part of the Ottoman Empire, but the year 1881 represented a pivotal moment in the early history of Zionism. First, in that year Alexander II, the Tsar Liberator, was assassinated, putting an end to any immediate prospects for the development of a modern liberal Russian Empire and dashing the hopes for any improvement in the position of Russia's five million Jews. Russian Jews both in reality and metaphorically lived on the margins of society (The Pale of Settlement), were officially classified as '*aliens*' and subject to state-sanctioned discrimination and the vast majority were desperately poor. Under the reactionary Alexander III (1845–94), the plight of Jews further deteriorated. As part of a programme of Russification, a wave of vicious police-instigated pogroms spread throughout the west and south of the Empire, notably in Kiev, Warsaw and Odessa. In total, it has been estimated that there were over 200 attacks on Jewish communities between 1881 and 1884, provoking a massive exodus of Jews particularly to America, but also to places like London, Manchester and Leeds.

The other landmark event of 1881 was the publication in Germany of Eugen Duhring's 'The Parties and the Jewish Question', which laid the foundation for scientific anti-Semitism. Anti-Semitism had disfigured European history since the Middle Ages, grounded in religious zeal, fear of difference and economic rivalries, but this new form of anti-Semitism was being legitimated by Science – that bearer of truth which had liberated society from tradition and prejudice and was the foundation of modernity and progress. This toxic coupling, as well as an economic downturn, unleashed a new wave of anti-Semitism not only in Eastern and Central Europe, but also, as the Dreyfus case (1894) demonstrated, in France, a country which prided itself on Enlightenment traditions and its revolutionary heritage.

The consequences of these developments varied. As mentioned earlier, one reaction was flight (2 million Jews fled Russia between 1880 and 1920), but there were other options: acculturation, assimilation, socialism and revolutionary activity. Another was what became known as Zionism. In an era of 'the national awakening of the people' ('*risorgimento*'), it was argued that, like other European ethnicities, the Jews had a right to their own ethnically-based homeland where their safety was ensured and their cultural identity preserved. Zionism in many ways provides a classic example of the role played by nationalism in the creation of the common sentiments and solidarities which are vital to the construction of nations.

Historians of Zionism chart two phases in the embryonic movement: 'Practical Zionism' and 'Political Zionism'. The former urged Jews to return to Palestine, and between 1881 and 1897 thirty Jewish settlements were established, often financed by wealthy and successful Jews such as Baron Edmond de Rothschild. A figure who provides a bridgehead between Practical and Political Zionism was Leon Pinsker (1821–91), a well-to-do physician living in Odessa. Until 1881, Pinsker favoured assimilation as an answer to 'The Jewish Problem', but the Odessa pogrom radically changed his views. No longer believing that Enlightenment values would defeat anti-Semitism, he argued in his *Auto-Emancipation* pamphlet that Jews must be transformed into autonomous agents in history, responsible for their own destiny, and they would only be truly free in a country of their own. In 1882, he founded Chovevei Zion (sometimes known as the Odessa Committee) to elicit funds for the purchase of land in Palestine and the organisation of emigration. A short-lived branch of Chovevei Zion existed in Leeds in 1883. The recognised apostle of Political Zionism, Theodor Herzl (1860–1904) published *The Jewish State* (1896) in the wake of the Dreyfus Affair, arguing that the Jews were a nation like any other and therefore required their own state. His unique contribution was to propose a strategy that was to transform Zionism into a serious international political force: the Great Powers must be persuaded to act together to provide a space for the Jewish masses to emigrate to and live in peace. Although personally agnostic about where this 'space' might be, in 1897 he organised the first World Zionist Congress (WZO) in Basle, which endorsed a four-point programme: the promotion of the settlement of Jewish farmers and tradesmen in Palestine; the strengthening of Jewish consciousness; the federation of all Jewish groups into local groups; and the attainment of governmental grants necessary to achieve Zionist purposes. Privately in his diary he confided,

Were I to sum up the Basle Congress in a word ... it would be this. At Basle I founded the Jewish state. If I said this out loud today I would be greeted by universal laughter. In five years' time perhaps and certainly in fifty years everyone will perceive it.[1]

The context

In 1841, there were no more than ten Jewish families living in Leeds, mostly of German origin; thirty years later the community numbered 900, but figures increased dramatically from the 1880s when migrants from the Russian Pale of Settlement and in particular from the province of Kovno, now in present day Lithuania, began to arrive. For some this migration represented a flight from oppression, pogroms and Russian conscription, but not all migrants were refugees, others were leaving home in order to benefit themselves economically, and it was the boom in the Leeds tailoring trade that was the major reason why so many settled in the town. We know, for example, that Herman Friend, a Jew of German origin and business colleague of John Barran who was the pioneer of mass tailoring industry, directly recruited labour in Kovno.[2] By 1891 there were 8,000 Jews in the city and perhaps as many as 20,000 by 1904. The following year, the passing of the Aliens Act reduced the numbers of new immigrants to a trickle yet, despite these restrictions, by 1911 Jews represented 12% of the population of the Leeds township.[3] The vast majority of these new immigrants were concentrated in the Leylands, a square mile of narrow streets and yards off North Street. Most worked in tailoring, not in the Gentile-owned tailoring factories which were springing up all over the city, but in small tailoring workshops usually owned by their co-religionists, which undertook a range of out-work for the larger factories.

An article in *the Jewish Chronicle* in 1924 referred to the Leeds Jewish community as 'a bubbling lava of chaos and disharmony'.[4] As elsewhere, there was friction between the Jews who had arrived before the mass influx and the Russian Jews. The latter referred to the former as '*the englisher*' while the newcomers were known as '*the grinner*'. As Rosalind O'Brien noted, 'a worker in a tailoring workshop from Lithuania and a member of the Marienpoler synagogue, would have little in common with, and seldom come across, and almost never identify with a Leeds Jew who was the master of a workshop, a member of the Great synagogue and of Polish origin'.[5] Despite their poverty the newcomers regarded themselves as much more pious and disdained the more long-established members of the community for giving up their *yiddishkeit*. The *Englisher* were often both the employers and landlords of working-class Jews, providing fertile ground for the class conflict which was detailed by Joseph Buckman in *Immigrants and the Class Struggle*.[6] Among the *grinner* themselves there was intra-communal sectarianism based on degrees of religious orthodoxy and different religious practices, political allegiances and loyalties to one's *landsmen*. According to O'Brien, 'Variations in dress, dialect, food preparation, forms of synagogue worship and social customs in general were enough to be the basis of sharp social divisions.'[7] Sometimes, newcomers on arrival in Leeds thought it wise to change their pronunciation of Yiddish in order to fit in.[8] By the outbreak of the First World War there were at least twelve synagogues in the city, representing different sections of the Jewish community and often named after the towns and villages where the congregation originated.

The origins of Zionism in Leeds

The first Zionist organisation to be established in Leeds was a branch of *Chovevei Zion* [Lovers of Zion] founded in 1883.[9] The organisation had been established in 1881–2 in response to atrocities in Russia, and it sought to promote Jewish immigration to Palestine through the purchase of land. Whether this fledgling Leeds branch survived seems doubtful, but it was certainly revived in the 1890s just before the man who deserves to be called 'the grandfather of Leeds Zionism' arrived in Leeds.[10] Dr Moses ('Jack') Umanskii (1862–1926) was born in Ekateroslav and, after medical studies in various European universities, came to Leeds in 1892 – the first Jewish medical doctor to practise in Yorkshire.[11] A year after his arrival, he founded the Leeds Hebrew Literary Society, which initially met in members' homes to discuss not only literary subjects but also philosophy and politics. Later, the Society acquired basement reading rooms in Byron Street and established a Hebrew School for children in Camp Road. Umanskii's other ventures were the revival of Chovevei Zion, which by 1898 had 200 members, and a branch of the Zionist friendly society The Ancient Order of Maccabeans. In 1897, he was one of eleven British Jews who attended the first Zionist Congress in Basle, where he met Jacob Moser from neighbouring Bradford. Together they embarked on two projects: the founding of the first 'political' Zionist organisation in the city, Agudas Hazionim [the Society of Zion],[12] and the establishment of a Jewish Hospital to commemorate the life of Theodor Herzl who died in 1904 (later to become known as the Herzl-Moser Hospital) in Leopold Street (the earliest Jewish organisation in Chapeltown). Dr Umanskii was to serve as its medical superintendent in 1905–26. Revealingly, a year before the opening of the hospital, a number of Leeds Jews contacted the local press, writing that they did not want a specifically Jewish hospital and were very satisfied with the service they received from the Leeds Infirmary.[13] At the 3rd Zionist Congress in 1899, Dr Umanskii and Sir Francis Montefiore were elected the English representatives on the Actions Committee established at the Congress.[14] In the same year he was a founder of the English

Zionist Federation and established Britain's first Zionist newspaper, *Dos Volk*, written in Yiddish.[15]

The first public meeting organised by Agudas Hazionim took place in February 1899 at the Grand Assembly Rooms (now the Howard Assembly Rooms). Dr Umanskii was in the chair and on the platform were the leading members of the English Zionist Federation founded in 1898: Joseph Cowen, Dr Gaster, Leopold Jacob Greenberg and Jacob de Haas - all disciples of Herzl.[16] According to the *Yorkshire Post*, the meeting was packed and resolutions were passed in favour of establishing a national home for Jews in Palestine. In the same year Mrs Henrietta Diamond and Mrs Umanskii formed the first Women's Zionist organisation (B'noth Zion) in the country.[17] Rebecca Umanskii shared her husband's interest in Zionist causes and was a delegate in 1898 to the 2nd Zionist Congress, accompanied by her small children. Usually excluded from positions of formal power in the community, Jewish women were to play a significant role in British Zionism. Just as the anti-slavery movement in the previous century had given British women the confidence to take part in public life, Zionism enabled Jewish women to step outside their conventional domestic roles and become key fundraisers and organisers of meetings, youth organisations and social activities.[18] On a less formal level, the formidable Mrs Sheinblum ran a regular Zionist salon in her kitchen in Brunswick Street which became so celebrated that most visiting Zionist notables attended when they had speaking engagements in the city.[19] The first Zionist hall in the country (later called the Herzl Institute) was opened in 1902 in St Luke Street, financed by Jacob Moser.[20] Later in the year, a Zionist synagogue was founded in St Alban's Street, and in 1907 it moved to new premises in Brunswick Street which cost £1,000 - £600 of which was contributed by Jacob Moser.[21] The Zionist Synagogue organised a youth club called Young Shomerin and held Sunday concerts every few weeks. In 1915, the synagogue had 190 seat holders. In the interwar years it moved again, to 307 Chapeltown Road next to the Zionist offices.

Building a movement: 1900-14

By 1899 there were twenty-six Zionist organisations in Britain, three of which were in Leeds; but in the opening decades of the twentieth century Zionists faced an uphill struggle. Far too busy earning a living and taking care of their families, most Jews in Leeds were indifferent to the issue of a Jewish homeland in Palestine. According to Walsh, 'only a minority of the community were Zionists. Many were indifferent and regarded the Zionists as scatterbrained ideologues, remote from reality.'[22] If they were involved in political causes at all it was to left-wing and anarchist politics they turned.[23] At the other end of the social spectrum, 'the top hats' of the *englisher shul* (their synagogue was in Belgrave Street) regarded Zionism as an ideology likely to do more harm than good, fearing that it would encourage anti-Semitism. Political Zionism was also anathema to the highly Orthodox. For them it represented a travesty of Judaism, only in the messianic era could the Jews return to Israel. The appointment in 1901 of Rabbi Israel Hayim Daiches (1850–1937) to the Beth Hamedrash Synagogue (situated in Upper Hope Street) did something to mitigate this situation.[24] Born in Lithuania, Rev. Daiches was considered one of the greatest Talmudic scholars of the day and, unusually for a highly Orthodox rabbi, he was also a Zionist. A year after his arrival in the city, the Rev. Daiches established the Leeds Orthodox Zionist Association and went on to found The Union of Orthodox Rabbis of England.

Apart from raising funds for Jewish communities in Palestine, the chief activity of Zionists in the city was to convert their fellow Jews by distributing literature, door-to-door collections, organising local events and holding public meetings. A meeting held on 30 March 1900 by the English Zionist Federation, with Sir Francis Montefiore in the chair, was not reported in the local newspapers; but thereafter the local press regularly reported large meetings held in the city centre sponsored by Agudas Hazionim, with national speakers from the English Zionist Federation. In May 1903, for example, two thousand Jews attended the Assembly Rooms. Under a banner declaring 'Pay your shekels, it may save lives' and a portrait of Herzl, Joseph Cowen spoke of how English Jewry had 'hung too much on the frock coat and silk hat' and said that Jews would always be regarded as aliens and 'the only practical solution to the Jewish problem is to provide a legally assured home in Palestine'.[25]

Herzl's quest for a Jewish homeland by seeking support from the great powers appeared to bear fruit in 1903 when the Colonial Secretary, Joseph Chamberlain, offered land in Uganda as a refuge for Russia's Jews. At the 6th Zionist Congress, Herzl urged the acceptance of this offer, and after acrimonious debate it was decided by a vote of 295 to 178 to investigate the matter further by visiting East Africa. Although the project was rejected at the 7th Congress (i.e. after Herzl's death), the Zionist movement was badly split, and in Britain Israel Zangwill, the Jewish novelist, formed the Jewish Territorial Society (IZO) to win support for the Uganda solution. A branch of IZO was established in Leeds in September 1905 at a crowded meeting at Lovell Rd School.[26] At the Theatre Royal in Hunslet Lane the following March a public meeting was held to support the Uganda solution – any territory was better than none – but a month later another meeting was held at the same venue to oppose the scheme.[27] Despite not being part of the mainstream of English Zionism, IZO survived until the 1917 Balfour Declaration.

In January 1910, Chaim Weizmann (1874–1952) paid his first visit to Leeds when, as President of the 9th Zionist Congress held in Hamburg, he made a report on its proceedings at a meeting at Lovell Road School.[28] Weizmann visited for a second time in 1914 when the Annual Conference of the English Zionist Federation met in Leeds. The formal proceedings of the AGM were held at the Queen's Hotel under the chairmanship of Joseph Cowen. In the evening there was a public meeting at the Albert Hall with all the luminaries of the English Zionist movement on the platform. Three resolutions were passed: support for a national homeland in Palestine; support for Jewish Schools in Palestine; and a resolution declaring that Hebrew was to be the official language of the Jewish people in Palestine.[29] According to J. S. Walsh's reminiscences, 'We organised a spectacular welcome for Dr Weizmann who was met by an open car to take him to the Queen's hotel. The route thronged with crowds.' Later in the evening, in Mrs Sheinblum's kitchen, Weizmann inveighed against liberal Jews and their leader Claude Montefiore.[30] In July, just before the outbreak of war, a national conference of Lady Zionists was held at the Herzl-Moser Institute under the chairmanship of Mrs Umanskii, and in the evening there was a mass meeting at the Leeds Jewish Institute.[31] However, as Ernest Sterne noted,

> Zionism was not by any means welcomed with open arms by the whole community. Many resented what they thought of as a desecration of the holy language, when the Zionists began to make Hebrew into a modern language ... One of the religious leaders of the community had befriended one of the younger immigrants and let him live in his own home. However, when he discovered that the young man was a Zionist, he promptly told him to leave the house.[32]

From the Balfour Declaration to 1939

As elsewhere, the Balfour Declaration galvanised Leeds Jewry, for no longer did a Palestinian homeland seem like an impossible dream. It was recorded nationally that membership of Zionist groups rose from 4,000 in 1917 to 30,000 in 1921, while the number of Zionist organisations affiliated to the English Federation increased from 61 to 234. In February 1918, before their investigatory visit to Palestine, members of the Zionist Commission visited Leeds to attend three functions organised by the Leeds Joint Zionist Council: a luncheon at the Queen's Hotel; an afternoon conference at the Grand Central Hotel on Briggate; and an evening meeting at the Theatre Royal. Weizmann, the chairman of the Commission, was indisposed so the principal speaker was Nahum Sokolow, the secretary of the World Zionist Congress who, with Harry Sacher, had written the first draft of the Balfour Declaration. In his speech at the luncheon, Sokolow told his audience,

> The Jews are going back to the east to establish their national home. Then they will be able to offer hospitality to hundreds of thousands perhaps millions of Jews who had wandered enough on the surface of the globe, and who rightly deserved at last to find a home.

Harry Sacher spoke at the evening meeting and a letter of support was read out from Sir Mark Sykes.[33]

The second development which greatly strengthened Zionism in Leeds was the arrival of the mathematician, Dr Selig Brodetsky (1888–1954), appointed to a post at the university at the end of 1919 where he was to remain until 1947. Born outside Odessa, in his memoirs Brodetsky recounted that 'I learnt Zionism on my mother's knee and over my father's knee'.[34] Already known in Zionist circles in the city, a grand reception was organised for him at the Zionist Hall. Brodetsky immediately joined Agudas Hazionim and the Zionist synagogue, and in 1921 began his work for the Joint Jewish Zionist Council (later the Zionist Central Council).[35] A tireless worker and inspirational speaker, Brodetsky re-organised the work of the Council by appointing a paid secretary and renting a suite of offices in Brunswick Street. Here he seemed to spend most of his evenings when he wasn't involved in speaking engagements. He was all too aware that the Zionist organisations in Leeds were largely middle class (probably lower middle class), and he deliberately tried to mobilise working-class Jews who formed the mass of the city's Jewry.[36] For example, subscriptions to provide funds for Palestine were usually set at 5s, and with this sum went the right to elect a number of delegates to the Zionist Congress, but Brodetsky insisted that subscriptions be lowered to 1s in order to make the movement more democratic.[37]

A mass of information about local meetings and social events appeared in the *Jewish Chronicle* and a great deal of time and effort went into fundraising. At the AGM of the Joint Zionist Council in 1923, a motion was passed to buy land in Palestine on which to establish a Leeds settlement, and a year later the first of the triennial Palestine Bazaars was held at the Town Hall in 1924 to raise money for this project. Opened by the Chief Rabbi, and addressed by the Leeds Lord Mayor, £2,300 was raised for the purchase of land.[38] As before the First World War, large city centre meetings continued, with speakers from the national and international movement such as Vladimir Jabotsky, Nahum Sokolow, Dr Gaster and Menachem Ussishkin – head of the Jewish National Fund. In 1922, Weizmann addressed the prestigious Leeds Luncheon Club on the question of 'Zionism and the Arabs'. 'The country has not been handed over to the Jew', explained Weizmann,

> but the British administration had to see fair play between Jewish and Arab interests there. The mandate recognised the historic connection of the Jews with Palestine and gave them a chance of trying to build up a national home ... The Jews were now doing the work of civilisation in interpreting the west to the east.[39]

In the afternoon, Weizmann spoke at the University Zionist Group and in the evening there was a meeting at the Town Hall chaired by the Lord Mayor,

Frank Fountain. In some ways it was not unusual for mayors to host public meetings in the city, but it did denote a mark of respectability and in turn bestowed a degree of legitimacy on their organisations. The key political figure in Leeds for over thirty years was the Conservative Sir Charles Wilson, who was a staunch supporter of the Leeds Jewish community. Montague Burton described him as 'the godfather of the Jews in Leeds'.[40] In 1925, Wilson chaired a meeting at the Coliseum addressed by Nahum Sokolow, and in 1929 addressed a rally at the Town Hall protesting about the Jews massacred in the Arab Riots.[41] In the same year, B'nai B'rith organised a complementary dinner for Wilson at the Queen's Hotel to celebrate his planting of 500 trees in Palestine which were to be known as Wilson's Grove.

However, Leeds Zionism was as prone to fracture as other sections of the Jewish community. Apart from Poale Zion [Workers of Zion], the left-wing face of Zionism founded in Leeds in 1902 and since 1921 affiliated to the Labour Party, Weizmannian Zionism (sometimes described as 'official' or 'General Zionism'), was attacked on two fronts: from 'Revisionist' Zionism associated with Jabotinsky and from Mizrachi, a religious Zionist organisation founded by Rabbi Astrinskii of the Burial Society Synagogue in Wintoun Street. In 1926, representing Mizrachi, Alter Max Hurwitz, a local barrister, unsuccessfully stood against Brodetsky in the election of the delegate to the Zionist Congress.[42]

Despite these rifts, the number of Zionist organisations was increasing. In 1923, Brodetsky recorded that 'there are currently ten Zionist organisations in the city including the old Leeds Society (Agudas Hazionim) working amongst working class people, one in Chapeltown, one in Roundhay, one consisting of those of Jewish orthodoxy, one associated with the Labour Party, two men's societies and three women's societies'. By 1937, eighteen societies were affiliated to Leeds Zionist Central Council.[43]

It is difficult to gauge how many Zionists there were in Leeds in the interwar period, or indeed quite what it meant to be a Zionist. Brodetsky wrote of up to 2,000 attending meetings, but audiences at these bumper meetings may not have all resided in the city.[44] Ernest Sterne, writing in 1982 about the year 1919, maintains that 'many Jews in Leeds were Zionists but little appeared in print about it'. Conversely, Louis Saipe in *A History of the Jews in Leeds* (1956) suggests that to 'give a list of names of all Leeds Zionists would be to give a list of almost every Jew in Leeds'.[45] In a paper presented to the Jewish Historical Society of England conference in 1975, A. S. Diamond argued that Zionism had a big impact in Leeds because 'the great bulk (of the community) had not yet put down deep roots as in London and other centres where a numerous, long-established and prosperous group was likely to oppose it'.[46] On the other hand, C. C. Aronsfeld, remembering his time in Leeds in 1935–6, believed that Zionist commitment was shallow and that the functions of the Zionist

Society were badly attended unless they were social.[47] Apart from the growth in the network of Zionist organisations, one piece of more solid evidence is the number of Jewish National Fund (JNF) collection boxes found in Jewish homes.[48] In 1901, 200 boxes had been distributed by Agudas Hazionim and by 1935, 3,000 boxes – with a Jewish population of approximately 25,000, this suggests that JNF collection boxes were a common feature of Jewish homes. But what such activity meant is another matter; was this fundraising seen as a political act or one that differed little from collecting for other Jewish charities?

We can catch occasional glimpses of other narratives of Jewish life in interwar Leeds – trade union activism, a significant strike at Burton's in 1936, activities in the Leeds Labour Party and the Communist Party – which perhaps suggest that the majority of working-class Jews had other political allegiances and preoccupations.[49] Anthony Clavane remembered his grandfather telling him that in the 1930s half the Leeds branch of the Communist Party were Jewish.[50] When Leslie Silver first came to Leeds in 1940, he joined the Young Communist League at 51 Francis Street, and later became a shop assistant at YCL's bookshop in Woodhouse Lane. According to John Fisher, Silver's biographer: 'There was wide support in the Jewish community for the Communist Party at all income levels, although the main support came from the working class and some professionals and academics.'[51]

Conclusion

It is understandable that the heroic days of Leeds Zionism are now celebrated and perhaps seen through rose-tinted spectacles. Even in the 1930s, the mass of the Jewish population were working class and some were still extremely poor.[52] Many of them, despite Brodetsky's endeavours, still felt that Zionism was a middle-class movement (associated, as one shop-floor worker at Burton's told me, with *'the toffs'*). Without any serious studies of the Leeds Labour Party and the Communist Party, it is difficult to know the extent of Jewish active involvement in left-wing politics in this period, or how far such involvement muted the appeal of Zionism. The growth of Fascism in Europe spurred both the left and Zionist causes in the second half of the 1930s. Ultimately, it can be argued, it was the Holocaust and the creation of the state of Israel that transformed Leeds Jewry's attitude to Zionism.

Notes

1   Quoted by N. E. Passachoff, *Great Jewish Thinkers: Their Lives and Work* (London: Behrman House, 1992), p. 98.
2   M. Freedman, *25 Characters in Leeds Jewish History* (Leeds: privately published, 2004), p. 10.

3 E. Krausz, *Leeds Jewry* (Cambridge: W. Heffer & Sons Limited for the Jewish Historical Society of England, 1964), pp. 4–9.
4 *Jewish Chronicle*, 18 January 1924.
5 The Great Synagogue was located in Belgrave Street, quoted in Aaron Kent, *Identity, Migration and Belonging. The Jewish Community of Leeds 1890–1920* (Newcastle Upon Tyne: Cambridge Scholar Publishing, 2015), p. 213.
6 J. Buckman, *Immigrants and the Class Struggle: The Jewish Immigrant in Leeds 1880–1914* (Manchester: Manchester University Press, 1983).
7 Quoted in Kent, *Identity, Migration and Belonging*, p. 174.
8 M. Freedman, *Leeds Jewry: The First Hundred Years* (Leeds: Jewish Historical Society of England, 1992), p. 7.
9 V. D. Lipman, *A History of the Jews in Britain Since 1858* (New York: Holmes & Meier, 1990), p. 120.
10 *Yorkshire Post*, 17 August 1891, reported a meeting at Gower Street School to establish 'a tent' in connection with the Lovers of Zion chaired by Paul Hirsch.
11 L. Saipe, *A History of the Jews of Leeds* (Leeds: Tercentenary Committee, 1956), p. 11.
12 Ibid., p. 28.
13 *Leeds Mercury*, 4 July 1905. Also Ernest C. Sterne, *Leeds Jewry 1919–1929* (Leeds: Jewish Historical Society of England, 1989), p. 12.
14 Samuel Landsman, *The History of Zionism* (1915 reprinted 2018 by Forgotten Books), p. 8. Samuel Landsman was a Leeds teacher and later solicitor who attended Mrs Sheinblum's Kitchen (see below).
15 W. D. Rubinstein and M. A. Jolles (eds), *The Palgrave Dictionary of Anglo-Jewish History* (London: Palgrave, 2011), p. 994.
16 *Yorkshire Post*, 14 February 1899.
17 Henrietta Daimond was the wife of the cantor at the Great Synagogue and owned a corsetiere shop in Albion Street. Freedman, *25 Characters in Leeds Jewish History*, p. 18. Mrs Diamond and Mrs Umanskii were close personal friends.
18 Mrs Diamond and Mrs Umanskii organised the first Palestinian Bazaar in 1912, and after the First World War the former was a stalwart organiser of the more regular Blue and White bazaars held in Leeds Town Hall.
19 J. S. Walsh, *Mrs Sheinblum's Kitchen* (Leeds: Jewish Historical Society of England, 1989).
20 *Yorkshire Post*, 17 March 1902.
21 *Yorkshire Post*, 7 October 1907.
22 Walsh, *Mrs Sheinblum's Kitchen*, p. 3.
23 See, for example, M. I. Lipman, *Memoirs of a Socialist Business Man* (London: Lipman Trust, 1980).
24 Freedman, *25 Characters in Leeds Jewish History*, p. 20.
25 *Yorkshire Post*, 18 May 1903.
26 *Yorkshire Post*, 29 September 1905.
27 *Yorkshire Post*, 27 April 1906.
28 *Yorkshire Post*, 24 January 1910.
29 *Yorkshire Post*, 16 February 1914.

30 Walsh, *Mrs Sheinblum's Kitchen*, p. 4.
31 *Yorkshire Post*, 6 July 1914.
32 E. Sterne, *Leeds Jewry and the Great War* (Leeds: Jewish Historical Society of England, 1982), p. 9.
33 *Yorkshire Post*, 25 February 1918.
34 Selig Brodetsky, *Memoirs from Ghetto to Israel* (London: Weidenfeld & Nicholson, 1960). Also see: Bernard Silver, *Three Jewish Giants of Leeds: Selig Brodetsky, Montague Burton and Jacob Kramer* (Leeds: Jewish Historical Society of England, 2000); Louis Teeman, *Footprints in the Sand* (self-published, 1976), pp. 458–60.
35 Although, as we have seen, Leeds Zionism was subject to internal feuds, the Joint Zionist Council was possibly the first example among Leeds Jewry of coalition building.
36 Amanda Bergen estimates that even in the 1930s, the Jewish community was overwhelmingly working class, and that the number of middle-class Jews in the city could not have amounted to more than 10%. Amanda Bergen, *Leeds Jewry. 1930-39: The Challenge of Anti-Semitism* (Publications of the Thoresby Society, Volume 10, 2000), pp. 2 and 7.
37 Ernest Sterne claims that Rabbi Mendelsohn was responsible for this change. Sterne, *Leeds Jewry 1919-1929*, p. 32.
38 Ibid., p. 32.
39 *Yorkshire Post*, 30 May 1922.
40 Sir Montague Burton was a close friend of Selig Brodetsky, he was Vice-President of the Zionist Federation of Great Britain and often represented the Leeds Zionist Central Council at various Zionist congresses.
41 Ibid., pp. 32–3.
42 Ibid., p. 33.
43 Krausz, *Leeds Jewry*, p. 20.
44 Brodetsky, *Memoirs from Ghetto to Israel*, p. 98.
45 Sterne, *Leeds Jewry 1919-1929*, p. 11; Saipe, *A History of the Jews of Leeds*, p. 28.
46 A. S. Diamond, 'Sketch of Leeds Jewry in the 19th Century', in Aubrey Newman (ed.), *Papers on Provincial Jewry* (London: Jewish Historical Society, 1975).
47 C. C. Aronsfeld, 'Reminiscences of Leeds', *Jewish Chronicle*, 22 October 1948.
48 The Jewish National Fund was founded in 1901.
49 Bergen, *Leeds Jewry*, pp. 3 and 16–17.
50 Antony Clavane, *The Promised Land* (London: Yellow Jersey Press, 2010), p. 24.
51 John Fisher, *Painting the Town Silver* (Leeds: Beecroft Publications, 2014), pp. 29–30.
52 Bergen, *Leeds Jewry*, p. 2.

9

The unwalled ghetto: mobility and anti-Semitism in the interwar period

Amanda Bergen

In 1925, a series of articles appeared in the *Yorkshire Evening News* entitled 'The Soul of the Leeds Ghetto'. The author, E. E. Burgess, noted how:

> The war brought a change. The post-war generation particularly, having peeped as it were into a world closed to their pre-war brothers, became dazzled with a new mental outlook, and their desires of things early took a more prodigious turn. They were soon to be seen knocking at the gates leading to new vistas hitherto denied them.[1]

The desire to move away from the ghetto, the 'new mental outlook' identified by Burgess, was the product of changing economic and social conditions. The first generation of Leeds Jews, for the most part of Eastern European origin, were distinctively foreign in their speech, clothing and outlook. Their children, educated in local schools, had been exposed to the culture and values of British society. Those who had served in the war had undergone a further process of immersion and integration within the armed forces. Now, in the immediate postwar period, increasing exposure to wider forces of change through the mass media brought access to an exciting range of new ideas. The repercussions of the war and the peace process, the people's revolution in Russia, the position of women, all hinted at a new world order. For Jews in particular, the Zionist movement and the Balfour Declaration opened up enticing prospects. Closer to home, the city's medical officers and town planners had their sights set on the slums of the Leylands, the heart of the ghetto. Leeds Jews now found themselves to be a sizeable and distinctive minority in the city. How would they fare in this modern world of possibilities?

The auguries were not immediately promising. In the dominant culture, Jews were delineated by familiar tropes that demeaned, humiliated and alienated them. Suspicions of 'international' or 'cosmopolitan' Jewry cast all Jews as potential revolutionaries, anarchists, conspirators, subversive elements in the body politic. In times of nationalist fervour or angst Jews continued to provide a convenient scapegoat. These entrenched beliefs and libels filtered down to a local level where they had a significant impact. As recently as 1917, Leeds Jewry had faced three nights of violence in which a mob, estimated at 3,000 strong, had attacked property and terrified residents (discussed in Chapters 4 and 7). The riot highlighted both the isolation and the vulnerability of the community. In addition, background anti-Semitism remained pervasive, restricting work and social life. 'No Jews Need Apply' was a familiar response to those who sought work, a property to let or purchase, or a club to join. Physical violence and intimidation on the streets encouraged some Jewish youths to adopt a macho toughness which in turn led to condemnation of Jews as thuggish or disreputable.

There were more hopeful signs in the way that Jews were shaping and influencing the city around them. In politics, education and the professions, in the arts and in business, Jews were beginning to make their presence felt. In 1918, the *Yorkshire Evening Post* published a series of articles on 'The Leeds Jews and Local Industries'; tellingly, community leaders felt it necessary to liaise with the editor to ensure they were not misrepresented in any way.[2] The Jewish community's impact on manufacturing and retailing stretched from the market to the high street, from the trade unions on the factory floor to the boardroom. Synagogues and communal offices, a kosher restaurant and a hotel, kosher shops, butchers and bakers, and the huge Burton's site and its innovative retail outlets, all contributed to the changing face of the city.[3] A burgeoning civic confidence could be seen in the opening in 1921 of the First Jewish Bazaar, a high-profile fundraising extravaganza, with a range of society patrons. This was an initiative of Professor and Mrs Brodetsky, whose arrival in Leeds in 1920 was to add a new dynamism to communal affairs and greatly strengthen the local Zionist movement.

In the immediate postwar period, many practical concerns were shared with the wider Leeds community. Families had lost husbands, fathers and sons, or had seen them return in ill health or disabled. The newly demobbed flooded the labour markets and the resulting economic volatility and uncertainty brought with it much hardship. However, the strength and prominence of the local tailoring industry provided some protection from many of the economic convulsions of the period. The city also faced a housing crisis; compared to other provincial towns there were an enormous number of back-to-backs and overcrowding was higher than average. The slums of the Leylands, the heart of the ghetto, were condemned as overpopulated and insanitary, a risk to public health. Local responses such as the building of council houses and improvement of transport links benefited all the city's residents. Existing welfare services were stretched to the limit and new organisations and charities arose to meet need. Jewish organisations often paralleled those in the wider community; there were, for example, Jewish branches of the National Federation of Discharged and Demobilised Sailors and Soldiers and of the Baby's Welfare Association. The opening in 1923 of a home for aged Jews and in 1928 of a children's convalescent home reflected changing communal demographics and priorities. Their separate existence is evidence not only of practical issues, such as the need to provide kosher food, but also of a strong tradition of self-help, generated in part by a desire to avoid adverse comment and anti-Semitism. Such organisations helped to cement relationships between Jews and reinforced their distinctive identity; more ambivalently they may also have served to prevent assimilation and delay integration.

The *Jewish Year Book* of 1922 suggests that Leeds Jews totalled 25,000 of the city's 445,000 residents, 5.61% of the total. However, more recent commentators see this figure as being somewhat inflated.[4] The community's status as the third largest in the country was undisputed. Originally strictly Orthodox, Leeds Jewry was becoming more traditional in its practice. Religious authority was often contentious and the subject of much infighting, leading the *Jewish Chronicle* to label the community the most disputatious in Anglo-Jewry.[5] The formation of a United Shechita Board in 1924, and the foundation in 1930 of the United Hebrew Congregation, might be seen as evidence of a diminution of earlier factionalism. A considerable diversity of religious practice was also beginning to emerge at an individual level. For many, working in their own businesses meant working on Saturdays, or even over high days and holidays, could not be avoided. Religious attendance was notably affected. The temptations of secular society and a natural desire to blend in with neighbours in matters of language, clothing and diet all impacted upon religious identity. English replaced Yiddish as the language of the sermon. A further challenge came from the impact of Zionist education and the emphasis placed on Hebrew rather than Yiddish. Most Jewish boys were expected to attend religious school; the education of girls was generally seen as secondary. Links to co-religionists on the continent remained strong: in 1919, Leeds Jews participated in a Day of Mourning in protest at pogroms then taking place in Poland. Despite the relative poverty of the majority of local Jews, there was a strong emphasis on charitable fundraising for causes at home and abroad to which the community responded with considerable generosity.[6]

As a consequence of the way the community had evolved, Leeds lacked elements of the infrastructure commonly found in other Jewish communities, such as a central charitable fund, an effective Representative Council and a local Jewish newspaper. An absence of coordination between organisations, in some instances due to religious factionalism, meant that there was an element of duplication of effort and confusion. The granting of a charter to a Leeds Lodge of B'nai B'rith in 1925 did much to remedy this situation, providing encouragement and support for a range of new ideas and initiatives. Local Zionist organisations benefited from the indefatigable energy of Professor Brodetsky, who reorganised the Leeds Central Zionist Council and found that local Zionists tended to focus on fundraising and education rather than more political or philosophical concerns. The most important communal organisation during this period was the Jewish Institute, which served as a source of entertainment and education and provided a focal point for all sectors of Leeds Jewry.

Another characteristic of Leeds Jewry in the early postwar years was its overwhelmingly proletarian nature. Few families had the resources or reserves necessary to tide them over even the shortest period of crisis. Many endured considerable hardship which left them dependent upon a mixed economy of welfare. The first recourse in times of need would inevitably be to family, friends and neighbours. Louis Teeman wrote of the weekly trip to the pawn shop, the desperate attempts to stave off a visit from the bailiffs and of the merciful charity of neighbours. He recalled his mother going 'from house to house "klibing" collecting coins, a few groceries, a packet of this, a tin of that, bread, cheese, butter, herring, all pushed into her upheld apron for someone who was in need or for an emergency'.[7] Thereafter, the destitute could turn to the strained resources of communal charity. The Board of Guardians offered loans and there were numerous friendly societies, works associations and synagogues which might also offer financial support. Some were a little too adept at accessing communal charities; 'visiting the Dorcas Society, the Ladies Benevolent Society, the Bikur Cholim, the Board of Guardians, and other institutions during the one week and receiving relief from each in turn'.[8] For others, entrenched notions of respectability meant that accepting charity was seen as deeply shameful. For those who were eligible, the gradual rolling out of social security payments for illness and unemployment, though inadequate in quantity and duration, provided a welcome safety net.

The tailoring industry, which had provided the initial impetus for Jewish migration to the city, continued to be the largest source of employment for Jews during the interwar years. Freedman suggests that as many as 62% of grooms in the 1920s gave their occupation as 'tailor'.[9] However, the majority of those who worked in the industry were female and, for example, at Burton's females outnumbered males by ten to one. During the First World War many businesses had been engaged in making uniforms, and in the immediate postwar years those who could make the necessary swift adjustments from war time to civilian production were able to capitalise as the demand for men's clothing surged. The transition was not smooth, as there were periods of economic dislocation and unemployment, but in the longer term not only did the larger concerns flourish, but certain of the smaller workshops were also able to take advantage of the favourable trading conditions. Distinctive and innovative businesses, many of them owned by Jews, developed niche markets and specialisms that enabled them to outpace their competitors. By 1935, it was claimed that the majority of the 200 tailoring firms in Leeds were Jewish owned, with Burton's the largest employer in the city. Firms such as Alexandre, Sumrie, Hipps and Berwin & Berwin all flourished during this period. The largest businesses were able to weather the seasonal fluctuations that were characteristic of the industry, offering their employees a steady income year round. The industry remained relatively impervious to the stagnation of the 1920s and continued to grow despite the depression of the 1930s.

The success of the larger concerns encouraged many Jews to abandon their practice of working at home for the better working conditions of the factory. That Jews owned many of these enterprises may have smoothed this transition, but Jews also worked for non-Jewish employers including Fifty Shilling Tailors. Thus it was that by the 1930s 'the traditional division of the industry between Jews and non-Jews had been considerably modified ... The segregation between the two races, both in the factory and in the workshop was lessened.'[10] This breaking down of barriers served as an important aid to integration. Burton's provided a protected working environment where the observant were able to practise their religion, and a sense of community developed with workers singing, eating, taking trips to the seaside, attending meetings of the League of Nations and engaging in sporting activities. Enlightened holiday and welfare provision meant 'Once you got a job at Burton's you were made for life'.[11] Honeyman noted that the success of the Jewish clothiers provoked resentment. There were clear anti-Semitic undertones in the industry press. Attempts were made to smear Burton on the basis of his origins as a 'peddler', mocking him for the anglicisation of his name, while his advertising campaigns were likened to those of a moneylender.[12] An element of disdain regarding Burton's proletarian background might also be detected, for he was transgressing boundaries of class as well as of ethnicity.

For those who did not wish to enter unskilled occupations, apprenticeships provided a means of accessing a range of vocational training. However, the cost was prohibitive for many poorer families. Apprenticeships in woodworking or cabinet making were popular choices. Again, Jewish firms such as Louis Lightman & Sons provided employment. Women worked in the markets, in factories, offices and shops. A few ran businesses, including Henrietta Diamond the corsetiere and Fanny Ziff who imported and sold shoes. Other women worked in hairdressing or in fashion. Many worked as seamstresses in family businesses. Some families took in lodgers for additional income.

The retail sector also provided many opportunities for advancement. Early experience gained working the markets could lead to work as a representative or sales assistant, or for the more able, to owning one's own business. The competitiveness of the sector meant cultural clashes could flare in disputes between trading rivals, and in the immediate postwar period disputes over the supply of kosher meat and the opening hours of shops led to allegations of unfairness.[13] Market stall vendors were criticised for unfair practices. The local press was quick to report on any negative publicity and to print hostile letters from their readers. Longstanding anti-Semitic stereotypes of Jews as being responsible for abuses in trades, of engaging in underhand business practices or of sacrificing principle in the pursuit of profit may well have inflamed the situation.

Notwithstanding lengthy periods of recession and depression, working-class income increased in real terms by between a third and a half during the interwar period. By 1939, the average working week had reduced from fifty-four to forty-eight hours and paid holidays had been introduced. Improved standards of living were reflected by an increase in life expectancy of fifteen years and a halving of the birth rate.[14] By the middle of the 1930s, a male factory worker would have been earning between £130 and £180, a railway clerk £225, a business manager £450 and a doctor £1,000 per annum.[15] Most Leeds Jewish families would therefore have benefited from rising standards of living. For those who were successful in business, or early entrants into the professions, there were tangible rewards. As early as the 1920s a few affluent families were living in large houses in the smarter suburbs; employing servants, taking foreign holidays and driving motor vehicles. By the 1930s a middle-class element was living in comfortable suburbia in semi and detached properties.

Improvements in the economic situation encouraged and enabled Jews to seek better lives for themselves and their children. Education was not only an end in itself, but also a means of acquiring social mobility. In an era where poverty forced the vast majority to leave school at 14, autodidacts saw education as a continuing process. Libraries and reading rooms, lectures, discussion groups and coteries such as that centred on Mrs Sheinblum's kitchen, book clubs and political engagement, all provided additional mental stimulation. On occasion, this extra-mural education could lead to professional advancement.[16] Julius Silverman MP, born in Leeds in 1905, left school at 16 to become a warehouseman but continued his studies at night school and was called to the bar in 1931, thereafter practising in Birmingham.[17] Of course, not everyone was keen or able to embrace the opportunities offered. C. C. Aronsfeld found the community parochial and limited in its ambition.[18] At the Jewish Institute, attendance at dances was sometimes made contingent upon a young person's presence at requisite lectures earlier in the week.

A fortunate and able minority of pupils were able to take advantage of scholarships. In 1925, pupils at Lovell Road gained twenty-five out of the 311 scholarships awarded in the city and in 1926, twenty-six out of forty pupils gained Leeds Junior City Scholarships.[19] A few pupils attended Leeds Grammar School. Senior City Scholarships or State Scholarships were awarded to those wishing to enter university. A Leeds branch of the Jewish University Students Association was founded in 1912. By 1923 it had more than seventy members.[20] However, these developments took a while to filter through. Fewer than 5% of bridegrooms in the 1920s were professionals.[21] Many families, perhaps bowing to cultural norms and expectations as well as economic necessity, continued to prioritise the education of their sons over their daughters. The experience of Gloria Yeates' mother was typical. 'Mam was the clever one, but she was taken from school at thirteen and sent "into the tailoring" though her teachers said she could win a scholarship. Education was for boys. For girls it was unnecessary, a positive evil. Girls who got educated didn't get married.'[22] However, a tiny minority of fortunate and exceptional women were able to take advantage of a university education. As early as 1915, Augusta Umanski had become the first woman to graduate from Leeds Medical School. Esther Sinovitch, born 1903, attended Leeds University where she graduated with a first-class degree in modern languages. A trickle of other females followed these pioneers, and there were early entrants into the professions of nursing, teaching and pharmacy. Learning the violin or the piano was also seen by some families as a skill that might enable a daughter to earn a respectable living.

Entry into the professions, medicine in particular, remained the ultimate goal. In 1931, a quarter of the students at Leeds Medical School were Jewish. However, for Jews, qualification – no matter how stellar – offered no guarantee of a career. Freedman quotes the example of Harry Eldelsten: 'Qualifying in Leeds in the early 1920s, he was top student of his year and would ordinarily have been first choice for a junior house position at Leeds General Infirmary. He was refused this and all he could eventually obtain was a post in what was then a lunatic asylum in Wakefield.'[23] Sterne cites Dr Shernovitz, the best qualified applicant for the post of Medical Officer to the Board of Guardians for one of the Leeds wards. Protests from the Catholic community, 'Jews must not treat our women', meant that he could not be appointed.[24] Julius Silman believed that the professions 'probably showed the most prejudice' and that 'No Jew could expect to be appointed consultant at the LGI before the war'.[25] Caught between working-class fears of Jews as predatory and middle-class cabals determined to exclude them, many Jewish doctors sought employment out of Leeds.

Jewish barristers and solicitors also faced prejudice in obtaining pupillage or articles in Leeds and in finding employment thereafter. This meant that lawyers had to head to other cities in order to qualify in their chosen profession. Alter Hurwitz, the city's first Jewish barrister, was called to the bar in 1924. Despite an outstanding academic record, he was unable to obtain pupillage in Leeds and had to go to Sheffield. He set up his own chambers in Leeds in 1926.[26] Silman, a solicitor, noted that 'no Jew was taken into partnership or even employed by the big Leeds firms ... So when young Jews qualified they set up on their own, creating successful firms.'[27] On occasion, anti-Semitic comments were made by other solicitors. Sterne suggests that the fact that local Jews were now entering the professions may have brought fears of 'Jewish competition' to the fore.[28]

Jews also faced difficulty in obtaining positions in the police force. In 1918, the *Jewish Chronicle* noted that Jews applying to join the Special Constabulary in Leeds had been 'declined without any apparent cause'.[29] Distrust of the police and suspicions that their sympathies lay with anti-Semites and Fascists remained a factor throughout the period and thereafter. These difficulties were compounded by a problematic relationship with the local press. It was felt that undue and unfounded emphasis was given to labelling those suspected of criminal activity as Jewish. Furthermore, when culprits were apprehended and proven to not in fact have been Jewish, no retractions were made. When the local press suggested that Jews were, 'acting as ponces', Teeman reported that: 'The community was heartsick and oppressed, and in the synagogues the Rabbis implored the congregation not to reply to the defamatory letters in the Press because by so doing they only prolonged the correspondence and therefore the vilifications ... in this and other ways was anti-Jewish feeling kept alive and nourished.'[30]

Outposts of artistic, avant-garde and advanced thinking were accessible to Jews and provided opportunities for them to flourish. Before the First World War, Jakob Kramer and Philip Naviasky had attended Leeds School of Fine Arts. Both were able to pursue artistic careers and later became teachers at the city's art schools. Kramer was a founder member of the Leeds Arts Club and remained associated with it until its collapse in 1923; subsequently, he was involved with the Leeds Luncheon Club. He was also at the centre of a clique whose members, Jewish and non-Jewish, comprised 'a Bohemian Group' defying existing 'social segregation'.[31] The university provided a positive environment with senior figures such as Sir Michael Sadler lending support to a variety of Jewish causes. The *Jewish Year Book* of 1922 mentions Professor Brodetsky and Myer Coplans, MD Demonstrator in Bacteriology and Public Health, as employees of the university. The stage provided Paula Ruby with a taste of fame. Other talented individuals chose to leave Leeds for London or North America where more opportunities were available.

Politics provided a way of achieving a degree of social parity at an elite level. Jews were able to make inroads into local government and obtain positions as aldermen and councillors. In 1941, Hyman Morris, a Conservative, became the city's first Jewish Lord Mayor. The size of the community may have given it political leverage, for in some city wards Jews constituted a significant proportion of the electorate. In the 1920s, there were allegations of a 'racist vote' from the Conservative press when a Mr L. Rosenberg stood for the Liberals in the municipal elections for the Brunswick ward.[32] For many Jews, parties of the Left, embracing ideas of communal working-class solidarity or brotherhood, were particularly attractive. By 1936, Jews constituted up to half the membership of the local Communist Party. Other Jews found different ways to perform civic duties on the boards of charities, as guardians or JPs. Abe Frais was elected President of the Leeds & District Union of Golf Clubs in 1929. Louis Godlove became President of the Leeds Law Society in 1941. Links formed at a civic level were important in building relationships between communities. Some private members clubs remained inaccessible; of course, not all the members of these organisations were anti-Semitic, but a determined element was none the less effective in excluding Jews.

For many Leeds Jews, the blatant discrimination practised by certain of the city's bars, restaurants and clubs was one of the most painful manifestations of anti-Semitism. Restaurant proprietors in particular seemed to take delight in 'slamming the doors in the face of the whole race'.[33] During the 1920s, the city's leading restaurant, Podolny's, had a 'No Jews Admitted' sign. This form of exclusion was notably experienced by both Issy Smith VC and Professor Brodetsky who was refused service by the Grand Restaurant because he was 'of the Hebrew persuasion'. Murray Freedman recalled an incident that occurred when he was a small boy at the cafe in Roundhay Park. Louis Teeman related a similar experience to Hyman Morris who was his employer at the time. He was enraged by Morris's laconic response – 'well don't go there'. There was a clear division between those who believed that drawing attention to the problem would only make it worse and those keen to challenge blatant discrimination. Some younger individuals took pride in besting racists by entering establishments illicitly, either as customers or as musicians. Occasionally, violence – in the form of vandalism against offending premises – took place.

Some sporting clubs and institutions also proved inaccessible. This was frustrating for, as Burgess noted, 'In no sphere has the local Jew proved more amenable to assimilative tendencies than in the realm of sport.'[34] This was particularly a problem in sports traditionally associated with the middle class, such as golf and tennis. Prior to the establishment of Moor Allerton Golf Club in 1923, 'Playing in Leeds was out of the question, the clubs having long made their attitude known.'[35] Interestingly, although Jews such as M. J. Landa, writing in the *Jewish Chronicle*, and H. Simans, interviewed by the *Yorkshire Evening Post*, were adamant that anti-Semitism was the reason for their exclusion, the *Yorkshire Evening Post* denied this allegation. The cause was simply that 'Jews and Britishers do not blend very well in a golf club ... [the Jew] has not yet acquired the appreciation of the traditions and spirit of the game that comes instinctively to the ordinary Britisher'. The Jew was also 'clannish' and insisted on bringing along his relatives, which proved 'irritating' to the serious-minded British golfer.[36] There is a suggestion here of disdain for the Jew as an *arriviste*, one who has yet to learn the rules of polite society, an outsider in terms of class as well as ethnicity. A similar situation prevailed with tennis, where Jews were prevented from joining local clubs. The Jewish community had to fall back on its own resources: 'If we are to be the Unchosen Race we must close up our own ranks.'[37] Jews played tennis at Moor Allerton or through the Maccabi Tennis Club. Teams from the Jewish Institute played billiards, draughts, chess, cricket and football in the local league. The Judean Club provided an outlet for youths aged 14–18. Other sports proved more amenable to Jewish participants, particularly boxing where Joe Fox and Harry Mason achieved considerable success. Leslie Goldberg (b. 1918) played football for Leeds United. Spectator sports such as rugby and football attracted a considerable Jewish following and allowed for the development of a powerful shared identity and sense of belonging to a wider community. (See Chapter 13 for further details.)

Although the community provided many opportunities for its members to socialise, much social activity, particularly for females, remained within the close-knit family environment. While this could provide comfort and security, it could also prove stifling and claustrophobic and operate as a means of policing behaviour. These restrictions promoted endogamy at a time when most Jews viewed marriage out of the faith harshly. A combination of social control from within the community, and exclusion and prejudice from without, meant that for many Leeds Jews contact with Gentiles was restricted to working or formal relationships. Silman reflected that

> It always seemed to me that Jews in Leeds lived in a kind of unwalled ghetto. Despite the fact that Jews achieved eminence politically … nevertheless socially we lived in a world apart. There was little overt anti-Semitism … yet there was an unspoken understanding that Jews weren't welcome in higher society … There was no social mixing.[38]

Silman, educated at The Perse in Cambridge and at Leeds Grammar School, chafed against both the parochialism and the exclusion that he found prevalent in Leeds. He refers to what he calls the '"You're Different" principle', whereby a token number of Jews might be accepted into the social realms denied to the majority of their brethren. Class almost certainly played a part in this 'difference', but exceptional talent might also smooth the way. The idea of the Jew as a class interloper, unaware of social convention, was clearly at play.

Economic and social change underpinned the geographical mobility which was characteristic of Jewish life in Leeds. The gradual move north, away from the Leylands – the area in which the community had sheltered in its earliest years – to secondary, more desirable areas of settlement, has been well documented.³⁹ The earliest immigrants and their families, 'the *englishers*', who worshipped at the Great Synagogue in Belgrave Street, were the first to move to more respectable locations. It was the newer arrivals, 'the *grinners*', who remained in the poorer inner-city areas. The Drapkin family moved to the Leylands in 1918:

> We moved into a house that had one room downstairs, a kitchen about 9ft by 9ft, and two small bedrooms above. There were my parents and nine of us children, all under 12. The toilet was about 20 yards down the street, shared between half a dozen families, and was absolutely disgusting. There was no dustbin, you used a big hole in the wall, called a midden, that filled a bucket. In one corner of the kitchen was a Singer sewing machine, which we hired by the week for about one-and-six, at which my father worked to support us.⁴⁰

During the same period the Sheinblum family lived in rather more comfortable circumstances in a four-storey property on Brunswick Street in the Camp Road area. There was a cellar kitchen, a paved back yard, a reception room, bedrooms and on the top floor Mr Sheinblum's tailoring workshop.

The process of slum clearance, which began in the Leylands in 1907, provided fresh impetus to the more recent immigrants to leave the ghetto. The return of the younger generation from war and the subsequent baby boom may also have encouraged this form of mobility. By 1919, the Leylands Council School in Gower Street had closed as a result of the decline in pupil numbers and its head was relocated to Harehills. For most, leaving the Leylands meant moving only a short distance, a few streets perhaps, to the back-to-backs that lined the bottom of the Roundhay Road or Sheepscar. These properties had shared outside toilets, cold water plumbing, scullery kitchens with a sink, an oven and a gas ring and a door opening onto a cobbled street with a view of the parallel terrace. Although most houses were solidly built, some families still lived in overcrowded, ill-furnished, cold and damp conditions. For others there was comfort to be found in a strong sense of community – which in some instances extended to Gentile neighbours, an obsession with cleanliness and respectability combined with the application of elbow grease that left front door steps shining, communal toilets spotless and pride intact.

Some families were more fortunate. The Raisman family, who moved after the First World War from the Leylands to a through terrace on 'the good side of North Street', now had electricity, hot water, a bathroom and a flush toilet, a back door, lace curtains, an electric bell and a tiny stained glass panel in the front door.⁴¹ In 1909, Julius Silman's middle-class family were living in Ramsden Terrace, Sheepscar; by 1914 they were in 'a rather nice semi-detached house' on Harehills Lane and subsequently moved to Chapeltown Road, where the family, who had several maids, 'acquired a chauffeur'.⁴²

As incomes rose, increasing numbers were able to move away from the back-to-backs, often in a series of small hops and jumps, to newer properties in Harehills or Chapeltown. In the late 1920s, Murray Freedman's family home was in Worth Street, off Camp Road. 'It was a small back-to-back house with shared outside toilets – typical of the thousands of such dwellings in Leeds ... [and] accommodated as many as seven of us.' In 1934, the family moved to Ellers Road in Harehills.

> Our new house was a 'through' house which unlike the Worth Street back-to-back, had both a front door and back door. There was a small front garden and a back yard. Most importantly, we now had our own toilet and bathroom. We had undoubtedly come up in the world by moving away from Camp Road. Like the vast majority of the property in those days our new house was rented, and though I don't remember the actual rent it could not have been more than a few shillings a week.[43]

For those who could afford to purchase their homes, a new semi-detached property in one of the middle-class suburbs such as Oakwood, Moortown or Roundhay cost between £600 to £750 in the 1920s. In 1931, Louis Teeman purchased his first home in Bentcliffe Mount, Moortown, with the aid of a building society mortgage. 'It was a fair sized brick built semi in a good residential district, £950 the price with 3 bedrooms, separate bathroom and lavatory and gardens in the front and rear, with the stout brick garage costing fifty pounds more.'[44] A few families, engaged in the professions or successful in business, were able to purchase larger detached houses in Moortown or Alwoodley. A number of ambitious Jews left the city in search of better prospects elsewhere and some chose to emigrate. Mr Coss, a clothing manufacturer, went to settle in Palestine where J. S. Walsh, on honeymoon in 1932, found 'him and his family living very happily indeed in the land of their aspirations'.[45]

As the population moved, so, inevitably, did its infrastructure: its synagogues, communal facilities and businesses. Its children moved schools and over time improvements in public transport meant that it was no longer necessary to live so close to one's place of work or to communal facilities. The move from neighbourhoods where the vast majority of one's neighbours were also Jewish to areas such as Chapeltown, where Jews now formed a large minority, must have impacted on both an individual and communal level. Opportunities for integration and assimilation opened up. At school and on the street, as well as in the shops and at work, people were able to develop a range of relationships. This movement was not always welcomed by non-Jewish neighbours. There were suggestions that communities did not mix and concerns for the character of the neighbourhood. Some of these concerns may have been motivated by a class element as well as an anti-Semitic bias. Working-class Jews were now moving into middle-class areas. It was not uncommon for landlords to refuse to rent to Jews or to sell land or properties to them. In order to purchase the land for the Moor Allerton Golf Club, Abe Frais found it necessary to use an agent. 'Abe bought it, not directly from the wealthy Lane Fox family to whom it belonged and whom he had good reason to know would not sell to a Jew, but through a Gentile builder whose fee was two hundred pounds.'[46]

Improved integration and bridge building were to prove increasingly important in the 1930s as the deteriorating situation in Europe came to dominate the communal agenda. Alliances and common interests forged in the workplace or through business, politics or academia meant that there was the potential for cross-communal initiatives. One early example was the Academic Assistance Council which was formed in 1933 in response to the dismissal of German academics from universities on racial or political grounds.[47] The founder of the Leeds branch of this organisation was a non-Jew, Professor J. H. Jones. The committee, which Jones wanted to be 'representative of all that is best in the district', included leading members of the Church of England and of the Quaker community, local aristocracy, Members of Parliament and other prominent citizens. Their support was primarily in lending their names to the cause but was significant as an early indicator of where allies might be found in the fight against Fascism. The Jewish contingent consisted of Professor Brodetsky, Hyman Morris and Rev. Abelson. Although the Council did succeed in sponsoring three academics, its success was limited with members having to tread a fine line to avoid arousing anti-Semitic comment. Certainly, stereotypes of Jews as wealthy, miserly and parasitic were expressed in letters to the local press.

Similarly, political alignment and engagement with parties on the left meant that common causes could attract wider support. Members of the Communist Party fought in the International Brigade during the Spanish Civil War. Their progress was watched anxiously by the local community who supported their efforts through fundraising and collections. Jews and non-Jews alike donated to appeals at Burton's, 'the most amazing thing ever seen in Leeds. Not one person refused to give.'[48] Anti-Fascists proved stalwart allies in the battle against political anti-Semitism which had gained new momentum with the formation of the British Union of Fascists in 1932. The most significant confrontation in Leeds was the 'Battle of Holbeck Moor' which took place on the 27 September 1936.[49] Mosley and 1,000 Blackshirts who had assembled on the Moor were confronted by a crowd numbering, according to *The Times* and the *Yorkshire Post*, up to 30,000. The *Manchester Guardian* suggested 25,000 were present, 'not all of them hostile'. It was clear to all commentators that the anti-Fascists were the more significant presence. Their heckling, 'Get Back to Germany', rendered Mosley inaudible and he and his followers were injured when stones were thrown by protestors. Jews had been warned by the community leadership not to attend the rally. However, some were present; as groups of lads – 'we liked a good fight with the fascists' – and at the counter demonstration organised by the Communist Party. For the most part the anti-Fascists must have included socialists, trade unionists, free thinkers, radicals and others who rejected Mosley's prejudice and abhorred his admiration of the Nazi regime.

As the situation in Germany deteriorated, a network of local Jewish refugee organisations developed to meet the task of rehousing, educating and finding employment for the incomers.[50] In the first instance, the Zionist organisations provided much of the necessary infrastructure. In 1934, the Leeds Jewish Refugee Committee was established under the Chairmanship of David Makofski and committees encompassing specific aspects of the crisis, such as the resettlement of child refugees and the immigration and welfare of trainees and domestics, followed thereafter. In 1938, the newly inaugurated Representative Council was able to assume responsibility for coordinating all activities relating to refugees. In Leeds, the principal device used to enable refugees to enter the country was the Trainee Scheme. This permitted male Jews aged under 35 to apply for a Home Office permit to take up a trainee position and was subject to payment of a deposit of £100 by the trainee and certification by an employer that no candidate was available locally. Makofski's papers list more than 150 businesses, the majority being small concerns, as providing placements for trainees. Females were found employment as domestics or nurses. Other refugees came to Leeds under the Guarantee Scheme, as illegal immigrants, as students or as part of the Kindertransport. In August 1939, 103 youths aged between 16 and 18 and twenty staff of the Berlin ORT technical school arrived in Leeds. Some sixty boys were accommodated at the Stainbeck Lane hostel and thirty girls at a hostel in Harrogate, with a further forty children placed in private homes. The community also raised substantial sums of money for national and local initiatives in aid of the refugees and there were significant donations of clothing and other forms of assistance. Most of the effort was internal, in part to disguise the extent of the influx and thus avoid arousing anti-Semitic comment. However, non-Jews including church groups, Quakers, educationalists, workers and businessmen also lent support. Some of the refugees were accommodated in non-Jewish homes and employment was found for youths on local farms. By the start of the war, more than 700 European Jews had been assisted by the Leeds committees.

By 1937 the slums of the Leylands were gone, and though many community members continued to experience financial hardship, increasing numbers had either joined the middle classes or stood poised to do so. Differences in class, politics and religious observance had continued to emerge during the period; however, the fierceness of internal religious sectarianism had declined. Although individual initiative retained its significance, effective leadership and infrastructure helped mobilise and coordinate wider community effort. The crisis of European Jewry saw Leeds Jewry acting in a concerted and purposeful manner. The presence of the refugees, many of whom were from middle-class non-Orthodox backgrounds, posed further challenges. However, the combination of internal evolution and hostile external forces drew the various strands of Leeds Jewry into a more cohesive whole.

The process of mobility, leaving the ghetto both psychologically and physically, brought Leeds Jews into closer contact with their non-Jewish neighbours and, in the longer term, increasing familiarity helped to improve relations and promote a more united city. An English education and acculturation combined with a desire to engage with the brave new postwar world improved the ability of Jews to integrate and assimilate with their neighbours. Changes in working practices, in particular leaving the home for the large-scale factory, moving to new neighbourhoods, attending new schools and participating or spectating in sporting or cultural activity, helped develop shared interests and identities with members of the wider community. Allegiances and friendships – through the universities, business and in local politics – brought the community valuable allies. By the end of the period, Leeds Jews, though retaining their distinctive identity, were no longer as isolated and as vulnerable as they had been at the start.

Anti-Semitism remained pervasive, but for most people registered merely as background noise. For those who were content to remain within the 'unwalled ghetto', the community provided a protective umbrella of parallel institutions and organisations which were a source of pride and security. Those who looked outwards found that mobility exposed them to new facets of anti-Semitism. Less physical in its manifestation, bourgeoise or golf club anti-Semitism was expressed via the snub, the entendre and other more or less subtle forms of exclusion. The respectable face of anti-Semitism still had the power to damage, wound and humiliate. To protest was to succumb to self-pity and hence further reinforce negative stereotyping. Those seeking access to the professions faced cliques determined to exclude them. Anti-Semitism cut across class lines, creating a perfect storm for early medics and lawyers. That many succeeded in forging successful careers was a tribute to their fortitude as much as their brilliance.

9.1 North Street premises of David and Annie Segal, c. 1913. The little girls outside are their daughters Ida and Esta

9.2 June 1939: Mizrachi card afternoon at the home of David and Annie Segal, 1 Moorland Garth, Moortown. The small child is Bernice Pearlman (née Olsburgh)

9.3 Harold Brostoff. Early 1930s

9.4 Wedding of Jenny Tagger to Benjamin Gothelf, c. 1926

9.5 Minnie Marks and Harry Tagger, c. 1938

9.6 A crowd of friends from Leeds on a walking trip, c. 1938. Minnie Marks and Harry Tagger are pictured on the right of the photo, which also shows their dear friend Ida Poyser

9.7 Minnie Marks seated bottom right on holiday with Leeds Jewish friends, c. 1935

Notes

1 E. E. Burgess, 'The Soul of the Leeds Ghetto', *Yorkshire Evening News*, 2 February 1925.
2 *Jewish Chronicle*, 22 March 1918.
3 Burton's Hudson Road site opened in 1922.
4 A. Bergen, *Leeds Jewry, 1930–1939: The Challenge of Anti-Semitism* (Leeds: The Thoresby Society, 2000), p. 2.
5 See for example, *Jewish Chronicle*, 1 March 1918 and 18 January 1924.
6 E. C. Sterne, *Leeds Jewry 1919–1929* (Leeds: Jewish Historical Society of England, 1989), p. 23.
7 L. Teeman, *Footprints in the Sand: An Autobiography* (Brighton: A. Manson, 1995), p. 3. See also G. Yeates, *A Daughter of Leeds: An Autobiography* (Castleford: Yorkshire Art Circus, 1997), pp. 9–11.
8 *Jewish Chronicle*, 1 April 1918.
9 M. Freedman, *Further Essays on Leeds & Anglo-Jewish History and Demography* (Leeds: Jewish Historical Society of England, 2005), p. 32.
10 J. Thomas, 'A history of the Leeds clothing industry', *Yorkshire Bulletin of Economic and Social Research*, Occasional Paper 1 (1955), 56–7.
11 G. Raisman, *The Undark Sky: A Story of Four Poor Brothers* (Newport Pagnall: Harehills Press, 2002), p. 183.
12 K. Honeyman, *Well Suited: A History of the Leeds Clothing Industry 1850–1990* (Oxford: Oxford University Press, 2000), pp. 72–4. Other leading Jewish clothiers faced similar prejudice.
13 Sterne, *Leeds Jewry*, p. 7.
14 B. Harrison, *A Century of Leeds: Events, People and Places Over the 20th Century* (Stroud: Sutton Publishing, 2007), p. 11.
15 See www.leodis.net/discovery.asp?pageLeodis (accessed 15 October 2018). The figures are for the mid 1930s.
16 J. S. Walsh, *Mrs Sheinblum's Kitchen* (Leeds: Jewish Historical Society of England, 1982).
17 N. Bush, 'Legal Leeds', *BIMA*, 282 (2013), 20–1. Silverman was a Labour MP for thirty-eight years.
18 C. C. Aronsfield, 'Reminiscences of Leeds', *Jewish Chronicle*, 22 October 1948.
19 D. Saunders and P. Lester, *From the Leylands to Leeds 17* (Leeds: Leylands Books), p. 156.
20 Sterne, *Leeds Jewry*, p. 27.
21 Freedman, *Further Essays*, p. 32.
22 Yeates, *A Daughter of Leeds*, p. 11.
23 Freedman, *Further Essays*, pp. 53–4.
24 Sterne, *Leeds Jewry*, p. 36.
25 J. Silman ... *Signifying Nothing* (London: Minerva Press, 1997), p. 67. LGI is an abbreviation of Leeds General Infirmary.
26 Bush 'Legal Leeds', pp. 20–1.
27 Silman, *Signifying*, p. 67.

28 Sterne, *Leeds Jewry*, p. 36.
29 *Jewish Chronicle*, 26 April 1918.
30 Teeman, *Footprints*, p. 363.
31 Silman, *Signifying*, p. 68.
32 Sterne, *Leeds Jewry*, p. 10.
33 Burgess, 'The Soul of the Leeds Ghetto', 16 February 1925.
34 Burgess, 'The Soul of the Leeds Ghetto', 2 February 1925.
35 Teeman, *Footprints*, p. 168.
36 T. Hyman, *A History of Moor Allerton Golf Club: 1923–1993* (Leeds: privately printed,1994), pp. 1–7.
37 *Jewish Chronicle* (19 April 1923), quoted in Hyman, *A History*, p. 2.
38 Silman, *Signifying*, p. 66.
39 E. Krausz, *Leeds Jewry: Its History and Social Structure* (Cambridge: Jewish Historical Society of England, 1964), pp. 23–4.
40 www.saperia.com/leeds/leeds_one.htm (accessed 15 October 2018).
41 Raisman, *The Undark Sky*, pp. 142–3.
42 Silman, *Signifying*, p. 15.
43 Freedman, *Essays*, pp. 50–4.
44 Teeman, *Footsteps*, p. 554.
45 Walsh, *Sheinblum*, p. 11.
46 Teeman, *Footsteps*, p. 169. Somewhat surprisingly, Col. Lane-Fox is recorded as having been elected an early member of the club. Hyman, *A History*, p. 15.
47 Bergen, *Leeds Jewry*, pp. 26–9.
48 Ibid., p. 17.
49 Ibid., pp. 12–15.
50 Ibid., pp. 29–37.

10

The Second World War

Ian Vellins

Leeds Jewry on the eve of the Second World War

By 1939, Jews had been living and working in Leeds for almost a century, with the largest influx between 1880 and 1914. There was still an older generation that remembered the move from Russia and Poland and spoke Yiddish, together with younger generations that had been born, educated and worked in Leeds. The Jewish population had spread from the Leylands to Chapeltown and Harehills, following the northern route from town up North Street, Chapeltown Road and Roundhay Road. By 1939, younger families and some more prosperous families were inhabiting the leafier suburbs, through the St Martins Estate built in the mid 1930s and the Dominions, and for a few up to Oakwood, Moortown (The Falklands, Southlands, Broomhills and the Talbots) and beyond. Very few moved to completely non-Jewish districts.

The late 1930s saw upward mobility, economic success and secular education, although many preferred to live with or near close family members, attending schools with a huge Jewish percentage of students, socialising solely with Jewish neighbours, family and friends, and often working in Jewish tailoring factories or sweatshops.[1] Family ties were still strong and social visiting to families at weekends was high on the list of activities. More intermarriage was occurring than in previous decades.

The contemporary estimate of the Jewish population of Leeds was 25,000 or 5% of the city population, always claimed to be the highest proportion of any British city. Later calculations suggest that about 20,000 was more realistic.[2] The synagogues were largely still situated in the areas where the Jews had first arrived and settled in Leeds, and the areas to which the first population movement had occurred – in the Leylands, in the Camp Road area and in Chapeltown.[3] Synagogue attendances had fallen except during the holy days. In the late 1930s, the Moortown synagogue was established. In the sphere of education, Jewish children filled many of the primary schools in the Jewish areas, such as the Gower Street, Cowper Street, Kepler Street, Compton Road and Chapeltown primary schools. Schooling terminated at the age of 14, although Jewish pupils excelled when going on to higher education at Roundhay School, the Leeds Grammar School and the City of Leeds High School. Religious education for children was well attended at various *chederim* teaching Hebrew and Barmitzvah classes.

Economic life was still dominated by the tailoring industry, sections of which were predominantly Jewish. Some of the original small tailoring firms grew into large concerns, the most celebrated of which was Montague Burton & Co. with its extensive chain of retail shops all over the country, and with its Leeds factory in Hudson Road Mills (opened in the early 1920s) at its peak occupying 100 square acres[4] and giving employment to over 10,000 workers,[5] its superb canteen facilities serving up to 8,000 people.[6] Silver records that during the years of the Second World War, Burtons produced 25% of all male and female service clothing,[7] coping with the fact that during the war well over 2,000 of the firm's personnel served in the forces. During the war, government orders for blankets and uniforms kept the woollen mills in Leeds busy.[8] Having clothed a quarter of the male population of Britain before the Second World War, Burtons also made a third of the de-mob clothing when it ended.[9] The de-mob clothing comprised a three-piece suit (jacket, trousers and waistcoat), a shirt and underwear, and became known as 'The Full Monty'.[10]

Many Jews were also involved in boot, shoe and slipper manufacturing, market trading, retail trading and furniture making.[11] Social conditions were improving from the squalor of the ghettos in which the initial Jewish immigrants had lived. Lipman's comments on the character of the wider Jewish community found their echo in Leeds:

> The rise in real earnings increased demand for Jewish employment in the service and distributive trade and in consumer-orientated industries, so Jewish hairdressers, taxi drivers, newsagents, tobacconists and confectioners were able to start their own businesses as self-employed workers, in retail shopping and chain stores ... Anglo-Jewish communities were ones in which the descendants of the Eastern European immigrants of 1881 onwards had been fully integrated, and indeed might be said to have taken over the community; and the Anglo-Jewish community itself had increasingly become integrated in British society.[12]

The Leeds Jewish population was the third largest Jewish population in Britain after London and Manchester. It was still overwhelmingly a working-class community with common cultural roots – linked by their race, their area of geographical provenance and their modes of employment. Leeds was almost entirely a Litvak community, hailing from the Baltic and Belarussian areas of the Northern Pale of Settlement and largely from the geographical region of the province of Kovno, which united the community; unlike London which was divided into at least two immigrant factions, the Litvaks and the Polaks, plus the Sephardim.

As Amanda Bergen has described in the previous chapter, Leeds had responded well to the appeals in the 1930s to raise money for the Central British Fund for German Jews[13] and to help establish the Leeds Jewish Refugee Committee to oversee the immigration and settlement of refugees in Leeds.

The war on the home front

The Second World War was genuinely a 'Total War' in which it was difficult for anyone, including civilians, to escape the effects.[14] As Winston Churchill said, 'the whole of the warring nations were involved, not only soldiers, but the entire population, men, women and children'.[15] In the period between 1938 and 1941, gas masks were issued, blackout restrictions imposed, evacuation was ordered, cinemas and theatres closed, and food and clothes rationing and conscription were introduced.

Ration books had pages with coupons for sugar, butter, cooking fats, bacon and meat. Jews would exchange their bacon page for the butter page with their non-Jewish neighbours. The booklets of instruction advised how to pick out tradesmen with whom to do business and register with them, which proved advantageous to the small Jewish corner-shop proprietors through maintaining loyalty. The consumer was exhorted to 'Grow Your Own Vegetables' and 'Dig For Victory'. Shoppers became used to rationing queues and making do with egg powder and margarine instead of butter.[16]

With regard to clothes rationing, material to make cloth was in short supply, as a great deal was needed in the war effort for uniforms, parachutes and other military necessities. As a result, clothes rationing had been introduced in May 1941. At first, sixty-six coupons were allowed per adult person per year. Later, in 1942, when material for clothes became even more scarce, the coupon allowance was reduced to forty-eight per adult per year. The *Picture Post* of June 1941 featured an article in which women were given advice on how they might use their sixty-six coupons, namely:

Dress or Dressing Gown or Jacket: 11
2 Pairs of Shoes: 10
6 Pairs of Stockings (4 Lisle, 2 Silk): 12
1 Nightdress, 1 Lingerie Set, 1 Slip: 14
2 Pairs of Gloves: 4
1 Jersey, 1 Cardigan: 7
1 Reserve for Apron, Scarf, etc: 8   Total 66.

People were encouraged to make do and mend. A Board of Trade Advice publication advised that from men's discarded shirts enough sound material could be salvaged to make a school blouse for a small girl and from old flannel trousers a warm little frock.[17] Leeds Jewish women were particularly adept at making clothes for their families, as most had been taught at an early age by parents and many had helped out with sewing duties in their family tailoring workshops.

Petrol and oil (imported through the ports) had to be used for the war effort, so there was very little petrol for the ordinary motorist. Petrol rationing was soon introduced, but it was limited to essential users and people had to learn to 'lay up' their cars. Accordingly, Leeds Jews were able to run few cars during the war, except, for example, butcher's delivery vehicles etc.[18] Coal shortages meant that houses were poorly heated and families would crowd together in the kitchen where the cooking took place, while other living areas were left unoccupied in the winter.

Teachers were in a reserved occupation from the age of 30, but permission was given for teachers between 35 and 50 to enrol, if they so desired, in the Army Officers' Emergency Reserve. Women in the war industries were paid half the wages of men. 'Many had to get up at 4 or 5 a.m. to fight and struggle for a bus. No wonder they don't exactly flock to work', wrote the *Picture Post* in December 1941. The Labour Research Department Report of 1942 reported that 'Thousands of women who want to volunteer find it difficult or impossible for them to undertake a war job. The most important reasons are low wages, insufficient day nurseries, long working hours, and consequent shopping difficulties, bad canteens and inadequate transport.'[19] This was particularly relevant in the case of Leeds Jewish women, where the locations in which the war work took place were some distance from the areas in which the Jewish community lived.

In May 1941, men between the ages of 17 and 65, not already in the forces or involved in Air Raid Precautions work, were invited to join the Home Guard.[20] The United Hebrew Congregation Bulletin of 13 May 1938 had already exhorted the Jewish community to perform their civic duties and, under the heading 'Air Raid Precautions. A Civic Duty and Responsibility', it wrote

> It is the duty of every responsible-minded citizen of this great city of Leeds to do his or her share in the Air Raid Precautions work which is now getting steadily under way. Men of over 30 are urgently requested to enrol in the course of training and those over 25 are offered the opportunity of volunteer service in the Auxiliary Fire Brigade and Ambulance Service. For women there are the opportunities of ambulance driving and other such activities.[21]

Indeed, many Leeds Jewish men enrolled in the ARP, and when one of the few bombs fell in Leeds on the Leeds Museum, next to the Town Hall, two

Jewish men, Dressler and Oscar Dytch (Dyson), were on duty in the vicinity and were shortly after at the scene; one man, Solly Belinsky, who was killed when a wall collapsed at the premises, was Jewish.

On 2 April 1939 there was a further appeal in the UHC Bulletin, signed by the Chief Rabbi and community leaders in London and Leeds, headed 'A Duty to Britain and a Duty to the Community. A Message to you from the Leaders of British Jewry':

> This month, every man and woman in Britain between the ages of 16 and 65 is being asked by Sir John Anderson 'WILL YOU VOLUNTEER FOR NATIONAL DEFENCE? WILL YOU PLEDGE YOURSELF TO SERVE YOUR COUNTRY ACCORDING TO YOUR AGE, PHYSIQUE AND SPECIAL SKILL?' Each one of you has to uphold the highest standards of life and conduct, and help us to present a solid wall of loyalty and courage. We must stand in line with the best elements of the whole of the country. All this is vital for the future well-being of the British people.[22]

The issue recorded that after a Jewish National Service rally held the previous week, 'about 110 enrolments were received as a result of the rally'. Indeed, throughout the Second World War the Leeds Jewish community supported unreservedly the efforts of the government and the country in defeating Germany and its allies.

The start of the war on 3 September 1939 was marked by 'great movements of population: throngs of young men in khaki being called to the colours, and children and mothers being evacuated from Yorkshire's supposedly endangered large cities'.[23] By the end of that September, the great migration – which involved over 3,500,000 civilians alone throughout Britain – ended and Yorkshire settled down to the war and new problems.[24]

After Dunkirk, Leeds saw the signs of the real war in the appearance of the new uniforms of the Canadian, French, Czech and Polish units. Real bombing came to Yorkshire in the autumn of 1940: in September, Bradford was bombed, as was Sheffield in December.[25] Leeds was bombed in air raids in March 1941 and in August 1942; the bombs hit areas where Jews were not living, although seventy-seven Leeds residents were killed. Leeds was fortunate that it was bombed less than many other cities.[26] Travel was highly dangerous, even for land-girls, as street lighting disappeared. By December 1941, unmarried women and childless widows between the ages of 19 and 30 became liable for call up. About a third of these women chose the alternative of factory jobs, but many were called into the three female branches of the forces, ATS, WRNS and WAAF.[27]

At first a whole range of trades, including elementary school teachers, were exempt from the forces, but as the years passed the deferment age was raised and various trades were removed from the list of reserved occupations. By

1942, most of Leeds elementary schools had been cleared of their male teachers, who were replaced by married women (before the war female teachers who had married had been forced to resign), and male pensioners.[28]

In 1936, the Jubilee Hall and Institute had been opened in Saville Mount Chapeltown, incorporating the Leeds Jewish Institute and the Jewish Young Men's Association. The outbreak of the war constituted a challenge to service which the Institute readily accepted – 748 members joined HM Forces. A forces canteen was established in the Institute which catered for serving men and women of all creeds who were given free access to the club's amenities.[29] The Leeds Zionist Council and the B'nai Brith lodges were important communal organisations providing war-related services.

The war years 'shattered the routines of Anglo-Jewish life, and, in particular, made the observance of Judaism, both domestic ritual and public worship and the regime of religious education that sustains it, haphazard'.[30] Interviews with Leeds Jewish soldiers – conducted by Simon Glass for his documentary film, 'The Last Tribe', and by Philippa Lester and Diane Saunders for their book *From the Leylands to Leeds 17* with Hymie Cohen, Izzy Pear and Frank Freedman – reveal their experiences of being thrust from the intimacy of their family and working lives in the ghetto of Leeds into the unfamiliar non-Jewish world of the forces, with prejudice encountered.[31]

In the United Kingdom, according to the Association of Jewish ex-Servicemen AJEX), some 50,000 Jewish men and women served in the British Armed Forces during the Second World War, of whom 14,000 were in the RAF and 2,000 in the Royal Navy.[32] The numbers for Leeds cannot be verified as no record was kept of the names or number of Jews serving, since religions were not noted by the authorities (presumably to avoid danger in the event of capture or invasion). Altogether, 3,024 British Jews were killed or severely injured. The AJEX memorial stone at Street Lane, Leeds, in the gardens of the Beth Hamedrash Hagadol (BHH) Synagogue, lists 120 names of Leeds Jews who were killed (Figures 10.1 and 10.2). (AJEX started in Leeds in 1946.) The most famous of Leeds Jewish war heroes claimed by the community was a pilot, Arthur Louis Aaron, who was awarded the Victoria Cross. However, he was not a practising Jew and even his putative Jewish grandfather is doubtful.

Bob Statman recalled in a memoir, *I Remember*, how he was called up on 1 November 1939 and spent a miserable night at Carlton Barracks between Snaith and Selby. Five members of his own family served in the forces, and one of his neighbours in Leeds had seven sons serving, two of whom were killed.[33] Marion Crollick, aged 21, living in Grange View, Chapeltown, kept the correspondence she had in 1944–5 with her fiancé Captain Michael Lipman.[34] In the same archive is a photograph of Louis Ellis in a fireman's uniform. He was in a reserve regiment, as he manufactured flying jackets for the RAF. Also in the archive is an interview with Hilda Mitchell who was conscripted at the age of 19 in 1942 as an RAF driver. The archives provide specific evidence that Leeds Jews played a full part in the war efforts.

As a result of the abnormal industrial conditions produced by the war, there was considerable application by the elderly for assistance from the Leeds Board of Guardians – including men unemployable by reason of advanced age – and the widespread distress which the war had brought placed an additional burden on the community.[35] Bombing of civilians brought into Leeds Jews who were bereft of all their possessions and in some cases their nearest relatives. The Board also created in 1942 a Post-War Emergency Fund, realising that, with the cessation of hostilities, the community would enter into a period of economic transition.[36]

Hostilities ceased on 5 May 1945. In Leeds, the Jewish community celebrated despite the rain. Everywhere there were street parties, parades, sing-songs and dancing. Averil Goldman remembers the street party in Manor Road Chapel Allerton, with trestle tables stretching the width of the street, and Jewish and non-Jewish neighbours with all their children celebrating together and smiling for the photographer of the *Yorkshire Post*. At the end of the war men and women returning from the forces needed help, as did many refugees who had become integrated into the Leeds community. Despite the creation of the Welfare State, Leeds Jewish charities still had an important role; for example, raising funds for the Victor Lightman Loan Fund, providing meal services and offering child care.[37] Such welfare organisations and their use were important factors in the maintenance of Jewish identity among members of the community.

As David Cesarani explained, referring to Anglo-Jewry as a whole, Anglo-Jewry emerged from the Second World War transformed. 'Evacuation and bombing had disrupted ... almost every communal institution and inflicted extensive damage on buildings ... Anglo- Jewry was facing a demographic disaster through the cessation of immigration, low birth-rate, the small size of families and out-marriage.'[38]

Religious observance was declining. Zionism was the most widespread and cohesive ideology among Jews, but was not providing an adequate check to secularisation and assimilation. Although the anti-Jewish feeling of 1946–7 and Fascist activity tailed off during the late 1940s, social anti-Semitism remained widespread in certain circles.

Children's experiences

Children's lives were considerably affected by the war. They suffered the trauma of an absent father, or even that of a father wounded or killed in action. Many Leeds Jewish fathers were conscripted or voluntarily served away from home for the duration of the war. Children were deprived of a male presence in the house and under school-age children often spent the day with grandmothers while their mothers worked, while schoolchildren waited in neighbours' houses after school until their mothers returned from work. (There was a lack of day-care and crèches.) School life was disrupted by evacuation. The quality of schooling was reduced by the mobilisation of male teachers and the re-recruitment of elderly retired teachers who were often 'past their best'. Blackouts and the absence of street lighting restricted the opportunity of children in the winter months to play outdoors, a restriction that was ignored by some more adventurous children.

Significantly, most children adapted well to the absence of fathers at war or having long hours of work, and of mothers at work. It was an era when the discipline of Jewish children was not adversely affected. Juvenile delinquency among Jews remained very low. Problems of travel and the timetable of family life, such as meals, disrupted the *chederim* system and fewer children attended than before the war. Family life revolved around the living room, listening to a radio with a mother, reading, visiting relatives at a weekend and, as a treat, cinema outings to the weekly Saturday morning screenings at the Forum of special children's cartoons and short films – which most of the children preferred to synagogue attendance.

Evacuation

The evacuation of Leeds Jewish children during the early period of the war threatened the maintenance of the Jewish faith. The billeting to non-Jewish areas and non-Jewish homes alarmed Jews. A letter to the editor of the *Jewish Chronicle* on 15 September 1939 was typical of that concern. 'It is feared that Jewish children will be lost to Judaism for ever.'[39] Leeds Jewry was not able to provide or arrange for Jewish hostels in the host areas.[40]

Leeds Jewish children, numerous in some Leeds schools, were evacuated in groups with their schools which were evacuated as whole units.[41] Evacuation did not necessarily save the children from the risks of the anticipated German bombing. Horace Black recalled that he 'and my pal Abe Saffer ... were bombed the first night we were there in Lincoln'.[42]

Children's memoirs of the period tend to avoid mention of hardships and discomforts. In retrospect they highlight the excitement of the danger, such as descending in the dark into the newly dug Anderson Shelter. Philip Feldman recalled his evacuation in September 1939 with his fellow schoolchildren to Retford in Nottinghamshire and being the only Jewish child in that town. He recorded his joy at being taken home to Leeds by his mother after a week, it having been decided that there was a lesser risk from bombs in Leeds. In that week he had developed a stammer which, he said, never quite left him. He wrote that 'otherwise life as a child in Harehills was enormous fun. I simply did not notice the grime or the cramped house in Hovington Terrace. At the knock on the door and "is your Philip playing out" I was away.'[43]

Chapel Allerton Primary School had a total of 870 children on the roll in 1939, quite a number of them Jewish. On 1 September 1939 the children were evacuated to an area around East Retford, Nottinghamshire, but 'there were more bombs flying around East Retford than there were in Leeds. The children and teachers were allowed to return home and the Leeds school re-opened on 5th December 1939.'[44] During war-time, children had to bring gas masks to school every day and if they forgot they were sent home to fetch them. 'A night watch was kept and teachers took it in turns to spend the night at the school, travelling there by torch-light. Although the harsh winter of 1939–1940 made daily living extremely difficult and air raid sirens during the following months left both teachers and children exhausted.' Despite this, the children's memories are not of the hard times but of the positive things they did, like raising money at school to adopt the *Ark Royal* ship.[45]

On 23 August 1939, small Jewish boys gathered with non-Jewish boys in City Square Leeds with 'more small boys to the square yard than all square yards in Leeds', to see Gene Autry, the Western-film hero, ride through the city of Leeds on a horse. 'A week later, on Friday 1st September, the Black Prince statue looked down on many of the same children as they returned to the square clutching their haversack, suitcase and pillowcases and carrying their gas masks ... more subdued ... about to undertake journeys to unknown destinations, to be cared for by unknown foster-parents, for unknown periods.'[46] Initially, the government had regarded Leeds as a whole to be an evacuation area and did not specify any particular zone as being neutral. The excessive secrecy that surrounded the location of the reception areas resulted from the Education Department's policy that the destination of primary schools should not be released prior to the actual evacuation; and many young evacuees, their parents and teachers only learned of where the children and teachers were going as the trains drew out of the station.[47] Plans to billet Jewish boys to Jewish families in Lincoln were abandoned because of the paucity of Jews living in that city,[48] a reality that could surely have been foreseen by a simple prior enquiry in either Leeds or Lincoln.

Children of City of Leeds High School, Thoresby High School, Roundhay School and Cowper Street School (which had over 350 dispersed pupils) were evacuated to Lincolnshire and children of Lovell Road, Roundhay Road, Kepler and Chapeltown Schools were sent to parts of Lincolnshire and North Yorkshire; with Roundhay High School to Otley, West Leeds High School to Tadcaster, West Leeds Boys High to Retford, Cockburn High to Knaresborough and Leeds Junior Technical and Commercial and Lawnswood High to Ripon, occasionally, therefore, siblings being so split.[49]

Jewish food was a problem. Previously, many of the Jewish children had not eaten in a non-Jewish household, and in the Lincoln villages there was a tradition of families keeping a pig, either at home or at a nearby farm, which was killed in the autumn so that the family could live on it through the winter.[50] The Chief Rabbi broadcasting on the BBC radio gave details of his emergency ruling on the observance of food laws, particularly 'forbidden meats' including any meat not slaughtered or cooked according to Jewish rites, but by mid November 1939 the difficulties raised by the Jewish parents and the protests of the foster parents had reached a stage when it was considered impossible to billet more Jewish children in Lincoln.[51]

Roundhay School – situated in the middle of fields, far removed from the factories of the city – seemed as safe a place as any, yet it was included in the evacuation scheme. On 1 September 1939 at 1 pm boys met at the school; it was recommended that they came to the rendezvous unaccompanied by parents, with their rucksacks and gas masks, with their labels round their necks stating name, school and city, 'and ominously their religion'. The headmaster, Mr Farrow, wrote to the parents that 'each boy should carry a pocket ration of food, e.g. dry biscuits, cheese, barley sugar, fruit. No bottles.'[52] Five hundred boys had registered for the scheme, but the roll-call on 1 September revealed that half of the parents had had a last-minute change of mind and only 237 boys marched off in columns of fours down to Oakwood and boarded special trams which took the party to Beeston Station. They were then taken by train to Lincoln, arriving at 7 pm hot, dirty and very thirsty. Because very few of the railway carriages had corridors, the children were denied access to toilet facilities, although stacks of buckets were provided and the stench was awful.[53]

According to Hinchcliffe, many parents brought their sons home after receiving alarming accounts of unsuitable billets, and as weeks went by without bombing those returning to Leeds grew in number. Boys who stayed in Leeds found places where they could in the unofficial schools which had sprung up and others at boarding schools. Many billeting hosts complained that they could not keep youths of up to 17 or 18 years on 10s 6p a week or 18s 6p for two. When plans were made to allow the boys in Lincolnshire to spend the Christmas holidays in Leeds and then return to Lincoln, it became clear that few intended to return, and reluctantly the Committee gave way and announced that Roundhay School would re-open in early January 1940.[54]

The headmaster of Leeds Central High School, Mr Worts, reported that parents taking back pupils from Lincoln at the end of September 1939 were his 'chief bugbear'. He considered that the majority of the twenty-three boys who were taken back to Leeds by their parents for – in Worth's estimation – 'no good reason' were Jewish, but 'their return to Leeds was due in part to the genuine and understandable difficulties that had arisen from being billeted with non-Jewish families'.[55]

The scheme of evacuation had begun to fall apart from its inception. In November 1939, provision was made for the elementary education of 6,500 children in Leeds as a whole. Many Leeds children returned with the re-opening of a number of the schools, and during Christmas 1939 foster parents also seized on the holiday period as a convenient time to offload their evacuees. By early January 1940, 45% of Leeds official evacuees had returned to Leeds, and with the re-opening of the Leeds schools no Jewish pupils remained in the reception areas.[56] Private schools such as Leeds Grammar School re-opened in February 1940. Parents had virtually brought the schooling evacuation to an end and brought their sons home from Ripon, Hartlington and Fairbourne to continue their education in Leeds. Some children were individually sent by their parents to other places during the war. The well-known Leeds architect, Cliff Barnett, recalls spending the war years in Ilkley, where there was a small but active Jewish community.

Leeds as reception area

As a result of enemy action in London, Liverpool, Glasgow, Manchester, Birmingham and Sheffield, a number of Jewish children were moved under private arrangements to Leeds. Later, in mid 1944 when the V1 'doodle-bugs' fell in London, Leeds became a reception area despite still being called an evacuation area.[57] Also in the war years, Leeds became a reception area for the families of the Armed Forces, Civil Service and business organisations whose professional duties had brought them to the city of Leeds, with their children causing more problems. The Head of Moortown School reported that she had been forced to refuse further admissions. 'We have neither room, staff or equipment to deal with more of them.'[58] In the period September 1944 to March 1945, the silent missile attacks by V2 rockets meant that evacuated children from London and other affected cities could not be returned until July 1945.

Education

It was claimed that Jewish children's educational levels during the war, as well as prewar and after, were much higher than their non-Jewish neighbours. Lovell Road School, under its Headmaster – a proud strict Christian, Thomas Bentley – harnessed to the full the energy of the Jewish population and its commitment to learning. Louis Teeman wrote of Lovell Road School that 'the whole school was Jewish and the headmaster, Mr. Bentley, absolutely superb'. Similarly, Leeds Central High School was described as 'the university of the original Leeds Jewry'.[59]

Home life

With regard to Jewish life in wartime, Mike Leigh wrote about his childhood in Gathorne Mount:

> Think of the opening credits of early Coronation Street and you have the picture – rows of back-to-back houses, cobbled streets and smoking chimneys from coal fires, with the air so polluted that pea-suit fogs were commonplace. Gas powered street lamps (not on at night during the period when air raids were expected). Going to bed during the winter was an ordeal. Feet were well catered for because of a stone hot water bottle. Otherwise there was about 30 minutes of uncontrolled shivering.[60]

He described the scullery as 'minute, consisting of a small sink and draining board, an oven, some inadequate storage cupboards and a bath covered by a bath top'. The cellar head was the 'fridge' where the family kept perishables. The bath top remained in situ because it was needed as storage for tinned stuff. 'Because the toilet was shared, the "gerry" was used. Otherwise it was going out with an overcoat and candle.' His aunt, he described, was worse off in her house in Enfield Grove, which shared an outside toilet with three other neighbours with large families.[61]

Anti-Semitism and crime

The war years were not marked by any lessening of anti-Semitism, even though there was an anti-Fascist agenda. There was a public belief that Jews were participating in black-marketing. The Leeds Jewish community during wartime was anxious to avoid any anti-Semitic reaction to perceived Jewish involvement in black-marketing of goods, whether real or imaginary, although there were no reports in the newspapers of the times that the Leeds Jews were any more involved than their Gentile neighbours. One incident, however, was gossiped about at the time – when a Jewish poultry dealer was transporting live chickens and eggs from a farm and was stopped by an inspector. The number of eggs in the vehicle exceeded that shown on the permitted documentation from the farmer. The dealer escaped without punishment with the excuse that the excess eggs had been layed on the journey. (One wonders how she explained away how the hens had deposited the eggs neatly in the cartons!)

Stories such as these no doubt fed a belief in stereotypes of Jewish misdemeanours. A recently published wartime diary confirms the existence in Leeds of a casual, reflex anti-Semitism. After tea with neighbours there was talk about Jews and a guest said:

> All bogus fires [presumably for insurance] and other such swindles would be traced back to a Jew, all storing of petrol etc that he had read in the papers had

been by Jews – in fact he as good laid all the evil in the country at their feet ... Jewish ideas on morality and honour are different from Western ones ... I have reported the anti-Semitic talk because so many people are taking up that line of thought these days and even blaming the war on to the Jews. My brother, who is an officer in the RAF, has extravagant views in this direction, and [said] all Jews should be sent into the front line because it was on their behalf we were fighting the war.[62]

When a Leeds by-election occurred in February 1940, the unsuccessful Fascist candidate included anti-Semitic sentiment in his campaign and Mass Observation, the recently founded polling organisation, found some anti-Semitic views among almost all interviewees, though not strongly held. They reported that Fascist support came from the 'unemployed or families with persons in jobs connected [with] or affected by Jews'.[63]

The notorious London gangster Jack Spot spent a short time in Leeds in 1943, having fled the Blitz in London and an impending prosecution for assault, buying a rail ticket to Leeds which he had heard was the black market capital of the north. However, in Leeds he indulged in 'mere gambling and assault', and soon returned to London.[64]

Evacuation caused further anti-Semitic problems, but the government was not prepared to deal with the issue of selecting the right evacuees for the right areas.[65] Food was a cause of conflict and some evacuees reported attempts by Christians to convert them from Judaism. The war and postwar did not bring any more violence to Leeds Jews than prewar. One murder was, however, widely reported in 1949, when Abraham Levine, a jeweller in Albion Street, was shot dead in his shop by two young men. They were convicted at Leeds Assizes in March 1950 of capital murder. The man who was under 18 went to prison while the other was hanged in Armley Prison on 30 March 1950.

Politics

Leeds Jewry, predominantly working-class, found a natural political home in the Labour Party, even though the first few Jewish city councillors were Conservative. The election of the Attlee Government in 1945, with its promise of radical social and economic policies, strengthened that connection. However, Jewish loyalty to Labour was vitiated by government postwar policy in Palestine. In particular, the apparently pro-Arab stance of Ernest Bevin alarmed the Jewish community and he was regarded in Leeds, as elsewhere in both the UK and the USA, as an anti-Semite. The delay in the recognition of Israel by Britain until February 1949 enhanced that perception. In Leeds there was anger and perplexity at the Labour Government's policies towards the Jews of Palestine in the Mandate, and towards those in Israel after the formation of the State. British Jews, including Leeds Jews, were encouraged 'to raise funds to finance illegal activities in Palestine, to help purchase and smuggle arms, and to smuggle refugees into the Holy Land, even to finance Jewish underground armies fighting against British troops. Many Jews gave generously to these causes without asking too many questions.'[66] The activities of the Jewish underground fighters in Palestine had led to widespread anti-Jewish riots throughout Britain and Mosley had attempted a come-back.

Zionism, both political and financial, became the main communal and social activity; the cause that transcended all divisions within the Leeds Jewish community. Zionism and the committees that supported it was strong in Leeds, as Zionism struck deeper roots in the new suburbs among middle-class Jews, while in the old immigration neighbourhoods interest in Zionism remained alive among those who had been born abroad and remained attached to religious tradition.[67] In Leeds, the presence of Leeds University Professor Selig Brodetsky, as a leader of the Zionist Council both on the national and local level, encouraged the Leeds community to unite in the support of the Zionist cause. The establishment of the State of Israel magnetised the Leeds Jewish community. A number of Leeds men in the 'Mahal' volunteered to serve in Israel's War of Independence and in later years. *Aliyah* [emigration to Israel] took place particularly among young adults in this period, such as through *Habonim* [Zionist youth group], to *kibbutzim* [collective farms] in Israel.[68] As Lipman states, Zionism 'filled an ideological vacuum which traditional religion was no longer able to fill'.

Refugees

The Second World War radically changed refugee work. Whereas in April 1933, British-Jewish leaders had guaranteed to maintain all Jewish refugees entering Britain as a result of Nazi persecution, this support was based on that leadership's estimation that it would only need support for around 4,000. However, the German occupation of Austria in March 1938 and of Czechoslovakia in March 1939 dramatically increased the number of Jewish refugees fleeing persecution (increasing to about 55,000 arriving in Britain by 1939, at a cost to the Jewish community of more than £3,000,000)[69] and furthermore the outbreak of war prevented Jewish refugees from returning. As a result, British Jews were faced with providing long-term aid to hundreds of thousands of Jewish aliens.[70] British Jewry was overwhelmed and, after an emergency meeting with the Home Office, it was agreed that the British Authorities would meet the costs for the maintenance of half of the Jewish refugees in Britain – but Jews in Britain struggled to raise funds to keep their side of the deal.[71]

The fall of France in May 1940, the evacuation from Dunkirk and the threat of imminent invasion were responsible for the imposition of dramatic measures against 'enemy aliens' in Britain. By stages the government 'was stampeded into interning 27,000 enemy aliens of all categories, the bulk of them German and Austrian refugees'.[72] The *Jewish Chronicle* considered the detention 'a sound measure'. Furthermore, the government's introduction of anti-alien restrictions and mass internment of enemy aliens in 1940 (Churchill's 'Collar the Lot'), further increased the economic dependency of Jewish refugees on British Jewry. 'Enemy alien travel restrictions resulted in the unemployment of 8,000 domestic servants, unable to follow their households during evacuation and threatened the livelihoods of aliens whose businesses depended on travel.'[73] Also, Jewish internees were often unable to pay bills and make suitable provision for their families, due to the rapidity of their arrest and detention, with the task falling on British-Jewish refugee organisations like the Central Office for Refugees.[74] Heinz Skyte considered that the Leeds Tribunal Chairman, who had to categorise the extent of the risk of the alien, was the harshest to Jews of all the Tribunals in Britain.[75]

However, the torpedoing of the British ship, *SS Arandora Star*, carrying internees to Canada on 2 July – and British MPs criticism of the internment policy – led to a reversal and to the release of nearly 10,000 internees before the end of 1941,[76] a release that included Heinz Skyte and Max Kingsley from Leeds. 'The Anglo-Jewish community went to great lengths to disperse the refugees across the country and advised them to keep a low profile so as to avoid the impression of a substantial and menacing Jewish body within England.'[77] Fear of domestic anti-Semitism also led British Jews to marginalise Jewish refugees. British Jews feared that any association with enemy aliens would erode their assimilated image and threaten their security. British Jews, on the whole, gave the German-speaking newcomers a mixed welcome. 'Some threw themselves into refugee work, helping the refugees to find employment, easing their way into the life of the community and taking in children who arrived on the Kindertransports. However, there were those as well who remained indifferent and did not respond to the appeals for funds, and, more importantly, for homes for unaccompanied children.'[78] Various estimates have been given as to the percentage of such children placed in non-Jewish homes nationally, varying from one third (Bolshover), to over 50% (Association of Jewish Refugees – AJR). Some refugees fought against the idea of learning English for many years and many middle-class refugees looked down on working-class British Jews with whom they were billeted, having come from a wealthy background, and found more in common with British Gentiles.

During the war, and after, the older refugees who came to Leeds mixed socially with their fellow German-speaking refugees but did not develop a communal life of their own. Unlike London, with its very sizeable refugee community, in Leeds 'of necessity they gradually tended to become absorbed into British society around them and associated with the existing local Jewish community, lacking as they did the critical mass to survive as an autonomous community with their own distinct German speaking cultural life and activities.'[79] Leeds, unlike London, did not have the Viennese coffee shops or the distinct districts which had large concentrations of the refugees, such as Belsize Park and Hampstead. None of the communities outside London were large enough to support a network of refugee organisations, businesses, retail outlets and other commercial enterprises comparable to that which developed across north west London.[80]

The refugees spread across Britain rapidly after the war, as it allowed refugees to move out of Leeds and settle across the country and those so desiring to return to London. After the war, with regards to the Displaced Persons (DPs) in Europe, Britain did not open any floodgates to survivors. Leeds saw hardly any DPs admitted. Whereas between 1946 and 1951 81,000 DPs were admitted to Britain under two schemes (many left on the completion of the schemes), hardly any came to Leeds. Initially under the Baltic 'Cygnet Scheme' Britain was to recruit 1,000 unmarried Baltic women DPs to serve as domestics in TB sanatoriums and hospitals. There is no record of any Jews coming to Leeds under this scheme. Similarly, the 'Westward Ho' scheme was aimed at DPs from Poland, Hungary, Bulgaria, and Czechs and Slovaks to work in Britain in the cotton, coal and agriculture industries, none of which had a special need in Leeds.[81]

A branch of the AJR was established in Leeds. Some refugees reported on the warmth of their welcome, but others felt isolated because of their different accent, language and social wishes. 'Certainly, the children of refugees found the pre-refugee German-Jewish communal life and views had little attraction to them.'[82] Refugees developed their own private and professional networks, no longer centred around other refugees. What remained were organisational ties with other observant or Reform Jews, with Jewish life in Leeds principally experienced through synagogues. The most observant were welcomed by the Orthodox synagogues, with the new Reform movement in Leeds – established after the war – attracting many refugees who remained there and who had experienced Reform Judaism in Germany.[83]

Nazism and the refugee crises had provided a challenge to the Jewish community, both in terms of what British Jews could do to combat Nazism and how they could influence British opinion favourably towards the arrival of Jewish refugees. Leeds Jewry, as a provincial community, found its own way of dealing with these crises, which often reflected the national approach, but occasionally differed because of the uniqueness of its own development. These crises 'raised once again the question about the fundamental nature of the Jewish presence in Britain and, more dangerously the question as to what political entity did the Jews in Britain belong? Was their much-vaunted patriotism nothing more than a sham, or in least in need of heavy qualification?'[84]

The reception and settlement of refugee children, who came unaccompanied on the Kindertransports, 'constituted a particularly painful episode. These children were initially traumatised by the experience of separation from parents, whom in many cases they would never see again, and by their journeys to Britain. Had they all been found billets in Jewish homes, their sufferings might have been lessened.'[85] Alderman considered that in Britain as a whole 'this could have been accomplished, but the will was lacking'. However, in Leeds, the Jewish response was far more positive. An examination of the lists of the names and addresses of the hosts and the names of the children, contained in the Makofski papers in the Leeds City Archives, reveals that, according to those lists, over fifty children were placed in private homes by the Leeds community, the vast majority in Jewish homes and many others in the hostel in Stainbeck Lane. The addresses of the foster parents were mostly in the working-class areas, but some were in the wealthier Moortown suburb. A further twenty more Kindertransport children who did not appear on the Makofski lists were also placed in Leeds. The response demonstrated the will and concern of the Leeds community, particularly bearing in mind that sponsors had to pay a £50 guarantee that the child would not be a cost to the public purse 'for the duration'.

When the children arrived in England, via the Hook of Holland and ship, those who had sponsors, guarantors and hosts already pledged were usually picked up either at Liverpool Street Station or Dovercourt Camp and then taken to Leeds. Those without pre-arrangements stayed at Dovercourt until hosts could be found – either through local initiatives, or through potential hosts arriving at the Camp and choosing a child. Those pre-arranged nationally in many cases involved non-Jewish foster-parents where the arrangements and finances had been made by the Red Cross, Quakers and other non-Jewish groups already established in refugee work in Germany, Austria and Czechoslovakia. Others were placed by the Jewish organisations in Berlin, Vienna etc. Those who came to Leeds were invariably arranged by Jews at both ends of the journey.

An example is that of Edith Michel (Goldberg), aged 11, from Germany, and her little sister Irmgard. Enquiries by their parents to families in Leeds resulted in Edith being taken by a Mrs Craskin into a working-class house in Grange View, Chapeltown, and her sister by Mrs Bloomberg a few doors away. Edith was then treated as 'one of the family' and had a hospitable reception. She went to Cowper Street school, speaking no English, and was later evacuated with the school to Lincolnshire (and promptly brought back by Mrs Craskin), but soon adapted. Ruth Reuben, with her husband serving abroad and with a small child, took into her small working-class house three of the children, whom she brought up along with her daughter.[86] Dorothy Fleming (originally Dorli Oppenheimer) arrived in Leeds, travelling on a Kindertransport on 10 January 1939, and recalled 'A lovely Jewish couple, Theo and Tilly Hall, agreed to take me in, and by doing so surely saved my life'. Ernst Simon travelled in January 1939 and was taken in by the Morris family in Sholebroke Avenue. Thea Skyte (Ephrian), aged 15, came from Berlin to Leeds on 12 January 1939 to a family Nagley. Elly Millet (Korn) came to Leeds, aged 15, on 13 March 1939 to the home of the Carr family in Street Lane, Mr Carr being a chemist with a shop at Moortown. Leisel Carter from Germany was sponsored by Jack and Mary Wynne at 12 Hustler Grove, Chapeltown.[87]

The hostel for young refugee boys in Stainbeck Lane Chapel Allerton Leeds – financed, planned and organised by the Leeds Jewish community – housed sixty boys, with thirty girls housed by the Leeds community in a Harrogate hostel. Both were organised on Jewish Orthodox lines, with kosher food and Hebrew lessons. Ernst Simon and his brother Kurt Simon, when interviewed in 2012, both recalled that they were very happy during their stay at the Leeds hostel;[88] whereas Kelly Bernard, when interviewed by a Holocaust Survivors' Association in America, did not describe his life in the Leeds hostel as pleasant 'due in part to a particularly harsh housemaster' (Bernard, VHA Interview 38097). Manfred Landau, who left Berlin on the first Kindertransport on 1 December 1938, stayed at the Leeds hostel until 1942 and had happy memories of his stay.[89] In February 1940, four refugee boys at the hostel celebrated their Barmitzvah – Egon Gutman, Hermann Indyk, Kurt Dukes and Pessach Moskovitz – who thanked the Leeds Jewish Community 'for giving them the happiness that had been denied to them in the land of their birth'.[90] At the Leeds hostel, the main organiser Mark Labovitch was friendly with the Chief Constable of Leeds, and called him in to verbally discipline any boy who was guilty of undue bad behaviour – a dressing-down which usually did the trick. At the Harrogate hostel, Ruth Heinemann felt that she was fortunate in the good care received there. She recalled that in December 1939 'I had a tonsillectomy at the Harrogate Hospital. On Xmas morning I received a beautiful gift from Mary, Princess Royal and Countess of Harewood. It was a large chintz-covered sewing box that I treasured.'[91]

The Hull Jewish community placed fifty-four Kindertransport children within the community in Jewish homes, an astonishing achievement for the small east coast Yorkshire Jewish community. The Bradford community established a Jewish hostel, much to the credit and efforts of the Jewish businessman Oswald Stroud, and there was a Jewish boys' hostel in Ilkley. The York committee was run by Quakers and Christians and the York Municipal Archives contain the committee's minutes revealing the effort and work put in by the members in placing the children and looking after their welfare, albeit that the children were placed in Quaker and other Christian households.[92]

At anniversary gatherings, the now much older child 'survivors' of the transports have repeated expressions of unqualified gratitude to the British Government for having saved them, despite the majority of their parents being killed in the Holocaust. Such gratitude appears on plaques in Parliament and on statues of the children at railway stations. However, the defects in the arrangements have been largely glossed over. The British Government refused to admit their parents (any pressure to do so may have led to a refusal even to allow the children), the programme was not funded by the government and remained overall under-funded, the admission was expressed to be temporary (leading to anxiety among the children) and the fostering in Britain was accomplished in haste by individuals and organisations not sufficiently experienced and organised for tasks of placement and welfare. Furthermore, the children were scattered throughout the United Kingdom to allay fears of anti-Semitism, and a substantial number of the Jewish children were placed in Christian homes causing alienation from their faith (although not in Leeds, Hull and Bradford). Some children suffered abuse (again not locally) and some older children suffered the unnecessary trauma of being interned as enemy aliens. Such negative features of the government's policy remain on the whole unexpressed in public.[93]

In addition, under a separate initiative, at the end of August 1939, 103 boys and 20 staff (including housemaster Clem Lorie) from the ORT technical school were accommodated with hostels and workshops in Chapeltown Leeds, arriving from Berlin – the boys being engineering apprentices between 16 and 18 years old (ORT is the recognised acronym from the German for the 'Organisation for the Promotion of Trade and Agriculture Among Jews').[94] The headmaster, Colonel Levey, had travelled with the youths from Berlin. He was a strict disciplinarian and kept them in order through tight instructions, although one youth recalled fights developing on the football pitch when the Vienna boys played the Berlin ones. The Regulations of the Leeds ORT school laid out rules to be followed.

> Although you passed the Tribunal you are, in the eyes of the Leeds Christian people, members of an enemy country at war with England. DO NOTHING at any time to arouse the slightest hostility and do not attract attention. The Jewish Community of Leeds expect you to show a splendid example of respect and thoughtfulness to the people of the City of Leeds for accepting you here in time of war.

The list of regulations consisted of twenty-six points. Number 1 read: 'Never speak German in the streets so that you can be heard. Try not to speak German at all if you can help it, and in any case speak very quietly.'[95] Once the school in Leeds was established it carried on the work and training that had begun in Berlin. It was divided into the same six categories: locksmiths, blacksmiths, plumbers, electricians, mechanics and welders. The boys and teachers were housed in two hostels in Chapeltown Road. Max Abraham, one of the Berlin ORT teachers who came with the boys and became a hostel-master, recalled that there were fifty boys sleeping in the hostels, six to a room in bunk beds.[96]

The reception of the Kindertransport children and the ORT boys shows Leeds Jewry acting with the very best of its endeavours, and contrasts with the lesser achievements of many other British Jewish communities.

10.1 War memorial at Street Lane

10.2 Sol Myers of Leeds. Killed in action, 1942

Notes

1. A. Kent, *Identity, Migration and Belonging. The Jewish Community of Leeds 1890–1920* (Newcastle Upon Tyne: Cambridge Scholar Publishing, 2015), p. 224.
2. E. Krausz, *Leeds Jewry, Its History and Social Structure* (Cambridge: Jewish Historical Society of England, 1963), p. 7.; *Jewish Chronicle*, 26 September 1952.
3. Krausz, *Leeds Jewry, Its History and Social Structure*, p. 23.
4. A. Kershen, *Uniting the Tailors 1870–1930* (Ilford, Essex: Frank Cass & Co. Ltd. 1995), p. 186.
5. M. Freedman, *Chapeltown and Its Jews* (Leeds: privately published, 2003), p. 13.
6. B. Silver, *Three Jewish Giants of Leeds: Selig Brodetsky, Montague Burton and Jacob Kramer* (Leeds: Leeds Branch Jewish Historical Society of Great Britain, 2000), p. 34.
7. Silver, *Three Jewish Giants of Leeds*, p. 45.
8. B. Nelson, *The Woollen Industry of Leeds* (Leeds: D. J. Thornton Press, 1980), p. 46.
9. Mick McCann, *How Leeds Changed the World. Encyclopedia Leeds* (Leeds: Armley Press, 2010), p. 41.
10. Ibid.
11. Krausz, *Leeds Jewry, Its History and Social Structure*, p. 17.
12. V. D. Lipman, *A History of the Jews in England Since 1858* (Leicester: Leicester University Press, 1990), p. 223.
13. A. Bergen, *Leeds Jewry 1930–1939, The Challenge of Anti-Semitism* (Leeds: Thoresby Society Publications, Vol. 10, 2000), p. 30.
14. Alastair and Anne Pyke, *The Home Front in Britain 1939–1945* (Brighton: Tressell Publications, 1985), p. 1.
15. Ibid.
16. Ibid., p. 16.
17. Ibid., p. 21.
18. Ibid., p. 22.
19. Ibid., p. 26.
20. Ibid., p. 28.
21. *United Hebrew Congregation Bulletin*, Vol 2, No 8 (13 May 1938).
22. *United Hebrew Congregation Bulletin*, Vol. 3, No. 5 (2 April 1939).
23. L. Kessler and E. Taylor, *Yorkshire At War, The Story of Fighting Yorkshire at Home and Abroad 1939–1945* (Yorkshire: Dalesman Books), 1980, p. 7.
24. Ibid., p. 10.
25. Ibid., p. 52.
26. R. Addyman, *A Leeds Family in the Second World War* (Leeds: R. Addyman, 2010), p. 2.
27. Kessler and Taylor, *Yorkshire At War*, p. 61.
28. Ibid., p. 71.
29. L. Saipe, *Leeds Jewish Representative Council 60th Anniversary 1906–1966* (Leeds: Rep. Council, 1966), p. 29.
30. T. Endelman, *The Jews in Britain 1855–2000* (Los Angeles: University of California Press, 2002), p. 222.

31 P. Lester and D. Saunders, *From the Leylands to Leeds 17* (Leeds: Leylands Books, 2015).
32 AJEX, Brochure for Remembrance Parade, 2015.
33 B. Statman, *I Remember. A Chronicle of Events in My Early Life 1923–1943* (Leeds: Self Published, nd), p. 11.
34 Interviews for *From the Leylands to Leeds 17* and Makor Archive, Leeds.
35 L. Saipe, *A Century of Care. The History of the Leeds Jewish Welfare Board 1878–1978* (Leeds: J. Jackman & Co., 1978), p. 34.
36 Ibid., p. 36.
37 H. Skyte, *Jewish Care in the Community. The Story of the Leeds Jewish Welfare Board and the Leeds Jewish Housing Association* (Leeds: LJWB, April 1999), pp. 28–33.
38 D. Cesarani, *The Jewish Chronicle and Anglo-Jewry 1841–1991* (Cambridge: Cambridge University Press, 1994), pp. 199–200.
39 *Jewish Chronicle*, 15 September 1939, p. 20.
40 K. A. Saunders, 'The Impact of the Second World War on British Jewry', MA Dissertation, University of Leeds, 2007, p. 15.
41 *Jewish Chronicle*, 15 September 1939, p. 13.
42 Interview, Makor Archives, 14 December 2011.
43 P. Feldman, *My Early Life 1933–1953* (Self Published, nd).
44 Chapel Allerton Primary School Leeds Parent teachers Association, *Chapel Allerton School, A Logbook of Memories 1871–1951* (Leeds: privately printed, 1994), pp. 28–9.
45 Ibid., p. 29.
46 R. Boud, *The Great Exodus: The Evacuation of Leeds Schoolchildren 1939–1945*. (Leeds: Thoresby Society, 2000), p. 41.
47 Ibid., p. 56.
48 Ibid., p. 57, quoting Report by Mr. B. Farrow, Headmaster of Roundhay School, 22 June 1939.
49 Ibid., pp. 96 and 135. *Jewish Chronicle* 22 September 1939, p. 14.
50 Boud, *The Great Exodus*, pp. 96–7, quoting Mildred Lipman.
51 Ibid., p. 97.
52 G. Hinchcliffe. *Roundhay School: The First Half Century* (Leeds: privately printed, nd) pp. 68–9.
53 Boud, *The Great Exodus*, pp. 72–3.
54 Hinchcliffe, *Roundhay School*, pp. 70–1.
55 E. Jenkins, *A Centenary History of Leeds Central High School* (Leeds: University of Leeds Press, 1985) p. 157.
56 Boud, *The Great Exodus*, p. 38.
57 Ibid., pp. 146, 149.
58 Ibid., p. 151.
59 Jenkins, *A Centenary History of Leeds Central High School*, p. 9.
60 M. Leigh, *Vignettes of Harehills 1940–1960* (Leeds: Self Published, 2006), p. 10.
61 Ibid., pp. 10–11.
62 'The Diaries of James and Tony Ridge', *Publications of the Thoresby Society* (26, 2016), pp. 29–30.

63 Ibid., p. 125.
64 Wesley Clarkson, *Hit'em Hard: Jack Spot. King of the Underworld* (London: Harper Collins, 2003).
65 T. Kushner, *The Persistence of Prejudice: Antisemitism in British Society During the Second World War* (Manchester: Manchester University Press, 1989), p. 65.
66 G. Alderman, *The Jewish Community in British Politics* (Oxford: Clarendon Press, 1983), p. 129.
67 Endelman, *The Jews in Britain 1855–2000*, p. 216.
68 Lipman, *A History of the Jews in England Since 1858*, p. 180.
69 R. Bolshover, *British Jewry and the Holocaust* (Cambridge: Cambridge University Press, 1993), p. 70.
70 Saunders, 'The Impact of the Second World War on British Jewry', p. 11.
71 Ibid., p. 12.
72 Cesarani, *The Jewish Chronicle and Anglo-Jewry*, p. 171.
73 Saunders, 'The Impact of the Second World War on British Jewry', p. 12.
74 Ibid.
75 Interview with Ian Vellins, 2015.
76 Cesarani, *The Jewish Chronicle and Anglo-Jewry 1841–1991*, p. 171.
77 Bolshover, *British Jewry and the Holocaust*, p. 50.
78 Ibid., p. 215.
79 A. Grenville, *Refugees from Germany and Austria in Britain 1933–1970* (London: Vallentine Mitchell, 2010), p. 40.
80 Ibid.
81 B. Shepherd, *The Long Road Home* (London: Vintage, 2010), p. 332.
82 Grenville, *Refugees from Germany and Austria in Britain*, p. 142.
83 Ibid., p. 144.
84 Alderman, *The Jewish Community in British Politics*, p. 281.
85 Ibid., p. 299.
86 Ian Vellins, 'The Kindertransport Children. Memory, Narration, Celebration and Commemoration', MA Dissertation, University of Leeds, 2013.
87 Interviews with Ian Vellins, 2013.
88 Ibid.
89 Interview with Ian Vellins, 2015.
90 *Jewish Chronicle*, 16 February 1940.
91 Ruth Heinemann, 'A beautiful gift', letter in *Association of Jewish Refugees Journal* (November 2016), p. 7.
92 Vellins, 'The Kindertransport Children'.
93 Ibid.
94 *Jewish Telegraph*, 23 May 1997.
95 S. Kavanagh, *ORT, the Second World War and the Rehabiliation of Holocaust Surivors* (London: Vallentine Mitchell, 2008), p. 18.
96 Ibid., p. 18.

Part III

The contours of the Leeds Jewish community

11

Jewish heritage in Leeds

Sharman Kadish

Bill Williams, the historian of Manchester Jewry, once observed that their history is like 'a walk up Cheetham Hill Road'. Likewise, the history of Leeds Jewry may be compared to a walk up Chapeltown Road, from the slums of the Leylands, the 'East End' of Leeds, through Chapeltown and Moortown Corner to Alwoodley ('Alyidly') and beyond. The settlement pattern of the Jewish community, whose presence in Leeds was built largely on the nineteenth-century textile industry, can be traced simply by a tour of the synagogues that they erected. Leeds Jewry is remarkable for its relentless suburbanisation – and its fractious congregational history; umpteen synagogues, none of which have survived from the Victorian era. Leeds Jewry has more than halved in size since 1945, today numbering about 6,850 (2011 Census). The historic city-centre Great Synagogue at Belgrave Street was closed in 1983 and blown up by a Jewish demolition expert. Happily, the stained glass windows were rescued and reused in the suburban Leeds United Hebrew Congregation (known as UHC or Shadwell Lane).

Since the Second World War, Leeds Jewry has built four big new synagogues that collectively give an interesting insight into contemporary synagogue architecture. Along the way, we shall meet some of the architects – most of them not Jewish – who designed Leeds synagogues and try to shed some light on how they came to undertake what remains an unusual commission and why they resolved design issues in the way that they did.

The case of Leeds affords an ideal opportunity to explore in miniature the issue of architectural style in relation to Jewish identity in Britain, and an attempt is made to place some buildings of local significance in a wider context. While the focus in this chapter is primarily on purpose-built synagogues, it will also touch on examples of other buildings converted for Jewish use, a phenomenon especially typical of first-generation immigrant communities in urban settings, but not confined to them. Mention will also be made of the surprising number of Jewish community buildings either erected or converted for secular purposes, given the limited size of Leeds Jewry.[1]

Jewish heritage in Leeds in the Victorian period

The earliest and most architecturally significant synagogue erected in Victorian Leeds was the Leeds Great Synagogue. This was the founding congregation in the city, the origins of which can be traced back to the 1840s. The original *minyan* began in a loft in Bridge Street at the bottom of Lady Lane. In 1846 they graduated to Back Rockingham Street, at Camp Road, and from there to Belgrave Street where 'the first purpose-built synagogue in Yorkshire' was constructed in 1860–1.[2] Nothing is known about the local firm, Perkins & Brockhouse, who were the architects. Information about the appearance of this earlier synagogue is also scanty: it was of brick and bore a tablet with the date of erection hidden in a chronogram. Inside, it had a gallery on three sides that faced the Ark with 'gilded pillars'.[3] Costing about £1,200 and with a capacity for 300 people, this first synagogue was soon demolished to make way for a larger building for 500, costing nearly £2,500.

Belgrave Street, in its second incarnation that survived for just over a century, dated from 1877–8 (Figure 11.1).[4] Established Leeds architect Stephen Ernest Smith (1845–1925)[5] came up with a vaguely Italianate design. Archive photographs show a series of large segmental-headed windows in eight bays on the long brick street facade, punctuated by two pedimented entrance bays.[6] One of these, situated at the far, western, end, presumably accessed the vestibule and a second, placed about halfway along the frontage, gave direct access to the prayer hall. Siting the long walls of a synagogue along the street was never the preferred plan when building a rectangular synagogue of the 'cathedral synagogue' type (see below) in Victorian Britain; the standard arrangement was for the front entrance, leading to the vestibule, to be situated on the short west front, giving off from the street. This allowed for entry into the main prayer hall facing towards the Ark without the need to change direction, as dictated by tradition. In practice, sometimes the restrictions of the building plot dictated otherwise. Smith's solution at Belgrave Street was imitated[7] several years later (1880–1) by the Healey Brothers at Bowland Street in Bradford where the Reform congregation (the first congregation in the town), likewise acquired a site in an existing terrace. Belgrave Street was spacious, with seating for 500,[8] to satisfy the needs of the rapidly expanding Jewish population – and, no doubt, in the hope of an amalgamation between several argumentative congregations already in the town.

Inside, the Ark was a simple but pretty whitewashed cabinet, with a decorative round pediment and scrolled banisters to the stairs (Figure 11.2). It must have been propped against the blind end wall at east.[9] A reproduction of this original Ark can still be seen in the Bet Midrash at the present-day United Hebrew Congregation (UHC), Shadwell Lane (see Figure 11.3). Otherwise, Belgrave Street was a low-budget provincial synagogue. The ladies' gallery, on three-sides, was very shallow.

Belgrave Street was the 'cathedral synagogue' of Leeds Jewry, that is, the landmark synagogue of the aspiring anglicised Jewish middle classes. Its erection slightly predated the influx of Yiddish-speaking Ashkenazim from Eastern Europe into the Leyland slums that began in the early 1880s. To them, Belgrave Street, with its formal dress and services, *hazan* [cantor] and choir, was culturally alien. In common with other big synagogues built in British cities in the second half of the nineteenth century – for example the umbrella United Synagogue in London (New West End Synagogue etc.), in Birmingham (Singers Hill), Manchester (Great Synagogue), Liverpool (Princes Road), Glasgow (Garnethill) and Dublin (Adelaide Road) – Belgrave Street came to be regarded as the *englischer shul* of Leeds.

The period from 1881 to 1914 saw the arrival in Britain of some 100,000 Jewish refugees from persecution and economic hardship in Tsarist Russia.[10] In Leeds, the 'point of arrival' was the Leylands, a neighbourhood just to the north of the city centre and Belgrave Street. By the late nineteenth century the Victorian terraces in this neighbourhood, many of which were 'back-to-backs' – never housing of the best quality – were deteriorating into slums. The Leylands occupied an area of less than a mile square below Sheepscar and bounded by North Street to the west and Regent Street to the east, and it was one of the most deprived neighbourhoods in the country. If there were a Leeds equivalent of Russell and Lewis's famous 1900 'Poverty Map' of the Jewish East End of London,[11] the Leylands would have been colour-coded deep blue.

Leeds perhaps holds the trophy as the most fractured – and fractious – Jewish community in the country. Its congregational history is highly complex. In the Victorian period, few Leeds synagogues were purpose built and, of those that were, none have survived. The Leeds 'Great Synagogue' at Belgrave Street was blown up in 1983 to make room for an office block.[12] Not very far away, the New Briggate Synagogue was nicknamed the *grinners' shul* – the 'Greeners' or 'Newcomers' synagogue – because it was built for the immigrants in the Leylands,[13] in juxtaposition to the *englischer shul* at Belgrave Street. Purpose-built New Briggate Synagogue, opened in 1894, represented the coming of age of the immigrant community. The antecedents of this congregation lay in a prayer circle founded in St Alban Street in 1869. They moved to a house in New Briggate in 1876. The new synagogue was first referred to as 'St John's Place', after the seventeenth-century St John the Evangelist Church (1634, Grade I) that overlooked the synagogue, just off New Briggate. (Today, St John is the oldest surviving church in Leeds.)[14] Only afterwards did 'Merrion Street' (to the north) become the popular name of the synagogue.

This was an ambitious project for a community that had grown from humble beginnings. Symptomatic of their aspirations, the congregation held an architectural competition (1889–90) for their new building, a happening rare even in the metropolis. The winning architect was William Henry Thorp (1852–1944)[15] who had previously won several other competitions for public buildings in Leeds, including the City Art Gallery (1886–8).[16] In 1890, he was elected president of the forerunner of the West Yorkshire Society of Architects. According to his obituarist, Thorp 'became one of the best-known architects in the North of England'.[17]

The *Building News* reported that the New Briggate Synagogue was intended to be 'in an Oriental style of a Saracenic type'.[18] 'Oriental' was the most fashionable architectural style associated with synagogues across Europe in the second half of the nineteenth century. By the 1890s it had caught on in provincial communities in Britain at a time when it was already on the wane in London. Indeed, 'Orientalism', in various guises, persisted longer outside the capital, albeit on a more modest scale. Leeds, as shall be seen, presents a good example of this time lapse in architectural fashions.

New Briggate Synagogue was not consecrated until 23 September 1894. It sat 500, only half the number originally intended.[19] Indeed, six weeks before the opening, the Leeds correspondent of the London *Jewish Chronicle* reported that the building appeal had met with 'a scanty response' and that there was 'still a deficiency of over £700'. 'Unless,' he warned, 'liberal aid be speedily forthcoming the building cannot be completed.'[20] In the end, the synagogue was opened anyway, even though it was 'not complete, through the insufficiency of funds'.[21] Presumably, the arriviste congregation had overstretched themselves financially.

Not surprisingly, as built, New Briggate Street Synagogue was a disappointingly plain building, from the outside at least. A rare archive image has recently come to light[22] that shows the synagogue in a streetscape photographed in 1929 prior to demolition. This was a two-storey, six-bay, end-of-terrace, brick building with stone dressings. The long street wall was on St John's Place with segmental-headed windows on both floors. The pedimented main entrance was at the far (west) end, up several steps. This was hardly the Oriental concoction anticipated, perhaps to compare with Bradford's exquisite little Islamic inspired Reform synagogue built in the previous decade. The south side of Merrion Street, including the synagogue, was demolished after August 1930 for road widening.[23] In 1933, the St John's Recreation Gardens (or Merrion Street Garden of Rest), was opened on the site opposite the church. Meanwhile, the Jewish congregation moved round the corner into St

John's Place proper and eventually merged with the big Leeds New Synagogue in Chapeltown Road (see below). Nothing is known of the interior appearance of the New Briggate building.

The Mariempoler Synagogue, a *landsmanshafter shul*, or congregation – whose members hailed from the same town of origin in *der Heim* [the 'Old Country'], which in Leeds usually meant *Lite* (Lithuania or Byelorussia) – was founded in 1886 or 1887. Mariempol (today Marijampole) is situated in Suwalki Province in the south west of modern Lithuania. The *Mariompoler shul* was officially called the Leeds Central Synagogue and afterwards the Leeds 'Old' Central, in order to differentiate it from the Leeds 'New' Central (see below). In September 1898, they opened a 'large' purpose-built synagogue in Templar Street for 700, the seating shared equally between men and women. This synagogue replaced previous premises that Chief Rabbi Hermann Adler, who presided at the opening, judged to have been 'quite unsuitable for prayer ... approached by a steep flight of stairs ... ill ventilated and badly lighted [sic]'. We may assume that the replacement synagogue was better equipped, but the cost was beyond the means of the 'majority of their members [who] were poor'.[24] They were left with a debt of £300. Nothing is known of the appearance of this synagogue that went completely unrecorded before being swept away in the early slum clearances of 1907.

From 1908 the Mariempolers were based at 20A St Alban Street and, after being uprooted again in the next round of slum clearances, moved out of the Leylands westwards to Little London. The neighbourhood around Camp Road was then becoming a secondary area of Jewish settlement. From 1929 to 1958, the Mariempolers were to be found at the former Victoria Hall at no. 4 Victoria Place. The Hall was a roomy two-storey Victorian building well suited to use as a synagogue. It was rendered and had a gabled entrance built into the terrace, while the long walls extended back into Villiers Terrace behind. It is unclear whether the roundel and pair of tall rectangular windows flanking it on the rear wall were inserted to accommodate the Ark or had been original to the Hall.[25] The orientation was certainly correct: to the south east. After the Second World War, the *Mariempoler shul* moved out to Newton Park in Chapeltown and finally merged with Leeds Beth HaMedrash in Street Lane, Moortown in 1959.

Little documentation exists on the early buildings of Beth HaMedrash HaGadol Synagogue, which, today, is the only functioning congregation in Leeds that retains its historical name. This name literally means 'the great study hall' and is written in what can only be described as a Leeds 'vernacular' mixture of Yiddish and Hebrew pronunciation![26] The congregation can trace its origins back to 1874 in Templar Street. From there they moved to 20A St Alban Street (1877–86) and thence to Hope Street, at two different addresses

(1886–1895–1908).[27] Immediately following the slum clearances and road-widenings in the Leylands of 1906–7, a purpose-built synagogue was constructed in 1907–8, apparently on the corner of Lower Brunswick Street with Bridge Street. Murray Freedman published a grainy photograph of the plain brick building in the 1990s, source not stated.[28] The architect remains a mystery. It was opened on 22 March 1908 and closed less than thirty years later (1936) on the move of the congregation to Newton Park in Chapeltown. The Edwardian synagogue was sold to the Salvation Army; both homes went virtually unrecorded.

The *mikveh* in Victorian Leeds Jewry

A 'magnificent' *mikveh* was opened at the Cookridge Street[29] Bathhouse in the centre of Leeds in 1882. The bathhouse had been built in 1866–7 by the commercial Oriental & General Baths Company at a cost of £13,000. Judging from his colour-wash perspective,[30] Cuthbert Brodrick (1821–1905),[31] today best known as the architect of Leeds Town Hall, had intended to create a splendidly appropriate Orientalist edifice for Leeds city centre. He designed a symmetrical low-slung Ottoman-style pavilion of six bays with a domed roof. The building was to have a projecting tripartite centrally-placed entrance with flanking side bays, all crowned by small domes. The roofline was to be crenellated and the walls of alternative courses of red and white brick. This feature is called *ablaq* in Arabic and was typical of both Turkish and Egyptian mosques. The most arresting element, according to plan, was a tall and slender 'minaret' rising above the dome.

Visual evidence is sadly lacking to determine how much of Brodrick's original concept was lost in building. An archive photograph (from 1928)[32] post-dates the 1882 extensions and alterations. In it, the 'minaret' appeared stockier than in the original design drawing. Indeed, it looked more like a church spire. The small domes, intended for the entrance bay, had been replaced by triangular pediments. The roof crenellation was reduced to a sort of Lombardic cornice. The extension may have involved the addition of a second storey to the originally single-storey wings, but of this we cannot now be certain. Either way, in reality, the building ended up more heavy Romanesque Revival than light and exotically eastern.

It was when the bathhouse was extended that the 'Jewesses' baths' were added to the new Turkish bath suite that was set aside for the exclusive use of women. The *mikveh* was apparently added at the request of Belgrave Street Synagogue and the technical specifications were supplied by the Chief Rabbi.[33] Separate entrances to the baths for men and women were provided for all users. The Oriental & General Baths Company obviously anticipated making a profit from this new facility. However, at the turn of the twentieth century the Leeds Corporation took over control of Cookridge Street and it became a municipal bathhouse.[34]

In view of the growing number of Jews and the concentration of the Jewish population, the Corporation decided to construct a new *mikveh* in the heart of the Leylands. Leeds was by no means the first example of a 'Jewish bath' provided by the local authorities; precedents existed in Hull, Birmingham and Glasgow, dating, in the first case, as far back as 1850.[35] However, the new *mikveh* opened in Leeds in 1905 is the only known example of a 'Jewish bath' in Britain actually paid for by the municipality, but built in complete isolation from a public bathhouse or swimming pool, as was the practice in other towns. The site chosen was on the corner of Albert Grove and Leeds Terrace just over North Street in Little London.[36] The architect engaged was a little-known local man called Thomas Adamson.[37] He designed a typically Edwardian dwelling house of banded brickwork with the single-storey *mikveh* facility attached on the Albert Grove side (Figure 11.4). There were two entrances, one on either side. The plain doorway on Leeds Terrace was into the live-in caretaker's three-bedroom house, while the other entrance leading to the *mikveh* had an elaborate Baroque stone door-case and wrought-iron gate. The pediment over the large corner bay window bore a date stone that proudly declared the building's function: '1903/CITY OF/LEEDS/JEWISH/LADIES/BATHS' with the word '*mikveh*' carved in Hebrew lettering beneath.[38] The facility offered two immersion pools served by eight 'slipper' baths. As was the practice in Victorian times, the bathrooms were graded: two 'first class' and six 'second class'. The official programme for the opening described the interior layout of the bathhouse, the building materials and decor:

> The Slipper Baths are in white earthenware, glazed all round, and supplied with hot and cold water. The *Mikveh* Baths are constructed in glazed ware. The main walls round porch, vestibule, corridors and Slipper Baths are lined with cream-coloured glazed bricks, relieved by coloured bands, and the bathroom divisions with cream-coloured patent tiles. The floors are formed with best quality floor tiles.

The bathhouse was equipped with the very latest in heating and ventilation technology, and inside toilets, delicately referred to as 'sanitary offices', were provided for both classes of bather and for the caretaker's house.

The cost of construction was £2,400, but ratepayers were assured that it would result in no extra charge to them. The baths were open daily from 10 am to 10 pm, a first-class bath cost one shilling (1s) and a second-class bath half as much, sixpence (6d), while 'non-bathers' were charged thru'pence (3d, i.e. three 'old' [imperial] pennies). Before the First World War, Albert Grove became well patronised; annual attendances stood at nearly 9,500 in 1909–10, that is, around 780 per month. Evidently, the new *mikveh* was financially profitable.

A prime mover in the construction of the Albert Grove *mikveh* was Rabbi Israel Chayim Daiches (1850–1937), who was appointed *Rav* of Beth HaMedrash HaGadol Synagogue in 1901. 'Generally regarded as the leading Eastern European rabbi in the provinces', he became embroiled in a *halachic* [Jewish legal] controversy over the technicalities of *mikveh* plumbing, with Rabbi Tsvi Hirsch Hurwitz (c. 1864–1946), who arrived in Leeds (New Briggate Synagogue 1911) from Sunderland (1903) before the First World War. In 1912, Daiches published a *Teshuvah* [rabbinical responsum] entitled *Mikve Yisroel* in which he defended the use of a water meter in the pipework of a *mikveh*, which was, it seems, common in English *mikvaot* of the time. This ruling, potentially, could have permitted the construction of *mikvaot* connected to the ordinary water supply of the city, rather than being largely fed by natural sources (*mayanot* or springs, ice, rain or snow water or groundwater) as was the usual practice. Both of these *Rabbonim*[39] had been born and educated in Lithuania. Indeed, Daiches was the son of the *Rosh Yeshivah*, or head of the prestigious Talmudical seminary in Kovno. Nevertheless, Rav Hurwitz enlisted the heavyweight support of the renowned *halachic* authority, known as the *Ohr Sameah*, Rabbi Meir Simha HaCohen of Dvinsk, and Daiches' opinion was overruled. Henceforth, use of the water meter was forbidden in Britain and, apparently, a number of provincial *mikvaot* were put out of use as a result.

Jewish burial grounds in Victorian Leeds

Rabbi Daiches' brick chest tomb, now a bit neglected and broken down, can still be seen at the Hill Top Jewish Cemetery that overlooks one of the main roads into Leeds, from the south west (the A62). Hill Top was not the first burial ground opened by the Leeds Jewish community in the second half of the nineteenth century. The earliest, known as 'Gildersome', is to be found almost directly opposite, on the other side of today's busy Gelderd Road. The dating and development of this site has been hard to determine because of the loss of vital records, especially communal burial registers, from the earliest days. This is a problem encountered all too frequently in Jewish communities where burial grounds were, and still are, often privately owned – especially before the advent of public cemeteries in the mid-nineteenth century.

An extensive and unremarkable site, Gildersome has three distinct sections, each of which originally had its own separate entrance in the high brick boundary wall facing the road as well as its own *ohel*. The *ohel* in the oldest section (at the far west) has been demolished, but the original ornamental red-brick gateway – with an inscription (now illegible) on the gable – survives. Here, legible tombstones (they mostly face north and west) date from the 1850s; complete surviving records start from 1854. However, it has been claimed that this cemetery was opened as early as 1840, before the formal establishment of the Jewish congregation in 1846, which evolved into the Leeds Great Synagogue at Belgrave Street. Gildersome remains the most used Jewish cemetery serving Leeds Jewry. Enlarged in the 1940s, there is plenty of unoccupied green space. The site is currently shared by the two rival amalgamated congregations: Beth HaMedrash HaGadol (now Street Lane) and the United Hebrew Congregation (now Shadwell Lane), about which we shall have more to say presently.

By contrast with the flatness of Gildersome, Hill Top is an isolated, elevated site, but well worth the steep climb for the views across the city. It is also something of a nature haven, uncommon among Jewish cemeteries. Hill Top was purchased at the beginning of 1873 by what became known as the New Briggate congregation and has been shared by at least five now defunct Leeds synagogues. Remains of the red-brick boundary walls that originally separated the various sections of this rambling cemetery are still standing, and traces of two ruined *ohalim* [prayer halls] are still visible. Headstones face in all directions. The oldest extant memorials (the earliest that our survey[40] identified are dated 1882) are clustered closest to the *ohalim*. Records prior to 1917 are missing, apparently destroyed by fire. The land was of poor quality, being located next to clay and limestone quarries, and in an area riddled with mine shafts. In 2006–7, engineers had to be called in when some graves on the lowest slopes collapsed. The last burial took place in the early 1990s and today visitors must negotiate the steep footpath (wearing stout shoes) and enter the uneven burial ground at their own risk.[41]

The youngest of the Orthodox Jewish cemeteries in Leeds is New Farnley, Whitehall Road (A58, south side), in a similar direction from the city centre. Acquired in 1893 by the 'Polisher' congregation, the first burial did not take place until 30 June 1896. However, the long lintel inscription on the old red-brick *ohel* (1913) on Whitehall Road (written in a not quite literate mixture of Hebrew, Yiddish and English), states that the main section of the burial ground was opened in 1901 by the *Anshei Poalim d'po Leedz*, known in English as the Leeds Jewish Workers' Burial & Trading Society, that was formally constituted in 1899 to pay for funerals for its poor subscribers. According to Murray Freedman, the founding of the new burial society was occasioned by a stand-off with the 'established synagogues' which refused to bury a young immigrant tailor who had been too poor to join. Afterwards claiming to be the largest burial society in Anglo-Jewry, this *hevrah kadishah* developed alongside the Polish *minyan* in Templar Street, although there was intense rivalry between them. Freedman claimed that the synagogue paid for the erection of the stone boundary wall around the cemetery and then unsuccessfully sued the society for half of the money, claiming that they were benefiting from usage of it.[42] The Polishers afterwards moved to Lady Lane (1913–24) and then on to Wintoun Street (1923–55) until they was swallowed up in postwar amalgamations.[43] New Farnley boasts no fewer than four *ohalim*, material testament to the historical divisiveness of Leeds Jewry. The cemetery is still in use by both Etz Chaim (which holds most of the original records) and UHC, Shadwell Lane (see below).

Founded in 1944, since the early 1950s Leeds Reform community (see below) have buried their dead in a plot set aside for them in Harehills Cemetery, Kimberley Road, LS9. In doing so they have continued the Victorian practice of many small Jewish communities (mostly Orthodox) in provincial towns, of taking advantage of facilities available in their local public cemeteries.

Edwardian and interwar Jewish heritage in Leeds

Slum clearance in the Leylands began as early as 1906–7. We have seen how difficult it has been to recover some of the early synagogues that existed before then. The Mariempoler (Leeds Old Central) in Templar Street, Beth HaMedrash HaGadol in Brunswick/Bridge Street and the New Briggate in Merrion Street/St John's Place remain ghostly despite being not insubstantial purpose-built synagogues. The displaced congregations tended to remain in the vicinity until after the First World War.

It was in the 1920s that Jews moved out of the inner cities to the suburbs, up Chapeltown Road, which then became the preferred area of secondary settlement. After the Second World War, the relentless migration northwards continued, to Moortown and, ultimately, Alwoodley. In the interwar years, Chapeltown was where most of Leeds' synagogues were concentrated. The largest of them all was the Leeds New Synagogue built between 1929 and 1932. Reinvented as the Northern School of Contemporary Dance,[44] this former synagogue perhaps represents the last flowering of the Byzantine Revival as reinterpreted in the era of Art Deco.

'Byzantine' Revival for synagogue architecture was a variant form of Orientalism because it was associated with the architecture of the Eastern Mediterranean, both early Christian and Islamic Ottoman. It shared elements in common with West European Romanesque: thick walls, round arches and decorative features such as cushion capitals, and so could be thought of as a kind of Eastern Romanesque, deemed suitable for Jews as ambivalent Europeans. The central plan was introduced into British synagogue architecture in the mid-Victorian period by Davis & Emanuel, who utilised a square plan at West London Synagogue (Reform), Upper Berkeley Street in 1869–70, and later (1896) at the Spanish & Portuguese Synagogue, Lauderdale Road, Maida Vale, where it was covered by a copper dome. Comparatively rare in England, the Byzantine style was more popular on the Continent, especially in Germany, and in the USA before and after the First World War. The shape of the dome and of the overall plan could vary according to taste and budget; octagonal, hexagonal or a square 'Greek cross', the dome deep or shallow. Sometimes these buildings sported a 'minaret' or several, a variation on the paired Oriental turrets of the preceding era. Back in England, over the Pennines, the young architect and developer Joe Sunlight put both a dome and a minaret on the roof of his South Manchester Synagogue, Wilbraham Road, in 1912–13 (Grade II).[45]

J. Stanley Wright & Clay's huge Leeds New Synagogue was also built on a Greek cross plan, with a reinforced concrete dome and minaret.[46] Wright, who had served in British Mandatory Palestine, was inspired by Turkish mosques but with what one commentator has described as 'the [concrete] portico of a neo-Egyptian picture palace grafted on to its front'.[47] Perhaps he was also influenced by the work of the modernist architects which he saw while serving in Palestine. He may also have visited the Palestine Pavilion at the British Empire Exhibition held at Wembley in 1924–5.[48] From the start, his ambitious synagogue in Leeds suffered from structural problems. Not yet complete, it opened unofficially for the High Holy days in 1932, but by 1938 the dome was in danger of collapse.[49] With a diameter of 63 feet 6 inches and a radius of 59 feet, it was quickly shored up at vast expense (£3,000) by a coating of copper. The synagogue was opened by the Chief Rabbi on 18 September that year. The Leeds New Synagogue surpassed in size the Victorian 'cathedral' at Belgrave Street and was quickly dubbed the 'Great' Chapeltown Synagogue by locals. The project set the community back about £28,000, in the days when a modest new suburban semi in London cost a few hundred pounds.

A much more typical suburban synagogue in 1930s Leeds was the *Chassidishe shul* [Hasidic synagogue] built at 46–48 Spencer Place in 1932–5.[50] This congregation had been founded in 1897. Although Ashkenazi, they worshipped according to the distinctive *Nusach Ari* (or variant 'Sephardish' – but *not* Sephardi) liturgy used by some Hasidic sects. Their original home was on the first floor of an 'old' gas-lit building at the corner of Hope and Bridge Streets. Street widening in 1907 and the creation of New York Road precipitated demolition of these premises and the congregation migrated into Bridge Street. In 1924, they started a building fund with a view to moving out altogether. They purchased 'Spencer Hall' in Chapeltown for £700, but this building proved unsuitable for their needs. Eventually, they engaged architects Kirk & Tomlinson of 63 Albion Street to build them a new synagogue from scratch. Construction took three years during which time the *minyan* met at the Continental Temperance Hotel at 16–18 Brunswick Place, at the invitation of the proprietor, Sholom Addleman. Spencer Hall was replaced with a simple, steel-framed building of red brick with a pitched slate roof. On the front was a capacious rendered and painted projecting porch with artificial stone dressings. The new synagogue was opened on 22 July 1935.[51]

The plans are in the West Yorkshire Archives and, more recently, a series of eight good quality but undated photographs of the interior have been discovered.[52] The substantial vestibule contained staircases in both corners that led up to the ladies' gallery. This was carried on steel girders. Below, the seating in the men's section surrounded a large rectangular *bimah*. Although the Ark was on the east wall, so too was the front entrance on Spencer Place; this awkward orientation was dictated by the site which was restricted by the terrace into which the synagogue had to be inserted, albeit set slightly back.

Recent research has identified the makers of the modest fixtures and fittings inside the building. In common with several other traditional synagogues that dated from the early part of the twentieth century – in the East End of London, Wolverhampton and Glasgow – members of Leeds *Chassidishe shul* furnished their building with the work of their own hands; many of them were cabinet-makers and upholsterers. Of course, tailoring was dominant, but cabinet-making was also a typical calling among first- and second-generation Jewish immigrants.[53] Here, the Ark was made by Barnet Feddy, the pulpit (placed in the centre of the *duchan* or Ark platform) was made by Max Kowalsky, cabinet-maker of Crawford Street, and the pair of flanking box pews for the rabbi and president were made by the three Collins brothers of S. H. Collins & Co., joiners, of 6 Lower Brunswick Street. The fifty-seater pews were 'provided' by Nathan Solomon of Larchfield Mills and upholstered by Mr Pitt of Northern Veneers, Leather Street (although his was another business based in the old Jewish quarter, judging from his name, this gentleman was a Gentile). The hinges for the doors and book-rests etc. were supplied by I. & H. Goldberg. Wives of members made the textiles: the Ladies' Guild sewed four mantles for the *sifrei Torah* [Torah scrolls] and 'Mrs Jimmy Lewis' and 'Mrs Maurice Leyton' made the white cover for the reading desk.

The *Chassidishe shul* closed in the early 1980s; services according to *Nusach Sephard* continued to be held at the Talmud Torah, Sandhill Lane. The Spencer Place building was afterwards converted into the Central Jamia Masjid [mosque]. In 1998, when a new mosque was in the process of construction in front of the old synagogue, eight barely legible marble foundation stones on the front wall were still extant, the only real clue to the building's former identity (along with some fragments of coloured window glass).[54] All have since disappeared. The gallery had already been removed and a *mihrab* inserted into the former Ark wall. The shell still survives in the grounds of the Islamic campus, scarcely visible at street level[55] from behind the new mosque, as viewed from the main gate on Francis Street which is now inscribed 'Leeds Islamic Centre'.

Converted buildings

Little remains of other Jewish places of worship which once existed either in the Leylands or the Chapeltown area; the latter is now enjoying a mosque-building boom. The practice of organising makeshift synagogues in private houses and workshops, afterwards transferring to rented or purchased accommodation that had been built for another purpose, was particularly prevalent in Leeds where it took some time for a largely 'working-class' immigrant cohort to prosper.

According to local historian Louis Saipe,[56] the *Lokever shul* was the first congregation to move out of the Leylands to Chapeltown on the eve of the First World War (1913). Like the Mariempoler, which had been founded about a year earlier, this was a *landsmanshaft* of Jews from the same town in Lithuania. Called Lokeva, Lowkeva or Loikeva in Yiddish and Laukuvas in Lithuanian, this small town is situated in Kovno (Kaunas) Province, to the south of the capital Vilna (Vilnius). The Lokevers began life in Concord Street in 1888 or 1889[57] and were peripatetic, moving from there, in succession, to Lady Lane, Templar Street, Bridge Street, Hope Street and Regent Street (from 1902 to 1913). In Chapeltown, they settled on 58–60 Francis Street (on the corner with Hamilton Place), two Victorian terraced houses that they remodelled into a synagogue by inserting steel girders to create an upstairs gallery.[58] Although heavily rendered and over-painted, clues to this building's original identity could be seen on the Francis Street elevation, where the first-floor fenestration was typical of Victorian housing for the lower middle classes.

A report in the *Jewish Chronicle* in September 1922 referred to the opening by the Chief Rabbi of a 'Chapeltown Congregation' and 'Beth HaMedrash' but, unfortunately, was very short on facts.[59] No street name was supplied. This may have been Francis Street, officially named Chapeltown Hebrew Congregation. However, local historian Ernest Sterne claimed that they merely 'expanded its buildings', which suggested that they had been holding a *minyan* in one of the houses in Francis Street before 1922.[60] Either way, the Lokevers, popularly referred to as Francis Street Synagogue, henceforth stayed put for almost forty years, finally closing in February 1961. The building had an afterlife as the 'Phoenix', an Afro-Caribbean nightclub.[61]

Another peripatetic *minyan* in Leeds was the Polish Synagogue or *Polisher shul* (pronounced locally as *Paylishi*). The Polish Jews or Polaks were distinct from the Litvaks who formed the majority of immigrant congregations in Leeds. The *Polisher shul* was established in Byron Street in 1891 or 1893. The associated *Anshei Poalim d'po Leedz* or Leeds [Jewish] Workers' Burial Society, as we have already seen, founded its own cemetery in 1896 at New Farnley. This *hevrah kadishah* expanded its activities into the economic sphere and in 1899, as we have also mentioned, officially became known in English as the Leeds Jewish Workers' Burial and Trading Society.[62] In the twentieth century, the Polish Synagogue decamped to Wintoun Street (1923–4), where it was known as the Leeds New Central Synagogue, and a decade later (1933) to the synagogue at no.1 Louis Street, near[63] to the newly opened large Leeds/Chapeltown New Synagogue that they acquired from the New Leeds Congregation. It has been claimed that Louis Street was the last synagogue in Chapeltown to close its doors, in 1985.[64]

Nevertheless, this is yet another poorly documented Leeds synagogue. It is likely that it was Louis Street (New Leeds Congregation), rather than Francis Street (Chapeltown Hebrew Congregation), that was the 'Chapeltown Congregation' that the Chief Rabbi opened in September 1922.[65] We also know that it was the New Leeds Congregation that engaged Jewish architect Marcus Kenneth Glass (1887–1932)[66] to design or remodel (which, is unclear) their synagogue in Louis Street. Glass, himself a Jewish immigrant to Newcastle upon Tyne, designed a string of synagogues, mainly in the North East, between 1915 and 1932, when he died prematurely at the age of 45. He employed a distinctively cinematic Art Deco style. He also made his mark on converted buildings. It has not been possible to establish into which category Louis Street fell. Judging by his other surviving work, this could have been a distinctive looking building, but no visual sources have come to light.[67] Glass was also responsible for the conversion of a former church hall into the first Harrogate Synagogue in 1925.

A Victorian house (c.1860) at 21 Leopold Street, Chapeltown, was home to the small Spanish and Portuguese Jews' Congregation, also known as the 'Federation Synagogue' from 1924 to the late 1940s. The Sephardi community was always a tiny minority in Leeds Jewry, the vast majority being Ashkenazi, of Eastern European origin. Sephardim are first recorded in Leeds during the First World War (1915) in Bridge Street.[68] In 1952, they sold Leopold Street to the young Leeds Reform Synagogue that stayed there until graduating to their own purpose-built home in 1960 (see below). The house then became the very first mosque in Leeds (1961–74). In recognition of the diverse occupants of 21 Leopold Street, it was designated 'House of Faith' and marked with a Leeds Civic Trust blue plaque in 2012.

It is worth pointing out that Leopold Street was not the only makeshift venue to be used in succession by several Jewish groups, as we have seen. No. 20A St Alban Street in the Leylands was home in turn to Beth HaMedrash HaGadol (1877–86), Agudas HaZionim (1902–1907) and the Mariempoler, Leeds Old Central Synagogue (1908–29). In 1933, New Leeds Congregation sold its synagogue at no. 1 Louis Street in Chapeltown for £4,000 to the *Polisher shul* (Byron Street) that henceforth became known as the Louis Street Synagogue.

The *Chevra Tehillim*, or Psalms of David Synagogue, at 38–40 Reginald Terrace, Chapeltown, was another conversion with a complicated building history. According to foundation stones still in situ in 1998, Reginald Terrace Synagogue opened in September 1938. It seems that this congregation had been founded in Bridge Street in 1884, moved to Lady Lane in 1903, and thence to Albert Grove, near the communal *mikveh*. The new suburban synagogue was modelled out of the shell of the Potter Newton Sports Club. The building was extended in various directions. Major structural alterations were carried out; steel girders were inserted that rested on new concrete pad foundations, and were supported by brick piers on the outside of the building. These piers also served to disguise the steel framing. The red-brick appearance was maintained, the long wall facing the street. The slate roof was given a swept hip over the curved west end. Inside, the ceiling had a shallow dome and a roundel lit the Ark wall. The major intervention was the insertion of a concrete and raked gallery on steel supports with a timber front. Kirk and Tomlinson were architects of the conversion scheme. They submitted a series of plans to the city council between 1937 and 1938.[69] The *succah* [temporary booth open to the sky erected to celebrate the festival of *Succot*] at the back was added in 1954.[70]

However, by the mid 1950s, *Chevra Tehillim* was rapidly losing members and absorbed the *Hevrah Shas* ['Talmud Synagogue'] (1890). Reginald Terrace closed in April 1973 and the combined congregations eventually merged with *Etz Chaim* in Moortown in 1980 (see below). In the 1990s, the Reginald Terrace building was in use as a community centre, the main space having reverted to its original function as a sports hall. The whole building was demolished in 2003. In this case, the foundation stones, recorded by the Survey of the Jewish Built Heritage (SJBH), were rescued and taken to the successor synagogue in Harrogate Road.

Synagogue conversions persisted in Chapeltown after the Second World War. The descendant of the Herzl Moser Zionist Synagogue, also known as Agudas HaZionim, together with the headquarters of the local Zionist organisation, was based in a terraced house at 307 Chapeltown Road from 1948 to 1965. This terrace was then known as St Marys Terrace and afterwards (1960s) as Mulligan's Mansions. In the 1990s, the roomy house was subdivided into six flats.[71] The Zionist Synagogue had been founded in 1894; its first recorded home was at 20A St Alban Street in 1902 (as we have seen), then at 17 Brunswick Street from 1907. Beth HaMedrash HaGadol's home in Chapeltown (1936–7) was a converted home at 'Parkside', 21 Newton Park View (opposite Harehills Avenue).[72]

Unlike in other big cities in Britain and America, Leeds Jews did not often convert churches or chapels – usually non-conformist – into synagogues. Nevertheless, several examples have been uncovered. In 1923–4 the

Polisher shul (Leeds New Central Synagogue, see above) acquired a former Baptist chapel in Wintoun Street. In 1937, a new congregation, calling itself simply the Moortown Synagogue, moved into a disused Methodist chapel at 8 Shadwell Lane. The solidly built stone chapel dates from prior to 1910.[73] By 1958, this congregation was fast outgrowing these premises to the extent that the building of a new synagogue in Alwoodley was under discussion.[74] Moortown Synagogue eventually (1986) amalgamated with the newly built United Hebrew Congregation further up the street. The 'Old Chapel' survives, having been used as offices from 1987 and it is currently (2017) a Montessori children's nursery. In the early 1950s, the *Mariempoler shul* (Leeds Old Central Synagogue) occupied the original chapel – then schoolroom – in front of which was later built the splendid Gothic Revival Congregational Baptist Union Church, at 281A Chapeltown Road (west side) (Archibald Neill, 1887, Grade II). The church itself was recycled as a Sikh temple in 1963.[75]

In 1955, the *Polisher* (Leeds New Central) Synagogue combined with the Vilna Synagogue (founded before 1885 at St Luke's Terrace, 1 Exmouth Street, corner of Camp Road) to form the Leeds New Central Vilna Synagogue. Litvaks and Polaks were at last cooperating! No doubt this rapprochement was necessitated by declining numbers, but it also reflected the fact that the subtle cultural distinctions and rivalries brought over from Eastern Europe meant little to the English-born second generation. Rather than looking for a redundant church, in 1959 this amalgamated congregation purchased the former Kingsway Cinema, 245 Harrogate Road, thus earning it the nickname the 'cinemagogue'.[76] The old cinema (1937, architect: James Brodie), was itself a local landmark and capable of accommodating 1,150 people. It was enlarged into 'the largest synagogue in Leeds', to hold 2,000. With its tall attached polygonal tower over the corner entrance and decorative brickwork, this was a real 1930s building, quite 'Scandi' Art Deco. It was vacated in 1991[77] and sadly was destroyed in a fire in the late 1990s. A block of flats named Beechwood Court now stands on the site. The rump New Central Vilna congregation continued to exist for several years at 7A Stainburn Parade, LS17 before being merged into *Etz Chaim*.

Jewish community buildings in Leeds

Jews in Leeds built a lot in relation to the size of the community. Arguably, this reflected both the schismatic character of the community and a plethora of parvenu patrons determined to make their mark. The volume of building for communal, as opposed to synagogal, use was quite exceptional for a regional community, perhaps partly an expression of rapid secularisation.

As early as 1910, the only known purpose-built headquarters in the country for a Jewish trades union went up at 25 Cross Stamford Street in Sheepscar (LS7), just north of the city centre.[78] The Leeds Amalgamated Jewish Tailors', Machinists' and Pressers' Trades Union was founded in 1893, making it the first independent Jewish trades union in the country, ahead of similar organisations in the East End of London. Immigrant Jews were heavily involved in the *schmatter* ['rag'] trade both in London and in the North. They struggled to improve pay and conditions in the 'sweatshops', not a few of which were run by Jewish bosses. The best-known Jewish boss in Leeds was ready-to-wear pioneer Montague Burton (1885–1952)[79] who sought to improve the lot of his workers. None of his menswear clothing factories, opened between 1915 and 1922, exist today; the last one, not purpose-built, in Concord Street (north side) survived long enough to be photographed by SJBH in 1998.

The Leeds Jewish Tailors' Union was noted for its radicalism and became the largest Jewish trades union in the country. Architect J. J. Wood of Leeds provided a solid Edwardian red-brick building with stone and/or faience dressings, heavily over-painted in red and black, with a Welsh slate roof.[80] Within five years of the construction of their headquarters, the Leeds' Jewish Tailors were absorbed into the United Garment Workers Union (1915) which, five years after that, became the umbrella National Union of Tailors and Garment Workers (1920).[81] The union building, now subdivided into commercial units, is chiefly of interest for the inscription on the facade that proudly declared its original purpose, but the word 'Jewish' has been deliberately obliterated (Figure 11.5).

G. Alan Burnett's Leeds Jewish Institute and Jubilee Hall at 21 Savile Mount in Chapeltown was the first in a sequence of quite ambitious Jewish community centres in Leeds. Built between 1934 and 1936, the moniker 'JCC' had not yet arrived in Britain from America; conceptually, Leeds was ahead of its time. The Jewish Institute had been founded in 1896. Its first and only purpose-built home was a substantial three-storey building with tall modernist metal-framed 'oriel' windows and a basement floor. The front was built in yellow brick with red brick to the rear.[82] The Institute enjoyed its heyday during the Second World War; some 2,600 members enjoyed sports, debating and dances there. After the war, recreational facilities followed the Jews out to Moortown. The Institute closed down in 1973 and for a spell served as a (non-Jewish) trades union club. Eventually, the attractive building was converted (with help from the Lottery, regional and local funding) into the Leeds Media Centre by Bauman Lyons Architects who also designed the new extension in 2000–1.

Turning now to schools: the Brodetsky Jewish Primary School had its origins in the Leeds Hebrew School set up in 1888 on the initiative of the Great Synagogue in Belgrave Street. In the wake of the 1870 Education Act, this new

Jewish school was meant to provide a mixture of religious and secular education for both boys and girls. However, it never had a building of its own, but was dependent on premises and staffing largely provided by the local Gower Street Board School in the Leylands, that had a high percentage of Jewish children.[83] Named after the Zionist leader Selig Brodetsky (1888–1954), who was a professor of mathematics at the University of Leeds, the successor school was established in 1957[84] and in the following year moved into 'new modern premises' in Sandhill Lane 'recently erected by the Leeds Talmud Torah Education Board'.[85]

The Leeds Talmud Torah remained a separate educational institution but shared common origins with the Brodetsky School. It could trace its roots to a religious school attached to the precursor of the Leeds Great Synagogue at Back Rockingham Street in the Leylands. This school operated in the context of the traditional system of *hedarim* and *talmudei Torah* brought over from Eastern Europe, in which *Yiddishkeit* exclusively was taught to boys only. In 1945, the Talmud Torah moved from Trafalgar Terrace in Little London to 'temporary' premises[86] in Cowper Street in Chapeltown, near the Home for Aged Jews. In June 1950, 'new buildings' were opened on this site at no. 70 Cowper Street.[87] Nevertheless, soon after the end of the war, the Talmud Torah spawned a suburban 'branch' in Sandhill Lane (nos 2–2A), Moortown, where a new building to accommodate 450 children, including girls, was erected in 1957 (architect or builder unidentified). This was a plain two-storey structure containing classrooms on both floors.[88] The large hall on the ground floor had folding doors, a flexible space solution widely employed in synagogues built in the 1950s and 1960s.

In 1971, the Brodetsky School became state aided. In 1973, nine acres was reserved for the building of a Jewish campus from land sold by Moor Allerton Golf Club to Leeds City Council. In June 1981, the new premises were finally opened and at the time were claimed to be 'Britain's most extensive Jewish day school complex'.[89] They effectively contained three schools in one: the Deborah Taylor Nursery, the Brodetsky Primary School and the experimental Morris Silman Jewish Middle School (begun on the site in 1973), accommodating some 400 pupils in total. In 2013, an expanded campus was reopened on the Moor Allerton site that incorporated a nursery, a primary school and the first-ever Jewish secondary school in Leeds. The Leeds Jewish Free School, funded by a £3m government grant, attracted controversy because it opened with only eight Jewish pupils.[90]

The extra-curricular Judean Club never enjoyed purpose-built premises. It was founded in a room in Brunswick Street in the 1920s and from there moved to former cavalry stables in Barrack Road, Chapeltown. The cost of this conversion was borne by Montague Burton and the philanthropic society B'nai Brith. A quarter of a century later, the club moved again to Street

Lane, Moortown, but eventually folded. After twenty years in abeyance, in 1999 it was revived, rebranded as 'The Zone' Jewish Youth Club, based inside the premises of the Leeds Jewish Education Board (Talmud Torah) at no. 2 Sandhill Lane. In 2013, that building was sold and the Judeans decamped to the Brodetsky School, Wentworth Avenue, in Alwoodley.[91]

None of the Leeds Jewish welfare institutions ever enjoyed purpose-built premises. The Herzl-Moser Jewish Hospital opened in converted houses in Chapeltown in 1905. The Leeds Home for Aged Jews (and Home of Rest) originated as a ward in the Jewish Hospital in 1923 and in 1929 expanded into a large house at 62–4 Cowper Street.[92] This was the forerunner of today's Donisthorpe that derives its name from the original classical-style Donisthorpe Hall on the Donisthorpe Estate, in Shadwell Lane, Moortown. The Hall was acquired in 1956 and formed the kernel of the repeatedly extended residential home that was formally consecrated in June 1960.[93] Donisthorpe also absorbed the Leeds and District Jewish Convalescent Home that had operated from a house on the Knaresborough Road in Harrogate.

By contrast, the privately funded Marjorie & Arnold Ziff Community Centre was opened in a well-appointed specially designed new building[94] (West & Machell 2005) at 311 Stonegate Road, LS17. The Ziff Centre also contains a small synagogue. However, the 1960s Queenshill Estate, to be discussed presently, remains the nearest Leeds, indeed Britain, ever achieved to compare with a truly American-style Jewish Community Centre (JCC) campus.

Jewish architects in Leeds

The Reform synagogue was the first synagogue in Leeds designed by a Jewish architect: Sinai Synagogue, Roman Avenue, LS8 (H. A. Halpern & Associates, 1959–60). How this commission arose is obscure because Hilary Halpern (1928–2013) was a commercial architect who specialised in high-rises and supermarkets and was based down in Chatham, Kent.[95] The Leeds Reform community had been formed in January 1944, in the middle of the Second World War. They had a peripatetic existence until (as seen) finding a home at 21 Leopold Street, purchased from the Spanish and Portuguese for £700. The site in Roundhay, slightly to the east of the increasingly popular suburb of Moortown, was acquired in 1950 but building did not commence for nearly a decade. Leeds' only Reform synagogue stands apart from its polygonal Orthodox contemporaries (see below). Its chief interest lies in its angled rooflines and mixture of facing materials: concrete, whitewash, stone and a contrasting red-brick east wall punctuated by seven windows forming the pattern of a menorah. The interior is a simple panelled box with acoustic tiled ceiling, utilitarian by comparison with its Orthodox counterparts. The original building sat 450; after extension in 1984–5 this number almost tripled to 1,200 people.

The only Jewish architect of note produced by Leeds Jewry was Basil Gillinson (1925–2001). He was 'senior partner of one of the largest architectural practices in the north of England'.[96] Gillinson & [Clifford] Barnett[97] employed 130 people and specialised in leisure complexes, an innovative concept in the 1960s.[98] Although he was never commissioned to design any of the postwar synagogues in his native city of Leeds, where he trained and practised, Gillinson did design the successor Bradford Orthodox Synagogue at Spring Gardens (1970, closed 2013) and had a hand in the new purpose-built Harrogate Synagogue (1966–8), both small-scale projects. The square, squat exterior of Bradford was covered in yellow ceramic. The large expanses of wall and vertical strip windows gave it a defensive appearance. The minimalist interior had exposed breezeblock walls and a timber panelled ceiling. The white curtains decorated with black stripes flanking the Ark deliberately recalled a woollen *tallit* [prayer shawl]. Similar decor is to be found in Leeds at Street Lane (see below) and had before the war been used at Ernest Joseph's Birmingham Progressive Synagogue (1938, demolished 2006).[99] Gillinson was also responsible for the interior design of the small synagogue at Donisthorpe.[100] This has exposed yellow brick walls, a light timber roof with matching furnishings and red upholstery, on the lines of Bradford, but of warmer and higher quality materials.

Gillinson had a strong interest in social architecture. For the Leeds Jewish Housing Association he planned the Queenshill Estate (1957–62), a sheltered housing complex in Moortown that 'became a model for Jewish social housing throughout the country'.[101] The Queenshill Estate, so named in 1957,[102] grew out of a project of the Leeds Jewish Housing Association that had been gestating since the early 1950s, to be built on thirteen acres of land around Stonegate Road earmarked from the Donisthorpe Estate. The project was made possible through loans amounting to almost 100% made by the Local Authority. The builders were N. B. Bell of Leeds and London. In the first phase, seventy-eight dwelling houses were planned and the first dozen tenants moved in March 1959. By the time of the official opening by Housing Minister Sir Keith Joseph in 1962, the estate comprised 187 dwellings, 'flats, maisonettes, bungalows and semi-detached homes' for over 350 residents in an 'attractive ... garden suburb' setting.[103] The campus then boasted as its 'focal point' a 'community centre' containing offices, kitchen, a TV lounge and library and, above all, a communal hall cum synagogue (1961–2) for 300 people. This building was crowned by a distinctive 50-foot square hyperbolic paraboloid roof, described at the time as 'unique' in the Anglo-Jewish context.[104] It was a form that became popular for new synagogues in Israel in the 1960s.[105] The whole project cost in the region of £270,000.[106]

Religious architecture in Leeds since the 1960s

In the 1960s, centrally planned synagogue spaces, based on a hexagon formed from the *Magen David*, caught on – especially in Leeds. The earliest example in the UK of this innovative plan, imported from America where much creative experimentation was going on, is in Belfast. Belfast Hebrew Congregation was designed by Czech refugee Eugene Rosenberg of Yorke Rosenberg Mardall in 1961–4 (Grade II).[107]

In Leeds[108] the hexagonal plan took root within mainstream Orthodoxy, probably related to developments in Catholic worship. A series of synagogues on a hexagonal plan has been built in Leeds since the Second World War. The precedent was undoubtedly the Leeds New Synagogue in Chapeltown Road that, as we have seen, was a 1930s update of the Byzantine plan (Figure 11.6). G. Alan Burnett designed Beth HaMedrash HaGadol Synagogue, Street Lane in Moortown in 1969[109] – reputedly the largest synagogue outside London. This was his second Jewish commission; the first came well before the war, as will be recalled, for the Leeds Jewish Institute and Jubilee Hall, across the road from the Leeds New Synagogue. Right next door to the New Synagogue itself was Burnett's simplified Romanesque Holy Rosary Roman Catholic Church (1940).[110] At Street Lane, Burnett cleverly combined the hexagon with the shape of a timber *Magen David* formed in the lantern.[111] The *bimah* stands directly beneath the lantern.

This plan became the norm for Leeds' large Orthodox synagogues of the United Synagogue type: at Etz Chaim,[112] Harrogate Road (Owen, Diplock & Associates 1979–81) and Leeds United Hebrew Congregation, Shadwell Lane (Peter Langtry-Langton, of J. H. Langtry-Langton 1986–7).[113] In the latter building, winner of an RIBA open competition in 1982, the *Magen David* theme is taken up, here in a dome above a yellow-tinted clerestory. Burnett was a Catholic while the Bradford-based Langtry-Langtons specialised in Catholic churches, a fact that may well explain their enthusiasm for centrally planned places of worship, much favoured following the Second Vatican Council of 1962.[114] J. H. Langtry-Langton's RC Our Lady and the First Martyrs Church, known as the 'Round Church', at Heaton, Bradford (1935), was claimed to be 'The first church in England designed with a central altar ... preced[ing] Vatican II, by twenty-seven years'.[115] The octagonal space with high ceiling lantern is strongly echoed at Shadwell Lane Synagogue (Figure 11.7). However, neither in Leeds, nor elsewhere in Britain, was the hexagon combined with an 'auditorium' seating plan, as became popular in American synagogues in this period.

Apart from the *Magen David* plan, little overt Jewish symbolism is to be found externally at the contemporary synagogues in Leeds. In the aftermath of the Festival of Britain (1951), public buildings tended to look alike – neutral rectilinear forms; this included places of worship. This increasing convergence was a legacy of prewar Internationalism. On the facade of a synagogue an architect might apply a discreet Star of David, *luhot* [tablets of the law] or a burning bush, perhaps accompanied by a Hebrew inscription rendered in an up-to-date square font. In Leeds, we have already noted the use of an abstract *menorah* at Sinai Reform. *Etz chaim* means 'tree of life' and this traditional Hebrew name was given to the new synagogue on the Harrogate Road. The name was not one inherited from any of the numerous Leeds congregations that were absorbed into it. Rather, it probably derived from the name of the semi-rural site on which the synagogue was built: Fir Tree Wood. A *Tu B'Shvat* [New Year for Trees] planting ceremony accompanied the laying of the foundation stone.[116] By and large, postwar Leeds demonstrates the fact that the days when the architectural style of the synagogue itself had to make a statement of difference were over.

At the Etz Chaim Synagogue, 'Pearl's' *mikveh* was added in the grounds as an afterthought in 1994.[117] None of the large Leeds synagogues erected between the 1960s and 1980s incorporated a *mikveh* into their building plans. The Edwardian Albert Grove *mikveh* remained open until the late 1960s. After the First World War, the Leeds Board of Shechita (responsible for kosher meat) took on financial responsibility for the *mikveh* from the Corporation and operated it at a loss. By 1935, attendances had dropped to 110 per month (women were charged five shillings a dip) and to forty by 1957. Oral testimony collected from Jewish women in the city in the 1960s, and written testimony in the 1990s from the '*mikveh* lady' attendant (Frieda Schiller, née Peretz), confirm that the practice of *mikveh* was being abandoned by the English-born children of Jewish immigrants in Leeds.[118] Added to the general decline in religious observance among the second generation was the fact that Albert Grove 'was in a rather bad state of repair and situated in a district which was not too salubrious so that many women preferred to go to Manchester *mikvaot* rather than use it'.[119] The *mikveh* was vandalised and rendered unfit for use and finally closed its doors on 5 January 1968 – and was swept away in the new round of slum clearance of the late 1960s. The replacement plan of a new municipal bathhouse that including an Olympic-sized swimming pool was never completed because of technical objections on *halachic* grounds (c. 1984).[120]

In any case, in 1967–8 a strictly Orthodox community opened a new *mikveh* of their own in an extension at the rear of the Shomrei Hadass Synagogue (c. 1961–2)[121] that was located in a converted house near Moortown Corner, at 368 Harrogate Road. The Board of Shechita elected to contribute towards the upkeep of the Moortown *mikveh*, which was by then far more conveniently situated for the suburban homes of the majority of Leeds Jews than was Little London. By the 1990s, the opening of a new women's *mikveh* at Etz

Chaim signalled a return to tradition among third-generation Anglo-Jews, a trend that did not leave Leeds unaffected – albeit on a very limited scale. The strictly Orthodox coalesced around the Shomrei Hadass and the outreach Hasidic organisation Chabad-Lubavitch that arrived in Moortown in 1975 and purchased what became the Leeds Lubavitch Centre at 168 Shadwell Lane in 1986.[122]

The future for Leeds Jewish heritage?

As has been remarked upon several times during the course of this chapter, Leeds was noted for the fractiousness of its working-class Jewish congregations, which spawned a multiplicity of little *shuls*, many of them in converted premises. Splits and mergers were rife. It has been quite a challenge to unravel this complicated congregational history, give the plethora of synagogues with similar, and a variety of, alternative names, in English, Hebrew or Yiddish. Moreover, for its size, Leeds Jewry has built a great deal and now owns too many big synagogues and other ambitious community buildings that represent serious over-capacity for its dwindling needs. The Jewish population has more than halved since 1945, today numbering about 6,850 (2011 Census), putting it a long way behind Manchester, Britain's 'second Jewish city'.[123]

Leeds' nineteenth-century Jewish heritage began to disappear almost as soon as it was created, with slum clearances in the city centre and the Leylands beginning as early as 1907. Further redevelopment, particularly of the street pattern and road networks, took place at the end of the 1920s. The Leylands almost disappeared in the wholesale redevelopment in Leeds, a fate that befell many other inner-city neighbourhoods in the 1960s, 1970s and 1980s; Glasgow's Gorbals is perhaps the closest parallel.[124] However, in Glasgow, thanks to the existence of the Scottish Jewish Archives Centre (established in 1984), the buildings of the old Jewish quarter are on the whole better documented. In Leeds, there are gaping holes in the historical record. Even some vital records, including burial registers, have disappeared. Recovery of the history – let alone reconstruction of the visual appearance – of most of Leeds' lost synagogues is now no longer possible.

Leeds Jewry has not been noted for its *frumkeit* [religious piety]. By and large formed of working-class immigrants, the process of secularisation was rapid, taking place within a generation – faster perhaps than in much larger communities, especially the East End of London. The Yiddish language and religious observance were abandoned as relics of an unhappy and impoverished past, a process hastened further by the social dislocation brought about by the Second World War. This loosening of traditional ties was mirrored in spatial terms – as in so many other cities in Britain and America – in the rush to the outer suburbs in the 1950s and 1960s.

As early as 1959, at the opening of the 'cinemagogue' in Harrogate Road, Chief Rabbi Israel Brodie 'wondered what the synagogue was going to be like in 25 years' time'. In an unusually candid speech, he complained that 'At the synagogue he attended the previous day [*Shabbat*, the Jewish Sabbath, Saturday morning] ... where a barmitzvah was being celebrated, it was infuriating to see the people arriving in cars and bareheaded ... and they could not even read the prayer book'.[125]

The majority of the third generation who grew up in the more affluent suburbs were disconnected from their 'small town' roots. They often left Leeds altogether for greater opportunities in higher education and the job market. The intense focus of their parents on upward social mobility left little time or inclination to document the past. At least the postwar synagogues of Moortown have now been recorded for posterity, whatever the future for Leeds Jewry may bring.

A note on sources and acknowledgements

This chapter is in part based on material published in the two editions of my architectural guidebook *Jewish Heritage in Britain and Ireland* (English Heritage/Historic England, 2006 and 2015) and my monograph *The Synagogues of Britain and Ireland* (Yale University Press, 2011). My research on the *mikvaot* dates back to the early 1990s, originally published in *Building Jerusalem: Jewish Architecture in Britain* (Vallentine Mitchell, 1996) edited by me.

I am indebted to the work of the late Murray Freedman who tracked the complex congregational history of Leeds Jewry. I have taken this opportunity to update and augment my previous work by the inclusion of recent literature and especially online resources that have developed or appeared since 2011, in particular JewishGen's JCR-UK and *Leodis*. Happily, Murray Freedman contributed factual corrections to documentation on *Leodis* of lost buildings in the Leylands. The genealogists have assisted in ironing out some of the confusion presented by the plethora of Leeds' synagogues, although JCR-UK still contains some inaccuracies. Thanks are due to John Minnis of the *Pevsner Architectural Guides* and to English Heritage photographer Keith Buck for their collaboration back in 2006 on documenting the post-Second World War synagogues of Leeds. Most recently, Rabbi Shlomo Katanka and editor Professor Derek Fraser kindly filled in the history of the Brodetsky School and the Leeds Talmud Torah. I am especially grateful to Antony Ramm of Leeds Central Library (Local and Family History) for his guidance and for supplying me with copies of relevant maps during 2017.

11.1 Belgrave Street Synagogue, undated

11.2 Belgrave Street Synagogue, the Ark, undated

11.3 The ark in the synagogue at Leeds UHC

11.4 Albert Grove *mikveh*. Photograph on the front cover of *City of Leeds, Jewish Baths, Opening by the Right Hon. The Lord Mayor, Wednesday 25th October, 1905*

11.5 Leeds Jewish Tailors' Building, inscription

11.6 The former Leeds New Synagogue, Chapeltown Road

11.7 Leeds United Hebrew Congregation, Shadwell Lane, the ceiling

Notes

1 However, private residences and business premises remain largely beyond the scope of this examination.
2 On www.leodis.net *Leodis: A Photographic Archive of Leeds* (cited henceforth as *Leodis*), entries for Leeds Great Synagogue, although there the building history fails to note the 1870s rebuild by a different architect.
3 *Jewish Chronicle*, 23 August 1861; for a brief report of the foundation stone-laying, see *Jewish Chronicle*, 29 June 1860.
4 *Jewish Chronicle*, 9 March 1877, re foundation; *Jewish Chronicle*, 27 March 1878 makes only a passing editorial reference on p. 11 to the fact that 'In Leeds the new Synagogue has just been consecrated by the [Chief Rabbi] Rev. Dr. H[ermann] Adler'. No report appeared.
5 W. H. Scott and W. T. Pike, *The West Riding at the Opening of the 20th Century*, Pike's New Century Series (London: 1902), p. 373; *RIBA Journal*, 19 September 1925, p. 619.
6 Black and white photographs in Manchester Jewish Museum, MJM 2491/10–16. Since originally viewed in the 1990s, some colour transparencies have disappeared from the collection; two photographs dated 1906 in E. De Haas, 'Men and Women of Mark', newspaper cuttings album 1892–1911 [De Haas *Album*] in the Jewish Museum London, JM catalogue no. C 1997.1, p. 239.
7 Although we have no documentary evidence of any link between the architects, it is likely that they were aware of one anothers' work, especially on so unusual a commission for Christian architects in a provincial town as a synagogue. Bradford's small Orientalist synagogue is far more interesting and architecturally important (Grade II* listed) than any of the heritage of Leeds Jewry and is still functioning. Despite its proximity, Bradford is beyond the scope of this book.
8 According to the Ordnance Survey [OS] map, Yorkshire (West Riding), Leeds, Sheet 218.2.17 (1891). The large scale 1891 first edition, on a scale of 10 feet to 1 mile, is the best contemporary source for mapping Leeds synagogues in the Victorian and Edwardian periods.
9 The western entrance shared a party wall with the existing two-storey caretaker's house (no. 15) next door, see images and comments posted on *Leodis*.
10 Refugees also came from Austrian Galicia and Roumania.
11 Map drawn by George E. Arkell, who had worked as a cartographer on Charles Booth's massive *Inquiry into Life and Labour in London* (1886–1903), for C. S. Russell and H.S. Lewis, *The Jew in London* (London: T. Fisher Unwin, 1901).
12 Ironically, this operation was carried out by a Leeds-born Jewish demolition expert, Richard Vann of RVA Consulting Engineers Ltd., Ipswich, see *Jewish Chronicle*, 12 November 2004. The stained glass was rescued and installed in the Leeds United Hebrew Congregation, 151 Shadwell Lane, LS17, where Mr Vann was a member. The architect Peter Langtry-Langton incorporated a great many segmental-headed window openings into his design (1983–7) to accommodate the glass from Belgrave Street, see below.

13 M. Freedman, *Leeds Jewry: A History of its Synagogues* (Leeds: privately printed, 1995), p. 18.
14 Now numbered no. 23 New Briggate, St John was rescued from redundancy by the Churches Conservation Trust, see www.visitchurches.org.uk/ (accessed 21 October 2018).
15 See the entry on W. H. Thorp in Christopher Webster (ed.), *Building a Great Victorian City: Leeds Architects and Architecture 1790-1914* (Leeds: Northern Heritage Publications for the West Yorkshire Group of The Victorian Society, 2011), pp. 399–402.
16 Alison Felstead, Jonathan Franklin, Leslie Pinfield, *Directory of British Architects 1834–1900* (London: Royal Institute of British Architects, 1993) [*DBA 1834–1900*]; Royal Institute of British Architects, British Architectural Library Biography File, Nomination Papers, [BAL Biog. File, RIBA Nom. Paps]; *Who's Who in Architecture 1914, 1916*; *The Builder*, 4 February 1944, p. 98; *Yorkshire Post*, 6 January 1944; Derek Linstrum, *West Yorkshire Architects and Architecture* (London: Lund Humphries, 1978), p. 385; Peter Leach and Nikolaus Pevsner, *Yorkshire West Riding: Leeds, Bradford and the North*, with contributions by John Minnis et al. (New Haven and London: Yale University Press, 2009).
17 *The Builder*, 4 February 1944, p. 98.
18 *Building News*, 17 January 1890, p. 93.
19 *Jewish Chronicle*, 3 January 1890.
20 *Jewish Chronicle*, 10 August 1894. The footprint of the synagogue is shown on OS Leeds (1891), 218.2.17, surveyed in 1889.
21 *Jewish Chronicle*, 21 September 1894.
22 On *Leodis*. The view is towards the entrance on the St John's Place/New Briggate side (at south). Another image, viewed from Merrion Street (at north), is only partial and both are dated 18 February 1929.
23 Comment by Arnold Zermansky on *Leodis* 28 July 2012. His parents were married at New Briggate Synagogue on 28 August 1930.
24 On 4 September 1898, see *Jewish Chronicle* announcement on 26 August and report on 9 September 1898 on which this paragraph is based. Labelled 'Central Synagogue', the rectangular building is located at the extreme east end of Templar Street (southside), near the junction with Quarry Hill, on the OS, Leeds, Sheet 218.2 (1908), 25 inches to 1 mile map.
25 See the three images on *Leodis* and a comment by the late Murray Freedman, undated.
26 Correctly speaking, it should be Beit HaMidrash HaGadol according to modern Israeli (Sephardi) Hebrew pronunciation or, alternatively, Beis HaMedrash HaGodol in the Ashkenazi Hebrew of Jews from Yiddish-speaking backgrounds.
27 A rectangular 'Synagogue (seats for 450)' is clearly identified towards the west end of Hope Street (southside) on the OS Leeds (1901), 218.2.17.
28 M. Freedman, *Leeds Jewry: A History of its Synagogues*, p. 27; *Jewish Chronicle*, 27 March 1908. There is some confusion about the precise location of Beth HaMedrash HaGadol which is not marked on the OS Leeds (1908). *Leodis* contains three photographs, all headed 'Lower Brunswick Street' and dated 9 June

1906, claimed to be of the existing dwelling houses on site being surveyed prior to their demolition. In one, Gower Street School is visible immediately behind 'the junction with Bridge Street' (i.e. to the south). This location does not square with a fourth image titled 'Back Nile Street Synagogue', dated 2 April 1908, identified as showing Beth HaMedrash HaGadol in a comment beneath made by Murray Freedman. Presumably, he was referring to the building just visible beyond the clothing factory in the foreground 'on Brunswick Row'. The gabled two-storey building, of brick with stone bands and a Venetian style window on the first floor, could well be the Edwardian synagogue.

29 S. Kadish, 'Eden in Albion: A History of the *Mikveh* in Britain', in Sharman Kadish (ed.), *Building Jerusalem: Jewish Architecture in Britain* (London: Vallentine Mitchell, 1996), pp. 101–54; on Leeds, pp. 120–3 and references cited there.
30 On *Leodis*; the original drawing is in the care of Leeds Libraries. It was reproduced in black and white in *Taking the Plunge: The Architecture of Bathing* (London: SAVE Britain's Heritage, 1982). This was a brief catalogue to accompany an exhibition at the RIBA which was the first attempt to document public bathhouses in Britain.
31 See 'Cuthbert Brodrick' in Webster (ed.) *Building a Great Victorian City*, pp. 181–96.
32 On *Leodis*.
33 See Kadish, 'Eden in Albion', p. 120, based on research carried out for me by Murray Freedman. Prior to the 1882 rebuilding, men and women had had different bathing hours, see generally Malcolm Shifrin, 'The Victorian Turkish bath and women's health', on his website www.victorianturkishbath.org/ (accessed 21 October 2018). See also Malcolm Shifrin, *Victorian Turkish Baths* (Swindon: Historic England, 2015).
34 It was closed in 1965 and subsequently demolished. The site of the baths was on the westside of Cookridge Street roughly where the road bends to the north east, just north of the redeveloped Millennium Square (2000).
35 See Kadish, 'Eden in Albion', pp. 119–20.
36 The site, at north, is visible on OS Leeds (1908) but is not identified on any maps of the period.
37 Named in the official programme *City of Leeds, Jewish Baths, Opening by the Right Hon. The Lord Mayor, Wednesday 25th October, 1905*, Leeds Central Library; research by Murray Freedman on my behalf.
38 The best-known photograph of the exterior is on the cover of *City of Leeds, Jewish Baths* (1905), first repro. in Kadish, 'Eden in Albion', p. 120; three images on *Leodis*. No images of the interior have been found.
39 See relevant obituaries in the *Jewish Chronicle* and entries in William D. and Hilary Rubinstein and Michael Jolles (eds), *The Palgrave Dictionary of Anglo-Jewish History* (London: Palgrave MacMillan, 2011).
40 Survey of the Jewish Built Heritage in the UK and Ireland (SJBH), mainly carried out between 1998 and 2001.
41 Leeds Beth HaMedrash HaGadol Synagogue (Street Lane) administers Hill Top and declared it officially closed in 2008. A prominent 'No Trespass' warning

notice has been placed at the roadside entrance: tel 0113 269 2181 www.bhhs.co.uk/ (accessed 21 October 2018). A database of burials, including a photographic survey, is available online at www.jewishgen.org/jcr-uk/ (accessed 21 October 2018).

42 M. Freeman, 'History of the Congregation' on Etz Chaim Synagogue website: www.etzchaim.co.uk (accessed 24 March 2017). His account of the rivalry to acquire land at New Farnley does not quite square with the dating of the early development of this site between 1896 and 1899; see also *Jewish Chronicle*, 6 January 1893, 17 May 1901.

43 In 1955, the *Polisher Shul* was absorbed into the New Central Vilna Synagogue, itself now part of Etz Chaim (see below). Behind the car park, at the south east, lies the cemetery (1935) of the Psalms of David Synagogue, which also amalgamated with the New Central Vilna (see below). See database at www.jewishgen.org/jcr-uk/ (accessed 21 October 2018).

44 The Art Deco doors to the Ark, marble grille work from the *bimah* and stained glass by David Hillman were all reused at UHC, Shadwell Lane, see below.

45 See the discussion in S. Kadish, *The Synagogues of Britain and Ireland: An Architectural and Social History* (New Haven and London: Yale University Press, 2011), ch. 13 'The Byzantine Revival'.

46 West Yorkshire Archives, LC/Eng BCP, Plan no 4, 24 July 1928, plus engineering drawings and calculations by K. Holst & Co. of Leeds and London; Susan Wrathmell, *Leeds: Pevsner Architectural Guides* (New Haven and London: Yale University Press, 2005), pp. 232–3; John Minnis with Trevor Mitchell, *Religion and Place in Leeds* (Swindon: English Heritage, 2007), pp. 21 and 77.

47 'Refurbishment: Dance School Leeds. Dancing Partners', *Building*, 27 February 1998, pp. 57–60.

48 See R. Fuchs and G. Herbert, 'Representing Mandatory Palestine: Austin St. Barbe Harrison and the representational buildings of the British Mandate in Palestine, 1922–37', *Architectural History*, 43 (2000), 281–333, photo: p. 308. For more on possible Palestinian influences on British synagogue architecture, see Kadish, *Synagogues of Britain and Ireland*, pp. 188–9.

49 *Jewish Chronicle*, 11 February, 16 September 1938.

50 West Yorkshire Archives, Building Plan no. 44, approved 27 February 1934. See copy sketches by Barbara Bowman in SJBH Archives at Historic England Archives in Swindon.

51 The Hebrew date 21 Tammuz 5695 was still visible on the corner stones in 1998.

52 On *Leodis* where the makers of the furnishings are identified, no sources cited.

53 See Kadish, *Synagogues in Britain and Ireland*. The excellent example of Leeds Chassidishe Synagogue only came to light during further research for this chapter in March 2017.

54 The lettering on the tablets showed signs of having been deliberately erased.

55 See Google Satellite for a good view.

56 Louis Saipe, *A History of the Jews of Leeds* (Leeds: Leeds Jewish Representative Council, 1956, 2nd edn, 1985).

57 A *pinkus* [congregational record book] dated 5649 [=1888–9] in 1995 was in the possession of Ella Freeman, granddaughter of Barnett Cohen, a founder member of the Lokever Synagogue; see M. Freedman, *Leeds Synagogues* (Leeds, privately published, 1995) n.p., note 101.
58 This is confirmed by West Yorkshire Archives, Building Plans, no. 56, unsigned, approved 9 May 1922; Plan 148, rejected 11 May 1937; Plan 27, rejected 25 May 1937; Plan 37, approved 2 January 1940 (the latter three pertaining to the 'Waiting room to synagogue'). These plans clearly show that this was a conversion of two terraced houses on Francis Street and Hamilton Place on behalf of 'Messrs B. Cohen, L. Simon, B. Young, L. Lurie, E. Simon, L. Cohen'. These plans were amendments to those previously approved on 3 January 1922, not seen. On 2 January 1940, at the third attempt, the Council approved a single-storey extension along the Hamilton Place boundary. This was to contain two waiting rooms. The architect was W. H. S Freeman AIAA of 11a Oxford Row, Leeds. Architect Barbara Bowman, who researched the building history for SJBH, guessed that a third terraced house was probably added on later, but it is unclear whether this was during the lifetime of the synagogue or subsequent to it. See also her copy sketches in SJBH Archive.
59 *Jewish Chronicle*, 8 September 1922.
60 E. C. Sterne, *Leeds Jewry 1919–1929* (Leeds: Jewish Historical Society of England, 1989).
61 The nightclub was still operating at time of SJBH in 1998; the building was derelict by a return visit in 2012. According to Google Streetview (accessed 23 March 2017) the corner site has been demolished.
62 In 1959 it was referred to as the 'Leeds Jewish Workers' Cooperative'.
63 No.1 Louis Street is not identified as a synagogue on interwar maps. I conjecture that it was located in a house conversion on the corner with Cross Louis Street, directly behind the Chapeltown Great.
64 *Leodis* gives the exact date of 29 September 1985. Murray Freedman added a comment that 'In the council school that served the district, Cowper Street, there were no Jewish children after 1966'.
65 *Jewish Chronicle*, 8 September 1922.
66 S. Kadish, 'Clapton Federation Synagogue' in Lisa Rigg (ed.), *Hackney: Modern, Restored, Forgotten, Ignored; 40 Buildings to mark 40 Years of the Hackney Society* (London: Hackney Society, 2009, 2nd edn, 2013), pp. 93–5; Kadish, *Synagogues in Britain and Ireland*, pp. 184–7; Kadish, *Jewish Heritage in Britain and Ireland*, 2nd edn. 2015, pp. 220–3. Acknowledgements to the architect's daughter Denise Williams and to architect Hedy Parry-Davies who, back in 1998, first drew my attention to this talented but unrecognised architect.
67 Freedman, *Leeds Synagogues*, p. 18 and n. 72.
68 According to the Jewish Communities and Records in the UK section of www.jewishgen.org based on the *Jewish Year Book*.
69 Plans: West Yorkshire Archives, Building Plans in Vol. 27 (1937) and Vol. 28 (1938), 'Reginald Terrace – Psalms of David Synagogue: Reginald Terrace'. Plan no. 115, rejected 8 June 1937 [Untraced] Alteration of Club Premises into

Synagogue. Plan no. 96, approved 22 June 1937 Alteration of Club Premises into Synagogue. Plan no. 79, approved 11 January 1938 Synagogue. Plan no. 104, approved 21 June 1938 (Amended version of Plan No 79). Plan no. 155, approved 16 August 1938 (Amended version of Plan No 79 with changes to WC layouts). See copy sketches by Barbara Bowman in SJBH Archives.

70 Opened 17 August 1954 according to a marble plaque on the outside wall: see also *Jewish Chronicle*, 16 and 23 June 1933, 23 September 1938.
71 Source: *Leodis*.
72 Source: *Leodis*.
73 Online resources: *Leodis*, Wikipedia Commons, Leeds City Council Planning Applications.
74 *Jewish Chronicle*, 12 December 1958, justified the new project 'to relieve pressure on the Moortown Synagogue in Shadwell Lane'. A decade passed until BHH, Street Lane was opened (see below).
75 Online resources: *Leodis*, Historic England, Register of Listed Buildings.
76 Freedman, *Leeds Synagogues*, pp. 41–3. Leeds (Etz Chaim) and Newcastle's Gosforth Synagogue both turned to the Rank cinema chain to provide comfortable tip-up seating for their congregations. Conversation on 28 November 2008 with architect Joe Gellert of Waring & Netts who designed Gosforth Synagogue (1985–6).
77 The cinema had opened on 28 June 1937 at a cost of £35,000 and closed in August 1958. The synagogue opened on 6 September 1959 and closed in October 1991, source: *Leodis*. See also *Jewish Chronicle*, 11 September 1959.
78 Now part of the A61 (Roseville Road) going north past the roundabout at the junction with Sheepscar Street South.
79 E. M. Sigsworth, *Montague Burton: The Tailor of Taste* (Manchester: Manchester University Press, 1990); Bernard Silver, *Three Jewish Giants of Leeds: Selig Brodetsky, Montague Burton and Jacob Kramer* (Leeds: Jewish Historical Society of England, 2000).
80 West Yorkshire Archives, Building Plans: Plan no. 14, approved 28 July 1909, 'Proposed Club Premises'.
81 J. Buckman, *Immigrants and the Class Struggle: The Jewish Immigrant in Leeds 1880–1914* (Manchester: Manchester University Press, 1983); A. Kershen, *Uniting the Tailors* (London: Vallentine Mitchell, 1997).
82 West Yorkshire Archives, Plan nos 102 and 105; *Jewish Chronicle* (1 November 1935, 11 December 1936); *RIBA Journal* (August 2001); M. Freedman, *Chapeltown and its Jews* (Leeds: privately printed, 2003); Wrathmell, *Leeds*, pp. 232–3.
83 A. S. Diamond, 'A History of Leeds Jewry in the 19th Century', in Aubrey Newman (ed.), *Provincial Jewry in Victorian Britain* (London: Jewish Historical Society of England, 1973), typescript, n.p.; D. Saunders and P. Lester, *From the Leylands to Leeds 17* (Leeds, privately printed, 2014), see www.leylandsls17.co.uk/ (accessed 21 October 2018).
84 *Jewish Chronicle*, 26 April 1957, p. 18, a passing reference in a report about Leeds Zionist Council. See n. 106 re postwar plan searches.

85 *Jewish Chronicle*, 11 July 1958. The Leeds Jewish Nursery School had already been set up at the same Sandhill Lane premises: *Jewish Chronicle*, 20 September 1957.
86 *Jewish Chronicle*, 20 April 1945.
87 *Jewish Chronicle*, 30 June 1950.
88 According to Rabbi Shlomo Katanka, email 31 March 2017. I am grateful to him for drawing attention to the Leeds Talmud Torah.
89 *Jewish Chronicle*, 26 June 1981; reminiscences by Rabbi Shlomo Katanka (by email 27, 28 March 2017) and Professor Derek Fraser who supplied the date of 1973 for the land sale; the *Jewish Chronicle*'s version was the 'mid 1960s'.
90 *Yorkshire Post*, 29 September 2014.
91 The Sandhill Lane building, its appearance hardly recorded, was converted recently and flats were being built on the site in 2017. See also www.1zone.org.uk (accessed 24 March 2017).
92 The Cowper Street premises were bought by Leeds Corporation and continued in use as the renamed Pearce House. See *Jewish Chronicle*, 3 April 1959, the day of the reopening by the Lord Mayor.
93 *Jewish Chronicle*, 27 April 1956, p. 31 carried an advertisement for a Housekeeper 'for the new Home at Donisthorpe Hall, Moortown'. www.DonisthorpeHall.org (accessed 20 March 2017) provides some history of this institution; clothing retailers Todd and Dick Goldberg (trading as 'Todd Richards') set up a charity that acquired the hall and seven acres of land from the Donisthorpe Estate. The deal was made possible through the good offices of the building company, Shutes, that initially purchased the estate and built housing on the rest of the site. In the 1950s, 13 acres of land were made over to the Leeds Jewish Housing Association for the Queenshill Estate (see below).
94 *Jewish Chronicle*, 24 June 2005. 'JW3' in London's Finchley Road does not contain any prayer space. Designed by Jewish practice Lifschutz Davidson Sandilands, the 'neutrality' of this so-called 'JCC' attracted criticism in the professional press, see review by Robert Bevan, *Building News*, 25 September 2013 available at www.bdonline.co.uk (accessed 21 October 2018).
95 *Jewish Chronicle*, 17 June, 11 November 1960, with additional research by John Minnis. Hilary Halpern: obituary *Jewish Chronicle*, 18 October 2013.
96 Obituary, *Jewish Chronicle*, 20 July 2001.
97 His partner Clifford Barnett was involved in neither synagogue project, email from Basil Gillinson's widow Lynda Gillinson to the author, 6 March 2007, SJBH Archives.
98 Bowling alleys, skating rinks, swimming pools (around the country) and a new all-seater spectator stand for Leeds United Football Club.
99 It is not known whether the textiles were part of the original scheme.
100 Email from Lynda Gillinson, 13 April 2007, SJBH Archives.
101 Obituary *Jewish Chronicle*, 20 July 2001. Gillinson & Barnett designed the clubhouse for Moor Allerton Golf Club, which was founded by Leeds Jews and, for Arnold Ziff – prominent Jewish businessman and philanthropist – the Merrion Centre in Leeds city centre.

102 *Jewish Chronicle*, 20 September 1957. Plans for the first phase had already been submitted and approved: *Jewish Chronicle*, 8 March 1957.
103 *Jewish Chronicle*, 14 September 1962. The report includes a photograph of Gillinson being presented to the minister.
104 *Jewish Chronicle*, 6 January 1961, with photograph.
105 For example, on Hai Taib Street, Har Nof neighbourhood, Jerusalem. Queenshill received a write-up in Rachel Wischnitzer's seminal book published a couple of years later: *The Architecture of the European Synagogue* (Philadelphia: Jewish Publication Society of America, 1964), pp. 274–5.
106 *Jewish Chronicle*, 13 November 1959.
107 See C. H. Krinsky, *Synagogues of Europe* (Boston, Mass: MIT Press, 1985), pp. 408–10; Kadish, *Synagogues of Britain and Ireland*, pp. 241–3; *Jewish Heritage in Britain and Ireland*, 2nd edn 2015, pp. 260–2.
108 Plans of all three buildings are in Leeds City Council Development Services (LCCDS), with acknowledgements to Richard Taylor and Chris Clarke. The collection of Leeds City Council Building Plans in West Yorkshire Archives does not extend beyond 1948. It was not possible in 2017 to conduct a further search for plans of postwar communal buildings at the council's offices.
109 *Jewish Chronicle*, 14 March 1969. Earlier plans had been submitted and approved in 1957, *Jewish Chronicle*, 8 March 1957.
110 By Marten & Burnett, see Wrathmell, *Leeds*, p. 232; Minnis with Mitchell, *Religion and Place in Leeds*, p. 32.
111 LCCDS Plan no. W4855; Isadore Pear, *The Beth HaMedrash HaGadol 1874–1994* (Leeds: privately printed by the Congregation, 1994).
112 LCCDS Plan no. 79/30/01058; not a pure hexagon, the north and south walls being longer than the rest.
113 Where it was oddly combined with segmental-headed windows to accommodate the numerous Victorian stained-glass panels salvaged from Belgrave Street in 1985–6. Shadwell Lane is also home to some glass brought from the Leeds New Synagogue, including a number of panels by London Jewish stained-glass maker David Hillman. LCCDS Plan no. 82/30/00378.
114 Research by John Minnis of the Leeds *Pevsner* on the Catholic architects; Bryan Little, *Catholic Churches since 1623* (London: Robert Hale, 1966); Christopher Martin with photography by Alex Ramsay, *A Glimpse of Heaven: Catholic Churches of England and Wales* (Swindon: English Heritage, 2006).
115 Leach and Pevsner, *Yorkshire West Riding: Leeds, Bradford and the North*, Plate 121 and p. 178, quoting P. F. Anson, *Fashions in Church Furnishings* (1960). This claim is repeated on the architects' website that also features Shadwell Lane www.langtry-langton.co.uk/places (accessed 22 December 2008).
116 *Jewish Chronicle*, 31 January 1986. The Leeds-born Jewish architect Stuart Leventhall worked for Owen, Diplock & Associates at the time, and now practises in Manchester. Regarding the *Etz Chaim* project, he cannot recall any office discussion of design significance attached to the hexagonal plan, only that the 'tree of life' motif was inspired by the wooded setting; telephone conversation with the author, 3 May 2006.

117 *Jewish Chronicle*, 18 November 1994, 15 September 1995; further information supplied in 1992 by Rabbi Meir Posen, *mikveh* consultant, of Stamford Hill and Jerusalem, see Kadish, 'Eden in Albion', pp. 122–3 and notes.
118 Ernest Krausz, *Leeds Jewry: Its History and Social Structure* (Cambridge: Heffer's and Jewish Historical Society of England, 1964), p. 110; letters from Mrs Frieda Schiller to the author, 6 March (postmarked), 29 March 1992, in response to a call for information on my behalf by Nigel Grizzard in the *Jewish Telegraph* (Leeds edn) in February 1992, in SJBH Archives.
119 According to Murray Freedman; *Jewish Chronicle*, 28 August 1959, 19 January 1968.
120 Letter to the author from Walter Rothschild, then minister of Sinai Synagogue, 8 September 1992. The use of fibreglass for the bottom and the shape of the pool was questioned by the rabbis.
121 Information from Rabbi Shlomo Katanka quoting Mr David Mankoff, email 28 March 2017. This *mikveh* is now used exclusively by men in accordance with Hasidic custom.
122 As stated on their website www.judaismlive.com, link kindly provided by Rabbi Shlomo Katanka by email 27 March 2017; see also *Jewish Chronicle*, 24 October 1986. The building was acquired two years previously.
123 Estimated 35,000 and the only community in the country that is growing overall, thanks largely to the *Haredi* [strictly Orthodox] sector.
124 See S. Kadish, 'Jewish heritage in Scotland', *Jewish Historical Studies* 47 (2015), pp. 179–216.
125 *Jewish Chronicle*, 11 September 1959.

12

Fellowship and philanthropy

Derek Fraser

Charity is one of the primary Jewish virtues, as exemplified in the intonation of the holy prayer on the Day of Atonement: 'Penitence, Prayer and Charity shall avert the severe decree'. As soon as the elements of even an embryonic Jewish community appeared, there was a philanthropic aspect in evidence. Each synagogue assumed responsibility for its poorer congregants, sometimes informally, sometimes organisationally through a benevolent society. At the same time, that sense of community which a common Jewish identity fostered also engendered ideas of mutuality at the family, geographic or trade level, in which those with some kind of kinship or occupational connectivity bound themselves together for mutual support. At its simplest level this might involve Jewish neighbourly succour for those fallen on hard times. More formally it led to a diverse range of mutual aid organisations which often fall under the umbrella term of 'friendly societies'. It is a sometimes overlooked fact of Victorian Britain that there were more people, almost all from the lower orders, enrolled in friendly societies than were in receipt of poor relief. Once a community need identified itself, the collective identity spawned a self-help approach in which the Jewish poor bound themselves together for mutual aid. This might be little more than a collecting club in which a few pence were contributed weekly to provide for some possible eventuality, such as bereavement, and one of the distinctive features of Jewish friendly societies was the payment of 'shiva money' during the traditional week of mourning. To facilitate the burials of poorer citizens, the Leeds Jewish Workers Cooperative Society was established as primarily a mutual aid burial club, later adding a butcher service and even acting as the sponsor of a synagogue.

As early as the 1850s the first Jewish friendly society was founded in Leeds, Ahabath Olam, which provided its members with financial support in times of illness. Its meetings were held in local taverns which enhanced the fellowship of the association. Sometimes the link of the *landsman* with the place of origin stimulated the wish for collective association, and in 1901 a group of immigrants from Dvinsk set up a lending club, which in 1906 became the Leeds Jewish Benevolent Society. Many had quaint or exotic names, such as the Abraham Fraise Lodge, the Samuel Lyons Independent Friendly Society or the Mount Sinai Beacon Order of Ancient Maccabeans. There might be a quasi-political agenda, such as the Zionist Anglo-Jewish Association's challenge to anti-Semitism; in other cases there was a social objective, such as the Leeds Jewish Institute or the Herzl Moser hospital or the Talmud Torah, for Jewish education.[1] These organisations' activities were regularly reported in the *Jewish Chronicle* and in 1910 a local journal argued that 'the Friendly Society – judging by the numerical strength and personnel of the membership – has become one of *the* institutions of the body politic'. It hoped to provide for 'the bettering of Jewish lodges ... a medium through which the voice of Jewish Friendly Societies will be heard'.[2] In their varied ways, these membership associations reflected a collective, mutual aid, fellowship philosophy, where funds contributed on a regular basis were then used for defined benefits or purposes.

There were two fellowship organisations established in the 1920s – the B'nai Brith and the Unity Lodge – which were distinctive through being part of a national and even international network. The timing is significant. By the 1920s, the Leeds Jewish community was no longer defined by immigration, which had largely ceased by the start of the First World War. The new generation were the children of immigrants, born and educated in Leeds, and they had already begun to move out of the Leylands 'colony' into Chapeltown. Many were building up businesses established by their parents and some had entered the professions. The Jewish community was no longer just a problem for Leeds civic society to deal with, as it had developed a range of social, educational and philanthropic organisations to meet its own collective needs.

B'nai Brith saw itself as a coordinating body, 'a communal clearing ground', whose mutuality and fellowship could bind together a community fragmented by the multiplicity of bodies and riven by religious fissures. The Lodge was convened in 1926 and received its formal charter the following year. Its initial membership comprised communal leaders and those willing to serve the Lodge's philanthropic purposes. Its first President was Hyman Morris, a Leeds City Councillor, and Vice-President was the distinguished Zionist academic, Professor Selig Brodetsky. One of its early successes was to sponsor a Jewish Children's Convalescent Home and its centralising role was confirmed in its initiative in launching the Jewish Representative Council as a forum for all local Jewish organisations. Because it was part of a national movement, it could use its good offices to call on support from elsewhere. For example, in 1928 a Leeds member sought the assistance of the District Grand Lodge to get a young girl into the London Jews' Temporary Shelter.[3]

Fellowship and philanthropy 217

Another chapter has explained how the difficulties Jews had in joining a golf club had led to the establishment of Moor Allerton Golf Club, and there were similar experiences for Jews wishing to join the freemasons. In the same year that the B'nai Brith received its charter, the Loyalty Lodge 4971 held its first meeting. It was not a wholly Jewish Lodge, but its specific purpose was to facilitate Jewish and Gentile members to meet within the fellowship of freemasonry. Many Jews joined the Lodge and its identification as a heavily, though not exclusively, Jewish Lodge was illustrated by the fact that the consecration oath at its inauguration was read by Rabbi Barnett Cohen. Like B'nai Brith, it attracted members from the business and political elite of the city and had overlapping membership. Samuel H. Lyons, founder of Alexandre the Tailor, was an early member of both organisations, as was Stanley Lightman, whose father Victor had established a successful furniture company. Other Jewish business leaders in the Lodge included Julius Friend, David Sandelson, Moses Myers and Jack Rose.[4]

The joining fee for the Lodge in 1927 was £11 and the annual subscription was 4 guineas – so it was beyond the reach of many – and even the working-class friendly societies presupposed a regular income from which to pay the modest subscriptions. There were always Jewish people in Leeds who were forced to resort to begging because of low or irregular income, and it was felt that '*schnorrering*' [the Yiddish word for begging, but which carries a derogatory implication] had become a public nuisance in the 1870s. While some could be sustained by the mutual aid developments discussed above, it was felt that a more systematic means of supporting the poor was required; and it is to the formal poor relief history in Leeds that the rest of this chapter is devoted

In an oft-quoted news item, the *Leeds Mercury* reported on a meeting in 1878 at which

> A Board of Guardians for the relief of the Jewish poor in Leeds was established. One of the objects of the proposed board is to carry out, on a broad and liberal basis, a system of relief by which all members of the Jewish persuasion, independent of nationality, may reap its benefits; to stop house to house begging; also by a system of loans, to encourage willing and able persons to obtain an honest livelihood for themselves and families and to lessen the burdens, so often put upon the Jewish community of house to house collections.[5]

Thus began an institution whose continuous history can be traced for the next 140 years.

There were two external developments which reinforced the decision to set up a Board of Guardians, a major national charity initiative and policy changes within the Poor Law itself. In 1869, the Charity Organisation Society (COS) was established, with the aim of rationalising and coordinating the multiplicity of charities which had sprung up in mid-Victorian Britain and to ensure that with proper vetting and enquiry the most appropriate assistance could be given to applicants. It was their overarching philosophy which struck a chord in Jewish philanthropic circles. The COS believed that charity had the power to move the poor from dependence to independence and their most famous adage was 'we must use charity to create the power of self-help'. This was an echo of the objective of the Jewish Board of Guardians, established in London a decade before the COS, 'to elevate poor Jews into self-supporting and self-respecting members of the general community'.[6] The distinguished Jewish philanthropist F. D. Mocatta believed in the administration of charity in such a way as not to demoralise the poor and he was an active promoter and Vice-President of the COS. The Leeds Board shared that approach, 'to encourage willing and able persons to obtain an honest livelihood for themselves and their families'.

Much more sharply focused and partly explaining the timing was the so-called 'crusade against outdoor relief' which flooded through the Poor Law system in the 1870s. The infamous New Poor Law of 1834 instituted the hated 'workhouse test' and generated a national psychological distaste for poor relief, which to some extent persists today – even though both the Poor Law and workhouses have long disappeared. In practice, however, during the middle decades of the nineteenth century relief outside the workhouse continued and those inside benefited from a range of medical and social services as workhouses increasingly became 'state hospitals'. To the zealots of the COS and the Poor Law minister who shared their philosophy, indiscriminate outdoor relief was preventing the implementation of proper social work practices in the dispensation of relief. Hence, a new dichotomy was promulgated during the early 1870s in which the 'deserving' poor were to be the responsibility of charities, while the 'undeserving' were to be consigned to the Poor Law with a newly acquired discipline, whose harshness, many historians feel, was even more severe than in the 1830s. Claimants who had previously been the recipients of temporary or permanent weekly payments now found themselves offered the workhouse, as outdoor relief was sharply reduced. The decision of the Whitechapel Guardians (with its heavy concentration of Jewish poor) to deny applicants anything but the workhouse was widely reported in the Jewish press, as was the need for more funding support if the explicit wish of Jewish philanthropy – 'no Jew should see the inside of the workhouse' – was to be fulfilled. To keep Jews out of the workhouse was a fundamental aim of Jewish philanthropy in Leeds.

Hence, the 1870s was a propitious time to launch a philanthropic initiative in Leeds, because of the desire to use proper modes of enquiry in place of unregulated doles and as a response to the renewed harshness of the Poor Law. There was also a pressing local issue to be addressed, which was

Fellowship and philanthropy

increasing foreign immigration. While not at the level of the floods of migrants in the 1880s, the Jewish population of Leeds had already been increased significantly by overseas arrivals. There was a concern that these impecunious, oddly dressed and rootless arrivals (sometimes called the 'stranger poor') might become a burden on the local state, with the risk of becoming an issue which might provoke anti-Semitic feeling among the host population. The clue to the importance of the foreign poor is the reference to creating a relief system 'by which all members of the Jewish persuasion, *independent of nationality* [my italics] may reap its benefits'. The creation of the Leeds Board of Guardians answered the well-known Jewish instruction: 'if you have the poor and needy in your midst do not let them become a charge on the Gentile community, look after them yourselves'.[7]

The newly established Board was led by Paul Hirsch for the first thirty years of its existence (Figure 12.1). He had been born in Mecklenburg and arrived in Leeds in the 1860s where he established a successful woollen business. He was a prime mover and President of the Belgrave Street Great Synagogue with which the Board was closely associated. He took leadership roles in many Jewish charities, but also integrated himself into local Leeds philanthropic circles, particularly supporting a number of hospital charities. He was made a magistrate in 1900 (the first Leeds Jew to be so elevated). His status as a respected member of Leeds civic society was reflected by the fact that the funeral in 1908 of this 'local prince of philanthropists' was attended by the Lord Mayor. (Although Jewish prayers were said at his home in Headingley prior to the cortege, he was cremated and not buried in a Jewish cemetery.)

Little is known about the early decades of the Board and Hirsch's views because of the lack of surviving sources, but something may be inferred from the fragmentary evidence. It would appear that he imbibed the COS philosophy and he highlighted the Board's policy 'to discourage the tramp and the professional beggar by granting relief after careful enquiry only'.[8] Hirsch also shared the view expressed by a luminary of the London Board that 'no relief will be given to foreign Jews until they have been here a certain time … to prevent needy foreigners attracted by the hope of relief'. In similar vein, Hirsch reported that 'the Board has discouraged the idea of permanent settlement of the refugees in this country, being of opinion that the labour market is already overstocked'.[9] The desire to keep Jews out of the workhouse was largely fulfilled and the Chairman of the Poor Law Guardians reported to the Select Committee on Foreign Immigration that there were no Jews in the Leeds workhouse in 1888–9. While the same Committee heard from a city Alderman that Jews had 'a society for relieving their own poor; they do not trouble the rates so much as the other portion of the population', evidence was presented on the numbers of Jews receiving some Poor Law outdoor relief in the 1880s. This was explained by the fact that 'they have the Jewish

Board of Guardians but they are not very wealthy and these poor people are frequently sent to our board'.[10] There may have been some shortcomings in the administration of affairs on Hirsch's death and the Charity Commission queried why the details of his bequest to the Board and the annual accounts for 1909 and 1910 had not been submitted.[11]

The close association between the Board and Belgrave Street was reinforced by the location of the office in a house adjacent to the synagogue. In a symbolic way the location of the Board reflected the changing demography of Leeds Jewry. The first office was in the inner urban area near the concentration of Jewish settlement. In 1930, the office was relocated to Brunswick Place in the heart of the new Jewish suburb of Chapeltown (Figure 12.2). In turn, that location became remote from the northward Jewish migration and the office moved in 1968 to its current location of Stonegate Road in Moortown.

After Hirsch's death, the leadership of the Board of Guardians passed to Victor Lightman, also an immigrant, who settled in Leeds almost by accident en route from his home in Vilna to his original destination of the USA (Figure 12.3). He was a highly skilled carpenter and founded a successful furniture business in Hunslet. Like Hirsch he was elevated to the magistracy and was also a prominent and active supporter of Leeds civic charities. One of the initiatives of his presidency was the establishment of a loan fund in the 1920s whereby aspiring businessmen could borrow interest-free loans to help in promoting their ventures – in the spirit of self-help the Board had always been keen to promote. Facilitated by an initial subvention of £500 from Montague Burton, the scheme was named the Victor Lightman Fund in his honour at Burton's suggestion. Other schemes dating from this period include the Jewish Girls Marriage Fund (later enhanced by the Dowry Fund) 'to provide small marriage dowries for poor Jewesses' and the Ladies Benevolent Society 'for the provision of food and clothing at Passover and the High Festivals'.[12] (An official return in 1963 shows the funds available in that year as Lightman £240; Dowry £215; Benevolent £118. Eventually all three were merged with Board funds.) Another feature of the Lightman years was the appeal in synagogues on the high holy days, which became a regular fundraising strategy which has persisted ever since. In 1919, such appeals raised over £1,000 (37% of the income) and this had surpassed £1,800 (43%) three years later. It would have been gratifying for Lightman to hear the Lord Mayor 'express his admiration ... of the self-sacrificing efforts made by the Jews of Leeds for supporting their own sick and poor'.[13]

Those words were spoken at the home of Hyman Morris after another successful musical concert, which also became a regular part of the Board's income-generating activities for the rest of the century. Morris succeeded Lightman as President on his death in 1928, having already served as Treasurer since 1914. Like his two predecessors, he was foreign born, having arrived

Fellowship and philanthropy 221

from Russia as a child, and like them he established a successful business – in his case in the manufacture of wallpaper. His shop in Vicar Lane promised 'cheap and artistic wallpapers' and from there he spread across the north of England. His civic career was stellar. He was a JP, a Conservative City Councillor from 1922, an Alderman from 1930 and the first Leeds Jewish Lord Mayor in 1941–2.

The growing status and integration of the Leeds Jewish community, as illustrated in Hyman Morris's career, was further reflected when the Lord Mayor chaired the Board of Guardians AGM for the first time in 1931. Many found that this added dignity to the proceedings and that, having heard at first hand of the valuable work of the Board, the Mayor would be favourably disposed towards the community in the award of grants. However, in an illuminating and robust exchange of views in 1934, a dissenting voice was raised. Nathan Cohen, President of the Harrogate congregation and also a Board Vice-President, thought that the presence of the Mayor 'stifles free speech, as no member likes to criticise and take the Board to task in the presence of the Lord Mayor and the Press'. When the Board Secretary, R. H. Hurwitz, confirmed that the presence of the Mayor had been unanimously approved, Cohen came back with all guns blazing. He wrote that the President was right to chastise the community

> What I object to is, that this should be done in the presence of goim (*gentiles*) and the press – as reports are not always accurate and it gives a handle to anti-semites. As to the dignity of the Chief citizen ... all I can say is that 'It is the stamp of the slave.' I have been present at dozens of meetings ... and it was not necessary to have a goy to give dignity to those proceedings ... The compliments usually paid to our Community by gentiles at such meetings leave me cold – as it reminds me of the story of Balem coming amongst our people to curse them, but commencing with compliments (*here quoting in Hebrew script the relevant biblical text*) ... I fully realise the tremendous relief you afford to the Public Assistance Committee ... I know we are entitled to their help, but this is the Jewish tragedy – we do not get what we are entitled to and the present is not the opportune moment to demand our rights.[14]

The minority view did not prevail and the presence of the Lord Mayor became a regular annual event.

The reference to the Public Assistance Committee (PAC) was in response to Secretary Hurwitz's comment that 'we have for too long ... taken longingly from the Public Assistance Committee an insignificant sum which has been grudgingly given us'.[15] Relations between the PAC and the Board were strained and it was claimed that 'there was an anti-Jewish bias. It was said that no public money would be given to set Jews up in business.'[16] Neville Chamberlain's 1929 Local Government Act had abolished the Boards of Guardians (a title retained in Leeds for another 42 years) and ended the term 'poor relief', both highly stigmatised by the association with the Poor Law and its workhouse test. It was felt that local authorities had none of the taint of the Guardians and Public Assistance was a value-free term. Indeed, it had been the term recommended by the Fabians Sidney and Beatrice Webb, in their Minority Poor Law Report of 1909. Yet in an odd way cultural attitudes became reversed and public assistance (provided by the local authority) became stigmatised in Jewish eyes, while the doles dished out by the Guardians (outlawed in the wider social administrative system) were preferable to the Jewish poor.

The Leeds PAC acknowledged that the Board was relieving a significant amount of Jewish poverty, in recognition of which the PAC made an annual donation of £300 (later £400) to Board funds – Hurwitz's insignificant sum. The Board of Guardians offered to deal with all the Jewish poor in Leeds in the 1930s, thus relieving the PAC of a burden, but the statutory responsibility of the PAC could not be delegated. The Board argued that it was humiliating for Jews to apply for public assistance with its hated family means test, an argument which fell on deaf ears. Hence the Board was limited to providing supplementary relief to many who were already in receipt of Public Assistance. The scale of this is illustrated in an enquiry submitted by the PAC in 1938 of 'a list of Jewish cases who are chargeable to this Committee', with a request for 'the amount of relief granted by your Board'.[17] (It is presumed that in the application process for public assistance there was a question about religion or how else would the Jewish cases be identifiable?) This survey of over 200 people showed that the Board was offering modest supplementary weekly grants to about a third of the Jewish poor who were already receiving Public Assistance. At a time when the maximum weekly public assistance benefit was 42s, most Board grants were in the region of 2s 6d to 7s 6d, given to recipients who were themselves on low levels of benefit. In only two cases was a grant paid to a public assistance beneficiary who was receiving above 20s per week.

The Depression of the 1930s placed a great strain on Board funds and it was felt necessary to pursue families to contribute to their parents' welfare, which included approaching overseas relatives. For example, in April 1933 the Board received an application from a man whose only income was a 10s per week pension. He would normally qualify for assistance, but as Hurwitz explained to the man's daughter living in Brooklyn USA,

> As a result of the abnormal distress which is prevailing in this Community … and the difficulty we are now experiencing in obtaining the necessary finances … especially since the organisation is entirely voluntary in origin, our task in assisting the great number of poor is all the more difficult, and consequently my Board unfortunately cannot extend the same measure of help which it has been in a position to give in past years. It is not, therefore, possible for my Board to

render such assistance to your father as might be commensurate with his need. We appeal to you therefore, to help your father in his unfortunate plight.[18]

Nor were these requests only in one direction. The Board received one approach from Kansas City and in February 1934 received an enquiry from the Chicago Unemployment Relief Service to trace the Leeds Jewish relatives of a family in distress in the USA to ascertain 'whether they are cognizant of our clients' circumstances, whether they are willing to assist, and to what extent they have assisted them in the past'. Three months later Hurwitz reported that he had tracked down one relative who had been in touch with her American family, but who could do no more than send 'small sums periodically which she, more or less, considered as a present for the children'. Three others were, on the basis of confidential information known to the Board, capable of rendering financial assistance, 'but, as you will no doubt appreciate, it is most difficult to persuade when they assume an indifferent attitude'.[19]

In such straitened times it was necessary to ensure that funds were given only to those in genuine need. In addition to the Board's own enquiries, there was occasionally information from what would later be called 'whistle blowers'. One woman reported that her husband had deserted her in London and was now living bigamously in Leeds. Another example survives in the Board's archives which casts light on contemporary attitudes and a particularly Jewish sense of fair play. Challenging the propriety of a woman being in receipt of Board relief, an anonymous correspondent reported:

> Firstly she has a lodger that she gets 5/- per week [*name given*]. Secondly she is not Yiddish as she has never been magire [*converted*]. Thirdly her husband worked Yom Kippur at a barbers shop near the Parish Church. Fourthly she says she keeps two children. Her mother keeps the eldest child so she has only one to look after. Fifthly her husband gets dole and he works ... What she has surplus money she pays in Christmas Clubs, Wine, Pork, Chicken and Cakes. Her mother is not magire and she has been getting loans for years. Hoping you will look into this.[20]

The outcome is not known, but there was always a slight undercurrent in Board thinking which was fearful of too generous a regime. Thus the Board was happy to approve small sums expended by the Ladies Welfare Committee in visiting the sick and aged, 'providing the maximum amount spent on any one visit does not exceed 5 shillings'. Similarly, responding to rumours that some were taking advantage of the free clothing distribution, the Chairman 'asked the ladies when issuing clothing to see that restraint was exercised [to prevent] ... excessive clothing issues'.[21]

This somewhat parsimonious attitude is in marked contrast to the open and generous manner in which support was given to those in difficulty. The members were much exercised by the sad case of an Austrian girl who had come to Leeds to take up domestic work with a distant relative and who then fell out with the family. She was threatened with deportation by the strict regime of the Home Office and, though not a Leeds citizen, was supported by the Board. That campaign was eventually unsuccessful and the Board was saddled with the costs of travel and visas when the girl was repatriated. A happier outcome resulted when a poor widow was threatened with a court order to pay toward the cost of care for a disabled son in a Halifax mental hospital. Hurwitz argued that the claim 'would result in great hardship as well as deprive her of some of her limited means of livelihood'.[22] When the Halifax officer pointed out that the late husband had owned two properties in the town, detailed enquiries were made to demonstrate that indeed 'this unfortunate woman is now in financial straits and is undergoing extreme hardship in maintaining her small home'.[23] These pleas were abortive and the PAC confirmed that it would seek the court order against the widow. However, a month later Hurwitz received the welcome news that 'the case came before the Halifax Borough magistrates this morning and they refused to make an order for her son's maintenance'.[24]

When Hyman Morris retired in 1947 after thirty-three years service, it represented a major watershed. It was remarkable to note that in the seventy-year existence of the Board there had been only three presidents (apart from a few months interregnum due to ill health in 1914). The baton passed from the last of the immigrant presidents to the first of the British born, Charles Sumrie. Moreover, the whole context within which the Board of Guardians operated was about to change. The creation of the Welfare State in July 1948 profoundly changed the character and direction of Jewish philanthropic activity in Leeds. The provision of 'cradle to grave' welfare benefits largely removed the need for regular financial maintenance which had been so pressing in the 1930s and during the war. Not that this would reduce charitable expenditure, as John Ellis (part of the postwar triumvirate which also included Charles Sumrie and Max Ziff) reminded members at the 1949 AGM. There was, he said, a mistaken impression that the new welfare regime would reduce Board costs, 'belied by the inexorable facts … expenditure during the past year increased by some £600 over the previous'.[25] There might be continued need for modest payments, and in the 1960s there were 130 families receiving weekly cash grants, usually a 10s postal order. However, increasingly, the bulk of expenditure would be directed to what Sumrie called 'the welfare requirements of the aged, the poor and needy members of our community'. The Board adopted a social care welfare agenda, as 'the Board's activities have now moved into a higher stage in which organised social and welfare work is in demand'. Treating the family as a whole and meeting their non-monetary needs was the best way, Sumrie argued, 'to supplement and help to coordinate the welfare services provide by the state'. As a local journal described it, the bulldozing of the old Guardians' offices in 1968 'witnessed the transformation from a purely almsgiving relief body into a modern welfare organisation'. By the 1960s this could not unreasonably be described as 'in microcosm a welfare state in its own right'.[26]

The meals on wheels service which, it was claimed, was the first to deliver a seven-day service (with two meals delivered on a Friday) was a good example of the new services – delivered to a poor clientele but meeting a need that was not primarily financial. Beginning in 1948, in a makeshift manner using volunteers' private cars, the service was delivering 14,000 meals annually in the 1960s and 40,000 in the 1970s, facilitated by a purpose-designed van that could carry sixty-five three-course hot meals.

The most obvious example of moving into new social welfare territory was the prescient decision to provide social housing, initially described by Sumrie in 1949 as an 'ambition fraught with difficulties'. There were three drivers underlying the decision. First, there was a growing appreciation of the appalling conditions in which some of the Jewish poor lived, augmented by the evidence and photographs provided by the many lady volunteer visitors. By the early 1950s the Board of Guardians had identified poor housing as 'a real and serious problem, one of the primary causes of difficulty and distress amongst our dependants'.[27] Second, the City Council was embarking on major slum clearance schemes which threatened to disperse much of the Jewish poor across the city, with the attendant problems of retaining Jewish identity and religious practice. The development of a convenient site near to the northward-moving Jewish population promised to be a stimulus to community coherence. Third, the Board was to some extent prompted by the prospect of others taking the lead, as both B'nai Brith and the Leeds Jewish Co-Operative Workers Society had plans afoot. These two organisations and others were represented as founding members when the Leeds Jewish Housing Association Limited (LJHA) was established under the aegis of the Board of Guardians in October 1953. Developed as a vibrant and successful housing charity in its own right, there was always a close relationship between the two organisations, with much overlap between officers and members, and the primary leadership role of the Board of Guardians was cemented by the grant of £10,000 toward the costs of the initial housing scheme.

The early years of the Housing Association were beset with difficulties over negotiations with the Council, the finding of a site and statutory requirements. Eventually the Queenshill Estate was developed and in September 1962 the housing scheme and the community centre (funded by Bernard Lyons) were officially opened by Sir Keith Joseph who was triply suitable – as a local MP, Jewish and the Minister for Housing (Figures 12.4 and 12.5). There were in all 187 dwellings providing varying accommodation, mostly flats, set in a park like environment, 'notable for the lack of fences and usual "front and rear gardens" ... situated in completely open landscape and all tenants enjoy the open space in an equal basis'.[28] This pioneering initiative was described as 'unique in its conception and magnitude in the Jewish community of this country', which enabled 'Leeds to claim the credit of being the first community in the country to have embarked on such a gigantic undertaking'.[29] The original project has been expanded successfully and in later decades the housing stock has grown both at Queenshill and at other sites, so that currently the LJHA has about 500 properties housing some 10% of the Leeds Jewish population.

The matter of the name of the organisation has an interesting history. As explained, the Boards of Guardians were abolished in 1929 and there was no immediate move in Leeds to follow suit. The first discussion of the name appears to have been during the war when, parallel to the 1944 great 'White Paper Chase' planning the Welfare State, the Board adopted a new constitution and laws. In developing the new laws there was some support for the name Jewish Assistance Board, but Charles Sumrie argued that a change of name would adversely affect subscriptions. So, the name was retained with the amended objective 'to assist the Jewish poor of Leeds ... and to ameliorate the condition of the Jewish poor of Leeds and district'.[30] At the 1946 AGM, the Lord Mayor commented that he thought the term Guardians carried the taint of pauperism. Indeed, at the 1949 AGM there was a formal resolution before the Board to change the name to Leeds Jewish Council of Social Service, but this motion was withdrawn after discussion.[31]

The matter was left in abeyance until the 1960s. It was a touch embarrassing when, at the 1965 AGM, Lord Mayor Hargreave advised

> The old association of 'poor law relief' with the words 'board of guardians' could be having an effect on the very good work of the Leeds Jewish Board of Guardians. A change of name would help many hundreds of people in conditions of penury because they would not ask for help as they wrongly associated it with the granting of poor relief.[32]

Albert Morris, who had succeeded Sumrie as President in 1964, emulating his father, replied that opinion was divided and a vote six months earlier by the Executive Committee had retained the name by 6–4, while a vote in the following year was tied 6–6 and the name retained only by the casting vote of the Chairman. By this time, opinion and practice was changing across the national Jewish philanthropy scene. London had changed and provincial charities were using a variety of names – United Benevolent Board (Birmingham); Welfare Board (Glasgow); Jewish Social Services (Manchester); Welfare Council (Liverpool); and Welfare Society (Newcastle). Leeds was out of step in still using Board of Guardians and it was not until May 1971 that the name Leeds Jewish Welfare Board was finally adopted. It was felt that 'the old name

Fellowship and philanthropy

no longer adequately reflected the Board's present-day function and that the new name would create a better image'.[33]

There was a legalistic postscript to this name change. The Board was advised that the change should be effected by the informal route of a resolution announcing the change of usage, a process which would have been familiar to many who had anglicised their surnames in a similar manner. There was no formal change of rules or constitution. Some sixteen years later, the eagle-eyed scrutiny of the Charity Commission noted that there had been a specific reference to 'informally' changing the name, which produced the query – 'could you please confirm when the title was *formally* changed for all purposes'.[34] This gave the Board's lawyers a conundrum, since technically there had never been a formal confirmation. They came up with the imaginative view that the rules formally adopted in September 1982 incorporated the new name 'and we would suggest that that be treated as a date when the title was formally changed for all purposes', which seems to have satisfied the Charity Commission.[35]

The story of Jewish philanthropy in Leeds exemplifies the changing relationship between charities and the state in the period from the late-nineteenth to the early-twenty-first century. These may be identified as four phases with differing characteristics:

- In the Victorian period charities were seen as an *alternative* to state action, often overtly aimed at demonstrating that there was no need for state involvement since voluntary philanthropy was preferable. The Leeds Jewish Board of Guardians were keen to show that the community could look after its 'own poor', not wanting the growing immigrant population to become a burden on the state, with the attendant risks of provoking anti-Semitism.
- After the Edwardian Liberal reforms introduced old age pensions, health insurance and unemployment benefit, charities became *supplementary* to state provision and in the first half of the twentieth century philanthropy plugged the gaps in what was sometimes called 'a social service state'. We saw that the Guardians in the 1930s were supplementing the income of some already in receipt of Public Assistance but at a level inadequate to meet their needs. The economic distress of the Depression reinforced the Board's character as still essentially a Poor Relief organisation.
- The welfare state effectively removed the need for charities to provide basic financial support and so, for about four decades after 1948, philanthropy offered services *complementary* to the welfare state. The Board of Guardians and later the Welfare Board provided a range of social services that were either not provided by or not easily accessible from state provision, including social housing, care for the elderly, mental health support, family advice and meals on wheels. As the benefactor, Bernard Lyons, put it, despite the

welfare state 'there remain a considerable amount of under-provision and of vacuum areas which are supplemented or provided by charity and voluntary effort'.[36]
- From the end of the twentieth century and into the present one, philanthropy entered into an *agency* relationship with the state, as charities became partners in delivering social care services. Government came to acknowledge that some services were better delivered by, and more acceptably received from, local voluntary bodies than from an impersonal state bureaucracy. Both the Welfare Board and the Housing Association received financial support to assist in the delivery of social policy objectives. This often enhanced the budgets of the Jewish charities but left them at risk in times of austerity and cuts in public expenditure.

12.1 First President of the Leeds Jewish Board of Guardians

12.2 Board of Guardians Offices in Chapeltown

12.3 Victor Lightman

12.4 Sir Keith Joseph visiting the Community Centre

12.5 Leeds Jewish Housing Association, Queenshill Estate, 1962. The Community Centre with its parobalic roof is at the top of the picture

Notes

1. Based on L. Saipe, *A Century of Care: The History of the Leeds Jewish Welfare Board 1878–1978* (Leeds: J. Jackman & Co., 1978) and E. C. Sterne, *Leeds Jewry 1919–1929* (Leeds: Jewish Historical Society of England, 1989).
2. *Ango-Jewry*, 15 April 1910, p. 15.
3. J. H. Taylor to D. Fox, 12 November 1928, LJWB Archives.
4. D. A. Friedman, *History of the Loyalty Lodge* (Leeds, privately printed 2002).
5. *Leeds Mercury*, 26 February 1878.
6. L. Magnus, *The Jewish Board of Guardians and the Men Who Made It* (London: Board of Guardians, 1909), p. 129.
7. Saipe, *A Century of Care*, p. 13.
8. *Annual Report of the Jewish Board of Guardians*, 1893–94, p. 3.
9. Magnus, *The Jewish Board of Guardians*, p. 20; *Annual Report*, 1893–94, p. 4.
10. Select Committee on Emigration and Immigration, Minutes of Evidence, July 1889, Mins 992, 1122.
11. H. W. T. Bowyear to LJBG, 1 May 1911, LJWB Archives.
12. Charity Commission return, February 1963.
13. *LJBG Annual Report*, 1919–20, p. 3; 1922–23, pp. 4–5.
14. N. Cohen to R. Hurwitz, 25 May 1934, LJWB Archives.
15. Hurwitz to Cohen, n.d. May 1934.
16. Quoted by H. Skyte, *Care in the Jewish Community: The Story of the Leeds Jewish Welfare Board and the Leeds Jewish Housing Association* (Leeds: Leeds Jewish Welfare Board, 1999), p. 11.
17. G. C. Brooke to R. H. Hurwitz, 15 July 1938.
18. Hurwitz to Mrs Lewis, 21 April 1933.
19. Illinois Relief commission to Hurwitz, 28 February 1934; response 20 June 1934.
20. Handwritten anonymous letter, n.d., LJWB Archives.
21. Minutes of the Executive Council, 18 August 1950; 14 November 1950.
22. Hurwitz to Halifax PAC, 28 May 1934.
23. Ibid., 8 June 1934.
24. Shepherd Whitley to Hurwitz, 11 July 1934.
25. LJBG Minutes, 17 July 1949.
26. *Leeds Jewish Observer*, 26 August 1949; *Jewish Chronicle*, 16 July 1954; *Jewish Gazette*, 28 June 1963, 4 October 1968.
27. *LJBG Annual Report 1953–54*.
28. *Queenshill Estate*, 1962 Brochure in LJHA Archives.
29. *Jewish Chronicle*, 17 June 1960; *Jewish Gazette*, 1 September 1961.
30. Laws of the Leeds Jewish Board of Guardians, 1943.
31. LJBG Minutes, 17 July 1949.
32. *Yorkshire Post*, 21 June 1965.
33. *Jewish Gazette*, 14 May 1971.
34. J. R. Young to Pearlman Grazin, 19 October 1987.
35. Pearlman Grazin to Charity Commission, 20 November 1987.
36. B. Lyons, *The Thread is Strong: The Memoirs and Reflections of Bernard Lyons* (London: n.p., 1981), p. 179.

13

At rest and play: leisure and sporting activities

Phil Goldstone

Introduction

There is a view that while British Jews have made their mark in many areas of economic, social and cultural life in Britain – particularly in the professions of law and medicine, the sciences, politics and business – sport has seen only a limited contribution. This view is erroneous and more recent research has shown to what extent the Jewish community has made significant contributions on both the playing and administrative sides of professional and amateur sport in Britain. Since the emergence of modern sport in the eighteenth century, Jews have played their part. Boxing was a particular sport in which Jews played a major role from the middle of the eighteenth century. Similarly, in the leisure arena, British Jews have contributed massively to the development of arts and culture and to the leisure activities of the nation.

In the introduction to his book on the British Jewish involvement in sport, David Dee sets a background that debunks the assertion that Jewish involvement and contribution to the development of sport and physical recreation generally is limited and not readily associated with the Jewish community.[1] Dee's book looks at Jewish involvement in sport on a national basis through the prism of 'Integration, ethnicity and anti-Semitism' between 1890 and 1970, but what he does not cover to any significant degree is the growth in involvement in those provincial cities with a major Jewish population: Leeds is one such city.

The involvement of the Leeds Jewish community in Leeds sport, both from a professional and amateur perspective, is far more extensive than David Dee had the opportunity to research; and this chapter will look at this involvement in association football, rugby league, boxing, cricket and several other sports from a local perspective and highlight the contribution of some notable individuals – both from a playing and behind the scenes perspective – whose contributions have not received the credit that is warranted. Leeds Jewry has produced writers, artists, playwrights and musicians, among others, who have made notable contributions to British culture and there has been a proliferation of community activities, with the establishment of Zionist organisations, scouts, guides and amateur dramatic groups.

The Select Committee on Emigration and Immigration in 1889 reported that some Leeds Jews passed their leisure time by visiting places of amusement, but they would not drink as they were sober in their habits.[2] The closeness of the community and the strictures of the ghetto acted as a brake on social, sporting and leisure activity. Jewish youths could not attend football matches which were played on Saturday, the Shabbat. Attendance at the theatre was forbidden as it was regarded as against Jewish Orthodox belief and adherence to Orthodox belief was paramount in an essentially Orthodox Jewish Community.[3] This is not to suggest that there was no Jewish interest or involvement in these activities. Stories abound within families of youths going to the synagogue on the Saturday morning and then disappearing in the afternoon ostensibly to see friends, but actually attending local amateur and professional football and rugby matches and, in some cases, playing.

By the early years of the twentieth century, Leeds was producing Jewish boxers, footballers and rugby players and was beginning to make its mark in many of the other growing areas of sport and leisure. The first serious involvement of the community in organised sports and leisure activities can be traced back to the formation of the Jewish Young Men's Association in 1896, later to be known as the 'Jewish Institute'.[4] The Institute based in Barrack Row was rehoused in 1936 in what became known as the 'Jubilee Hall', which became a focal point for community gatherings and both public and private social events.

In 1923, the Moor Allerton (Jewish) Golf Club was founded and the Judean Club was opened in 1929 to cater for the social needs of the younger members of the community. It was founded by a group of young Zionists who met to discuss Zionism and to hold social events and who wanted larger premises than the small room in Brunswick Street where they met. With the assistance of Sir Montague Burton and the B'nai B'rith, the Judean Club opened in Barrack Road and later moved to Street Lane.

Football

As the Jewish community prospered in the city, there was an interest from many in not just supporting the local football and rugby league clubs, but also in playing for them and even becoming involved in management and ownership.

Probably the most important influence on professional sport by the Jewish community in Leeds is that played out at Leeds United, Leeds' only professional football club. From the dressing room to the boardroom, the role of the Jewish community has been prominent in their involvement with the club.

Leeds United was formed in 1919 in the offices of a Leeds Jewish Solicitor, Alf Masser, after the collapse of Leeds City. Leslie Goldberg was the first and only Jew to play for Leeds United 1st team. He attended Leeds' Elland Road ground in 1932 to train for School Boy Internationals against Wales and Scotland and afterwards signed amateur forms for the club before joining the ground staff in 1934 and becoming a professional in 1935. He was the first Jew to play for England Schoolboys and he was the first Jew to captain Yorkshire Schools.

Goldberg was born in 1918 went to Lovell Road School – where 95% of the pupils were Jewish; he joined the Leeds Jewish Institute where sport and involvement in physical training were championed. He was encouraged in his sporting endeavours by his sports master, Nat Collins, who tried to disprove the charges of disloyalty, cowardice and unmanliness that anti-Semites made regularly against young Jewish men. He had his first game for Leeds United in Division 1 in 1937 on 4 December in a home game against Sunderland, which Leeds won 4–3. In that game he replaced Bert Sproston, the England full-back. It was clear that Goldberg was an England international in the making.

The Second World War intervened. The Football League was suspended and Goldberg, who served in India, played wartime fixtures for Arsenal. After the war he played a few more games for Leeds before being transferred to Reading in 1947. It was in Reading that he changed his name to Les Gaunt to avoid anti-Semitism. There were few Jews in Reading and he lacked the protection of a close Jewish community as he had in Leeds. He became detached from his Jewish roots. His playing career came to an end in 1950 after seventy-one games for Reading. He stayed in football scouting for Reading and Oxford, managed Newbury Town and then returned to Reading to assist the then manager Jack Mansell. On leaving football he worked in the food industry in the South of England and later moved to Australia, where he died in 1985. He is buried in Perth.[5]

Leslie Goldberg was a one-off as a local Jewish boy playing for his hometown club as no other Jewish player has followed him into the 1st team; but Jewish involvement in Leeds United escalated from a growing level of support to that of involvement in general management and positions on the Board of Directors. In September 1956, the West Stand at Elland Road was destroyed by fire and appeals were made for cash to rebuild the stand along with Leeds City Council. One of the cash-raising initiatives was the formation of the 100 Club, the objective of which was to raise money by charging £100 to watch matches from a club room to be incorporated into the new West Stand. This was an early example of corporate sponsorship and it allowed many Jewish supporters to join one of the major sporting institutions of the city at a 'corporate level' from which they had previously been barred. Jewish members of the 100 Club, like Manny Cussins, Albert Morris and Leslie Silver, all successful local businessmen, joined with other successful members of the Jewish community to comfortably rub shoulders with non-Jewish members' in a convivial environment. It was to these men that the club turned in difficult times for finance and other assistance in running the club.

The club's manager Don Revie met many of the club's Jewish members, socialised with them and even joined the Jewish golf club. The era of emancipation within the national game had begun thanks to initiatives by the Leeds club, all brought about by their need for finance and direction. In 1961 the club was on the verge of bankruptcy. Who better for the board to turn to for assistance than members of the 100 Club? Albert Morris and Manny Cussins answered the call, as did Sydney Simon. They became directors and each lent substantial funds interest free to stave off the club's possible demise. Albert Morris was briefly the Chairman, but it was two other Jewish men who were to become the boardroom giants of Leeds United. Manny Cussins and Leslie Silver were the most influential in restructuring and refinancing the club and became synonymous with the club's successes over a period of twenty years. Both of them regarded their involvement as a matter of civic duty.

Manny Cussins, who made his fortune in the furniture retail business, was determined 'to give something back' to his home town, as were many members of the Jewish community who had been successful in their careers in the city. Hence Cussins was willing to lend money to Leeds United and join the Board, eventually becoming the Chairman in 1972. When Cussins became Chairman, Leeds United were at the height of their powers. Don Revie was the Manager, the club had just won the FA Cup and played in the European Cup-winners Cup the following season and the First Division title was to follow in 1974. Leeds were runners up in the European Cup the following season. The Revie/Cussins era brought great success to the club and this was reflected in the success of the city and its enhanced international reputation.

In July 1974, Don Revie left Leeds to become England Manager. A period of unfulfilled promise ensued, overseen by a succession of relatively unsuccessful managers, and the club was eventually relegated in 1982. Manny Cussins was desperately looking for investment. He met Leslie Silver at a charity event hosted by another successful Leeds Jewish entrepreneur, Arnold Ziff. He approached Leslie Silver and said 'I hear you're a football fan and particularly interested in Leeds United. Would you like to join the United board?' Silver cautiously enquired 'What is it going to cost me?' to which Cussins replied

'Absolutely nothing.'[6] Silver joined the board and loaned the club £2 million, believing that he could make a difference and that he was in a position to give something back to his adopted city.

Beset by hooliganism, the club's reputation as well as its finances were in the doldrums. In 1983, Silver became Chairman. He put in place a business plan. He restructured the finances by way of a share issue and sold the freehold of the ground to the city council with an agreement that the club would commit to working with local community initiatives. Silver believed that this commitment from the council would mean that the club would be treated as part of the city's culture. The aim was to play a positive role in improving community facilities in the south west of the city. Black players were recruited, which helped to eliminate racial chanting and abuse. Players were contractually obliged to give 7 hours a week to community service in schools and youth clubs. Efforts were made to make attendance at matches a family occasion with the opening of a family stand and a fully staffed creche. The unemployed were provided with facilities, and training in basic skills was introduced, including reading and writing in conjunction with the Apex Trust to assist in securing employment. Women were encouraged to attend aerobic classes. Identity card schemes and all-ticket away-game involvement reduced hooliganism. Finances were stabilised.

The issue of management of the team was difficult. Allan Clarke, Eddie Gray and Billy Bremner had all failed to revive the club, which by 1988 was close to relegation again. Silver was able to convince Howard Wilkinson, who was managing Sheffield Wednesday, to come to Leeds with a transfer fund of £2 million. He was to be Leeds' eighth manager in fifteen years. With the club in a mess, Wilkinson introduced his brand of meticulous pre-planning and ruthless strict training. Nothing and nobody were sacred. The club was saved from relegation, promoted to the First Division in 1989/90 and in 1991/92 won the League. Wilkinson and Leslie Silver produced results on the field and off the field. They put together a wonderful team. The stadium was modernised, a state-of-the-art training academy was established and the club – now financially sound – had rebuilt its reputation both on and off the field. In April 1996, Leslie Silver announced his resignation and his intention to sell his substantial stake in the club. He left with his reputation as a business leader and communal visionary substantially enhanced.

With the departure of Leslie Silver the golden period of Jewish involvement with professional football in Leeds came to an end. Various directors and chairmen followed until in 2004, with the club heavily in debt after borrowing vast amounts to finance a 'dream of European success' and in administration, it was acquired by Adulent Force Limited, a consortium led by Gerald Krasner, the Jewish head of a local accountancy practice. After a year reducing debt, the consortium sold out to Ken Bates, the ex-Chelsea Chairman.

How did the Leeds public, both Jewish and non-Jewish, react to the involvement of members of the Leeds Jewish community in the city's football club? Anthony Clavane claims that he personally experienced very little anti-Semitism as a Leeds United fan in the 1970s – although he does recall taunts of 'Yid' being heard from the supporters of other Yorkshire teams when they came to Elland Road, and chants of 'Does your rabbi know you're here?' made him feel somewhat proud.

That there was anti-Semitism on the terraces was apparent, but it was being expressed as part of the culture that pervaded society generally at this time. The Jewish community itself was proud to support the Leeds United team and felt that their support was part of their acceptance within the city. There were few expressions of concern from the wider community about the Jewish business community's involvement in the running and ownership of the club, as their involvement had saved it from financial ruin and also brought success on the field.

The only real anti-Semitism expressed at Board level were the sentiments and prejudices of the Chairman of Burnley Football Club, who made many enemies during his involvement with football at a time when the leading clubs had in all three Jewish directors, one of whom was Manny Cussins.

Stories abound of Jewish supporters following and playing both codes, but what of the local youth? Was there an involvement in local amateur football and, if so, how did this manifest itself? There was never any encouragement for young Jewish boys to play sport for both religious and cultural reasons. Playing on the Sabbath was forbidden and the playing of sport was regarded by the elders of the community as not being something that Jews did.

At Lovell Road School in Leeds, with a predominantly Jewish intake, the sports master Nat Collins (the mentor of Leslie Goldberg) encouraged all the pupils to get involved in sport and PT. Mr Collins, who was Jewish himself, wanted the children to shed their parent's Old World ideas and face the outside world and integrate using sport as their vehicle. As part of this strategy he entered the school into the Leeds Schools Cup and they made it to the final. Football had become a very popular pastime for young Jewish boys and Lovell Road School had a very successful team in the 1920s. From the late 1940s, the Leeds Jewish Institute had an excellent team, playing in their green and white squares at Soldiers Field. Other successful local teams followed, including the Judean Club, Ajex, Lions and Maccabi and eventually a girl's team, the Amazones, was formed.

Mick Adler, 'the John Charles of the Jewish soccer scene', was one of the finest Jewish players in the country, playing for the Institute first as a centre half and then as centre forward. He was approached by semi-professional clubs, but never left the Institute. Similarly, Alan Preston had professional trials but stayed with Jewish football, playing for the Institute for fifteen years and captaining representative sides. Other players included Mel Rubin, Cyril Skolnick and Cyril Villiers (whose career in sports administration is discussed later), Brian Jackson, Anthony Kelvin and Ronnie Mackler, who also played as a semi-professional. Whether representing the Institute, the Judean Club, Ajex or the Lions, Leeds Jewish football flourished and developed a great rivalry with Manchester Jewish teams, with games being played in the Manchester Jewish Soccer League and the Northern Jewish Soccer League – which was much stronger, with teams from Southport, Blackpool, Liverpool, Leeds, Sheffield and Manchester. The mantle of Jewish football in Leeds is now held by the thriving Leeds Maccabi Football Club, which plays football from junior to senior level in several Yorkshire and Lancashire leagues.

Rugby league

Jewish involvement with rugby began well before its involvement with association football. In order to encourage people to attend church and to be good Christians, in 1874 Leeds Parish Church formed a rugby team to bring inner city youths into the church and under the influence of the Church of England. The same year had seen the Saturday Half Holiday Act become law, and this was a catalyst for the popularity of rugby. Workers were now free on Saturday afternoons to indulge in leisure activities, and due to increases in prosperity had the means to enjoy them. As rugby became more popular, so the demography in the area close to the Parish Church was changing. The Leeds Parish Church Rugby team in the 1880s became the focus of support of Leeds' growing Jewish immigrant community, as the result of the closeness of the Jewish area of the city to the Church. They became some of the most committed and partisan spectators and in the 1890s the Jewish support was so prominent that the Church teams' supporters were known by the anti-Semitic term 'sheenies'. The Parish Church team became infamous for crowd violence and intimidation of referees, but there were also accusations of paying players in direct contravention of the RFUs amateur rules. In 1901, this misconduct resulted in the team being closed down, with most players moving to Leeds RL, being followed by their Jewish fans.

One of the earliest known Jewish players in Leeds was Eli Hyman Jacobson, who first played for Leeds Parish Church in 1892. He made his debut playing for the A team against Otley A. He also played for Hunslet, Holbeck and Leeds and won representative honours, playing twelve times for Yorkshire between 1896 and 1898. Jacobson, a local butcher, had his athletic prowess rewarded with a medal presented by the Leeds Jewish community in 1897. He was sentenced to ten years penal servitude for attempted murder in 1901 and died in 1932 from injuries sustained after 'slipping on a cabbage leaf'.[7]

The sport had become so popular in Leeds that Professor Selig Brodetsky, who was Professor of Applied Mathematics at Leeds University, wrote in his 'The Intellectual Level of Anglo-Jewish Life': 'the road in which I live in Leeds, leading to and from the famous Headingley ground, is crowded every Saturday by … wandering Jews, upon whom the "packele" of the Torah seems to sit very lightly indeed.'[8] Reports suggest that the sound of Yiddish songs was heard ringing out from the South Stand in the 1930s.

Jewish players were evident in other cities such as Hull, where Louis Harris made 255 appearances for Hull KR scoring seventy-six tries between 1920 and 1928. He was a Yorkshire Cup Winner in 1920, a Championship winner in 1923 and a Challenge Cup runner up in 1925. His long career with the club culminated in the 1960s when he retired as a Director and Chairman.

The number of Jewish players declined after the Second World war, but Leeds RL signed probably the most famous of all Jewish players, Wilf Rosenberg, in 1959 (Figure 13.1). The son of a South African Rabbi, he became only the fifth Jew to represent South Africa when he played for the Springboks against the British Lions in 1955. He had been scouted by Leeds and he learned of his record £6k transfer while on honeymoon. Rosenberg, who was a medical student back in South Africa, switched to dentistry at Leeds University on his arrival, hence his nickname of 'The Flying Dentist'. He played at centre initially but was successfully switched to the wing with devastating effect. He had a memorable three-year stay at Leeds helping the club to win its first Championship in season 1960/1, scoring forty-eight tries. He played eighty-one games for Leeds, scoring seventy-three tries, before moving on to Hull in 1961 (Figure 13.2). In an interview with David Saffer of the *Jewish Telegraph*, Rosenberg said of his stay in Leeds:

> The club were not *schmocks* (fools). They knew a Jewish boy could draw the crowds and on my first appearance the number of Jewish fans was incredible. The Jewish community was fantastic. We were often asked for Friday night supper and it is something I've never forgotten.[9]

As the numbers of Jewish players in rugby league declined, Jews began to make their mark as administrators in Hull, Liverpool, Swinton and in particular in Leeds – where Ronnie Teeman, Bernard Shooman, Tony Sugare, Jeff Wine, Melvyn Levi and Jeff Walton (a current Director of Leeds Rhinos) have all had a part to play in the Leeds rugby league story. These changes, which can be seen in other sports such as boxing and football, have reflected the changes within the Jewish community, which after the Second World War became more affluent and upwardly mobile and where careers in the professions and business, rather than in professional sport, are seen as the path to a prosperous future.

When he retired in 2013, Ronnie Teeman had been practising as a solicitor for over sixty years and had been involved in many high-profile cases. After graduating from Leeds University, he was articled to a Leeds solicitor before starting his own practice in 1952; he is best-known in sporting circles, though, for his representation of many well-known sportsmen and sports bodies. While he would never describe himself as an 'agent', he represented many sportsmen in their negotiations with clubs regarding their contracts, wages and terms of employment. He is probably most remembered for his involvement with professional football. He represented Billy Bremner, for example, in his libel action against *The Sunday People*, which accused him of offering a bribe to a player in a vital match. Teeman secured for Bremner £100,000 record damages. He also represented Johnny Giles in his action against the publishers of *The Damned United*. The publishers paid Giles damages and corrected the untruths told about Giles in subsequent editions of the book.

Both codes of rugby, though, were Ronnie's real sporting love and as a young man he had a great interest in amateur rugby league in Leeds. He was introduced to the Leeds and District Amateur Rugby League by referee Bernard Lester and began to advise young players; as a result he was elected to the Committee and came into contact with the professional game and professional players. He became legal advisor to the Rugby League and eventually was appointed the League's President. His wise counsel was particularly valued by David Oxley, who became the Secretary General of the Rugby League in 1975. Oxley said of Ronnie in his Foreword to Ronnie's autobiography:

> From my earliest days at Rugby League headquarters in the mid-1970s Ronnie proved to be a staunch friend, a wise counsellor and a fine advocate, whose skills were as influential in the game as they were celebrated in the courtroom.[10]

Ronnie was involved in establishing the New Hunslet club, following the demise of the old Hunslet RL, and secured them a ground at Leeds Greyhound Stadium at Elland Road; he also undertook the introduction of tuning-fork goalposts, which were eventually replaced by traditional rugby posts as a result of objections from visiting clubs. He hired a helicopter to hover over a waterlogged ground to ensure that a lucrative Challenge Cup tie went ahead guaranteeing national publicity for the club and for the game of rugby league. Ronnie was instrumental in convincing a sceptical Rugby League Council in 1986 that the game's flagship matches should be staged at Old Trafford. This has proved to be both a commercial and marketing success with the Premiership Final being played annually at Old Trafford now one of British sports' iconic events. His legal and persuasive powers were seen at their peak when he convinced the clubs to adopt a standard playing contract clearly outlining rights and obligations of both players and clubs. This was a landmark moment for rugby league for which the game, according to Oxley, should be eternally grateful.

Jewish characters abounded in rugby league in the 1960s and 1970s, including Syd Cohen who played for Dewsbury, Darren Cohen who played for Castleford and Dewsbury and Leeds-based Pinky Klein who played for Hull. One of the most enduring characters in the game has been Bernard Shooman, who has been involved with amateur and professional rugby league since his childhood as player, grade one referee, coach, scout and in various administrative roles at professional and amateur levels (Figure 13.3). After playing rugby at school and in the RAF in the 1950s, he started to watch Leeds RL in 1961 and played for Leeds Judeans – one of the three Jewish amateur rugby league teams in the city, the others being Leeds Jewish Institute and Leeds Maccabi. He became so dismayed with the standard of refereeing that he decided to become a referee himself and joined the Leeds & District Referees Society, eventually becoming a Grade 1 referee in 1974 and refereeing mostly in the amateur game. He had taken an RL coaching course at Lilleshall in 1971 and became a qualified amateur rugby league coach. He got involved in rugby league broadcasting with Radio Leeds in 1976, and later worked with Radio Aire, Pennine Radio and Red Rose Radio as well as reporting on a number of televised games.

In 1979, Bernard resigned as a senior referee to take up the position of Secretary/ Manager at Dewsbury RL – a position which he held until resigning in 1985. In 1987, he was appointed Chief Scout at Leeds RL by the then Manager Maurice Bamford, bringing such players to the club as Francis Cummins, Paul Anderson and John Bentley. He was sacked in 1992 by Dougie Laughton. Bernard has continued his involvement with the sport and still works on many organisations and committees involving rugby. In 2016, he was given the ultimate accolade and was awarded the John Holmes Memorial Trophy for his services to rugby league in Leeds.[11]

Cricket

Involvement in professional cricket has been limited for the Jewish Community. No Jewish professional players have played for Yorkshire CCC, but the late Recorder of Leeds Judge, Brian Walsh – one of whose major leisure pursuits was watching cricket – was elected to the County Committee in 1984 and became Chairman in 1986 in the aftermath of the Geoffrey Boycott affair. 'His charm and diplomacy did much to heal the rifts at a difficult time', according to the *Daily Telegraph*. At the end of his Chairmanship in 1991 he was made a Life Vice President.

Young Jewish boys played cricket in the local parks, but it is not until the early 1930s that there is any record of organised cricket. In 1931, there are reports of regular cricket being played by Jewish boys in Potternewton Park, in the heavily Jewish populated Chapeltown area of Leeds. In 1932, calling themselves Potternewton Juniors, they played well in a competition run by a local newspaper and many of the boys subsequently attended a Rover Scout camp; it was there that the New Rover Cricket Club was formed, playing its first game at Soldiers Field on 16 June 1934. For fifty years the team played on the same No. 11 pitch on Soldiers Field, using an old garden shed which cost £20 as a pavilion. The only games were friendlies and recruitment was normally via the introduction of player's sons and nephews. Bernard 'Seggy' Seaton, one of the original organisers of the cricket matches and a stalwart of the club, kept contact with all of the players during the war which ensured that when peace came and there was a return to normality, the New Rover club was able to pick up where they left off. A successful businessman, Seggy's great passion was New Rovers which he served in every capacity for the next forty years. The club developed a thriving junior section, and by the late 1980s a decision was made to abandon friendlies and to become involved in league cricket. In 1988, an application was successfully made to join the Dales Council Cricket League.

Continued success in the League put increasing pressure on the limited facilities at Soldiers Field, which was hampering the club's ambitions. In May 1993, a 7.5-acre piece of land was acquired in the Adel suburb of North Leeds with the financial help of the Richmond family, who were passionately interested in cricket as well as in football. The aptly named Richmond Oval was transformed into a superb cricket ground. Geoffrey Richmond, whose son Michael played for New Rover, was a successful Leeds-based entrepreneur who acquired control of Bradford City Football Club, becoming Chairman in 1994 and taking them into the Premier League in 1998.

New Rover were promoted as Division B Champions in 1995 with Michael Richmond establishing a new league batting average of 97.5 and opening bowler Richard Stevens taking an exceptional 99 wickets in the league. Higher standards of cricket were aspired to with the club's acceptance into the Leeds League in 1998. A new pavilion was opened, partly funded by a lottery grant. Entry into the Whixley Evening League and the Harrogate Evening League brought more success, with the club winning the Leagues and the MMP Cup. In 1999, there developed a unique partnership with Yorkshire County Cricket Club as the County's Academy squad began to use the ground as its mid-week base. The arrangement with Yorkshire coincided with the full-time employment of Keith Boyce, the ex-County groundsman, to the position of the club's full-time groundsman. The County provided additional equipment as well as a scoreboard from Headingley and a small bungalow was built for the groundsman. The county were using the ground on a regular basis and in 2000 played the United States national team and the Indian State Team Delhi

Blue at the Richmond Oval. The club joined the Wetherby League in the 2000 season and won the Third Division Championship at a canter with three players being picked for the league's representative team.

When 'Seggy', the then President of the club, died in 2001, the club lost someone who had devoted virtually all his spare time to the development of cricket in the Leeds Jewish community and who had been instrumental in establishing and guiding New Rover since its formation in 1934. Born in November 1914, he was a successful businessman, but his commitment to cricket far outweighed virtually everything else in his very busy life. He was the club Secretary, he looked after the ground, he organised the fixtures, looked after the club's finances, he even made the tea and kept in regular contact with all the players. No task was too lowly for him if it meant it was beneficial to the club. He was not looking for thanks or reward. He saw that in the huge numbers of youngsters who joined the club over the years and in the development of its facilities, culminating in the ownership and development of the Richmond Oval. What Seggy or any of those passing through the club could not have foreseen was the development of Leeds Jewish cricket from the pitches of Potternewton Park to the magnificent ground in Adel, a remarkable tale.[12]

Boxing

Boxing is a sport that has had Jewish participants since the early eighteenth century, with such famous names as Daniel Mendoza, Samuel Elias, Aby Belasco, Barney Aaron and Elisha Crabbe; and if one sport epitomises the efforts of the Jews to lift themselves out of the ghetto, it is boxing. The youth of Leeds were no different to those in any other Jewish community as young men strived to better themselves. From the deprived areas of the Leylands, young Jewish men saw the opportunity that success in boxing could bring in terms of fame and fortune.

Above a warehouse in Bridge Street a room existed that during the day was used as a gymnasium and in the evening was used as an illicit gambling club. From this very basic facility, Leeds developed into a recognised boxing centre with a number of well-supported boxing venues close to the city centre, including The National Sporting Club, The Beaufort Club, clubs in Crimbles Street and one located at Cross Harrison Street off Vicar Lane. One club at the top of Skinner Lane featured unlicensed boxing. The most well-known club was the Brunswick Stadium, which featured regular boxing bills every Sunday afternoon. It was initially run by Percy Fox and later by 'Barber' Ben Green and his brother Jack, who became major promoters of boxing in the city and started a dynasty which for many years was synonymous with boxing in the city. The Brunswick was well run, with doctors in attendance including Dr

Samuel Samuel. The Master of Ceremonies was Mott Green and the referee was Ben Green.

The Commercial Club in Vicar Lane, the Lonsdale in Brunswick Terrace, owned by Dave Goodman, and the other clubs were close to each other and became the centre of professional boxing in Leeds in the 1920s. All were close to the Leylands, which meant that many of the boxers who frequented these clubs were Jewish, including Tolly and Rufky Solomon, Louis Ruddick, Cockney Samuels, Harry Mason, Tom Sharkey, 'Cockney' Cohen, 'Cockney' Buxton, Myers Stringer, Alf Mansfield, Lew Taylor and the most famous of all, Joe Fox. Most trained at the gym of 'Professor' Louis Marks, so called because of his great skills as a trainer.

Joe Fox became both the Bantamweight and Featherweight Champion of Great Britain. Born in Leeds in 1894, he began fighting in fairground booths in 1908 and started his professional career at the age of 16 in 1910. He lived with his parents in the Leylands. In 1914, Fox travelled to America with his brothers – who acted as his manager/promoter and trainer – to gain experience and fought in Madison Square Garden and became a great crowd pleaser. He boxed extensively in the United States where he toured three times and he also fought in Australia. He won a Lonsdale Belt outright by the time he was 23.

Harry Mason, who was born in London but came to Leeds as a child, made his professional debut in August 1920 and fought over 200 fights. In 1923, he won the British Boxing Board of Control Lightweight title and later in the year became European Champion. In a career that lasted until 1937, when he lost his final fight to Jack 'Kid' Berg, he won 145 fights, twenty-six by knockout. Mason was known for his astonishing confidence and aggression and also for his showmanship. He often played the violin or recited poetry from the ring before a fight, and in 1926 he appeared in vaudeville at the Holborn Empire, singing, dancing and conducting a band.

Ben Green was a very popular referee in the city and became a Grade A referee of international repute. He refereed many international championship fights which featured many distinguished fighters, including Benny Lynch and 'Kid' Berg – both of whom were world champions – and Bruce Woodcock. Ben was the first ever radio commentator on a match that was being broadcast from Leeds Town Hall. In 1965, Ben was made President of the Leeds District Ex-Boxers Association. Ben's eldest son, Mott, was a Boy's Yorkshire Area Champion and his youngest son, Danny, boxed for his Battalion during the war and became Brigade Flyweight Champion.

Around 1935, Jewish involvement in boxing was at its height, but the period immediately after the Second World War saw a decline in interest which was reflected in the Leeds boxing scene. The two remaining viable venues were the Brunswick and the National. Boxing was still promoted at the

Town Hall by Jack Green, brother of Ben who had now retired, and Jack's son Arthur, but these were mainly charity events.

Leeds Jewish involvement in boxing continues today in the work of Alan Alster, who is an official British Boxing Board of Control Inspector (Figures 13.4, 13.5 and 13.6). Alan recalls listening to boxing on the radio with his father in the late 1940s and being interested in the sport; and going to a tough school in Harehills he learnt to box to defend himself. As a young man he continued his interest in the sport and became a fixture on the Leeds boxing scene, attending fights and writing reports for *Boxing Monthly*. He became involved with the Leeds Ex-Boxers Association and has been on the committee for over thirty years. In 1987, he was asked by the Chief Inspector of the Board of Control if he would like to become an Inspector. On accepting the role Alan undertook training, which included seminars on the rules of boxing, and had a twelve-month probationary period which he successfully completed. Alan as the Inspector is the 'eyes and ears' of the Board of Control. His job is to ensure that all the relevant medical safeguards and controls are implemented at a tournament. The Inspector supervises the weighing of boxers and ensures that the ring dimensions are in accordance with the regulations. He confirms gloves are the correct standard and in good condition; he is in the boxers' dressing room when hands are bandaged and signs the bandage to confirm that all is correct before gloves are put on and laced up. Alan has been the Inspector at hundreds of fights in the North of England and still carries out his role at several contests each month.[13]

Wrestling

Arthur Green of the famous Green family, who were engaged in boxing and boxing promotion in Leeds, was to develop his own career in promotion via the sport of wrestling. He met George de Relwysko Junior, the son of George de Relwysko who was a double wrestling Olympic Gold Medal winner. George Jnr himself was a wrestler and teamed up with his brother after the war to promote wrestling along with Arthur. Their business and five others formed an alliance in 1948 called Joint Promotions, which promoted wrestling across the UK with Arthur as the Secretary. Every major town had a show every month. Joint Promotions established a strict set of rules for a clean and technical sport. By the mid-1960s this cartel, which virtually controlled the professional wrestling business, was promoting 4,500 live events every year.

Relwysko and Green kept their independence, and from 1969 until the early 1980s live wrestling took place in the now demolished Astoria Ballroom on Roundhay Road, having previously been held at Leeds Town Hall. It was the exposure of the sport on television that gave wrestling a truly national profile. Arthur, George and the other promoters negotiated with the new commercial television companies and came to an agreement to show wrestling on ABC and ATV – the weekend franchise holders on ITV. The first show appeared on 9 November 1955 from West Ham Baths. It was a success and wrestling became a main attraction every Saturday from Autumn to Spring, and in 1964 became a full-time feature on ITVs main sports programme World of Sport. The shows were compered by Kent Walton and televised every week until 1988.

Relyskow and Green became household names. They put Leeds on the sporting map. They were running up to forty shows a week in thirty cities in England and Scotland. Arthur travelled the world, even visiting Arab countries to sign up wrestlers. Wrestlers were feted wherever they went and became the sporting superstars of the day. Arthur continued to promote boxing, promoting Londsdale Belt Championship bouts in the 1950s, and brought Floyd Patterson over to the UK to fight Henry Cooper in 1966. He became involved in the promotion of pop music concerts with Bernard Hinchcliffe and in 1963 they launched 'all night' concerts where breakfast was available if audience members stayed after midnight. An early show in 1962 featured the Beatles before they went to Hamburg. Arthur was closely involved with Leeds charities and was instrumental in establishing the Leeds Jewish Sportman's Committee which, through boxing events at Leeds Town Hall, raised substantial sums for Leeds Jewish charities.[14]

Golf

Sport witnessed social, non-organised expressions of anti-Semitism from the 1890s onwards. A number of scholars have termed this the 'anti-Semitism of exclusion' and it ran alongside the organised anti-Semitism of the right-wing and the Fascists.[15] The *Jewish Chronicle* and *The Yorkshire Post* ran articles which evidenced cases of direct exclusion and blackballing in golf clubs in Leeds and surrounding areas. There were, though, clubs like Garforth that welcomed Jewish members, although there were still ongoing issues with membership. As far as Leeds was concerned, ongoing anti-Semitism practised by local golf clubs was a catalyst for the establishment of the first Jewish golf club in the United Kingdom in 1923.

Abe Frais, a member of a club outside Leeds, asked for his wife to be made a member and was refused. That for him was the final straw. Abe and his business partner Hirsch Rosenthal had often talked of the need to have a golf club for the Jewish community. A large piece of land came up for sale in Alwoodley, consisting of 108 acres. Hirsch Rosenthal took a six-month option at approximately £40 per acre. An initial visit to view the land was arranged and a number of interested individuals were invited – including Hyman Morris, Abe Benedict, B. Harrison and Louis Godlove – all of whom joined Abe Frais and Hirsch Rosenthal and his wife. This visit was followed by a number of meetings with other golfers where expressions of interest were confirmed and agreements with regard to contributions made. The decision to take over Hirsch Rosenthal's option and go ahead with the purchase of the land was taken. Negotiations took place with Colonel Lane-Fox MP to purchase 110 acres of land. The acquisition of the land and buildings known as Pykeley Hill Farm was carried out in the name of Mr Willie Naylor, an associate of Abe Frais, as it was feared that a Jewish purchaser might be problematic. The course was designed by Dr Alistair McKenzie along with his brother Major Charles McKenzie, who later was involved in designing the Augusta course the home of the US Masters.

The course opened on 27 March 1923 with twelve playable holes and a number of tennis courts. The early history of the club reveals that there were 170 founder members and the constitution stated that membership would be open to all, irrespective of religion. Early members included Col. Lane Fox, Major Lipscomb, Dr McKenzie and Rev. Buchanan. By the end of the 1920s, the club had consolidated its position in the Jewish community and also in the wider golfing community to the extent that Abe Frais was in 1929 elected President of the Leeds & District Union of Golf Clubs. (He was later followed in that prestigious office by Hyman Morris (1938), David Fox (1952), Doddie Aber (1965), Marshall Bellow (1973), Stanley Fingret (1988) and James Denton (2007).) Probably the most influential figure in Jewish golf in the United Kingdom, Abe died in March 1935. He had inspired the opening of the first Jewish golf club, was an ambassador for Jewish golf and had promoted the cause of the Leeds Jewish community on a local and national basis.

By 1951, the golf club reported 700 members and had one of the best courses in the region. In April 1958, a new clubhouse was opened which contained some of the finest facilities of any clubhouse in the country. Due to the popularity of tennis in the prewar years, the golf club had been opened with a number of tennis courts, and by the mid-1930s there were a number of outstanding players.

The 1950s and 1960s saw the club booming from both a golf and social perspective and membership had risen to over 800; a new Professional Shop and Club Store were completed in 1962. In 1964, Bernard Lyons, a successful businessman and club member, identified a piece of land of 220 acres – Blackmoor Farm – adjacent to his own property which was to be auctioned, and he realised that it would be an ideal means of securing the future of the golf club, which was 3 miles away and surrounded by suburban housing in an area that was ripe for further housing development. Irwin Bellow, the club Chairman, took responsibility for furthering the opportunity and with the full support of the members the project proceeded. The investment was made and a new course was ready for use by October 1970. The official opening of the new club by the Minister of Sport, Mr Eldon Griffiths MP, took place on Sunday 2 May 1971.

The new course designed by American golf architect Robert Trent Jones consisted of three loops of nine holes, tennis courts, a bowling green and a ranch-type clubhouse. The professional was now the internationally renowned Peter Alliss, the seven times Ryder Cup player, winner of innumerable European tournaments and BBC golf commentator. The 1970s and 1980s had seen the club go through many ups and downs with changes in its administration and in its finances, while the 1980s also saw a decline in the Leeds Jewish community from over 20,000 to approximately 10,000 by 1986. Junior membership reduced as other interests overtook golf, including the priority of education, the pressure to leave the city to go to university and the desire to pursue careers – particularly in London and the South East. This impacted on the willingness and ability of those with knowledge of the club to take responsibility for its future by becoming involved in its administration.

The number of applications from non-Jewish members began to exceed those from Jewish members. This was a concern as it might mean at some time in the future that the majority of members would be non-Jewish – which might in extreme circumstances lead to Jewish applications for membership being turned down: members of the Jewish faith might not by right be able to join the club. A similar predicament faced other Jewish golf clubs around the UK. Legal advice was taken and it was agreed that individual shares would pass into the hands of Trustees who would uphold the original objectives of the club to provide a safe place for Jewish golfers unable to join other clubs, which is a situation that still exists today. This resolution was passed on 6 April 1995.

While junior golf declined, promotion of the ladies' game by the club in the 1990s was a major success, bringing in many new members. The club is promoting many ancillary activities and increased investment in its facilities to compete with increasing competition for the interest of potential members, such as the growth of new local golfing facilities based on a different financial structure allowing for occasional use as opposed to full membership. The development of a website and the increasing use of social media has been an attempt to promote the club and to retain and promote club membership and its availability to outside organisations for competitions.

The club has produced some fine Jewish golfers. For example, Stanley Fingret was in 1965 the first Jewish golfer to win the Leeds and District Championship, followed in 1972 and 1981 by Howard Taylor, who also won the individual gold at the Maccabiah Games in 1973. Moor Allerton was also represented regularly in the Maccabiah Games by Stanley Fingret and Johnny Lawrence. More recently, Johnny twice reached the semi-finals of the Yorkshire Amateur Championship and also represented the Yorkshire Team.

As a senior he was a member of the Yorkshire Senior Team which won the English Senior County Finals in 2017.[16]

Tennis

The history of tennis in the Leeds Jewish community is inextricably linked with Moor Allerton Golf Club and the Maccabi Tennis Club, but the way into competitive tennis was always via the Parks Teams which were represented in the divisionalised Parks League. The best players from the Parks League were selected for the city team, which played in the Yorkshire League. A number of Jewish players were involved with the Parks Teams, including probably the most successful of the Leeds Jewish players, Sam Seagal. He was the first Jewish player to win the Leeds Parks singles tennis championship, which he won three times; he also won the mixed doubles five times and the men's doubles seventeen times. He was chosen for the British Maccabiah Team in 1933 but was unable to take part. He was Chairman of the British Parks Lawn Tennis Association and Chairman of the Yorkshire and Leeds Parks Lawn Tennis Association. Sam, a tennis promoter, brought world-class tennis players, including Lew Hoad and Ken Rosewall, to play charity events at the Roundhay Park Arena in the 1950s and 1960s, with the initial event drawing nearly 10,000 spectators.

As golf grew at Moor Allerton, so did tennis, producing some fine players including Esther Wineberg (Nee Nagley), one of the best Jewish tennis players in the country who, interestingly, never played for the Yorkshire County Team. Esther, along with husband Maurice and Sam Seagal, was selected to play for England at the Maccabiah Games in Prague in 1933 but they were unable to accept the invitations, although Esther and Pat Morris played for England in the 1950 Maccabiah Games. Phyllis Barnett (Mrs Glick) was Junior Champion of Wales and a regular in the Yorkshire County Team. Maurice Wineberg represented Leeds in the Inter City Games in the late 1920s and 1930s, winning many trophies in this and other competitions. He was regarded as one of the finest players in the county. David Shulman won the Yorkshire Boys Championships in 1936 and 1937.

Tennis developed strongly at Moor Allerton in the 1950s and 1960s, with one member, Robert Appleson, qualifying as a professional tennis coach in 1972, though the 1970s saw the slow decline of tennis at the club as a result of the poor siting of courts at the club's new location. Neil Frieze became a notable figure on the tennis scene in the late 1960s, becoming both a prominent player and a Lawn Tennis Association qualified coach. Neil was a Yorkshire League title winner in the early 1980s and represented both Yorkshire and Great Britain Veterans. He formed the North Leeds Tennis Club in the early 1990s with a large group of Jewish and non-Jewish players and the club ran until 2011. Neil's son, Simon, was an exceptional tennis talent who represented Yorkshire and the North East Region before playing tennis in the USA and Israel. In more recent years, Rhona Glucksman (nee Rapaport) has been the most prominent individual on the Leeds Jewish tennis scene as a qualified LTA Coach and a promoter of Pro-Ams at the David Lloyd sports centre.

Athletics

The most famous UK Jewish athlete is undoubtedly Harold Abrahams. While the city of Leeds cannot boast a Jewish athlete with the prowess of Abrahams, it did produce an athlete of some note in Dr Frank Aaron, who was the older brother of Leeds' only Second World War VC, Arthur Aaron, and a national athletics coach who coached athletes to Olympic, World and European medals. Frank was a member of Leeds St Mark's Harriers, which became one of the constituent clubs of Leeds Athletic Club which was formed in 1967. He was an English International cross-country runner and has the distinction of being the only man in the twentieth century to win three consecutive English Cross Country Championships (1949–51). The club subsequently founded the Aaron Trophy races in his memory. (Although the Aaron brothers are regularly cited as 'Jewish', recent demographic research has cast doubt on their Jewish identity and affiliation.)

Jonathan Rosenthal, who was coached at school by some of the country's leading athletics coaches, had a career as a junior athlete which took him to County Championship titles in Long Jump, Triple Jump, Javelin and Decathlon and was ranked in the top ten in the UK Triple Jump. Inspired by visits to all the Olympic Athletics events in 1972, 1976 and 1980, Jonathan took up a voluntary coaching position at Leeds Athletic Club, eventually qualifying and later being responsible for coaching in the Northern Counties Area. In 1986, he was appointed Great Britain Coach for both the Horizontal Jumping Events, first for the junior age group in the Triple Jump and later as the senior group event coach for the Long Jump. Over his ten-year career as a National Coach, he was responsible for some thirty athletes who were to become both junior and senior internationals and win national titles.

In 1983, he became coach to a 14-year-old athlete from Derby. Fiona May later came to live in Leeds and attended Trinity and All Saints College. Her career as an athlete took off and she won two Olympic Silver Medals, four World Championship Gold Medals, three European Championship Medals and was ranked as No.1 female long jumper in the world for five years. Jonathan's career included the positions of Great Britain Coach at the Seoul (1988) and Barcelona Olympics (1992), European Athletic Championships (1990), the Commonwealth Games in 1986 and 1990 and at the 2012

Olympics as Advisor to the Brazilian Athletics Team. In 1988 he won The British Association of National Coaches 'Coach of The Year Award'.[17]

In November 2007, Cyril Villiers was awarded an MBE for his services to sport and in November 2012, Cyril and his wife Joan – who had been awarded an BEM in 2012 – were awarded a Lifetime Achievement Award by the Yorkshire Awards Committee. These awards were given by a grateful country and a grateful county for their years of unstinting service to the promotion and the administration of sport and their charity work in Yorkshire and Humberside. Cyril's sporting interests developed as a young man as a footballer playing for the Judean Club/Leeds Jewish Institute, as a table tennis player and even as a sprinter and long jumper. Having qualified in PE and Teaching at Carnegie College he taught PE and maths locally, as well as being involved in leadership at the Judean Club, before moving to Birmingham in 1960 where he became Director of Solihull Athletic Stadium. Returning to Leeds in 1965, he took up the position of Youth Community Officer for West Riding Education Authority. In 1967, he was appointed to the position of Regional Director of the Sports Council responsible for Yorkshire and Humberside. His work in the development of sport between 1967 and his retirement in 1996 saw him become responsible for the sporting development of a region consisting of 5.5 million people, involving all sports and in particular rugby league, rugby union, basketball and table tennis. In 1976 he co-founded the Sports Aid Foundation which raised over £2.5 million over 40 years in Yorkshire and Humberside to assist athletes to meet the costs of their sporting careers.[18]

Leisure

As a consequence of the restrictive conditions under which they lived, and the close family and communal ties that were a function of Jewish life, the Jews of Leeds socialised among themselves and enjoyed a communal leisure experience. Not only were religious, charitable and educational institutions established in the community, but there was also the foundation of a club for young people –The Jewish Young Men's Association, formed in 1896, which later became the Jewish Institute. The Institute became a centre for social and sporting activities, including dances, debating, drama, singing, billiards, draughts and chess, football, cricket and table tennis. By 1936, enough money had been raised to open the Jubilee Hall which became the social centre of the community until its sale in 1984.

The Judean Club was formed in 1929 to provide for the youth what the Leeds Jewish Institute was providing for adults. Both the Young Zionist Society and the B'nai B'rith were closely involved in setting up the Judean. Suitable premises were eventually bought on Barrack Street as a result of local fundraising and the assistance of Montague Burton. The Judean was an early pioneer of mixed clubs – an idea that led to a visit by Basil Henriques, head of the Boys' Club Association of London. The club served juniors, intermediates and seniors and by the late 1930s had grown quite significantly and was known for its progressive policies. The war years saw the formation of a Cadet Corps and a Girls' Training Corps. The end of the war saw the real beginnings of the movement north of the Jewish population and the club began to consider acquiring a sports field and new premises. In 1949, Bernard Lyons became involved with the Judean and with his father's involvement set up a trust fund to be used to establish a Youth Centre in North Leeds as the new focus of the community. A property called The Spinney on Street Lane was acquired in 1954 and officially opened by Edwina, Countess Mountbatten, in 1957 after various alterations and extensions. There was now a ballroom/hall with a stage, gymnasium, changing rooms and showers as well as the original house and grounds.

As the emphasis on sporting activities increased, the Lyons Sporting Association was formed in the late 1970s and sporting activity continued to develop with twelve table tennis teams, gymnastics, football, judo, badminton, gymnastics, weight lifting and shooting sections and keep-fit classes. The Judean celebrated its Golden Jubilee year in 1979, but in 1984 – after a period of decline in numbers and with the property in a state of disrepair – the land and premises were sold to property developers, ending an era of vibrant Jewish youth development from a moral, social and physical perspective. The sale of the Judean property resulted in £500,000 being put into a trust fund which was to be used to develop a replacement property, but it was not until 1998 – with the establishment of the Zone at the Talmud Torah building on Sandhill Lane – that Jewish youth had a replacement for the Judean Club.[19]

Under the leadership of Stanley Cundle and Ian Delroy, the Zone made efforts to find volunteers who would assist with the development of programmes to engage the youth of the community in the new facility. Volunteers came forward, but many had little knowledge or direct experience of youth work. By a process of 'trial and error' programmes were put together and a working philosophy was established. One of the volunteers who continued her involvement with the Zone was Raina Sheaf, who started as a volunteer in 2003 and later became the full-time Operations Director.

As interest from local youth in using the Zone developed, numbers grew substantially. The numbers of children visiting the Zone and taking part in its activities ranged from 120 to 140 per week in the summer to 250 per week in the winter. Facilities were outgrown and the Trustees started to look for alternative premises, with interest in using the free space on the Brodetsky Campus a preference. However, it took several years of discussions and negotiations for this to become a viable option. Money had to be raised, plans agreed and planning permission obtained and most critical was the agreement of the education authorities and the school administration. Success was heralded by the opening of the new Zone in 2014.[20]

The demise of the Judean Club saw a decline in the organised development of many of the sports and activities that had become synonymous with the Club. Some sports, though, took on a 'life of their own' and developed autonomously, like football and table tennis – the latter being reconstituted as the Leeds Judean Table Tennis Club at the Moor Allerton Sports and Social Centre and is still run and administered by many of those who were prominent in developing the sport at the Judean Club, including Cyril Villiers, Alan Taylor, Alan Myerson and Robin Gilmore. Football eventually came under the banner of Maccabi in 1989 after an application to Maccabi GB by Ian Selwyn and Richard Norman. Although there have been 'breakaways' over the subsequent years, local football is now firmly under the Maccabi banner and recent developments have included the awarding of a major grant to develop football pitches and a pavilion on the Henry Cohen Campus where many of the new facilities for the youth of the community, like the Zone, are being centralised.

While the Judean Club and its successor the Zone provided facilities and social activity for the youth of the Jewish community, there has long been a history of the development of other organisations which catered for the youth – and none more so than scouting. Jewish scouting celebrated its centenary in 2009. Formed in 1909, and possibly the oldest Jewish Scout Troop in the world, the 7th Central Leeds (Jewish) produced the 1st Jewish King's Scout, Louis Hobits, in 1913 and found its first permanent home at the Judean Club in 1929 after holding meetings for many years in various premises. Now called the 15th (Northvale), it merged in 1992 with the second Leeds Jewish troop – the 22nd North Leeds (Hillel) – which was formed in 1951 to meet the growing need from the community. This troupe eventually built a Scout and Guide Hut in Fir Tree Wood on Fir Tree Lane.

The development of the game of bridge in Leeds has been a factor in the development of the game across the UK. A leisure activity much loved by Jewish people, it was played in the Jubilee Hall after the Second World War and the Leeds Jewish community provided many exceptional players who played for the Yorkshire County Team. The team was renowned nationally with famous players coming from the city – including Harold Franklin, who played for England and became a leading international Tournament Director and was responsible for changing the laws of the game. Harold invented the Swiss Teams Scoring System. Irving Manning was likewise a fine player who played for Great Britain in the Tenerife Olympiad in 1974. Other notable players included Joe Bloomberg, Eric Newman and Alf Finlay. Leeds Bridge Club formed in 1978, based in many venues, but is now run from the Moor Allerton Sports and Social Centre.

The arts

Jewish immigrants to the United Kingdom brought with them a keen interest in the arts, and those coming to Leeds showed enthusiasm in supporting all areas of cultural activity, which included professional and amateur theatre, music, painting and much more. The community has produced writers, artists, musicians, actors and actresses and has been keen to promote and support all aspects of the community's cultural development, with certain families being at the forefront of this patronage.

Often unable to speak or understand the language and culture, the growing Jewish population relished visits to the city from groups of travelling Yiddish actors whose performances were a popular distraction from the humdrum lives they led; but it was not until the late 1930s that the first signs of interest in creating a local Jewish theatre company appeared. Alec Baron, who had always had an interest in theatre and cinema, had been fascinated by the London-based Unity Theatre and wanted to create something similar in Leeds. The war interrupted his plans, but he quickly re-kindled his interest and established the Leeds Citizens Theatre. He put on a number of plays for charity and was soon asked to assist in setting up a Jewish drama group, The Proscenium Players. One of those first members was Cecil Korer, who was later to become a TV Producer and Commissioning Editor for C4 and produced many programmes, including Jeux Sans Frontiers, The Good Old Days, Ask The Family and Countdown. The Players' first production was J. B. Priestley's *An Inspector Calls* in November 1948. Others quickly followed and their reputation grew. Along with Cecil Korer, others in the team included Cyril Livingstone, Doreen Barnett, Zelda Black, Gerald Coleman, Minnie Marks and Max Gordon. The philosophy of the group was to put on four productions a year with one having a Jewish interest, and the Leeds Women's International Zionist Organization (WIZO) agreed to be their sponsor.

The company became known as the 'Pross' and the most momentous production tackled was *The Dybbuk*, which had a cast of over forty and a set designed by Cyril Livingstone. Although it was staged in December 1950, it is still remembered as a highlight of the Pross' twenty years of productions and the pinnacle of Alec Baron's career. Great successes were achieved in the 1950s, 1960s and the 1970s as the popularity of amateur theatre grew across the city and the professionalism of the Pross and other local theatre companies increased. Critical success attracted many actors who were to turn professional, including Pamela Cowan, George Cooper, Barbara Kellerman, Ronald Pickup and Beverley Callard – who was later to star in Coronation Street for many years as Liz McDonald.

New, younger, members were taking over from those who had founded the Pross and they carried on its traditions well into the mid-1990s. A new theatrical group which came to be known as Limelight was established in 1977 by members of the Beth Hamedrash Hagadol Synagogue. After several successful productions, Limelight entered its first drama festival in Bradford winning the Best Actress Award. Other festivals followed, and in 1987 and 1988 Sydney Levine and Lawrence Gorsden won Best Actor Awards. Young Limelight was formed in 1995 to encourage youngsters from the Jewish community to experience the theatre. The production of *Kindertransport* in 1997 brought great press and local television interest, with Yorkshire Television's Calendar showing rehearsals and interviewing members of the cast. Emma Gordon won the Best Actress and the play won the award for Best Drama Production at the Leeds Civic Arts Guild Award Ceremony – the 'Oscar' ceremony for Leeds amateur theatre. Two productions a year were presented at the Civic Theatre and in 2001 Limelight were a major element in setting up the Leeds Jewish Theatre Festival. In the same year they acquired their own premises at the Street Lane Gardens Synagogue.

In 2006, the Civic Theatre closed and productions were moved to the new Carriageworks Theatre. Limelight also presented productions at the Marjorie and Arnold Ziff Community Centre. Further awards followed at festivals including at the Wharfedale Festival of Theatre. By 2010, difficulties were regularly being experienced in casting productions and in finding committed backstage crews and many older members, some of whom were founder members, were looking to retire. At the AGM in 2011, Harry Venet was awarded the Limelight Cup for 14 years sterling service as Chairman and the feeling was that unless a miracle occurred the group would close down. There was no miracle and after thirty-five years and nearly seventy productions Limelight was no more.

The professional stage has seen actors and actresses and writers from the Leeds Jewish community have very successful careers. Actresses like Thelma Ruby and Kay Mellor, who is also a successful scriptwriter, and her daughter Gaynor Faye have all become nationally recognised figures. Thelma trained to be an actress in the USA during the Second World War and then worked for ENSA entertaining wounded soldiers round the UK before starting serious acting in repertory theatre. She appeared in several films during the 1950s and 1960s and in major television series – including Doctors, Comedy Playhouse, Minders and Dempsey and Makepiece and Z Cars – and is still working. Kay Mellor started her writing career on Coronation Street with Granada Television in the 1980s.

One of the world's most famous music teachers is Leeds-born Fanny Waterman. A talented pianist and teacher, she launched the Leeds Piano Festival in 1961 with her friend Marian, the Countess of Harewood, and it has become one of the paramount piano competitions in the world. The first winner of the competition in 1963 was Michael Roll who was just 17. Fanny was the competition's Chair and Artistic Director until her retirement in 2015.

Although not Leeds born, Eta Cohen spent many years in the city as a wife and mother and as a teacher of violin and viola to many talented students who went on to have successful careers in music. Her own daughter, Maureen, had a career as a successful soloist. A mainstay of the Leeds music community, she wrote a series of textbooks which have become one of the world's best-selling series of instrument tutor books. The Eta Cohen Violin Method continues to be an inspiration for violin teachers throughout the world.

Leeds Jewry has also been well represented in the national popular music field, with Frankie Vaughan, Julie Grant, Jeff Christie and the group Outer Limits – of which Christie had been a member – all achieving popular acclaim. Jeff Christie's most famous song – Yellow River, written and recorded in 1970 – became an international hit, selling over 30 million copies, and was followed later in the same year by San Bernadino – another hit for the band, now called Christie. The Yellow River theme was later to become part of a famous television advertising jingle.

The Leeds Jewish community's contribution to the arts has rarely been promoted. Artists and writers have been prolific and their Jewish backgrounds have not been over-emphasised, although in many cases the theme of their work has reflected their ethnic and Jewish background which they have used to complement the content and veracity of their work. Jacob Kramer's most recognised work, for example, is *The Day of Atonement* (1919) closely followed by *The Jew* (1916).

Two art exhibitions took place in Leeds in 2013. One was the '100 Years of Jewish Art in Leeds' exhibition, curated by Helen Frais of Makor, the Leeds Jewish cultural organisation, and asked the question 'What is Jewish Art'. The second was the Jewish Artists in Yorkshire exhibition, which was based on works by the major Jewish artists held by the Leeds University's art collection and loans from local public and private collections, and which took place at the the Stanley and Audrey Burton Gallery at the University. Curator Layla Bloom said that the exhibition was not just about the local area, but about the contribution that many of the artists had made both nationally and internationally. Artists' works exhibited included those by Jacob Kramer, Philip Naviasky and Willy Tirr, Bernard Weninsky and Joash Woodrow. Works by contemporary artists like Gillian Singer and Judith Tucker were also included.

Conclusion

This chapter has demonstrated that the popular conception of Jewish indifference to and exclusion from sporting and leisure activities is erroneous.

A rich variety of personalities and achievements has enriched the life of Leeds Jewish society over the generations. Sport and leisure provided opportunities for personal fulfilment and added no little kudos to the Leeds Jewish community.

13.1 Wilf Rosenberg

13.2 Wilf Rosenberg scoring for Leeds RL

13.3 Bernard Shooman receiving his award

13.4 Alan Alster with Larry Holmes

13.5 Alan Alster with Mohamed Ali

13.6 Alan Alster with Antony Joshua

Notes

1. D. Dee, *Sport and British Jewry* (Manchester: Manchester University Press, 2013).
2. E. C. Sterne, *Leeds Jewry 1919–1929* (Leeds: The Jewish Historical Society of England, 1989), p. 19.
3. E. Krausz, *Leeds Jewry. Its Historical and Social Structure* (Cambridge: Heffer, 1964), p. 29.
4. T. Collins, *1895 And All That* (Leeds: Scratching Shed Publishing, 2009), p. 61.
5. A. Clavane, 'The strange disappearance of Leslie Goldberg', *The Blizzard*, 7 December 2012.
6. J. Fisher, *Painting The Town Silver* (Leeds: Beecroft Publications, 2015), p. 81.
7. *Leeds Mercury*, 22 October 1932.
8. Quoted by S. Kadish, *Good Jews and Good Englishmen* (Abingdon: Routledge, 1995).
9. *Jewish Telegraph*, 11 June 2011.
10. R. Teeman, *A Lawyer For All Seasons*, foreword by David Oxley CBE (Leeds: Scratching Shed Publishing, 2011).
11. Interview with Bernard Shooman, 27 January 2017.
12. Interview with Clive Sullivan, 28 March 2017.
13. Interview with Alan Alster, 20 January 2017.
14. Interview with Margaret Cohen (neé Green), 17 April 2017.
15. Dee, *Sport and British Jewry*, p. 174.
16. Ted Hyman, *A History of Moor Allerton Golf Club* (Leeds: privately printed, 1994).
17. Interview with Jonathan Rosenthall, 28 February 2017.
18. Interview with Cyril Villiers, 30 January 2017.
19. Interview with Alan Myerson, 24 March 2017.
20. Interview with Reina Sheaf, 25 May 2017.

14

The influence of personalities
Michael Meadowcroft

Introduction

Every society has its personalities, individuals who stand out, some who inspire and some who change the course of events. Not all of them are pleasant men and women – sometimes to achieve vital changes requires more toughness than diplomacy. What is significant about the Jewish community in Leeds is how soon the poor, Yiddish-speaking immigrants from the Russian empire in the late nineteenth century onwards produced remarkable leaders. Also, it is noticeable that many of the key figures used their leadership more to impress the city of Leeds than to interpret the community, and its Jewishness, to its citizens. Some, though far from all of them, with that understandable wish to impress, seemed to emphasise their ability to identify and compete successfully with the broader community, rather than to demonstrate a Jewish identity which was of itself beneficial to the city of Leeds.[1]

The casual anti-Semitism that was latent in Leeds as elsewhere was a catalyst to the work of Jewish leaders within the city whose work and example provided a consistent antidote. It is notable that so many impressive Jewish individuals adopted Leeds with a passion and became identified with the city. For first-generation immigrants that was far from being automatic, as their initial priority was to achieve economic survival which often required them to travel before finally settling in Leeds.

The selection here of key Jewish figures in Leeds is inevitably subjective, but the criterion has been those who made an impact on the city rather than those whose contribution was, no doubt commendably, chiefly within the community.

The first notable Jewish leader in Leeds was Gabriel Davis, who came to the city from Germany about 1815 and by 1837 had succeeded in buying a plot of land for Jewish burials among the fifty or so Jewish residents in Leeds, in Gelderd Road, Gildersome – still in use today. He died in October 1851.[2]

The early Jewish community in Leeds was largely of German origin and mainly middle-class wool merchants. They have largely been ignored by Leeds Jewish historians, partly because the overwhelming majority of Leeds Jews came as a consequence of the persecution of Russian Jews following the assassination of Tsar Alexander II in 1881, and also because, once Bradford had overtaken Leeds as main centre of the wool trade, many of the early immigrants moved to Bradford. One such individual was Jacob Behrens (1806–89) who settled in Leeds in 1834.[3] He soon became involved in 'establishment' organisations in the city, becoming a proprietor of the Leeds Library in 1837[4] and an early member of the Leeds Club.[5] Interestingly, though there was later a de facto bar on Jewish members, Behrens' grandson, Edgar, became a member in 1942. The bar was finally broken in the 1970s by Peter Fingret,[6] with the support of a number of younger members who persisted in nominating him.

Paul Hirsch (1835–1908)

One immigrant from Germany who did not move to Bradford was Paul Hirsch, who become the first member of the community to have a significant influence on the civic life of Leeds. He was born in 1834 in the spa town of Waren in the present German state of Mecklenburg-West Pomerania. He came to Leeds 'early in life' and set up in business as an export woollen merchant in partnership with Henry Josephy, whose family was also from Mecklenburg. After Paul Hirsch's death in 1908, the original company only survived until 1913 – although there was a successor business which continued until 1930.

The company was initially based in Hunslet but it soon became established in Cookridge Street, variously at numbers 27, 29, 33 and 35 – premises which for many years housed the main bookshops of Austicks and are currently occupied by a hairdresser and a cafe. Paul Hirsch was living in Brunswick Terrace, off Camp Road, in 1870, in Reginald Terrace, Chapeltown, in 1881 and, finally, in 1901 in Alma House, on the corner of Alma Road and Otley Road, Headingley.

He married Caroline, who was also from Mecklenburg, and they had a daughter, Anna Bertha, in early 1874. He was naturalised in 1866. He became closely involved in Leeds Jewish organisations and was an acknowledged leader. He was President of the Great Synagogue in Belgrave Street from 1878 to his death in 1908; was Vice-President of the Leeds branch of the Anglo-Jewish Society from 1881; and was also President of the Leeds Jewish Young Men's Association. Most important of all his civic roles was the inaugural presidency of the Leeds Jewish Board of Guardians, serving from 1878 to 1908. He was also involved in the wider Leeds society, being a member of the Leeds Literary and Philosophical Society from 1881 and a Proprietor of the Leeds Library – share number 448 – from 1879 until his death. He was active in Conservative Party politics but, most significantly, he was the first Jewish magistrate in Leeds, being appointed a JP in 1899.

After Paul Hirsch, all those who had influence on the wider Leeds life had their origins in the Russian Empire. This term encompassed one of the largest empires ever which stretched from the Baltic in the west across to the Pacific, including Central Asia and the Caucasus. It lasted as a centralised monarchy from 1721 up to the first Russian revolution in February 1917. The persecution of Jews included severe restrictions on where they could live. The 'Pale of Settlement' in most of which Jewish settlement was allowed, was located in the south west of the Empire and included much of present-day Lithuania, part of Latvia, Belarus, Ukraine, Moldova and Poland. As more and more Jews fled from persecution, the natural route to Northern Europe – and, in theory, eventually to America – was from the Baltic ports to Hull and then by train cross country to Liverpool in order to embark for the USA. Though they came originally from different regions, it was not surprising that many stayed together with those from their original province and linked up with other neighbours when they arrived in Hull, Leeds and Manchester. The result in Leeds is that a remarkable number of original immigrants came from the Kovno province of present-day Lithuania, and particularly from the one town of Joniskis. Some records of former days in the country have been preserved at the provincial level, but efforts to seek evidence of Jewish life in Kovno come up against the annihilation of that community and the murder of the remaining Jews by the Nazis, assisted by many of their Gentile fellow citizens. Other Jewish refugees into Leeds came from Belarus or, as in the case of Herman Friend, from Poland. None of them spoke English, their lingua franca being Yiddish.

Herman Friend (c. 1820–1905)

Although arriving in Leeds in the early 1850s – before the main influx of immigrants – and being responsible for significant innovations in the tailoring industry, Herman Friend is not as well known as some later arrivals. He had a curious relationship with the Liberal politician and clothing manufacturer John Barran. Barran would not employ Jews in his factory but was happy to subcontract work to Herman Friend, who developed the use of the bandsaw to cut a considerable number of pieces of cloth in one operation and began to divide the manufacturing into a number of separate but interlinked processes. Ironically, the prejudice of Barran, and other major clothing manufacturers, plus the low prices they paid for the outwork done by Herman Friend and by other Jewish enterprises that sprang from Friend's small factory, made entrepreneurs out of them and, by the mid-1930s, led to the domination of the Leeds clothing trade by Jewish-owned businesses.

Michael Marks (1859–1907)

If Herman Friend had a largely anonymous contribution to an innovation that transformed the clothing business, Michael Marks' name is still borne and respected by hundreds of retail stores across Britain and abroad. He was born in Slonim in an area disputed between different central European countries. Essentially its history is Polish, though after the break up of the Soviet Union it became part of Belarus. Michael Marks was clearly a very significant Jewish figure, but his influence was entirely economic and his entrepreneurial genius ensured that he concentrated on developing the business that still bears his name.

Marks arrived in Leeds penniless and alone soon after the start of the Russian regime's pogroms of 1881–4. His original idea was to find employment in tailoring which was his family background. This was happily pre-empted by one Isaac Dewhirst, a wholesale haberdasher, who lent Marks £5 to enable him to buy goods from his warehouse for re-sale. He intended to be an itinerant peddler, but his health wasn't up to it. Instead he took a stall in Kirkgate open market and at Castleford and Wakefield markets which between them were open every day. His stall carried the famous sign: 'Don't ask the price – everything is a penny.' The suggestion that he had to resort to this tactic because he could not speak any English is probably apocryphal. What is true is that it was the original Poundstore, with one old penny approaching £1 today.

Marks soon saw the need to expand the business and he recruited assistants to run the stalls while he gave his attention to buying and distribution. He developed stalls at markets across the north of England and then began opening shops. He moved to Wigan in 1891 and to Manchester in 1894. He then realised that he needed a partner and, when his original mentor, Isaac Dewhirst, turned him down, he formed a partnership with Dewhirst's cashier Thomas Spencer. When the partnership turned into a limited company in 1903, Spencer retired, leaving Marks with a problem. His skill was a unique understanding of the market and of what customers wanted, but he had no accounting competence and it was left to his managers to run that side of the business. This they did even after his death in 1907, until his son, Simon, eventually assumed the main responsibility and developed the company into the huge business that it is today. Even though he lived in Leeds for less than a decade, Michael Marks is always claimed as part of the city's history and the picture of his barrow in the Leeds market, complete with the well-known sign, has become an iconic image.

Victor Lightman (1859–1928)

Victor Lightman built up a reputation as a supporter of a range of Leeds charities, by no means confined to Jewish organisations. A quiet man of firm views, he was the acknowledged lay leader of the Leeds Jewish community for some twenty years from 1908 as President of the Leeds Board of Guardians in succession to Paul Hirsch. He was the second Jewish magistrate in Leeds, appointed in September 1909.[7]

With his mother, his younger brother Louis, and three sisters he came to Leeds from Vilnius, Lithuania, in 1880,[8] just before the assassination of Tsar Alexander. His obituary states that he came to Leeds by accident:

> He had arranged to sail for America, but meeting another emigrant on the boat bound for Leeds, he changed his mind and eventually found work in the city as journeyman cabinet maker at 8d an hour.[9]

The furniture trade was very much a minority occupation among immigrants in Leeds, yet clearly Victor was both a skilled cabinet maker and businessman, as by 1888 he had his own business in the Leylands. Lightman's great innovation was to develop a wholesale furniture trade. At the time, most furniture was bespoke to order and poorer people had to buy secondhand. Lightman developed the machinery to supply furniture in bulk. By 1899, he had opened a factory in Hunslet to meet orders placed by retailers. His development of the trade in Leeds led to him becoming a nationally recognised figure in the furniture industry.

Lightman was a dedicated Liberal and an office holder at the local level. He was a financial mainstay of the Leeds party at many levels and was an active member of the Leeds and County Liberal Club in Quebec Street. Curiously, he never stood for public office, though his nephew, Harold Lightman, contested the Bramley ward unsuccessfully in 1927 at the tender age of 21.[10] Victor was also an active Freemason and a generous donor to a number of Jewish, civic and Christian charities. One successful innovative charitable project he established in 1923 was the 'Victor Lightman Loans Fund'. Through this fund, small interest-free loans were made to those in need, to be repaid in weekly instalments.

His leadership within the Jewish community began when he became President of the main Belgrave Street Synagogue, for which he made and presented a pulpit. In 1908, he became President of the Leeds Jewish Board of Guardians and thus de facto became the lay leader of the community. He was a popular leader and it was a surprise when, in 1914, he was challenged for the post by Abe Frais.[11] The election was keenly fought and, although Victor Lightman won by 190 votes to 154, the strength of the vote against him was a surprise. He then suddenly resigned the post just one month later, ostensibly on the grounds of ill-health; however, when his successor, Abraham Feldman, resigned following his removal to London a bare year later, Victor was prevailed upon to take up the post again – which suggests that there was more to his resignation than health grounds. Victor continued in the post for a further thirteen years, until his death in 1928.

A key event in Leeds during his leadership was the riot in June 1917 when Gentile youths attacked the Jewish community in their Leylands neighbourhood (see Chapters 4 and 7). The local papers were clear that the Jews were the innocent party and one notes that there were no Jewish names among those arrested. It was a serious disturbance, but it was a unique occasion, never repeated. Victor played a key role in calming the community and his perception of the situation was demonstrated when he congratulated the police on their handling of it.

At his death he left a wife, two sons and six daughters. It is some indication of his reputation that the company that bought the furniture business on his death maintained it as Victor Lightman Limited through to the 1950s.

Montague Burton (1885–1952)

If Michael Marks was very footloose and had no great affinity to Leeds, save as recognising it as his original opportunity,[12] the opposite was true of Sir Montague Burton who developed and maintained his main clothing manufacturing empire in the city and who was a philanthropic donor to the Leeds arts world and to its local organisations generally. Charities established by the family continued until recently, when their funds were finally distributed.

Moshe Dovid (not David) Osinsky was born in Kurkel in the province of Kovno, in what is now Lithuania, on 13 August 1885, to a family of Russian subjects whom he described as 'Clothiers' – though his father has also been recorded as a bookseller. He was a shy and reticent man and the valiant efforts to delve into his personal life have always been reduced to inferring events from the few available clues and the comments of friends and acquaintances. The diversity of the accounts of youth, despite much research by his biographers, is largely explained by his consistent reticence as to his early life. The sparseness of his entry in *Who's Who*, written by himself sometime after 1943, demonstrates the problem.[13] The progression from Osinsky to Burton, with a succession of first names, from Morris to Maurice and finally to Montague, is remarkably vague. His naturalisation papers in February 1910 had him as Osinsky 'known as Morris Burton'. A year later he filled in the census form as

Maurice Burton, but by 1910 the business was styled 'Montague Burton' and his knighthood was gazetted in 1931 in this name. Finally, his probate was registered in 1952 in the name of Montague Maurice Burton. Given his attention to detail and his business efficiency, it is odd that there is no evidence of any name change being documented legally, but even so none of this is significant in his progression to prominence – based in his adopted city – but is simply curious. His remarkable business success is down to sheer entrepreneurial skill allied to a powerful determination and to his ability to analyse business practices and the accounts that underpinned them.

Before leaving Kovno in 1900 at the age of 15, Montague Burton had had a *yeshivah* education and this religious background and a love of learning stayed with him all his life. His application to study also helped him rapidly to acquire a knowledge of English. As with so many young Jewish men, he had to make an initial living from peddling, but he found this particularly difficult as a result of his poor health – suffering on and off all his life from chronic nephritis – and in 1904 he opened a retail shop as a 'hosier and draper' in Chesterfield. This was hardly a natural town in which a 19-year-old Jewish man would start a business but, with few overheads and an extremely ascetic personal life, including studying late into the night by candlelight, he made a success of it and opened a second shop in Mansfield in 1908. Somehow, he found time just one year later to marry Sophie Amelia ('Cissie') Marks, the daughter of a businessman in Worksop, just twenty miles from Chesterfield. Sophie was also chronically ill but was able to accompany her husband on later voyages to New York and to Durban.

In common with other Jewish businessmen, Montague Burton believed in expansion rather than consolidation, and by 1919 he had forty shops and was living in a pleasant detached house on the edge of the centre of Harrogate, in which he lived until his death over thirty years later. One of his shrewd moves had come around 1908 with the purchase of a small clothing factory, Progress Mill, in Leeds. Typically, this soon became too small and the production side moved to Elmwood Mills near to Camp Road – the second Jewish area chronologically in Leeds – and then to a site in Concord Street, on the edge of the Leylands, the original area for Jewish immigrants on the edge of the city centre. This dual approach of production alongside retail was the key to Montague Burton's economic success and, indeed, dominance in the clothing sphere. In a way, the Burton shops were the forerunners of the present-day factory shops, and the link between knowing what sells and having the capacity then to produce it, put the business ahead of most of its competitors. Other separate factories sprang up in Leeds to meet demand, and by 1921 Burton saw the need to consolidate all production in one large factory. He acquired a site in Hudson Road, Harehills, and began building the works that became the largest clothing factory in the world at the time, employing 10,500 employees at its height. By the end of the 1930s, some 25% of British men were clothed by Burtons.[14]

The Hudson Road factory was a remarkable place. It catered for the social and welfare needs of the workforce with an excellent canteen, medical and dental clinics and sports facilities, together with cultural opportunities – all governed by committees elected by staff. Above all, Burton staff had regular and permanent employment, with paid holidays, rather than the equivalent of zero hours contracts which were the norm across much of the clothing trade at that time. During the Second World War, over 2,000 of the company's employees served in the armed forces. Typically, Montague Burton ensured that every one of them had his pay enhanced by contributions from the firm to enable his wife and family to live a decent life.[15] Entering the factory for the first time was a shock for the visitor, with sewing machines, steam presses and cutting equipment as far as the eye could see and with every member of the staff clearly knowing his or her workplace and role.

All this remarkable business success – from the one small shop in 1904 and the tiny production unit a few years later, to the huge production enterprise in Leeds little more than twenty years later, plus 364 shops within the same period – came from Montague Burton's determined work ethic, often with an eighteen-hour day, allied to keen observation of his clientele and a shrewd judgement as to what its future dress taste would be, a keen eye for where to site his shops and attention to detail in how to cut costs.

His life outside of business was varied. He played bridge and golf and was a voracious reader, particularly of women novelists and of Hebrew writers. He enjoyed travel and went on many cruises. He was a devoted family man, taking care of his wife when she became bedridden, and having his younger brother Bernard in partnership with him from the mid-1920s. He wrote long epistles to his eldest child, Barbara, from his travels and he took his sons – Stanley, Arnold and Raymond – into the firm. He was a committed and supportive Zionist who was a close friend of the Leeds academic and active campaigner, Selig Brodetsky. Burton also endowed the Weizman Chair of International Peace at the Hebrew University of Jerusalem. He succeeded Dr Chaim Weizman as President of the Zionist Federation of Great Britain and Ireland.

Montague Burton was generous sponsor of academic development. Above all this was shown in his support for the Hebrew University of Jerusalem. He also established a number of scholarships in honour of the Jewish poet and co-founder of that university, Chaim Nachman Bialik, whom he knew personally. His passionate interest in promoting peace was expressed by endowing chairs of international relations in Oxford and Edinburgh, plus lectureships in Nottingham and Leeds and support for the continuation of the chair in international relations at the University of London, originally established by Sir Ernest Cassel. He followed his longstanding concern for good working conditions and for constructive relationships between workers and management by establishing chairs in industrial relations at Leeds, Cardiff and Cambridge universities.

He never advertised his support for the Liberal Party, which he supported quietly by donation.[16] It was the opinion of Liberal, and later Labour, politician, Joshua Walsh, that one reason for the decline of the Liberal Party in Leeds was that leading Liberals, 'such as Montague Burton', were not prepared to be City Council candidates.[17] In 1930, it was the Liberals' turn to nominate a Lord Mayor and Alderman George Ratcliffe, the Leader of the Liberal Group on the City Council, and his key colleagues, approached Montague Burton to invite him to accept nomination and to become Leeds' first Jewish Lord Mayor. Even though there were expressions of support from the leaders of both Conservative and Labour parties, it was said that Burton turned it down because the Liberals themselves were not unanimous.[18] When Burton became a Justice of the Peace in 1924 he is likely to have been a Liberal nominee. He was a passionate believer in international cooperation to prevent war and he sponsored the largest League of Nations Association in Europe at the factory in 1928, with eventually 6,000 members, and after the war transmuted the organisation into a United Nations Association. At every luncheon meeting in the huge Princess Royal canteen, lowly speakers such as myself were somewhat awed by the menu card which listed all the speakers back to the association's beginning, including many leading national personalities. To reach the canteen we walked through the huge workshop. His knighthood, awarded in 1931, was for 'services to industrial relations'. Despite his shyness he spoke at many public meetings on a whole range of topics and many of his speakers' notes survive in his archive.[19]

Before the establishment of the Hudson Road factory, Burton spread his factories around Leeds and, after a strike in 1936, he moved some of the production to Lancashire.[20] By 1939, he had a dominant position both in manufacturing and in retail.[21]

Montague Burton died suddenly at the Great Northern Hotel in the centre of Leeds, at a dinner for his senior managers and executives on 21 September 1952. So intensive was his personal leadership of the company that he had not trained successors. Katrina Honeyman's conclusions are very stark:

> In the case of Burton the tenacity of the tradition established by the founder, and the controlling influence of the family, impeded factory closures. The absence of a suitable successor to Montague Burton ... led to a merger with Jackson ... It was not until 1969 that Burton's first manager from outside the industry was appointed.
>
> For much of the 1970s Burton's manufacturing made a loss and the overall profit of the group depended on the property division. Manufacturing never

recovered. The Burton family members, who because of its two-tier structure retained control of the business, were seen as a constraint on the group's development. The Burtons strongly resisted factory closure, which was the preferred option of the new managers. In 1979 family control of the business was lost as non-voting shareholders were enfranchised, and manufacturing was abandoned within the year.[22]

Montague Burton's death came just before the changes in men's clothing styles in the 1950s and this, together with the beginning of imports of clothing, were bit by bit disastrous for the Leeds clothing industry. There were vain calls for protectionist policies and manufacturing wound down at Hudson Road from the 1970s. Within two years of Sir Montague's death, Burtons had merged with Jacksons the Tailors who brought new management perceptions. Over the next decade, despite the family's emotional attachment to production, the inexorable importation of cheaper clothing from Eastern Europe and South Asia led to the decline in British manufacturing, and by 1981 all production at Hudson Road had ended. Burton's sons did not possess their father's entrepreneurial flair and their slow estrangement from the company led them, particularly Stanley and his wife Audrey, to find a new role in philanthropy, particularly in regard to the arts in Leeds.[23]

Moshe Dovid Osinsky – Sir Montague Maurice Burton – left a huge mark on Leeds and, though small in stature and of a retiring disposition, he was – in Bernard Silver's words – one of the 'Giants of Leeds'.

Selig Brodetsky (1888–1954)

Uniquely among the distinguished Jewish individuals of Leeds, Selig Brodetsky achieved his fame as an intellectual and a scholar. He was also a highly committed Zionist at a time when this was much more controversial than it has become over the seventy years since the establishment of the State of Israel. Brodetsky came to Leeds in 1920 on his appointment as Reader in Applied Mathematics at the university and was promoted to Professor in 1924. He remained in Leeds until 1947, when he retired from his university post at the age of 60 in order to devote more time to Jewish affairs. He then moved to a flat in London; but went to Jerusalem in July 1949 to take up the post of President of the Hebrew University, becoming an Israeli citizen. He had consulted his doctor as to his health before taking up the post, but in 1950 he suffered a heart attack and shortly afterwards was forced to give it up and to return to his home in London, where he died on 18 May 1954. Brodetsky was involved in a number of Leeds organisations, but it was his academic distinction, his dedication to promoting Jewish identity and particularly his skilful leadership of the Zionist cause which marked him out as a Jewish leader.

In August 1893, Brodetsky's mother and her four children from nine down to 18 months managed to smuggle themselves across the Ukrainian–German border together with some hundred other Jews determined to escape from the Russian pogroms. The family travelled by train to Berlin and then on to the port of Bremen, where they managed to get on a boat to London. His father had arrived in London a year earlier, but had been unable to find a steady job and had only managed to rent one room in a house in Brick Lane, into which parents and four children were crammed until they found larger accommodation nearby. At the age of 5, and knowing no English, the young Selig started at the local primary school. A year later he transferred to the Jewish Free School and age 8, at his own request, also attended the local Talmud Torah. He soon acquired a reputation as a scholar and, within three years, as a teacher. Brodetsky's academicism was quickly recognised and when he was 10 his headteacher obtained his father's permission to enter him for an examination through which he was able to enter, successfully, for a scholarship to the Central Foundation School for Boys in the City of London. By his own confession, Brodetsky was not one for the playground, preferring 'reading and studying'. He says that he had no leisure time and quite happily spent his days in study and religious observance.

Remarkably, in 1905, only a little more than a decade after escaping from the Ukrainian ghetto, Brodetsky became school captain. Five years on, at 16, he was successful in gaining a scholarship to Cambridge University. Once again his academic brilliance was noted and in his third year, in 1908, he became 'Senior Wrangler', being first in mathematics. This opened up a whole world of prestigious meetings and of invitations to speak. He carried on his education, often unfunded, until he was in a stronger financial position, not least because of his determination to continue with Zionist and other Jewish lecturing. Finally, in 1914, he became lecturer in Applied Mathematics at Bristol University with a steady income plus lucrative vacation work. By the end of the war he was earning enough to marry Manya Barenbaum, whom he had met two years earlier.

In 1920 came the move to Leeds, which was to be his base for the next twenty-eight years. On his second day in the city, together with two friends, Brodetsky visited a city centre cafe. Despite the place being barely a quarter full, no one came to serve them. Eventually Brodetsky called a waitress and asked for coffee for the three of them. The waitress went away and spoke to the manager who proceeded to tell them that Jews were not served in that cafe. A very different reception came from the University's Vice Chancellor, Sir Michael Sadler, who, on their first meeting, asked whether Brodetsky would object to him being proposed for membership of the prestigious Leeds Luncheon Club, of which Sir Michael was President. This was the beginning of a continuing friendship between the two men and ensured Brodetsky's acceptance in Leeds' academic community.

Brodetsky was a man of wide cultural and community interests and he participated in a number of non-Jewish organisations – including the University Labour Club, the local League of Nations branch and the Association of University Teachers – but his key focus was on promoting the Zionist cause, which at the time was much less accepted than it became in later years. In 1917, even before he came to Leeds, he applauded the Balfour Declaration.[24] He immediately established a Zionist Council in Leeds with a paid secretary, as well as heading the list of delegates to the first postwar Zionist Congress in Carlsbad.

He entered into an increasing number of demanding national and international commitments in the Zionist cause, and such was his value to the university that his senior colleagues were flexible in the scheduling of his lectures. Even so, he was under great strain, compounded by his wife's demands for emotional support following the death in infancy of their first two children.[25] As the threats to world peace increased and the persecution of Jews advanced, Brodetsky was active in assisting the welfare needs of the Jewish students in Leeds and in the care of refugees from Nazism. He also struggled in vain to get the British parliament and the League of Nations to act on the persecution of the Jews. Later, in the 1930s, the British Board of Deputies, a key organisation within British jewry, was divided by internal disputes and personality clashes, often over Zionism. His Zionist colleagues pressured Brodetsky to accept nomination as its president, but he was reluctant to take office in such divisive circumstances and insisted on being elected unopposed. His key anti-Zionist opponent was Anthony de Rothschild, who recognised that Brodetsky's standing and reputation would provide the necessary leadership and withdrew his nomination, thus paving the way for his election. Characteristically, Brodetsky immediately proposed that de Rothschild be elected to the Executive Board and the two men worked cooperatively throughout Brodetsky's period of office.

Brodetsky continued with a heavy round of academic, Zionist and more general Jewish activities until April 1949, when he announced that he would not stand for re-election as President of the British Board of Deputies. This presaged the final phase of his career. He had been a firm supporter of the Hebrew University of Jerusalem since its foundation in 1925. He had raised a considerable sum, particularly from Montague Burton, to endow professorships, and a chair in mathematics and related subjects had been established. Now he achieved a dream: in April 1949 at the age of 61 he was elected unopposed as the University's President. Three months later he arrived in Jerusalem to take up his duties and shortly afterwards received his identity book as an Israeli citizen. Not long afterwards, in 1950, he suffered a heart attack. He carried on with his duties but became ill again and was advised to give up his university post. Reluctantly he did so and returned to London where he died on 18 May 1954.

Bernard Silver included Brodetsky in his booklet *Three Jewish Giants of Leeds*[26] and few would quibble with this designation, his eminence deriving not from his influence on the city's affairs, but rather from the reflected glory of his academic brilliance, his highly respected role within the Jewish community and, particularly, as a Zionist leader.

Hyman Morris (1873–1955)

It is doubtful whether anyone, even his family, really knew Hyman Morris. Some aspects of his life are clear enough – he was, for instance, a tenacious and successful businessman who started from nothing and developed a large and profitable wallpaper merchant business. He was also a consistent supporter of Jewish organisations in the city. Beyond these anchors, everything is rather obscure. He collected positions both in Leeds civic life and within the Jewish community, but never appeared to have any real enthusiasm for the duties these positions required. And within the Morris family there appears to have been little contact; indeed, as in a small way his biographer, I found myself the only person in touch with all branches of the family. Even within the wallpaper business there was little central direction and each member of the family had his own territory to run with a separate limited company.

Like many Leeds Jews, Hyman Morris came to the city around 1882 from the Kovno province of present-day Lithuania. As such, until his naturalisation in 1902, he was officially a citizen of the Russian state. Five children came with their parents under the family name of Samuels (five more children were born in Britain) and the change of name originated with the second son, Samuel Morris Samuels, who simply dropped the 'Samuels' – thereafter 'Morris' became the accepted family surname.

Hyman was reticent about his personal background, as if to hark back somehow diminished the 'Englishness' which he emphasised as a Conservative candidate for the City Council. He sometimes described himself as a 'native of Sheffield' and placed his age on arrival in the UK as being 5 rather than 10. He was the only Conservative in the family as his brother, Sam, was a Liberal Councillor and later Mayor of Doncaster and the youngest brother, Harry – a lawyer and the only sibling not to go into the wallpaper trade – was a Labour Sheffield City Councillor, MP and finally a Labour peer.

The family arrived at the port of Hull and went directly to Sheffield where there was already family member, David Samuels, listed in an 1884 directory as a 'paperhanging dealer', which was presumably where the family business originated. Hyman's mother, Fanny, provided for the family by running a market stall; his father apparently never worked, regarding himself as a scholar, invariably occupied with reading the Talmud and expounding it to the family – who respected him for this. Hyman began in business with £5 borrowed from his uncle, David, and started up in Wakefield with his wife, Annie Blashky, whom he had married in 1897 (Figure 14.1). Hyman soon wanted to move to Leeds, but Annie made him wait to be established in Wakefield before tackling the much bigger city. Certainly, by 1906, he was well established in Leeds with offices in Harrison Street, at the side of the Grand Theatre, and with two shops in the city.

He soon became involved with Jewish organisations and by 1914 he was Treasurer of the Jewish Board of Guardians and President of the Leeds Jewish Institute. He later became founding President of the Leeds B'nai Brith and, in 1923, he was an active supporter of Abe Frais in the founding of Europe's first Jewish golf club, at Moor Allerton.[27] Much later, in 1941, he became the President of the Jewish Representative Council.

He was soon setting his stall out in the wider Leeds establishment, becoming a Freemason and a Rotarian and the first Jewish member of the Conservative Club. In 1922, he was elected as Conservative Councillor for the Central ward.[28] There is no record of him expressing any political opinion or explaining why he was a Conservative representative. Reports of his election meetings detail the speeches on party policy made by Conservative worthies on his behalf. Hyman Morris' only reported words relate to comments on the alleged anti-Semitism of his Liberal opponent. He was a poor speaker and there are no reported speeches in the City Council except for the routine introduction of the minutes for the minor committees for which he had responsibility. He was nevertheless sufficiently popular to be appointed a magistrate in 1929, to be given one of the Conservatives' aldermanic seats in 1930 and to be elected as the City's first Jewish Lord Mayor in November 1941 (Figure 14.2).

His first major task as Lord Mayor was to deal with the disaster of the Royal Navy's flagship, the aircraft carrier *HMS Ark Royal*. Just a week before being elected as Lord Mayor, the city of Leeds had adopted *Ark Royal* as part of a national effort to encourage fundraising for the war effort. Then, just one day after coming into office, *Ark Royal* was sunk in the Mediterranean by a German torpedo. Leeds' target immediately changed from £3.5 million for a replacement hull to £5 million for a replacement ship. Just three months later, from 30 January to 7 February 1942, under the leadership of a committee on which Hyman Morris played a key role, the City raised the astonishing sum of £9.3 million – over £400 million today.[29] Linton Andrews, the editor of the *Yorkshire Post*, commented that 'The Lord Mayor has created an excellent impression by his work for the *Ark Royal* week.'[30] Hyman Morris carried out his Lord Mayoral duties with considerable assiduity and the year was particularly notable for adding a civic dimension to a number of Jewish functions.

It would be nice to finish the Hyman Morris story here but, unfortunately, there is another darker side to him. His wallpaper business was extremely successful – by 1947 he had six shops in Leeds – but he ran his business in an authoritarian way, very different to his public image. Louis Teeman worked for Morris for many years and he describes a very different man to that seen in the newspapers. He recounts favourably how Morris started from the bottom in business but calls him a 'hard man', isolated in his office away from his staff, and summarises his view of him thus:

> Morris was no hero to me. I saw the warts where others saw no flaw. I saw meanness where others saw generosity, but, for his rise from poverty to riches, from obscurity to prominence, from petty market trader to tycoon, from being, literally, without a shirt to his back to becoming City Councillor, then Alderman, and then to wear the Lord Mayor of Leeds's chain, for all these progressions, and hard work and endurance, and resolution, I doff my cap. But it does not alter my opinion of the harshness of his real nature.
>
> He deserved all the encomiums but to me who also saw the other side of the coin he was a man, an employer who paid low wages, a cold unsmiling man who functioned best in the spotlight.[31]

Flawed or not, Hyman Morris certainly achieved a great deal and, to the Jewish community in Leeds, he was in politics what Montague Burton was in business, Jacob Kramer in the arts and Selig Brodetsky in the academic sphere. He died in 1955 at the age of 82.

Jacob Kramer (1892–1962)

Jacob Kramer (Figure 14.3) was a man of paradoxes. He was a restless Bohemian, a gregarious man always in need of companionship but unable to settle for any length of time; unreliable even to the extent of failing to turn up for exhibitions of his own work; an individual regularly in need of financial support but lacking the discipline to assure it; a non-practising Jew who produced some of the most powerful paintings of Jewish subjects of his time; and an artist who was an early exponent of Cubism but who was happy to produce fine naturalistic portraits. Finally, he succumbed to an increasing and debilitating dependence on alcohol, despite his awareness that it was damaging to his artistic work. For all his failings, he had a loyal coterie of friends in Leeds plus the support of leading artists, such as Jacob Epstein and Mark Gertler. His great patron in the city was Sir Michael Sadler, the Vice-Chancellor of Leeds University, who regarded Kramer as a genius and whom Kramer exploited over many years, even after Sadler had moved on to Oxford University in 1924. Kramer's behaviour towards Sadler and his other friends was not malign but simply the careless acts of an artist who found it difficult to cope with twentieth century civilisation.[32] Sadler's son's biography of his father[33] generously omits to mention the difficulties he had with Kramer.

Unusually for immigrants of the period, Jacob Kramer was born in 1892 in modern day Ukraine to an artistic middle-class family; his father, Max, and an uncle were accredited Court artists. It was this background that led the family to move to St Petersburg. His mother, Celia, though from a more Orthodox family, was an accomplished opera singer and an authority on Slavonic music.[34] St Petersburg prior to the revolutions was a hive of political foment and, despite their life amongst the intellectual elite, it was likely that family members were involved in political activity. This, compounded by being Jewish, put them at risk and the Kramers decided to emigrate; they ended up in Leeds in 1900 where they joined the small group of Ukrainian Jews who were already there. Jacob retained a strong Germanic accent.

Jacob's rebellious nature was evident at his first school, and at the age of 10 he ran away to Liverpool and signed on as a cabin boy, going to sea for six months. His artistic talent had already been recognised and at 12 he obtained a scholarship to the Leeds College of Art.[35] He made sufficient progress there for Sir Michael Sadler and members of the Jewish community to provide funds for him to go the prestigious Slade School in London.

Kramer was extremely well read and wrote impressively on the philosophy of art.[36] In the years after the the First World War, the final two years of which he spent in the trenches and latterly as an interpreter, he lectured to arts groups and luncheon clubs and became a much sought-after arts teacher. He enjoyed lecturing and particularly delved deeply into his philosophy of portraiture in which he sought to express the spirit of the sitter. He described his art as 'symbolic', though this did not assuage some of sitters who intensely disliked the non-naturalistic portraits he presented them with. His efforts to broaden the appreciation of art and to encourage involvement and discussion of the subject were shown when, in 1931, he formed the Yorkshire Luncheon Group. When Kramer contacted distinguished artists and philosophers they usually came to speak and it became a well-regarded and intellectually stimulating gathering. Inevitably, given Kramer's roving spirit, it latterly met only sporadically, and its last meeting was in November 1934 at Whitelock's bar in Leeds.[37]

In addition to his painting skill he was also a fine and sensitive pianist, though almost entirely self-taught. He was a gentle man and, while he spent time in London and Paris as international centres of art, he was unable to settle in either city and always returned to Leeds, even though he thought that in comparison to Bradford its art world was philistine, particularly after Sadler had left.[38] His last years were increasingly sad as his alcoholism deepened and he was all too often to be found in his favourite city-centre hostelries. The art historian, Frances Spalding, refers to a friend of Kramer's who, 'with painful accuracy', wrote to him in 1938:

> What you want is a renaissance, you have certainly got talents in you, but they have got lost under a heap of beer bottles, talk, women, a touch of laziness and ordinary worldly habits that are no use to you as an artist.[39]

There are sad parallels with another famous Leeds artist, Phil May (1864–1903), 'the father of caricature', who achieved fame immediately before Kramer. Like Kramer, Phil May travelled a great deal but always returned to Leeds. He also succumbed to alcoholism and was reduced to drawing quick sketches of companions in Leeds pubs for the price of his drinks.[40] Jacob Kramer died in a Jewish care home in London on 5 February 1962; but appropriately for an artist of whom the distinguished art critic and his great friend and supporter W. T. Oliver wrote, 'Jacob Kramer performed his greatest service for art in Leeds simply by being in the city', his body was brought back to Leeds for burial in the Jewish cemetery at Gildersome.[41]

The Leeds Art Gallery has fourteen of Kramer's paintings, including his masterpiece, *The Day of Atonement*, and his portrait of Frederick Delius. Leeds University has three of Kramer's works, including his famous *The Jew*, and his portrait of Selig Brodetsky. He remains well known and respected in the city that was his home for over sixty years.[42]

Joshua Walsh (1902–84)

Joshua Walsh – known always as 'Jos' – was Leeds' pre-eminent educational reformer of the post-Second World War era. He was the Labour chair of the City Council's education committee for two long periods, 1945 to 1951 and 1953 to 1967. He was a passionate advocate of comprehensive education – though according to Labour colleague, Alf Tallant,[43] he was 'a late convert' – and embarked on a twenty-year programme of comprehensive schools. Only four were built before he left office in 1967 – Foxwood in Seacroft, Matthew Murray in Holbeck, John Smeaton in Swarcliffe and Allerton Grange in Moortown.[44]

The Walsh family followed the time-honoured path from the Russian Empire, in the Walsh case from modern-day Latvia. His parents married in Leeds in 1900 and their first home was in the Camp Road area. Like just about all Jewish families, the Walshes regarded education as the key means of improving their situation and their children were very 'driven'. Jos was a brilliant student. He went on from Lovell Road Primary School to the Leeds Central High School. From there he took articles and became a student in the Law School of Leeds University. In his first year he won the Law Society's Studentship, the top prize of a national competition. In his final year he obtained a First in the Ll.B examination – the first ever awarded in that examination. During his time at the University he was a member of the first Jewish Students' Association there.

Leaving university with such glowing results, Jos could have expected to find a position with one of the established Leeds law firms, but such was the insidious anti-Semitism of the period that none employed Jewish solicitors, forcing Jos, and his contemporary Joe Wurzal,[45] to set up their own practices. It might be thought odd that he did not join with Wurzal who, though some eight years older, was very much Jos' political contemporary and who had set up as solicitor in Leeds one year before him. But the fact that Jos and Joe did not get on at all meant that they were more competitors than colleagues.

Jos set up his plate in 1923 in Vince's Chambers, 53 Park Lane – directly opposite the Town Hall. His younger brother joined him as a partner in 1932 and they remained at the same address until Percy left the partnership in 1968. Very typically of the Walsh family, the two brothers did not get on, and spent most of their long years as partners not speaking to each other and passing messages via secretaries.

By the time Jos was playing a leading role in Leeds politics he had ceased to be active in any Jewish organisations in the city but, according to his only published work, he had in his young days been active in community matters and had been a committed Zionist. His booklet, 'Mrs Sheinblum's Kitchen',[46] is not recipe book but an account of the religious, educational and cultural activities that were held in the house of the Sheinblum family. Even after Mrs Sheinblum died in 1925, the house continued as a Jewish centre into the 1930s. Jos was interviewed on television in 1981 and he spoke on his and other Jewish children's educational history in the early part of the twentieth century, at the same time as the Sheinblums' house was a centre of Jewish cultural activity.[47]

Jos Walsh's first Leeds City Council election was as a Liberal in the Brunswick Ward in 1928,[48] in which he came third. This was the year that Labour first gained control of the City Council and Jos realised his future lay with that party. Political Jews remained with the Liberal Party longer than others who switched soon after the First World War. One reason for this was a residual loyalty to the party whose governments had been responsible for Jewish emancipation from the mid-nineteenth century. It was also the case that a number of prominent early Labour pioneers, including James O'Grady, the first Labour MP in Leeds, were anti-Semitic. Walsh then unsuccessfully contested the strongly Conservative ward of Cross Gates and Templenewsam in 1930 and 1931 before being elected for the Central Ward in 1932 – and re-elected there at every election until 1951. The ward boundaries were redrawn that year and Jos was selected for the supposedly safe Labour Blenheim Ward, which he promptly lost. The following year he became a Labour Alderman and kept that office until he retired in 1968. Despite his sharp mind and political skills, he never became a fluent public speaker. Jos was a great fan of the Reverend Charles Jenkinson, the Leeds Labour Councillor and housing pioneer. He told me that he was 'the outstanding leader of the time who transformed Leeds' and was a man of 'tremendous imagination'.[49]

In 1966 he became Leeds' second Jewish Lord Mayor. The community was, of course, proud of his appointment and celebrated it, including a civic visit from the newly appointed Chief Rabbi, Immanuel Jacobovitz, but there were criticisms of him for his lack of involvement in the Leeds Jewish community. It was alleged that he did nothing for the Jewish community during his years in charge of education and would not allow schools to observe Jewish religious days, nor did he appoint any Jewish headteachers.[50]

Jos Walsh's civic achievements rather hid his difficult family relationships, which were symptomatic of estrangments within the wider Walsh family. In 1932, he married a Liverpool actress, Rachel Ada Wolfe. Jos walked with a limp and almost always used a stick, the reason for which was curious: on his honeymoon in Israel he fell and broke his femur. The only available local infirmary happened to be a maternity hospital, at which he was treated. The bone was not well set, leaving him with a permanent limp. His wife never used the name Rachel and felt that Aida was better suited than Ada to her life as an actress and dancer. Their daughter, Janice, was born in 1934. She did not 'get on' with her parents and was sent away to boarding school, which certainly did not suit her as she was expelled twice and left without any qualifications. After Jos' death and the increasing ill health and deteriorating sight of her mother, Janice's estrangement meant that it was her husband, John Sinson, who had the responsibility of caring for Aida. Janice trained as a sculptor but became a noted psychologist.

Jos' obituary in the local Labour paper, the *Leeds Weekly Citizen*, said that 'he was a dominant and sometimes a controversial figure'.[51] He was certainly a big man whose determination to leave his mark on his native city succeeded. He was a socialist more concerned with practical change than class war, hence his concentration on educational reform over leadership or parliamentary ambition. His lord mayoral year was a fitting conclusion to his political life – and he recognised it.

Fanny Waterman (born 1920)

No one in contemporary Leeds has made a more lasting impact on the city's cultural life than Fanny Waterman. The global status of the Leeds Piano Competition and the glittering team of judges assembled for each competition are a continuing testimony to her dogged perseverance and to the respect that she is held in throughout the musical world. In 1961, Fanny decided that

Leeds should have an international piano competition – and simply set about establishing one. She recruited Marion, the then Countess of Harewood, to whose son Fanny gave piano lessons, as her partner in this project. Marion was herself a concert pianist and was a great friend of Benjamin Britten, whom she persuaded to write a piano piece – 'Nottorno' – as a compulsory piece for all the Leeds competitors.

Fanny's father, Myer, was born in Russia around 1893. He came to Leeds at the turn of the century, having started training as a diamond setter. His first shop was in Trafalgar Street on the edge of the Leylands, moving from there to Wade Lane and eventually to New Briggate, opposite the Grand Theatre, where he remained until his retirement. In 1915, Myer married Mary Behrman, born in Leeds to Russian parents, and in their first home, typical of the Leylands, they shared the toilet with five other families. Despite the family's poverty they had a piano and Fanny started playing it around the age of 5. Her first teacher was 'terrible' and, when it became clear that she had talent, her parents scraped together the cash to send her a couple of times a month to Tobias Matthay, a controversial piano teacher at the Royal College of Music.

Fanny had an elder brother, Harry,[52] and their parents taught them both not to value people by their wealth. Myer followed this stricture in his jewellers business; according to Fanny, he 'didn't like his customers' and if he felt that they were pretentious he 'wouldn't open the safe' to sell them his jewellery.[53] Fanny has always shared this radicalism and berated me throughout the 2010 Coalition Government for the Liberal Democrats' support for Conservative measures!

Fanny was set for a career as concert pianist and was already much in demand as a soloist when, in 1944, she married the 21-year-old doctor, Geoffrey de Keyser. When her two sons arrived, Paul in 1950 and Theodore in 1956, Fanny and Geoffrey were unable to afford nannies and she exchanged her solo career for teaching and 'never regretted it'. Geoffrey was a perfect partner for Fanny being, in her words, 'never ambitious for himself', but a supportive organiser and background strongman. She became an internationally renowned piano teacher and continued to teach into her 90s. In addition, together with Marion Harewood, she published a series of piano tutors. She was awarded the OBE in 1971, CBE in 2000 and was made a Dame in 2005. In March 2004 she was made a Freeman of the City of Leeds.

Her drive and her international contacts made the triennial Leeds International Piano Competition a success from its inception in 1963, and it has increased its status on each successive occasion. She has herself also served on competition juries across the globe. She controlled the whole operation in detail until finally handing over the reins at the age of 95, following the 2015 competition. By her own admission she was 'difficult to work with'.[54]

Her name will be permanently associated with the Leeds Piano Competition and her impact on the cultural life of Leeds has been formidable.

Conclusion

The choice of individuals to portray as the key Jewish movers and shakers is bound to be invidious and others will no doubt challenge my choice. What I have endeavoured to do is to look at those who were most prominent in their time and who were particularly influential in the life of Leeds. Other members of the community were significant as Jewish leaders but not necessarily as civic figures; others did not have the same longevity as those chosen. It can be well perceived that Leeds Jewry has been blessed with many leaders of note: Murray Freedman was able to produce a book with biographies of twenty-five of them[55] and the definitive dictionary of Anglo-Jewish history has entries for thirty-six Leeds Jews.[56] The fact that Fanny Waterman is the only woman in the lists is very noticeable. It cannot be as a result of a lack of personality or ability and has to be put down to the mores of the time or to Jewish tradition, including constitutions of organisations that expressly limited officers to men.

Among those who deserve mention and might have been included are Irwin Bellow (1923–2011) who was the first Jewish leader of the Leeds City Council and, as Lord Bellwin, became a minister in Margaret Thatcher's government; Bernard Lyons (1913–2008), businessman and philanthropist, and a Conservative city councillor and Leeds magistrate; Karl Cohen (1906–1973), known always as 'KC', who was the highly influential chair of the city council's housing committee for twelve years and was knighted in 1968; Leslie Silver (1925–2015), manufacturer and philanthropist, who became chair of the Leeds United Football Club board and chair of the board of what was then the Leeds Metropolitan University; and Arnold Ziff (1927–2004), businessman and philanthropist, whose development company established the Merrion Centre which was among the first shopping malls in Britain.

14.1 Hyman Morris with his wife

14.2 Alderman Walsh as Mayor

14.3 Sketch of Jacob Kramer, 1918

Notes

1. All present-day historians of Leeds Jewry are indebted to a number of predecessors, in particular Murray Freedman.
2. See chapter on Davis in Murray Freedman, *25 Characters in Leeds Jewish History* (Leeds: privately printed, 2004).
3. See *Oxford Dictionary of National Biography*, article on Behrens by D. T. Jenkins (accessed 14 June 2018).
4. The Leeds Library, 18 Commercial Street. Established in 1768 and in its present premises since 1808. It is the oldest continuing subscription library in Britain. In 2008 it became a charity.
5. The Leeds Club, 3 Albion Place, was a members' club from 1849 to 2004, when it became a proprietary club. In 2017, it closed and was sold to Marstons brewery who propose to reopen it as a pub and restaurant.
6. Peter Fingret, Conservative member of Leeds City Council, 1967 to 1974; Solicitor, 1960–82; Stipendiary Magistrate, 1982–5; appointed as Recorder in 1987 and Circuit Judge from 1992 until his retirement in 2005.
7. Appointed at the same time as Frank Leslie John Zossenheim.
8. Three further sisters were left behind in Vilnius. One escaped to the USA but the other two are presumed not to have survived the Holocaust.
9. *Leeds Mercury*, 25 July 1928.
10. Harold Lightman (1906–98) was pressed to be a Liberal parliamentary candidate in three different constituencies at the 1929 General Election, but he chose instead to pursue what became a distinguished a career at the Bar.
11. Abraham (Abe) Frais (1876–1935), the prime mover in the establishment of the Moor Allerton Golf Club in 1923. He was a director of a clothing company in Leeds.
12. Leeds benefits greatly from being the home of the remarkable Marks and Spencer Company archive (https://marksintime.marksandspencer.com/home) but its collection and exhibition of material shows the remarkable expansion of the company across Britain and beyond as opposed to an organic connection to Leeds.
13. 'Burton, Sir Montague', *Who Was Who* (A & C Black, an imprint of Bloomsbury Publishing plc, 1920–2016; online edition, Oxford University Press, 2014; online edition, April 2014): http://www.ukwhoswho.com/view/article/oupww/whowaswho/U235321) (accessed 23 June 2017).
14. Bernard Silver, *Three Jewish Giants of Leeds: Selig Brodetsky, Montague Burton and Jacob Kramer* (Leeds: Jewish Historical Society of England, 2000). I am indebted to this publication for much other information.
15. Silver, *Three Jewish Giants of Leeds*.
16. Information to author from Albert Ingham, Secretary, Yorkshire Liberal Federation, 1945–67.
17. Author's interview with Honorary Alderman J. S. Walsh, 31 May 1978.
18. *Yorkshire Evening Post*, 24 July 1930 and *Leeds Mercury*, 25 July 1930. Until local government reorganisation in 1974 it was possible for the Lord Mayor to be elected from outside the sitting Aldermen and Councillors. The Liberals had

in fact done this in 1916 to nominate Edmund George Arnold of the educational publications family, a Liberal sympathiser but not openly affiliated with the party. They later also used it to nominate Miss Beatrice Kitson in 1942, the first woman Lord Mayor; she occupied the same political position as Burton and Arnold.

19 West Yorkshire Archive Service, Nepshaw Lane South, Gildersome, Leeds LS27 7JQ.
20 Katrina Honeyman, *Well Suited: A History of the Leeds Clothing Industry, 1850–1990* (Oxford: Oxford University Press, 2000), p. 224.
21 Ibid., p. 56
22 Ibid., p. 245.
23 Ibid., p. 102.
24 The sentence following, which states that this could not prejudice the civil and religious rights of existing non-Jewish communities in Palestine, is less well-known.
25 They later had a son, Paul, and a daughter, Adèle, who outlived him.
26 Silver, *Three Jewish Giants of Leeds*. The other two were Montague Burton and Jacob Kramer.
27 This move came as a consequence of Jews being prevented from joining the Moortown Golf Club. The Moor Allerton Club was as a matter of principle open to all.
28 He was not the first Jewish City Councillor. This distinction fell to Liberal Jack Lubelski, elected in South Ward in 1904. The first Conservative Jewish Councillor was Moses Myers in Brunswick Ward in 1908.
29 Leeds' involvement with *Ark Royal* continued; the fourth *Ark Royal* was given the Freedom of the City in 1973 and, following the final decommissioning in 2011 of the fifth ship, a room in the Lord Mayor's suite in the Leeds Civic Hall was named 'The Ark Royal Room' to commemorate the seventy-year civic connection.
30 William Linton Andrews diaries, Special Collections, Brotherton Library, entry for 6 February 1942.
31 Louis Teeman, *Footsteps in the Sand* (self-published, 1976), pp. 455 and 529.
32 David Manson, *Jacob Kramer: Creativity and Loss* (Bristol: Sansom, 2006). I have relied on David Manson's biography for a great deal of background information. His analysis of Kramer's paintings is extremely valuable.
33 Michael Sadler, *Sir Michael Sadler: A Memoir by his Son* (London: Constable, 1949).
34 I am indebted for much material on Kramer's background to Silver, *Three Jewish Giants of Leeds*.
35 Established in 1846, it was renamed the Jacob Kramer College of Art in 1968. It was granted university status in August 2017.
36 See, for instance, his contribution to the catalogue for an exhibition in 1984 of his work, quoted in Silver, *Three Jewish Giants of Leeds*, pp. 49 and 53–5.
37 Manson, *Jacob Kramer*, pp. 67–177.
38 Ibid., p. 152.
39 Quoted in Silver, *Three Jewish Giants of Leeds*, p. 62.

40 See D. Cuppleditch, *Phil May: The Artist and his Wit* (London: Fortune Press, 1981).
41 Manson, *Jacob Kramer*, p. 196.
42 For further reading, ibid.
43 Alfred Tallant (1908–2003), Labour Chairman of Leeds Education Committee 1972–74. (For his obituary see www.bramley.demon.co.uk.)
44 The scheme was completed, via a middle-school structure, in 1972 under a Conservative chair, Paddy Crotty, who was equally keen on comprehensive education.
45 Joseph Wurzal (1892–1963). Admitted as solicitor January 1916, Leeds. Served in First World War, 1917–19. Set up as solicitor in Leeds in 1922. Labour City Councillor, 1933–6; Labour Alderman, 1936–45. Wurzal was not the first Jewish solicitor in Leeds; that distinction went to Frederick Blackston who set up his practice in Albion Street more than twenty years earlier.
46 Hon Alderman J. S. Walsh OBE, LlD, *Mrs Sheinblum's Kitchen* (Leeds: Leeds Jewish Historical Society of England, 1981).
47 Video supplied by family member; available on YouTube at https://youtu.be/gc8RoFt3Cjs (accessed 20 April 2015).
48 Joe Wurzal also first fought as a Liberal, in the Central Ward, in 1924 and 1927.
49 H. J. Hammerton, *This Turbulent Priest* (London: Lutterworth, 1952).
50 Information from Ronnie Teeman, 7 September 2015.
51 *Leeds Weekly Citizen*, 10 March 1984.
52 Harry Mordecai Waterman (1917–73). Leeds solicitor and Labour politician. Leeds City Councillor, 1952–67, and parliamentary candidate, Leeds North East, 1955, 1956 (by-election) and 1959. Leading member of the Campaign for Democratic Socialism, 1962.
53 This and other information from Fanny Waterman interview on *Desert Island Discs*, Radio 4, 9 July 2010.
54 Ibid.
55 Freedman, *25 Characters in Leeds Jewish History*.
56 *The Palgrave Dictionary of Anglo-Jewish History*, ed. William D. Rubinstein, Michael A. Jolles, and Hilary L. Rubinstein (London: Palgrave, 2011).

15

Spaces of Jewish belonging

Irina Kudenko

This chapter offers an alternative conceptual framework for looking at the diversity of individual experiences of Jewish identity in the Leeds Jewish community, at present and in the past. Borrowing from the field of citizenship studies and identity politics, it argues that to understand local expressions of Jewish belonging, they need to be framed in the wider context of the national discourse on Britishness and citizenship. This means that changing notions of national identity inevitably trigger changes in how people express and experience their Jewish 'selves'. However, this ongoing dialogue between one's sense of Jewishness and Britishness is also mediated by the local circumstances, which explains why Leeds Jewry is simultaneously similar yet distinct from other Jewish communities in the UK.

My research interest in the past and present of the Leeds Jewish community was sparked when my family moved to Leeds in 2002 and settled in the suburbs of LS17, home to Britain's third largest Jewish community. I embarked on a continuous journey of discovery, attending communal events, researching local archives, reading into community's history and – above all – meeting and talking to members of the Leeds Jewish community. The evidence collected in this research included twenty-seven in-depth interviews, a stratified survey of local residents ($n=73$), personal vignettes gathered during private and communal meetings, as well as numerous historical and contemporary documents and media sources.

Although previous chapters have revealed a divided community, by the late-twentieth early-twenty-first century the Leeds Jewish community seemed more united. Indeed, one of the first things I learned on my arrival to Leeds was the reputation of local Jewry as a closely-knit provincial and ageing community renowned for their traditionalism, continuity of identities and practices. This image of stability and unity painted a very different picture from the still visibly fractured communities of London and Manchester, where the intra-communal *sinat chinam* [a Talmudic term denoting hatred between Jews] is strongly articulated both institutionally and discursively. No less surprising was how people of different ages and religious outlook frequently describe Leeds Jewry as traditional and unchanging, yet also acknowledge that compared to the past the community has changed considerably:

- people now are more open about their religion. Before – you wanted to merge with the crowd, today there is a choice, but then, many don't use it (male, 75)
- it is easier because there is more democracy, but at the same time more difficult because Judaism is pushed away by many (female, 45)
- traditions have changed and so has practice (female, 14)
- there is more involvement of all types of Jews (female, 15)
- Judaism has become far more secular and more diverse as people marry out more (male, 16).

Although there is no agreement on what had changed and whether it was for better or worse, there is a growing acceptance that Jews today feel free to construct, live and publicly display their identities in multiple different ways. This finding challenged the image of Leeds Jewry as a monolithic stronghold of traditional Judaism and prompted further investigation.

Setting the scene: Jewishness and Britishness

Compared to most other minority groups of immigrant origin living in the city, Leeds Jewry is often described as a model minority, who have successfully completed their integration into the social and economic mainstream and presently enjoy stable and unproblematic identities. Yet, using contemporary understanding of identity as relational and contextual,[1] Jewish identities have to be viewed as social constructs which are 'continually being defined and redefined according to different social circumstances, including the effects of other cultures, economic and technological developments and political conditions'.[2] A distinct feature of Jewish identity is its simultaneous connection to religious, ethnic and cultural dimensions, which enable many competing definitions of Jewish self and Jewish community. In the words of a famous Jewish historian, Horowitz, Jewish identity is 'akin to a multi-flexed phenomenon moving in a variety of historical as well as structural directions'.[3]

Jewish life in Britain is commonly identified with London and Manchester, while small provincial communities, like Leeds, are often viewed as their regional extensions. Although Jewish perceptions in small provincial communities are shaped by national and international developments, they are also mediated by the local circumstances. While members of large-sized communities could be relatively secluded from outside influences, smaller enclaves of minorities are more exposed to their external settings, which makes their study particularly interesting.

Jewish life in diasporic communities outside Israel is to a great extent shaped by the terms of engagement between local Jewish and non-Jewish populations. A useful concept, which captures the terms of national engagement, integration and belonging is the concept of *national citizenship*. Understood here as a form of collective identity and, simultaneously, as a set of institutional and discursive practices,[4] the concept of citizenship allows us to explore how particular expressions of Jewish identities become responses to specific socio-economic and cultural circumstances. Consequently, when the terms of national citizenship change, past expressions of Jewish identity may no longer fit the new circumstances, calling for new 'readings' of Jewish belonging.

During the early stages of the settlement (1880–1914), Leeds Jewry was in many ways typical of London or Manchester communities: many poor immigrants from Eastern Europe living in segregated areas and working in sweatshop industries. The identities of the first generation of immigrants were shaped by their experience in their countries of origin and reflected the main ideological divisions of the time, in which the supporters of socialism and nationalism challenged the traditional, pre-modern vision of Jewishness. Like everywhere in Britain at that time, Leeds Jews faced a hierarchically racist worldview, institutionalised anti-Semitism and national identity deeply rooted in white English culture. The pressures for cultural assimilation were incredibly strong, while public expression of non-Englishness led to marginalisation and stigma. Integration in the society and socio-economic ascent were impossible without the abandonment of visibly 'alien' identities. However, since religion was viewed as a private matter, the expression of Jewishness through Judaism resulting in a formula of 'private Jewishness and public Englishness' offered the way forward. Indeed, confining one's Jewishness to the private realm of personal faith helped reduce the barriers to socio-economic integration into the British mainstream and offered a chance for upward mobility. Yet it came with a high price of assimilation which allowed Jews to drift away from their community, faith and identity.

In Leeds, where the Jewish community had the highest concentration of foreign-born Jews, mostly working in the tailoring industry and living in a close neighbourhood, this acculturation process took longer than in London. Nevertheless, by the 1950s and 1960s this transformation was accomplished and most people in the community joined the British middle class, embracing the identity of the 'Englishmen of Jewish faith' and becoming respectable and loyal members of the society. Known at the start of the twentieth century as a 'bastion' of Orthodoxy,[5] very observant yet 'narrow and unimaginative',[6] the community drifted towards traditional middle-of-the-road Judaism, still Orthodox in its outlook, yet often pragmatic in its religious practice. As acculturation and economic integration progressed, the socio-economic ascent of Leeds Jews was mirrored in the changing geography of a community that was steadily moving northwards to suburbia and in the gradual dilution of minority identity, which was becoming more symbolic.[7]

The arrival of other immigrants in the Second World War period problematised the old notion of citizenship and challenged the old formula of social inclusion. The last quarter of the twentieth century saw the formation of a new national discourse on multicultural society, diversity and inclusivity, which redefined the status of racial and ethnic minorities in Britain. To ensure minority rights, new legal institutions, such as Race Relations Acts (1965, 1967 and 1976), were created. Britishness has become viewed as an act of belonging to the national political community rather than the sharing of white English 'culture'. Finally, the prevalence of 'identity politics' gave legitimacy to minority groups' collective representation in the public space, with at least some of their citizenship rights being group based. These developments have taken place in the context of declining class-based politics, rising levels of secularism and increasingly consumer-oriented attitudes to social policies and identities. As a result, mainstream British society, which in the past was strongly associated with white Christian English middle-class culture, has been challenged and fragmented, creating multiple identity representations.

In these circumstances, Jews, individually and communally, found themselves challenged by the growing inconsistency between the established Jewish identity model (i.e. private religious identity) and the new socio-political reality, which enabled and encouraged identity politics, diversity and pluralism.[8] This prompted revisions to the meaning of Jewishness and led to a revival of ethno-cultural markers in self-presentation, such as Jewish cultural traditions, family and local histories, participation and activism in community affairs, Jewish friends and support for Israel.[9] This ambiguity regarding the importance of religious, ethnic and cultural markers for Jewish identity has become endemic and has been acknowledged in the Jewish discourse nationally[10] and internationally.[11] Qualitative evidence collected in this research and presented in the next section shows that these processes have also affected Jewish individual and collective representations of 'self' in Leeds, producing complex, diverse, fragmented and frequently incongruent identities.

Contemporary spaces of Jewish belonging in Leeds

Although past Jewish 'identity packages'[12] have been challenged by the new national formula of citizenship and belonging, they are still viable and being actively used in the community. In an interview, a self-identified Jewish 'Loiner' in his 80s confessed:

> I'll tell you something interesting: all Jewish children strived to achieve academically ... Unlike the Muslims today we wanted to integrate. Jewish people practised their faith discreetly.

At the same time, many Jews now use these packages in an eclectic and contextualised way: people 'mix-and-match' different visions of Jewishness, as well as different concepts of Britishness, to support a particular argument or point they want to make. They seamlessly blend in narratives from the non-Jewish discourse, like issues of racial equality, gay rights, environment protection, etc. into their visions of Jewish 'self' and Jewish world. This finding is consistent with the research findings of Heilman and DellaPergola,[13] who identified the destruction of the fixity of established models of Jewishness as a worldwide trend.

Quite telling in this regard was the loyalty split in the community when Israel and England were drawn in the same qualifying group for the 2008 European Football Championship. Some even saw it as a Jewish version of Tebbit's cricket test of loyalty.[14] Ahead of the first game in March 2007, the Jewish press published a series of interviews with local Jews, asking who they intended to support. The answers differed greatly, but more importantly they illustrated how differently people chose to define their sense of Jewish identity. For some, who saw Jewishness strictly as a matter of religion, their unquestionable loyalty was to the English team; for others, who ethnicised their Jewishness, it was 'a coming together of two home nations'.

An article in the regional Jewish newspaper, 'Question of Support: It's England v. Israel ... but who will you be cheering on?',[15] featured a full range of positions. A Leeds United fan, Mike, was firmly on the English side: 'I am definitely going to be supporting England – I am English, after all.' To ascertain the strength of his Jewish identity he added: 'if Israel were playing any other team apart from England, then I'd support them.' Yet, many other Jews, interviewed in the newspaper, backed Israel and wished them victory, although to explain their allegiances they used contrasting models of Jewish 'self'. Simon of Leeds supported Israel because he saw it as a home country for all Jews: 'I am Jewish and I support Israel rather than England without a doubt, they are number one.' For Richard, a coach of Leeds Maccabi football team, it was a strong religious identity that made him favour Israel: 'I will definitely be supporting Israel because that is where my heritage lies. My religion is my priority.' Stephen of Leeds emphasised his Zionist allegiance to Israel: 'I like to see England do well, but on this occasion, as a Zionist, I would like to see the underdogs win. It will also help to raise a more positive image of Israel.' Some interviewees, who felt uncomfortable with the situation, which split their affinities, hoped for a draw as way out: 'A draw would be best all around as I'd love to see both teams qualify,' confessed Sheldon, a co-manager of Manchester Maccabi. Sensing this tension, the newspaper columnist Doreen Wachmann in a follow-up article, entitled 'Flag is not a loyalty badge',[16] played down the role of sympathies in spectator sports and offered another measure of Britishness: '... whether or not one enjoys spectator sports is a totally private matter for each individual ... what matters is that I keep British law.' This, according to Wachmann, makes Jews, who contributed to Britain 'on a scale far disproportionate of their numbers', model citizens.

The illustrated diversity of opinions shows not only a continuing pluralisation of Jewish space,[17] but an increasing public acceptance of this process as legitimate. What is qualitatively different about the present communal discourse is that Jews are no longer afraid of looking disloyal and openly air their support for the Israeli team at the expense of the English team. This is rooted in the new formula of the national citizenship: although assimilationist pressures still exist and perhaps have even intensified since the declaration of the 'war on terrorism' in 2001, they are different from the past. Now they are about political unity and the acceptance of liberal democracy as the foundation of the state, rather than about giving up one's ethnic, cultural or religious identity.

Not surprisingly, 83% of the surveyed community members agreed with the statement 'Nowadays Jewish people are free to choose and to change their own identities', while only 9% actively disagreed with it. The reasons given by those who disagreed were often mutually exclusive. People with strong religious conviction saw Jewishness as a G-d's given identity, hence to change or abandon this identity was a transgression against G-d. Explanations given by more secular respondents ranged from anti-Semitism, which 'does not allow Jews to forget who they are' (male, 67) to a purely ethnic definition of Jewishness, which makes it an in-born permanent characteristic that is impossible to alter.

This is how one of the interviewees, 21-year-old Alex,[18] explains his doubts about the permanency of one's Jewishness: 'One can change their image, and even maybe their identity, but can never change the fact that they were born, and therefore are, Jewish.' As the interview continues, Alex switches from this ethnic definition of Jewishness to a more traditional, religious vision of Jewish identity. Although by his own admittance Alex is a passionate secular Zionist, who does not consider religious belief and observance necessary for his sense of Jewish self, he nevertheless constantly refers to Judaism, accepting and even praising the importance of religious commitment for the continuation of Jewish identity:

> There will always be extreme forms of religion: extremists Islamists, Lubavitch Jews. But I think it is essential to have this kind of people because they are the

ones who really, really care and drive the religion forward, the sort of people who will debate the religion until they die. Yet it is essential for non-Jews to mix with Jews and Jews to mix with the non-Jews, it is the only way to reach complete understanding of all faiths and cultures.

This statement blends together a centuries-long Jewish appreciation of *tzadikim* [religiously righteous people] and a modern secularist anxiety over staunch religious observance, hence the term 'religious extremists'. Both are then crafted into a complex 'multicultural' narrative, which emphasises the importance of mutual respect and cross-cultural dialogue. The latter enables Alex to show his tolerance to the expressions of Jewish identity that he personally does not share; it also enables him to draw a parallel between Jewish and other minority identities and to identify inter-communal relations as a means to combat prejudice and bigotry.

To understand the historical continuity and the present variety and consistency of personal identifications it is useful to distinguish analytically between the religious and social dimensions of Jewish identity. Alex's example nicely illustrates that even for self-identified secularists, Judaism remains a focal point of reference. At the same time, the absence of a strong religious anchor makes Jewishness one of many social identities of a person, creating a peculiar 'identity bag' in which initially disjointed narratives of 'self' interact and influence each other. Depending on how important the religious dimension is to one's sense of Jewishness, its interaction with other existential spaces (work, family, politics and social relations) could be of various natures, leading to different ways of building and narrating Jewish identity.[19]

Making sense of Jewish identity attributes

To capture the interplay between the religious and social elements of identity, the survey contained two questions which prompted respondents to assess the importance of different identity items to their feeling of being Jewish. The list included religious attributes (belief and observance) and socio-cultural elements (friends, neighbourhood, participation in communal life, Jewish knowledge); in addition, the list contained Zionism and anti-Semitism, both of which historically had a profound significance for Leeds Jewry. Table 15.1 summarises the rank scores of attributes based on the answers to these questions.

Predictably, such characteristics as religious outlook, age, involvement in Jewish communal life and the type of school attended (for teenagers) give some insights into why people ranked identity items in one way or another. Yet, there were certain unexpected or ambiguous results, which were further investigated through interviews and document analysis. This approach

Table 15.1 Ranking of Jewish identity attributes by different groups of community members

Q1: Could you, please, rank the following attributes according to their importance for feeling Jewish? (1 – the most important, 8 – the least important)
Q2: Could you, please, state the significance of each of the following aspects to feeling Jewish?

Attributes of Jewishness		Adults* (n=26)	Community Youth Leaders* (n=5)	Youth club members (n=17)	Young people** Grammar school students (n=21)	Young people** Jewish Independent school students (n=4)
Socio-cultural space	Knowledge of history, culture and traditions	1	2	1	1	2
	Jewish friends	3	2	2	1	7
	Participation in Jewish social life and communal events	3	2	5	6	3
	Living in a Jewish neighbourhood	6	6	6	5	4
Religious space	Religious belief	3	7	3	3	5
	Religious Practice	5	8	7	5	1
Zionism		7	4	4	7	8
Anti-Semitism		7	5	8	6	6

* Jewish activists were in the age range of 19 to 23 years, and adults were in the 25 to 85 age range.
** School students and youth club members were between 14 and 17 years old.

proved very useful as it showed that the same ranking order of Jewish identity attributes was often grounded in different identity models. It also demonstrated inconsistencies and fragmentation of personal Jewish identities as well as the ease with which individual respondents, just like Alex, were able to shift narrative spaces and combine different identity models.

Socio-cultural attributes

As expected, and in line with the national trends identified in the 2013 National Jewish Community Survey,[20] most respondents to the survey viewed socio-cultural attributes as the main identity items. However, they disagreed over the importance of particular social and cultural items. The least controversial was '*knowledge of history, culture and tradition*': virtually everyone placed this category at the top and no one thought of it as unimportant.[21] '*Jewish knowledge*' is such an encompassing category that it easily becomes a central point for people with otherwise conflicting views on Jewish identity. It is congruent with a religious outlook, which assigns high value to Jewish learning. Equally, those with a more secular outlook seek Jewish knowledge, albeit of a different sort. They wish to learn about Jewish history, culture and politics, viewing this as a foundation for their identity and a sense of belonging. Slightly more contentious was the importance of '*Jewish friends*', as secular respondents considered this category of high importance while more religious people thought of it as unimportant. All survey respondents admitted having Jewish friends and 80% of them said that at least half of their friends were Jewish,[22] yet respondents with strong religious outlook and strict observance viewed 'friends' as a consequence of being Jewish and living Jewish life rather than an independent identity item which could define their sense of Jewishness.

All adult respondents, regardless of their observance and outlook, thought that participation in community life was just as important as Jewish knowledge and friends. At the same time, younger respondents, with the exception of students from a strictly Orthodox Jewish school, assigned low priority to this category. In a follow-up interview, some of them pointed out that community life was akin to 'boring activities for grown-ups' (male, 15). In their view, younger community members require a wide range of specifically targeted activities.

The final socio-cultural attribute of Jewish identity that was included in the survey, residence in a Jewish neighbourhood, has become an equally contentious issue. Although nearly all of the survey respondents stated that presently they lived in a Jewish neighbourhood and felt happy about it, they often expressed contradictory views on the value of this identity category. As a rule, religiously observant people who require daily access to Jewish infrastructure placed this category significantly higher than non-observant people, many of whom commented on the irrelevance of this category for their sense of

Jewishness. Explaining their answers, some secular respondents were concerned that living in close proximity to other Jews could jeopardise personal anonymity, which was a very important factor for their sense of wellbeing. For instance, Hannah, a pupil from a local comprehensive school, confessed that what she liked about living in Leeds was that her feeling of being part of the Jewish community did not come at the expense of personal liberties. She explained that 'You always feel like a part of the community but at the same time [as] "an individual".' Another reason for dismissing the role of Jewish neighbourhood was linked to a declining importance of physical proximity due to modern means of communication. This sentiment was especially strong among younger respondents and members of the Reform movement, who did not accept the prohibition to drive or carry on Shabbat.

Ironically, low priority assigned to personal residence in a Jewish area went hand in hand with a perceived importance of having a clearly distinguishable Jewish neighbourhood (buildings, landscape objects and people), which reinforces Jewish identity and pride in the community. For instance, for Eddie (66), the Leeds Jewish community was embodied in its physical infrastructure, as his listing of the community's main elements included 'different synagogues, Jewish shops; community and youth centres; Jewish welfare agency, B'nei B'rith, Hillel etc.; Jewish education and Cheders; Jewish Housing'.

Overall, the importance of socio-cultural space comes as no surprise in a community that historically had a very high level of occupational and residential concentration and a high density of social interactions among its members. With a general decline of religious observance, cultural attributes and 'social capital'[23] have become the most important and uncontroversial assets of Jewish life in Leeds. This is also supported by the finding that most respondents (84% of adults and 55% of youngsters) considered family history as important for one's sense of identity and expressed a strong interest in their own family history (88% and 76% respectively).

Zionism

Another surprising survey finding was a relatively low priority ascribed to Zionism in the community that historically was considered a Zionist stronghold. Only a few survey respondents, most of whom were community youth leaders, ranked Zionism as important for their identity. Angela, a community youth leader, who was born and has lived in Leeds all her life and who self-identified as a secular Jew, shared her strong sentiments about Israel: 'I feel like it is my true motherland, I need to do everything to promote its course and it makes me feel proud.' However, other respondents were reluctant to select Zionism as an identity item because of its ambiguous meaning. Zionism could be interpreted simply as love of Israel and support for Jewish people in Israel, but it could also mean the support for Israeli politics, or as an obligation for all Jewish people to 'return' to Israel. This is how Helen, a middle-aged female – who grew up in Leeds and, in the past, had been involved in many Zionist activities – explained her current position:

> It depends on what do you mean by Zionism: Zionism as an 'ism' is not important, but Zionism as a love of Israel is intrinsic to Judaism. I don't like Zionism as an 'ism' because, unfortunately, with some people it replaces Judaism. If you call the love of Israel being a Zionism, then I am a Zionist, but I do not like to refer to myself as one, because it is like Communism or Socialism, and it is not like that.

Secular interviewees were also keen to distance themselves from the term Zionism, albeit for different reasons. Some indicated that widespread liberal criticism of Israel's policies compromised Zionism as a basis for identification, while others were not happy with the old Zionist appeal to all Jewish people to make *aliyah*[24] and to settle in Israel for good. In an interview to a local Jewish newspaper after spending a gap year in Israel, 19-year-old Leeds-born Chana speaks about the importance of staying in a diaspora and supporting Israel from abroad:

> During my stay in Jerusalem, someone said that it was better to be a Jew in Diaspora than in Israel, because if all the Jews have lived in Israel, who would defend and protect us? The statement stuck with me and now that I am back I feel it even more so.[25]

On the whole, the evidence collected in this research points to a decline of Zionism as a ground for self-identification in Leeds and, according to a national research on Jewish attitudes to Israel,[26] this is a general trend affecting many communities. Nevertheless, Israel remains central to the identity of the local Jews: 72% of the survey respondents and nearly all interviewees stated full support and love of Israel, although among young respondents this was less popular (52%).

Religious belief and practice

Analysing how various community members judged the value of religious practice to their sense of Jewish identity predictably showed a strong correlation with their religious outlook. This identity attribute scored high on the list of more observant people, while for somebody like Alex it was close to the end of the list. A 15-year-old female from a strictly Orthodox family gave the following explanation for why for her observance was non-negotiable: [being Jewish] 'is not a coincidence or nice thing to be, but a job and a way of life'. According to a strictly Orthodox point of view, religious space is as an encompassing dimension of human life, penetrating and regulating other existential spaces. This model is considered the only 'true' way of living: all aspects of Jewish life should be structured by the Jewish law leaving virtually nothing unregulated – dietary habits, dress code, social relations, business ethics, family life, etc.

Interestingly, when it came to predicting the ascribed importance of religious belief, the dichotomy between observant and non-observant was not sustained: belief was ranked as moderately important for those who identify with strict Orthodoxy, yet it featured even higher on the 'identity list' of some less observant members of the community. This conundrum was explained by a local Orthodox rabbi who simply stated that practical observance has to come before belief: 'one would never know all the answers and never understand everything, but a Jew has to follow the laws of Torah, because that is what being Jewish is about'. This axiom guides the lives of the religious and motivates the upbringing of children who are taught to tame their desires in accordance to the Jewish law. Consider the episode that took place in a local Jewish primary school during a sports event. A girl of 9 from an observant family was crying out loud because she felt hungry and did not have any money to buy food that was sold on the premises. Another concerned parent offered her a kosher chocolate bar and the face of the girl sparkled with delight, but she could not hide her disappointment when it turned out to contain milk: 'I've recently had a burger [which contained meat], so I am not yet allowed any milk' and the girl moved away.

For less observant Jews, however, these Orthodox complexities of adjusting the spaces of modern life to religious commitments proved to be less of a problem and often involved an inverse relationship of adjusting religious space to fit the necessities of the modern world. They usually hold a more secularised view that considers religious space as one of many dimensions of human life. How much of the religious dimension is permitted in one's life and how it coexists with other existential dimensions is a matter of personal conviction and frequently is open for ad-hoc negotiations. Despite the secularisation and lack of observance, the majority of Leeds Jewry did not want to totally abandon the religious dimension and consider religious belief a significant attribute of their sense of Jewishness. This is consistent with the results of other national surveys,[27] showing that people search for 'spirituality' and sacredness in Judaism, but approach religious customs pragmatically. The religious dimension is seen as a way to spirituality, while rituals are seen as conventional, hence optional, entry points to this religious space. Responding to the debate about the Halachic prohibition to use a wheelchair to get to Synagogue on Shabbat, an elderly *Jewish Telegraph* reader, who identified as an Orthodox Jew, wrote:

> The Torah, which has been the source of our guide to a good life for over 2000 years, should supply a solution to our problems and not a prohibition to our needs.[28]

For those who see the religious dimension as an autonomous space, there exist certain entry–exit points into and out of this space. These may be associated with material objects like the synagogue, the community centre or the Torah, or there may be behavioural and spiritual triggers, like saying certain prayers, celebrating holidays and engaging in Jewish learning. This often leads to a fractured mentality whereby different normative and behavioural frames of reference are used in different circumstances. For instance, when describing Leeds Jewry as a whole, many interviewees pointed to the large numbers of friends, relatives and acquaintances, who kept kosher at home, but did not hesitate to break the laws of Kashrut when going out. In another interesting confession, some female interviewees, who belong to Orthodox synagogues, admitted dual standards with regard to women's rights: they may be supporters of gender equality in a secular world, but would not even consider the possibility of having a female rabbi or cantor (service conductor) in their synagogue.

Anti-Semitism

The final item on the list of identity categories was anti-Semitism and, although most respondents acknowledged the importance of this phenomenon and felt concerned about the rising levels of anti-Semitism, they refused to make it a determinant of their Jewish 'selves'. In the age of positive identities, it is understandable why anti-Semitism (i.e. fear and/or experience of anti-Semitism), which is associated with externally imposed negative conception of Jewishness, scored very low in a personal hierarchy of identity items. At the same time, most of the respondents showed awareness of the role social prejudice and stigma played in the past and expressed concern about its potential growth in the future.

The diversity of contemporary views on Jewishness and Britishness became more apparent when people described anti-Semitism and offered strategies to combat the phenomenon. Some employed an age-old conception of anti-Semitism as a unique, timeless and almost irrational hatred of Jewish people, which is destined to hurt Jewish people forever. The following citations from two Jewish females with very different backgrounds share the same emphasis on the permanence of anti-Semitism. For a very observant middle-aged female, 'anti-Semitism is a creation of God, there is no rationale behind it, just blind hatred on the side of other people'; equally for a Reform-affiliated 26-year-old community leader, anti-Semitism 'is always around [for] … we are constant "other" in Europe'.

On the other hand, a growing number of Jews, especially among the younger generation, define anti-Semitism as a manifestation of racism and use a general multicultural narrative to describe it:

- it is just abuse of a minority due to ignorance or a small amount of knowledge. People hate things that are different, no matter what it is! (female, 21)
- people are anti-Semitic for the same reasons as to other ethnic groups; they cannot understand how people are different to them (male, 17)

Consequently, they don't believe that hiding Jewishness and 'keeping their head down' – the dominant mode of Jewish existence in Britain for more than a century – would solve anti-Semitism. Instead they encourage open resistance to anti-Semitism and public celebration of one's Jewishness. Likewise, they demand communal and national recognition (and equal representation) of alternative ways of defining and living Jewish identities.

Conclusion

Behind this new, more assertive and celebratory display of Jewish identity is a desire to belong and to feel proud about one's heritage and community. This is a common thread that links members of the Leeds Jewish community as they speak of their pride in being Jewish:

- I enjoy the feeling of belonging – a sense of community – a sense of connection to a rich and long history (female, 50)
- it's my identity and heritage (male, 15)
- because I feel I belong to a special community rather than being an individual in a religion (male, 19)
- I feel I have a certain identity and I enjoy it (female, 17)
- because I am proud to be Jewish (male, 16)
- it is a big part of my life, it is my identity, looking back many years, Jews had a colourful history and most necessary, it has to have a bright future (male, 20)

These views are very different to the sentiments publicly expressed by Leeds Jewry in the first half of the twentieth century. They are the product of the new formula of national citizenship and belonging, which from the late 1980s has been used to validate ethnic, cultural and religious pluralism and legitimise public display of differences. Observing this national change, one of the interviewees, a middle-aged male, pointed to a staggering difference between his and his daughter's experiences in school. In his childhood, when Jewish children were the only minority pupils, they aspired to blend in and be like English kids, but in the twenty-first century the mainstream has become very diverse, so in his daughter's school it was acceptable and even 'cool' to be something else than English: Sikh, Muslim, Jewish or Black.

Throughout the history of Jewish diaspora, Jewish life has always been community-bound; and in present day Leeds, just like in the past, the sense of physical and metaphysical togetherness remains important for Jewish identification. However, the bases for this unity, as well as the functioning and the meaning of modern communal life, have become very different. This is true about individual Jewish 'selves' as well as about collective representations of Jewish community. The narration of Leeds Jewry as a community of people with the same cultural, economic and religious characteristics and a shared sense of local history is a powerful way of representing its unity, but it does not reflect a growing diversity of its members and make it unsustainable in the long run, especially in the face of a very real threat of demographic shrinkage.[29] Acknowledging this situation, communal organisations headed by their main representative body, the Leeds Jewish Representative Council (LJRC), since the turn of the twenty-first century have actively promoted an alternative, more pluralist and inclusive image of the community. In 2006, the LJRC used its newly created website to publicly acknowledge the need to 'enhance the unity and mutual cooperation of Jews living in Leeds and its surrounding districts' and to support Jews 'irrespective of their political or religious affiliations'.[30]

Later, this approach was captured in a new mission statement to make Leeds 'a great place to be Jewish' and became part of a joint communal policy to build community's resilience.[31] It was supported by a number of specific policy actions aimed at making Leeds more welcoming to all Jews, including those who don't fit the traditional image of Jewish Loiners and who previously found themselves at the physical or spiritual margins of the community. In his 2017 AGM report, the LJRC President Laurence Saffer reinforced this message:

> It is our aim that people are able to live here as Jews in whatever way they see fit rather than simply reside here. To some it is going to shul or attending a shiur. To others it is playing bridge, football, or golf, with a Jewish group, or singing in a Jewish choir. Others still want to see an Israeli film or learn Ivrit. Others may want to do charitable work. They are all valid expressions of Jewish identity and all show a commitment to and involvement with our community.[32]

There are some encouraging signs that this approach is paying off and the community has turned a corner – it is buzzing with events and activities for people of all ages and outlooks.

Notes

1. K. Woodward (ed.), *Identity and Difference* (London: Sage, 1997).
2. E. Krausz and G. Tulea (eds), *Jewish Survival: The Identity Problem at the Close of the Twentieth Century* (Abingdon: Routledge, 1998), p. 262.

3   I. L. Horowitz, 'Minimalism or Maximalism: Jewish Survival at the Millennium' in Krausz and Tulea, *Jewish Survival*, p. 3.
4   S. Marston and K. Mitchell. 'Citizens and the State: Citizenship Formations in Space and Time', in C. Barnett and M. Low (eds), *Spaces of Democracy: Geographical Perspectives on Citizenship, Participation and Representation* (London: Sage, 2004).
5   E. Sterne, *Leeds Jewry and the Great War 1914-1918: The Homefront* (Leeds: Jewish Historical Society of England, 1982).
6   A. S. Diamond, 'A Sketch of Leeds Jewry in the 19th Century' (a paper presented at the JHSE conference Provincial Jewry in Victorian England, 1975), p. 2.
7   H. Gans, 'Symbolic ethnicity and symbolic religiosity: towards a comparison of ethnic and religious acculturation', *Ethnic and Racial Studies* 17 (1994), pp. 577-92.
8   P. Weller, 'Identity, politics, and the future(s) of religion in the UK: the case of the religion questions in the 2001 Decennial Census ', *Journal of Contemporary Religion*, 19:1 (2004), p. 12.
9   D. Graham and J. Boyd, *The Attitudes of Jews in Britain towards Israel* (London: Institute for Jewish Policy Research, 2010).
10 S. Miller, M. Schmool and A. Lerman, *Social and Political Attitudes of British Jews: Some Key Findings of the JPR Survey* (London: Institute for Jewish Policy Research, 1996).
11 S. DellaPergola, 'World Jewish Population at the Dawn of the 21st Century', in E. Ben-Rafael, Y. Gorny and Y. Ro'i (eds), *Contemporary Jewries: Convergence and Divergence: Jewish Identities in a Changing World*, Vol. 2 (Leiden and Boston: Brill, 2003).
12 J. Webber (ed.), *Jewish Identities in the New Europe* (Liverpool: Littman Library of Jewish Civilization, 1994), p. 83.
13 S. Heilman, 'Building Jewish Identity for Tomorrow', in Krausz and Tulea, *Jewish Survival*, p. 83; DellaPergola, 'World Jewish Population at the Dawn of the 21st Century', p. 49.
14 In 1990, Lord Tebbit suggested that the loyalty of British Asians could be measured by who they supported in international cricket matches.
15 *Jewish Telegraph*, 3 February 2007, p. 20.
16 *Jewish Telegraph*, 30 June 2007, p. 7.
17 N. G. Hofman, *Renewed Survival: Jewish Community Life in Croatia* (Oxford: Lexington Books, 2006).
18 This and other names of the people who were interviewed and quoted here have been changed.
19 A. J. Winter, 'Symbolic ethnicity or religion among Jews in the United States: A test of Gansian hypotheses', *Review of Religious Research* 37 (1996), pp. 137-51.
20 D. Graham, L. D. Staetsky and J. Boyd, *Jews in the United Kingdom in 2013: Preliminary Findings from the National Jewish Community Survey* (London: Institute for Jewish Policy Research, 2014).
21 The only person who marked '*knowledge*' as unimportant was a grammar school student who also marked other categories as unimportant and later explained his position by his secular outlook and a general indifference to Jewish matters.

22 This finding was supported by the results of the 2001 Institute for Jewish Policy Research survey of Leeds Jewry which were published in S. Waterman, *The Jews of Leeds in 2001: Portrait of a Community* (London: Institute for Jewish Policy Research, 2003). In their sample, three-quarters of Jews with a secular outlook and more than 96% of people with somewhat religious/religious outlook had more than half of their friends who were Jewish.
23 R. D. Putnam and A. K. Leigh, 'Reviving community: what policy-makers can do to build social capital in Britain and America', *Renewal: A Journal of Labour Politics*. 10:2 (2002), pp. 15–20.
24 A Hebrew word that means to 'go up', which originally referred to ascending to Jerusalem to celebrate the Jewish Feasts, but today has come to mean the return of the Jews to the Land of Israel.
25 *Jewish Telegraph*, 15 September 2006, p. 2.
26 Graham and Boyd, *The Attitudes of Jews in Britain towards Israel*.
27 According to the JPR Survey of Leeds Jewry in 2001, around 60% of the respondents described their religious observance as 'traditional', most of whom considered their outlook as 'somewhat religious' (60.7%) and 'somewhat secular' (23.7%). Another 22% defined their practice as 'just Jewish', whereas only 6% thought they were strictly Orthodox and 7% confessed to a secular lifestyle (Waterman, *The Jews of Leeds in 2001*, p. 9).
28 *Jewish Telegraph*, 24 August 2007, p. 7.
29 D. Graham, M. Schmool and S. Waterman, *Jews in Britain: A Snapshot from the 2001 Census* (London: Institute for Jewish Policy Research, 2007), p. 42.
30 www.ljrc.org (accessed 17 May 2007).
31 Jewish Joint Distribution Committee (JCD) – Europe, *Community Resilience Profile: Leeds Jewish Community*, http://ljrc.org/useful-links/jdc-community-resilience-report/ (accessed 14 October 2018).
32 L. Saffer, 'President's report at the Leeds Jewish Representative Council annual general meeting' (March 2017), www.leedsjewishcommunity.com/join-in/2017/03/15/ljrc-president-agm-report/ (accessed 10 May 2017).

16

The community today and its recent history

Derek Fraser

There were three main developments which characterised the Leeds Jewish community in the decades after the Second World War: social mobility; relocation to a new 'unwalled ghetto'; and numerical decline. For much of the twentieth century, as previous chapters have illustrated, Leeds Jewry was predominantly a proletarian community. When the writer first came to Leeds as a student in the late 1950s, he lodged with a family in Chapeltown where the householder was a cutter at Burtons, among the elite of the skilled workers there. Thousands of Jewish men and women worked at Burtons and at other Jewish-owned tailoring firms, as well as at the countless outsourcing and subcontracting workshops. At its peak, Burtons employed 10,000 workers and during the war the firm supplied 25% of all male and female service uniforms, as well as a third of the de-mob clothing. The de-mob clothing comprised a three-piece suit (jacket, trousers and waistcoat), a shirt and underwear and became known as 'The Full Monty' (after the name of the firm's founder) and this term has gone into the common parlance.

By the third quarter of the twentieth century, profound changes were affecting the clothing industry, which were to lead to a rapid decline in employment and the removal of much clothing manufacture overseas. Yet, as this was happening, the Leeds Jewish community itself was changing, influenced by the rising standard of living of the wider society, as encapsulated in Harold Macmillan's winning election slogan, 'You've Never Had It So Good'. In celebrating the centenary of the Leeds Jewish Board of Guardians in 1978 (by then the Leeds Jewish Welfare Board), its President, Arnold Ziff, identified 'the continued and accelerated change of the Leeds Jewish community from a predominantly working class community to a middle class society'.[1] His opinion was confirmed in the census statistics. In 2001, 44.5% of employed Jews were in managerial and professional occupations and a further 32% in technical and administrative roles, with only about 5% in operative and elementary jobs. This contrasts sharply with the other identifiable Leeds immigrant communities, such as South Asian, Black Caribbean and Irish people.

Moreover, the social analysis also revealed geographical contrasts. The Jewish population's rising economic status was accompanied by its northward migration, in contrast to some, if not all, other immigrant communities. As a major geographical survey revealed:

> The thriving Black Caribbean and Asian enclaves of Leeds still largely coincide with the relatively deprived inner areas where the first immigrants from these groups settled. In contrast, the Jewish population, which came to Leeds in the middle of the nineteenth century as poverty-stricken refugees, has migrated northwards from the slums of the Leylands, through Chapeltown to the affluent outer suburbs of Roundhay, Alwoodley and Shadwell.[2]

The 2011 Census (which recorded a 17% drop in the community since 2001 from 8,267 to 6,847), demonstrated the concentration in the contiguous suburbs of Moortown, Roundhay and Alwoodley, with outlying satellites in Harewood and Scarcroft. Perhaps surprisingly, there were Jews who identified themselves as such in every ward of the city, ranging from 9 in Morley South to 3,270 in Alwoodley. The 650 identified in the Headingley, Woodhouse and City wards were no doubt predominantly students, probably in effect temporary residents. The majority Jewish residential choices are clearly shown visually (Figure 16.1). It will be seen that the community infrastructure coexists with the residential zoning.

While the Jewish community was upwardly mobile and moving to the more affluent suburbs, it was declining in numbers. The peak claimed Jewish population of 25,000 and 5% of the city in the early and middle decades of the twentieth century had declined to some 7,000 and no more than about 1% of Leeds citizens by the present. The factors cited for this decline (which affected other cities and led to the disappearance of many smaller communities) include inter-marriage, young people moving to London (often followed by their parents), relocation to Israel, declining birth-rate and a general secularisation of society, with its attendant loss of faith and erosion of religious commitment. The last may also account for the noticeable decline in *kashrut* [keeping of dietary laws], often said to be the result of Jews joining the forces during the war and during national service. (Those who wish to may now eat at the kosher restaurant at the community centre, an option denied to the community for half a century.) It may be that the numerical decline has been halted and the population has now stabilised. Indeed, the career opportunities offered by the blossoming Leeds economy open the prospect of new incomers, which might reverse the trend of the last half century. There was to be no repeat of the migration of Jews to Leeds which had been so significant both in the 1880–1900 and 1930–45 periods. The 1956 Suez crisis did lead to a small number of Jews arriving from Egypt, followed by a few from Iran and Russia. Once the state of Israel was created it was there (and perhaps the USA) which was the preferred destination of persecuted Jews. Support for Israel gave a new focus to opinion among Leeds Jews and was a unifying force, which in many ways healed some of the fissures in Leeds Jewry, which had been a characteristic feature of its previous history. The Zionist communal meetings in Leeds in October and November 1956 voiced general unanimity that Israel was justified in attacking Egypt, to bring to an end years of terrorist incursions across the Gaza strip. Similarly, the Leeds Jewish community was supportive of Israel in the Six Day War of 1967 and the Yom Kippur War of 1973. Zionism acted as a unifying force because it allowed people to express their Jewish identity without reference to their religious observance, and support for the Jewish National Fund (JNF) or the Joint Israel Appeal (JIA) was almost a religion-free statement of Jewish commitment. Today there are strong and active Zionist organisations, such as United Jewish Israel Appeal (UJIA) and the Women's International Zionist Organization (WIZO).

It had indeed been the level of orthodoxy (or laxness) which had damaged Jewish unity in Leeds for many generations and its divisiveness had become almost its most compelling feature. As a visitor to Leeds in 1959 put it in a piece on 'The Enigma of Leeds':

> Leeds Jewry obtained a reputation for quarrelsomeness. Congregations split off continually; shechita rivalries were endemic; rabbi would not sit with rabbi. The reputation has stuck.[3]

An example of the fissures in the Leeds Jewish community occurred in the 1960s, after the private purchase of a nursery in Street Lane, Moortown, which was then offered to the Beth Hamedrash Hagadol Synagogue (BHH) as a new site for removal from their premises in Newton Road. As early as 1958, the BHH President offered the Street Lane site so that 'all the congregations within the community should band together to build one large synagogue'. Negotiations were opened with the Moortown Synagogue (UHC) and plans were developed for the UHC to move from its former chapel in Shadwell Lane to amalgamate with BHH into the new Street Lane building. This was widely welcomed, and Bernard Lyons predicted:

> The community is entering one of the most important phases of its history. The Street Lane Synagogue and Community Centre project will have the effect of bringing together in amalgamation and common interest the two major synagogue groups ... we now enter upon a year when the considerable efforts put into the creation of communal unity will begin to show results ... The historian of the future will no doubt quote 1966 as the year when 'unity within the community' ceased to be a meaningless cliché.[4]

But the project foundered when, at a very late stage in the process, the UHC withdrew from the scheme, leaving the BHH alone to finance it by means of a large bank overdraft which took years to repay. (Similar negotiations in 2017 were also reputedly terminated by the UHC.)

Lyons wrote in his role as President of the Leeds Jewish Representative Council, in which he served for over a decade. Undoubtedly the Rep. Council has been a unifying force, with a long and somewhat confused history. In 1966, the Council published a pamphlet to commemorate its 60th anniversary, thus dating its establishment in 1906. However, in 1987 the *Jewish Telegraph* had a feature marking 50 years of the Council, suggesting a 1937 start date. Even more puzzlingly, the Council published its 2017 'Annual Directory' with the title, *Centenary Year Book ... 100 Years Working for the Community* (1917 is deemed to be significant in the Council's history as it is the first recorded reference to a 'Representative Council' after the anti-Semitic riots). It was indeed in 1906 that, at the suggestion and leadership of Rev. (later Rabbi) Moses Abraham, a Communal Council was established whose purpose was 'the protection of Jewish interests and the cultivation of mutual feeling between Jews and Gentile'.

Though active before and during the First World War, the Council fell into abeyance in the postwar years. It was revived in the late 1930s under the aegis of B'nai Brith, whose President, Alter Hurwitz, became the Council's first chairman when it adopted a new constitution in 1941. The Council has always sought to bring together under one umbrella (now its visual symbol) the diverse range of organisations and interest groups which make up the community. In the mid-1960s there were over 100 affiliated bodies, today about half that.

The Leeds Jewish community was and remains a 'broad church', with a mainstream of varying observance, sandwiched between an ultra-Orthodox wing at one end and a progressive liberal wing at the other. The Rep. Council has sought to encompass that broad range and to develop a unified single voice, willing to speak for all who identify themselves as Jewish and promoting dialogue with other faiths (such as with Islamic leaders in Bradford) in the interests of mutual understanding and community harmony. This ecumenical approach poses some difficulties, given the underlying tensions. The ultra-Orthodox (often now referred to as the Charedi) community is largely self-referential, almost a community within a community, prioritising the contiguity of geographical and religious space. This branch of Leeds Judaism is based around the established Lubavitch community, with its self-financed facilities in Shadwell Lane, and a *Kolel* [joint enterprise association] of a small cohort of outside rabbis and their families who re-located to Leeds in 2015 to devote themselves to Torah studies and such lifestyle, hoping to influence greater orthodoxy in Leeds (so far without great success, save as a saviour to the daily *minyans* of the three orthodox mainstream synagogues). The Council publicises details of the Lubavitch synagogue, but it is not an affiliated body, although the *Kolel* has recently subscribed.

To represent the interests of this sector of Leeds Jewry alongside, for example, the Reform movement poses many challenges. The Sinai Reform synagogue dates from 1944 and since 1969 has been an affiliated organisation of the Rep. Council. Both lay and religious Sinai leaders complained regularly about being stigmatised by the wider Leeds community and many communal events have denied Sinai participation. The inter-synagogue annual football and cricket competitions are a rare example of the four main synagogues joining together on an equal footing. This overt anti-Reform prejudice has not prevented Sinai members from playing active and leading roles in charitable, inter-faith, political and Zionist organisations and, for example, Sinai member Tim Friedman (whose family can boast three generations of office holders) was Rep. Council President for three years. For the Orthodox mainstream, Reform Judaism has posed a problem both locally and nationally. This was brought into sharp focus in a spectacular way at the opening of the Street Lane BHH synagogue building (discussed above) in 1969 and may be cited as an exemplification locally of the similar tensions revealed nationally at the funeral of Rabbi Hugo Gryn in 1996.

It fell to Lyons, as Rep. Council President and in effect the lay head of the Jewish community, to make the civic arrangements for the consecration of the synagogue. The Chief Rabbi (Dr Jakobovits), the Lord Mayor, civic officials, architects and contractors were invited and agreed to attend. Also included was Reform Rabbi Henry Brandt, which the Sinai synagogue took as a symbolic acceptance of its status in the community. On learning of this, the four rabbis of the orthodox synagogues, including the one to be consecrated, gave Lyons an ultimatum: that he must withdraw the invitations or they would not attend. He rejected their ultimatum as 'unacceptable ... improper and unreasonable'. He recorded his critical thoughts in his autobiography:

> The effect of this was that no Leeds rabbi would be present to conduct the service. They took their decision in spite of the fact that the Chief Rabbi, fully aware of the situation, intended to be and was, in fact, present on the day. Here were four religious leaders who, preaching harmony and love from the pulpit, not objecting to conducting a religious service with Christians in attendance, refused to do so in the presence of a Jewish rabbi of a Reform congregation ... They boycotted the event and attempted unsuccessfully to persuade influential members of the laity to do likewise.[5]

In a lower key reverse snub a quarter of a century later, Orthodox clergy refused to attend the 50th anniversary of Sinai synagogue in 1994. Rabbi Walter Rothschild believed that this illustrated the weaknesses and divisions of the Leeds community and that he was 'the single rabbi who is prepared to meet the challenges of dealing with those divisions'.[6]

One of the drivers of the social mobility which transformed the economic character of the community was the entrepreneurial spirit of the first- and second-generation families. Much of the early history of the Leeds Jewish community involves sweat shops in tailoring and its later history is often unduly influenced by the mid-century dominance of the large-scale manufacturers in the men's clothing industry. However, Jewish employment diversified, with the development of small- and medium-sized businesses which flourished even during the depression of the interwar years. North Street, later Chapeltown Road and still later Moortown Corner and Street Lane, were bustling retail locations, characterised by a variety of Jewish-owned shops and businesses. Until well into the third quarter of the twentieth century (and in some cases beyond) were to be found Jewish butchers, bakers and poulterers, grocery shops, furriers, jewellers, textile, drapery and fashion stores, chemists, hairdressers, cosmetic and beauty salons. These suburban SMEs complemented many similar larger retail businesses with their city centre locations.

One of the industries which had a disproportionate Jewish presence was furniture making and upholstery. Many families record the stories of their forebears (like Victor Lightman) arriving in Leeds with just their woodworking tools. One such was Shlomo (Sam) Waldenberg, who established the well-known furniture-making firm in Templar Street, later expanding into New York Road. The firm's bright new showrooms were opened by the Lord Mayor in 1933 and its 1949 advert shows an impressive factory. The company survived until 1960 and an associated family company, Waldens Sleep Shops, continued until the end of the century. Among dozens of other similar Jewish firms in the furniture trade were Vulcan Upholstery, Bridgecraft, Simpson Solk, Northern Veneers and Kelvins, which as late as the 1990s was employing around 100 people making reproduction furniture; while Manny Cussins was for many years the leading Leeds retailer, with his John Peters store. By the present century, furniture manufacture had gone the same way as the clothing industry and ceased to be a mainstay of the Leeds Jewish economy.

As the Jewish presence in manufacturing declined, it was balanced by an increased participation in the professions, notably in law. Leeds Jewry produced two distinguished lawyers who made their mark in the wider legal word and who had been born into immigrant Leeds families before the First World War. Arthur Diamond, the son of the *chazan* at the Great Synagogue, ultimately became Master of the Supreme Court, while Julius Stone became a leading legal theorist and was for thirty years a professor at the University of New South Wales. They were followed by many distinguished lawyers who remained in Leeds. There were obvious barriers to overcome and, for example, Alter Hurwitz (mentioned earlier as a prime mover in the relaunch of the Rep. Council) could not find a pupillage in Leeds in the 1920s, although he had been ranked third nationally when called to the bar and was eventually to become Recorder of Halifax. The first Leeds Jew to secure a legal appointment was Rudolph Lyons QC (cousin of Bernard Lyons), who in 1957 became Recorder of Newcastle. Later he was Recorder of both Manchester and Liverpool and was knighted. Other Leeds people who achieved national legal distinction included: John Dyson, who became Master of the Rolls; Sir Harry Ognall QC, who was a High Court Judge; Geoffrey Rivlin QC, senior judge at Southwark Crown Court and later legal advisor to the Serious Fraud Office; and Brian Walsh QC, who was Recorder of Leeds for four years prior to his death in 2000. By the second half of the twentieth century, such barriers as there may have been had been successfully surmounted and there were a large number of Jewish lawyers in Leeds and a significant number of both barristers and solicitors became judges, including the first female Leeds QC and Recorder of Leeds, Louise Godfrey.[7]

There was a similar story in the medical profession. When Herman Friend died in 1905, one of his sons was identified as a medical practitioner and he was probably one of the first Jewish doctors in Leeds; while the first female graduate in medicine in Leeds was Augusta Umanski in 1915. It was always alleged that there were Jewish quotas at the Leeds University Medical and Dental Schools (and anecdotally at Leeds Grammar School and Leeds Girls High School) and it was common for newly qualified doctors to be unable to find their initial postings in Leeds. Anecdotally, it was said that Anglicising a Jewish surname helped to insidiously weaken the alleged anti-Jewish prejudice by the appointment of consultants who, in effect, concealed their overt Jewish identity. The creation of the NHS and developments in equal opportunities regulations gradually promoted a climate in which Jewish doctors were able to have careers in both hospitals and general practice. In 1966, it was estimated that some 16% of Leeds doctors were Jewish, with double that percentage for Jewish dentists. Illustrating the mid-century social mobility of the community, it was also suggested that 25% of Leeds chemists were Jewish, 20% of Leeds solicitors, with 7% of chartered accountants and 3.5% of teachers.[8]

The same survey identified that 8% of the Leeds City Council was Jewish at a time when the Jewish community was probably no more than 3.5% of the city's population. Political participation was an indicator of the gradual transformation of an immigrant community into an embedded cohort within the host society. Given the heavy concentration of the Jewish migrants in the inner-city wards, there were early attempts to align political commitment with Jewish identity. For example, in 1919, campaigning under the slogan of 'Jews for the Jews', Louis Rosenberg, the Liberal candidate for the Brunswick Ward, complained that 'it was a crying shame that the Jewish people were not represented on the Council'. His sponsor Alderman Brown was even more direct and said,

> I say to the Jews of this ward that they ought to be ashamed of themselves if they do not vote for a man of their own faith.⁹

The following year, a more oblique and less overt strategy was employed when Joe Cohen's sponsor, Alderman Perry,

> Appealed to Jews in the ward not to vote for Mr Cohen simply because he was a Jew but because he was the right man representing the right principles.¹⁰

Thereafter, the involvement of Jewish political activists was to stress their ability and ideology rather than their religious identity. Although both in Leeds, as nationally, there was strong identification with left-wing politics (including the radical trade unionism of people like Moses Sclare), in fact Jewish city councillors have represented all three major parties. There have been three Jewish Lord Mayors (two Conservative and one Labour) and after the 2017 election Leeds had two Jewish Labour MPs (for Leeds North East and North West), following in the footsteps of the Conservative MP and minister Sir Keith Joseph. Among those who originated in Leeds and were MPs elsewhere may be mentioned Julius Silverman, Gerald Kaufman, Jack Diamond and Edward Lyons. Two Leeds Jews have sat in the House of Lords: Irwin Bellow, leader of Leeds City Council and a minister in Margaret Thatcher's government and the Labour peer Joyce Gould of Potternewton.

Jewish participation in political activity – just as with involvement in wider civic, charitable, regional and cultural organisations – is evidence of a growing integration of the Jewish community into Leeds secular society. In many, possibly most, cases this was not accompanied by assimilation. Thus, integration without assimilation has been one of the defining characteristics of the Leeds community, where economic and professional success has permitted active involvement in Leeds affairs without sacrificing Jewish identity. A prime example of this was the life and career of Arnold Ziff. Entering the Stylo family shoe business in his twenties, he inherited the leadership of the business in 1966, following his father Max who died in 1954. Arnold took the business to new heights, such that Stylo and the later acquired Barratts shops were to be found on every high street. By the 1990s, there were nearly 900 retail stores, mostly by then under the Barratts banner, as well as Hush Puppies and Stylo Instep. Sadly, a Jewish Leeds business that could date its company history back to 1936 (and its origins to the 1920s) was unable to survive the turmoil of the 2008 financial crisis. In 2009, Stylo went into administration and two further attempts by Arnold's son Michael to rescue the rump of the business also foundered. The third administration at the end of 2013 marked the end of the Stylo story.

By contrast, Town Centre Securities, the property company Arnold Ziff formed in the 1950s at a critical stage of the British postwar recovery boom (as he sometimes joked, as a hobby), is still prospering as a Stock Exchange listed company. His greatest Leeds achievement was to build the Merrion Centre, which temporarily in May 1964 was the largest covered shopping centre in Britain (until overtaken by the Bull Ring Centre in Birmingham). Some said that his project was a white elephant in the wrong part of town, but he had both patience and confidence and in time the Merrion Centre thrived; at the time of writing it is the site of a major further expansion. Arnold Ziff often mentioned the gratitude he felt towards his native town for giving refuge to his grandparents when they arrived in Edwardian Leeds from Kovno with their eight children. He generously supported many Leeds projects, including the first body scanner for the NHS in Leeds, the developments at Canal Gardens at Roundhay Park, the building of the cricket school at Headingley, professorships at both universities and even the restoration of Leeds Parish Church. (The Ziff Building at Leeds University is paralleled by the Leslie Silver Building at what is now Leeds Beckett University.) Ziff was a Leeds JP for thirty years and in 1992 became the first Jew to be appointed as High Sheriff of West Yorkshire. Such was the wide-ranging scope of Arnold Ziff's involvement and achievements that he was accorded a full-page obituary in the *Times*, possibly the only Leeds Jew to receive that accolade. Though well-known in London business circles, it was his life in Leeds which was his main focus. As his biographer summed it up:

> Arnold seemed to have links with everything that made Leeds tick. As well as the city's thriving Jewish community, its universities, art gallery, parks, parish church, county cricket club and international piano competition were among the many organisations which benefited from his generosity and active involvement. Highly respected in the worlds of property development and shoe retailing, he became so well known in his native city that some suggested he deserved to be called 'Mr Leeds.'[11]

The Ziff family legacy to Leeds is the community centre which bears the name of Arnold and his wife Marjorie, which opened in 2005 and is now colloquially known as 'the MAZ Centre', the home of the Leeds Jewish Welfare Board. Arnold Ziff was President of the Welfare Board for 18 years (1968–86) and it was during his time that the charitable focus of the Board changed to meet the demographic and social challenges of the late twentieth century community. At his instigation and under his leadership the Jewish Day Centre opened in 1973, which at its peak had 600 members and which by the 1990s had a budget of £160,000. It was created to address the needs of the old and the lonely and, as at the successor MAZ Centre, offered a wide range of leisure, educational and health promotional activities. Statistical analysis suggests that the Leeds community has a higher proportion of elderly citizens (about 30%) than the national Jewish community as a whole, and the Welfare Board has an active programme targeted on this sector, as well as pioneering professional services to deal with mental health and family breakdown.

Welfare Board presidents continually bemoaned the fact that only one in four Leeds Jewish households supported the Board financially, and imaginative strategies were needed to meet the growing demands on the budget. From the early century there had been a music or theatrical event and by the late twentieth century the Variety Show had become not only a major community event, but also the source of around half of the Board's income (partly from ticket sales, but mainly from the advertising brochure which doubled as the concert programme). As Arnold Ziff commented, it was a 'problem raising 50% of the total income that we require for the annual budget' and, as two colleagues confirmed,

> Without the Variety Show the [then] Jewish Board of Guardians would cease to exist in its present form and would not be able to carry out the vast amount of work that it is doing continually throughout the year.
>
> The Variety Show raises almost half of the income of the Board. Without it … the Board would find it very hard to carry on without drastically curtailing the scope of its work.[12]

Hence, the Variety Show was an essential cog in the wheel of philanthropic endeavour, but also, in attracting a wide range of Jewish sponsors, advertisers and ticket holders, had a unifying effect in reinforcing Jewish identity.

In the early 1970s, the programme comprised local cultural groups, such as the Leeds Jewish Choral Society led by Monty Simons, together with semi-professional artists. Later, the organisers became more ambitious and successful and were able to attract nationally known entertainers. Ken Dodd appeared four times (1975, 1979, 1981, 1988) and Victoria Wood twice (1991, 1992), while other genuine 'stars' included Frankie Vaughan (himself from Leeds, 1983), Stephane Grappelli (1980), Jimmy Tarbuck (1982), Marti Webb (1986) and Little and Large (1987). By the end of the century, it had ceased to be financially viable to take over a whole theatre and so the strategy changed to the purchase of blocks of tickets for an existing show, while still retaining the very successful fundraising brochure. More recently, the policy has diversified further to the organising of dinners with national speakers, such as Ruby Wax (2014) and Michael Portillo (2017).[13] The Welfare Board and its income generating activity have acted as a powerful source of Jewish cohesion and identity.

The Leeds Jewish Welfare Board, celebrating its 140th anniversary in 2018, has been an important part of the Jewish community infrastructure and plays a vital role in meeting individual social needs. Thanks to state welfare there is little need for basic poverty relief, but there is a large and growing requirement to enhance the quality of life for the elderly, the isolated, those with mental problems or dealing with the traumas of family breakdown. The Board is but one (though a vital one) of the institutions and organisations which serve and sustain a viable and active Jewish community in Leeds. Where in previous generations Jewish educational provision was limited to the after school and Sunday morning *cheder*, there is now a full complement of all age Jewish schools – the Deborah Taylor Nursery, the Brodetsky Primary School and the Jewish Free School for secondary education (reducing the need for Orthodox parents to send their children to King David School in Manchester). The Free School, which started with painfully small numbers in 2013 (now about 100 pupils), is seen as a key to the future and, for example, the *Jewish Chronicle*, ran the headline 'High school raises hopes for stability in the long term'.[14] All the schools are located on the Henry Cohen campus (formerly the George Littleton) in Alwoodley, on a site provided originally by the departing Moor Allerton Golf Club when it relocated to Wike. Now co-located on the campus is the Zone, which provides a range of child and youth social activities, together with the scouts, the Maccabi football teams and four Jewish youth groups. It is also the location for the Welfare Board intergenerational project of the community allotment.

The campus is a valuable community asset, as is the MAZ Centre which is busy daily, serving kosher food, providing exercise and health classes, organising educational and leisure events and providing a home to several charities, thus facilitating coordinated philanthropic initiatives. Adjacent to the Centre are the sheltered flats and houses of the Leeds Jewish Housing Association, a pioneering social housing organisation with a deserved national reputation. The Association now houses some 10% of the Leeds Jewish population, mostly in rented properties specially designed to meet to needs of the elderly and infirm, with on-call support. For those Jewish men and women unable to sustain independent living, there is the Donisthorpe Hall care home providing some 180 beds. In recent times, Donisthorpe has had some serious quality concerns, following critical quality inspection reports. Recovery plans have been put in in place to permit this high-quality care facility to survive and prosper.

The religious life of Leeds is sustained by four main synagogues, all conveniently located within walking distance (an important aspect of Sabbath observance) of the main areas of Jewish residence. One synagogue supports a Jewish bakery, while another sustains the remaining kosher butcher. All the synagogues have extensive programmes of educational, leisure and Zionist activities. It is estimated that synagogue membership comprises about 4,300 people, with a further 2,500 or so identifying themselves as Jewish but without current synagogue affiliation. The very active and successful Leeds Jewish

Representative Council speaks for the whole Jewish community, irrespective of religious commitment or observance.

Despite falling numbers, all these institutions help to sustain and give form to a viable community. As Waterman concluded from the household survey conducted in 2001,

> The Leeds Jewish community is still robust and active ... and comprises myriad voluntary associational activities, all of which contribute to the accumulation of social capital within the Jewish community.[15]

The history of the Jewish community in Leeds is a story of social mobility and economic success. Much of that progress has been sustained by the educational achievements of successive generations. The noted educational proficiency of second-generation pupils in the predominantly Jewish schools, such as Lovell Road, is now echoed in the fourth generation, where 80% of Leeds Jewish school leavers go on to higher education, more than double the national average. Abject poverty and unemployment among the Jewish community are now a thing of the past, though the work of the Welfare Board explodes the myth that all Jews are wealthy. In common with the wider society, the community is ageing, which not only generates increasing welfare needs, but also reduces the pool of volunteers to keep some organisations active. Some stalwart bodies such as B'nai Brith are dwindling in numbers and a few ladies Zionist groups have dissolved as members have aged. Yet if some beloved and previously active cultural bodies – such as the Jewish Orchestra, the Proscenium Players and Limelight – have disappeared, there are now annual cultural and educational events, such as Millim or Limmud, which attract large numbers.

The success and social progress of the community since its late-Victorian refugee origins were the result of the industriousness, dedication, entrepreneurial flair and inventiveness of the people themselves. Yet this was not achieved in a vacuum and we should not underestimate the importance of Leeds itself in providing a supportive and open environment in which the Jewish community could thrive. Despite occasional incidents of anti-Semitism (small in comparison with the frequent derogatory insults common in the 1930s), Leeds is a relatively trouble-free and tolerant host urban community. Above all, its changing and growing economy produced the ideal context for the talents of the immigrants and their children to flourish. It was and continues to be a diverse economy and this can be illustrated in the range of businesses which produced some of the noted benefactors to the Jewish community and its institutions, such as Montague Burton and Bernard Lyons (clothing), Arnold Ziff (shoe retail and property), Manny Cussins (furniture), Leslie Silver (paint) and Louis Harris (building). The transformation of the Leeds economy from manufacture to services now provides new opportunities in the professions and internet-based industries, in which the grandchildren and great-grandchildren of the original families (as well as Jewish incomers) can build successful careers. Less divided than in previous generations, the Jewish community remains viable and thriving, geographically compact and cohesive, enabling those who are Jewish to express their Jewish identity and commitment in the manner most satisfying to themselves. And it is Leeds where they live and it is Leeds that has sustained them. As the Lord Mayor of Leeds commented after attending a play as part of the Welfare Board's 140th commemoration: 'How blessed we are, as a city, to have all these disparate communities, and how blessed we are that they can all live in harmony.'[16] That is a fine postscript to this history of the Jewish community in Leeds.

Conclusion

Looking back over nearly two centuries of Jewish life in Leeds, it is possible to discern some key developments and themes which have illuminated this narrative.

The most important feature of the community's past is its *demographic history*. This is characterised by slow initial development, intense rapid growth in a single generation, a plateau of three or four decades, followed by a half century of steady decline. Late-Victorian and Edwardian Leeds received a flood of East European migrants and refugees, which increased the Jewish community more than tenfold in some twenty years. This posed enormous challenges of absorption both by the city and the community. Some contemporary estimates put the size of the community at 25,000 as early as 1914. This is probably an over-estimate, but this figure was commonly quoted from the 1920s through to the 1950s and the mantra of 5% of the Leeds population being Jewish (the highest proportion of any British city, though not of course the highest number) became something of a self-righteous test of community confidence. It is noteworthy that those historians who challenged this often quoted figure, such as Krausz and Freeman, were sometimes roundly criticised by community leaders. Estimating the Jewish population without reliable census data is beset by methodological difficulties around such issues as synagogue membership, family size, birth, marriage and death rates, and the particular algorithm used to calculate the statistical relationship between them and community size. Whatever the figure (and it was probably about 20,000 rather than 25,000), there has been a slow and steady decline from the mid-twentieth century to the present, which has resulted in the current community being no more than one-third of the size of its peak population. This is not unique to Leeds, and many traditional centres of Jewish life, such as Birmingham, Liverpool, Glasgow and Hull, have experienced a similar or even more severe decline.

Most of the chapters of the book refer to *fragmentation and division* as historically important, and perhaps distinctive, features of the Leeds Jewish community. There were, as elsewhere, tensions between the existing community and the newcomers, whose arrival disrupted existing urban relationships. The latter disparaged the former as the *englischer* whose religious observance contrasted sharply with the orthodoxy of the incomers. Nor were the new arrivals themselves united. Though most, if not all, hailed from the same broad region of the Russian Empire – which gave the Leeds community its 'Litvak' character – there were geographical loyalties which expressed themselves in divided activities in the new country, echoing the distinctive urban identity of their former home. Reference has been made to the countless small synagogue communities which differentiated themselves by references to faraway names and places. The *landsman* nexus also spawned friendly societies and social activities which divided Jew from fellow Jew, now living side by side in Leeds, but retaining their previous birthplace identity. This was the fertile context in which religious fractiousness could grow and there were decades-long struggles to get universally accepted institutions, such as the *Beth Din* [religious court] or the *Shechita* Board [for ensuring the provision of kosher meat]. Even in the third quarter of the twentieth century, it could be said that the distinctive feature of Leeds was the much-quoted saying that 'rabbi refused to talk to rabbi'. With the passage of time and generational change, these divisions faded and fragmentation is no longer a feature of the modern community, having been replaced by a greater sense of coherence. Some divisions do remain and, for example, the Reform Sinai Synagogue is excluded from many community initiatives while the ultra-Orthodox remain cocooned in a religious space largely unaffected by the rest of the Leeds community. However, the sharp divisions which featured so prominently in this history are now very much a thing of the past.

In contrast to this historical fragmentation, the Jewish community has always been geographically characterised by its *residential concentration*. During the period of dramatic growth, from 1880 to about 1920, the Jewish presence was concentrated in the insalubrious Leylands, spilling over into Camp Road and North Street. Then, most Jews, often the second generation, decamped into Chapeltown, where the building of the splendid New Synagogue presaged a permanent home, but which turned out to be a forty-year sojourn to more distant suburbs. From the 1960s, the northern migration to Moortown and Alwoodley left the Chapeltown institutions, such as synagogues, the Jewish Institute, the Guardians and Zionist offices, marooned in a religiously barren environment, deprived of their lifeblood as their patrons moved away. In each of the three geographical locations (which correspond to three broad historical periods), the Jewish community has been marked by collective residential choices which clearly identified Jewish districts, in turn spawning a distinctively Jewish social and retail infrastructure. It is true that the 2011 census revealed Jews who identified themselves as such in every ward of the city. Yet, while the current Jewish population is no more than 1% of Leeds' overall population, in the Alwoodley municipal ward 15% of the voters are Jewish. Moreover, in Alwoodley and its adjacent suburbs are to be found a whole Jewish infrastructure, comprising four main synagogues, the Ziff community centre, the school campus with three Jewish schools and the Zone youth activities, the Jewish Welfare Board, the Jewish Housing Association and Donisthorpe Hall old age home.

The northerly migration up the A61 was made possible by *economic progress and social mobility*, which themselves were essentially two sides of the same coin. Examples have been given earlier in this chapter of entrepreneurial success, where Jews established the classic small- and medium-sized enterprises which underpinned the increase in income, which in turn permitted moves to higher priced housing. Already in the 1920s, Hyman Morris, with a successful wallpaper business, was living at 185 Chapeltown Road, as one of the pioneers of a trend which would become well established. It was from there that in January 1921 his daughter left to be married at a splendid wedding ceremony held at the Majestic Hotel in Harrogate, an example much emulated since.[17] Economic success allowed Jewish citizens to purchase terrace houses in Chapeltown for perhaps £600–£800 in the interwar years and a semi-detached in Moortown for £2,000–£3,000 in the 1950s and early 1960s. Economic progress was a prerequisite for the social mobility which distinguished the Leeds Jewish community from some other of the city's immigrant groups. For over three quarters of a century the Leeds community was predominantly proletarian, with the characteristic association with trade union activity and mostly left-wing political affiliation. By the end of the twentieth century, the Leeds Jewish community had become almost wholly middle class, exemplified in the successful retail, manufacturing and property businesses owned and managed by Jews and in the Jewish penetration into the professions of law, medicine (including dentistry and pharmacy), accountancy and teaching. Ironically, this social mobility contributed to the decline in numbers, since as Jews became upwardly mobile so their family size reduced. Large families were a characteristic feature of the first generation of incomers. For example, Reverend Davidson, who officiated at the Great Synagogue for over forty years, had thirteen children,[18] and many can recall extended families with multiple uncles, aunts and even more cousins. However, as in the host community, economic success and social mobility was accompanied by family planning (except among the ultra-Orthodox) which reduced the Jewish birthrate.

This economic and social progress facilitated *Jewish integration* (not assimilation) into Leeds urban society and its institutions. No doubt assimilation played some part in the reduction in the size of the community. Marrying out of the faith, which became far more common after the Second World War, inevitably weakened Jewish identity, which was often diluted further in subsequent generations, so that by the time individuals had but one Jewish grandparent or great grandparent, they were probably lost to the community. But most Leeds Jews managed to retain their Jewish identity, while at the same time living fulfilled lives within their chosen business or professional careers. The contributions of Jews to the social, economic, professional, cultural and civic life of Leeds have been significant and of a scale disproportionate to the size of the community relative to the city as a whole. Nor has anti-Semitism been a barrier to active Jewish participation in the secular life of Leeds. There were the terrible riots in 1917, increased tension in the 1930s and intermittent daubing at cemeteries or synagogues. However, Leeds has been a friendly and supportive environment in which Jews could practice their religion free from harassment, while at the same time playing a full part in the wider society. Just as these words are being written there has been well-publicised concern about alleged anti-Semitic sentiment within the Labour Party. This led Fabian Hamilton, the Jewish MP for Leeds North East, to comment,

> We want our Jewish supporters back because in my experience, the North Leeds Jewish community has not only contributed so much to the Labour Party over more than a hundred years, but also has a strong social conscience and sense of social justice. It cares deeply not only about its own community but also about the health and welfare of the whole city of Leeds and has made such an enormous contribution to it.[19]

The comment on social conscience reflects a continuous strand in the history of the community from its very beginnings in a strong sense of *social solidarity*. The commitment to charity and mutual aid exemplified not only a religious and moral obligation, but also a community social imperative. Philanthropy was in many ways the glue that bound the Jewish community together, transcending and counteracting the many fissures in Jewish society. The early creation of the Board of Guardians was partly a consequence of the desire of the community to look after its own poor and ensure that Jewish poverty should not become a burden on the city authorities. There was always an element of worry in Jewish philanthropy, often unstated, which desired the community itself to solve its own social problems, for fear that the 'Jewish question' might become a controversial issue in public debate. Sometimes this was explicit, as in the 1938 offer of the Jewish Board of Guardians to assume responsibility for the Jewish applicants for relief from the Public Assistance Committee. More often it was implied in the self-help attitude which spawned such a rich diversity of charitable and mutual aid organisations. The numerous charitable groups which addressed (and still do) a range of social, medical

The community today and its recent history 327

and physical needs, together with the collective and mutual aid bodies – such as the Jewish Institute, the Herzl Moser hospital or the B'nai Brith and the many fellowship lodges – all provided cohesiveness to the community and created social capital as a resource for community support. It was the flowering of philanthropic and collective endeavour which led the President of the Rep. Council, itself the focus of community cohesion, to conclude that the Jewish community in 2018 was 'proud, robust, confident and frankly brilliant … there is more of a communal outlook and more cases of organisations of working in collaboration'.[20]

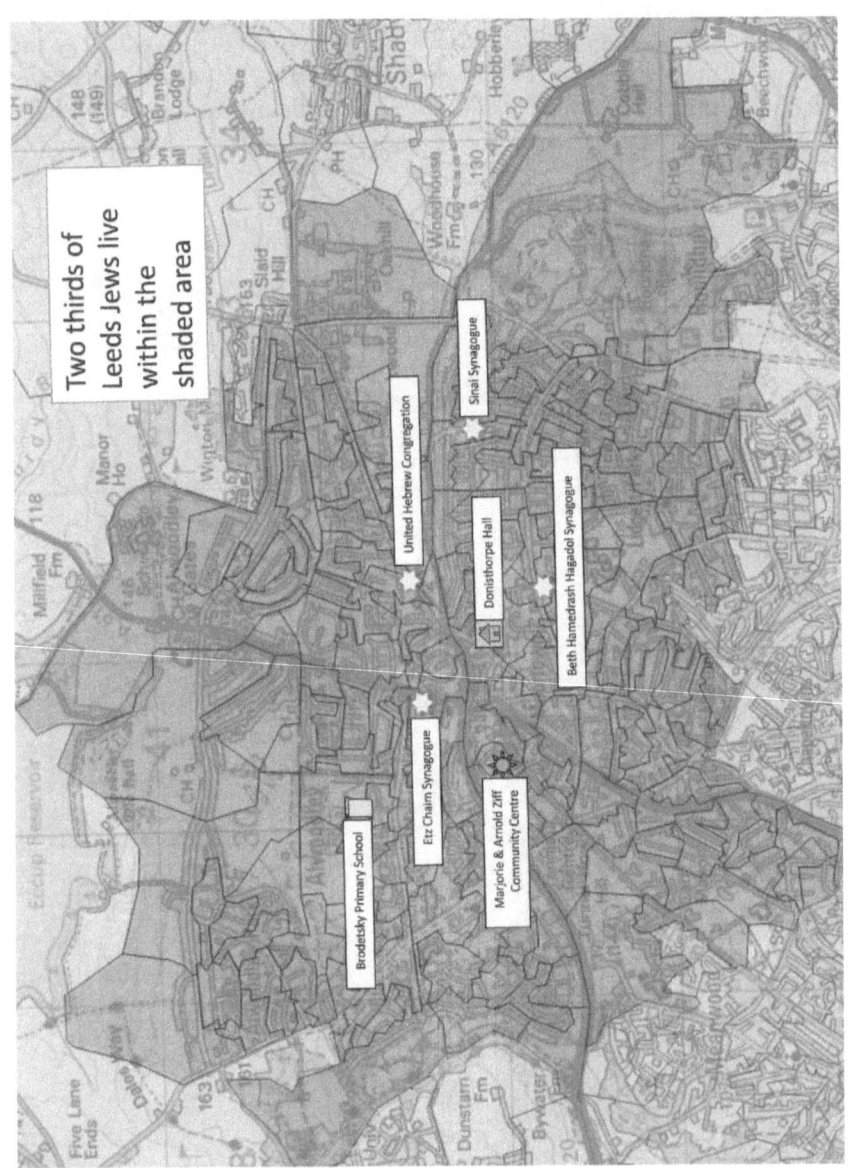

16.1 Map of main Jewish area, 2011

16.2 Sketch of Rev. M. Abrahams, 1909

16.3 Waldenberg poster, 1949

16.4 Malcolm Shedlow at work in North Street, 1953

Notes

1. L. Saipe, *A Century of Care: The History of the Leeds Jewish Welfare Board 1878–1978* (Leeds: Leeds Jewish Welfare Board, 1978), p. 10.
2. R. Unsworth and J. Stillwell (eds), *Twenty-First Century Leeds: Geographies of a Regional City* (York: PLACE Research Centre, York St John College, 2004), p. 63.
3. *Jewish Chronicle*, 4 September 1959.
4. *Leeds Jewish Representative Council. Sixtieth Anniversary* (1966). President's Report. See also BHH, *Annual Report*, 1958, p. 3.
5. B. Lyons, *The Thread is Strong: The Memoirs and Reflections of Bernard Lyons* (Leeds: np, 1981), p. 204.
6. *Jewish Chronicle*, 7 January 1994.
7. N. Bush, 'Legal Leeds', *BIMA*, 282 (2013), 20–1.
8. Figures calculated by Louis Saipe in *Leeds Jewish Representative Council. Sixtieth Anniversary* (1966).
9. *Yorkshire Evening News*, 31 October 1919.
10. *Ibid.*, 14 October 1920.
11. N. Watson, *Arnold Ziff: The Making of a Great Yorkshireman* (London: Vallentine Mitchell & Co Ltd, 2005), p. 1.
12. 56th Annual Variety Show 1970 (Brochure), p. 5; *Ibid.*, 58th 1972, p. 5.
13. Information supplied by James Denton, who was for many years chairman of the Variety Show committee.
14. *Jewish Chronicle*, 21 July 2017.
15. S. Waterman, *The Jews of Leeds in 2001: Portrait of a Community* (London: Institute for Jewish Policy Research, 2003), pp. 3–5.
16. *Leeds Jewish Telegraph*, 16 February 2018.
17. *Yorkshire Evening Post*, 19 January 1921.
18. *Leeds Mercury*, 29 December 1919.
19. Text of undelivered speech, quoted in *The Jewish Weekly*, 26 April 2018.
20. Speech of Laurence Saffer at the end of his term as President, Rep. Council AGM, 23 April 2018.

Index

Aaron, Arthur 154, 253
Aaron, Frank 253
Abrahams, Moses 52, 74, 314, 329
acculturation 139, 296–7
Adler, Hermann 16–17, 19, 21, 179
Adler, Michael 106
Adler, Nathan 13, 16, 19
Albert Grove *mikveh* 181–2, 196, 202
Alderman, Geoffrey 64, 71, 165
Ali, Mohamed 264
Aliens Act (1905) 15, 37, 56, 92, 100, 102, 115
Aliss, Peter 251
Alster, Alan 248–9, 263–5
Alwoodley area 5, 325
Amalgamated Jewish Tailors', Machiners' and Pressers' (AJTMP) trade union 55, 92–7, 191, 203
Amalgamated Union of Clothing Operatives (AUCO) 93–5
anarchism 92, 117
Andrews, Linton 280
anglicisation 71–2
Anglo-Jewry (journal) 105
anti-Semitism 4, 19, 37, 41, 56–9, 118, 126, 129–39, 160–3, 167, 216, 219, 227, 267, 280, 284, 299–300, 306–7, 326
  of exclusion 249
  institutionalised 296
  'respectable' face of 139
  'scientific' 113–14
  social 155
  in sport 237, 240, 249

Appleson, Robert 252
architects 193–4
architectural style 175, 178, 184, 195–6
Aronsfeld, C. C. 121–2, 130
art exhibitions 259
the arts, interest in 257–9
Ashkenazi Jews 11, 51, 177, 185, 188
assimilation 5–6, 12–13, 64–6, 70, 97, 114, 126, 136, 139, 155, 163, 296, 299, 318, 325–6
Association of Jewish ex-Servicemen (AJEX) 154
Astrinsky, Yehuda Leib 104, 121
athletics 253–4
Autry, Gene 157

Baden-Powell, Robert 73–4
Baines, Edward 26–7
Balfour Declaration (1917) 119, 125, 278
Barran, John 30, 84, 115, 269–70
Behrens, Edgar and Jacob 268
Bellow, Irwin 250, 287, 318
Beth Hamedrash Hagadol (BHH) Synagogue 103, 118, 154, 179–80, 183–4, 187–8, 195, 258, 313–14
Bevin, Ernest 161
Bevis Marks synagogue 11
Bialik, Chaim Nachman 274
Birmingham 4, 18, 194
Black, Horace 156
black-marketing 160–1
blood libel 10

B'nai B'rith 121, 127–8, 154, 192, 216–17, 225, 236, 254, 280, 314, 322, 327
Board of Deputies of British Jews 12–13, 278
Boards of Guardians, national and local 14–15, 51, 72, 218, 221, 226
see also Leeds Jewish Board of Guardians
bombing 153
boxing 235, 246–8
Boy Scouts 72–5, 256
Bradford 106, 153, 166, 176, 195, 268
Bradford Orthodox Synagogue (Spring Gardens) 194
bridge, game of 256
British Jewry Book of Honour (BJB) 58, 106–7
Britishness 294, 297–9, 306
Britten, Benjamin 286
Brodetsky, Manya 126, 277–8
Brodetsky School 191–3
Brodetsky, Selig 57, 120–2, 126, 132–3, 137, 162, 192, 216, 242, 276–9, 274, 281, 283
Brodie, Israel 19, 198
Brodie, James 190
Buckman, Joseph 104, 115
Building News 178
Burgess, E. E. 56–7, 125, 133
Burnett, G. Alan 191, 195
Burton, Arnold 65–6, 72
Burton, Sir Montague 65, 121, 191–2, 220, 236, 254, 272–6, 278, 281, 322
Burton's (company) 4, 122, 126, 129, 137, 150, 273–6, 311
Byzantine architectural style 184

cemeteries 182–4, 197
census records 6, 85, 102, 175, 311–12, 323, 325
Cesarani, David 2, 155
Chamberlain, Joseph 118
Chapeltown 102, 136, 149, 184, 187, 189, 216, 220, 312, 324–5
Charity Commission 227
Charity Organisation Society 217–19
Chassidishe Shul Synagogue 185–6
chevroth 51–2
Chief Rabbinate 16, 19–20
children's experience 65–8
in the Second World War 155–60
Christie, Jeff 259
Churchill, Winston 151, 163
Clavane, Anthony 50, 122, 240

clothing industry 4, 18, 43, 53–9, 83–6, 95, 104, 115, 126, 129, 149–50, 269–70, 273–6, 311, 316
Cobbett, William 26
Cohen, Barnett 217
Cohen, Darren 244
Cohen, Eta 259
Cohen, Karl ('KC') 287
Cohen, Nathan 221
Cohen, Syd 244
'Cohen count' 39–40
Collins, Nat 237, 240
communal outlook 66, 327
Communist Party 122, 133, 137–8
community coherence 225, 324
community cohesion 5, 69, 127, 139, 327
conscription 108, 151, 154
contraception 40
Cookridge Street *mikveh* 180–1
'Cousinhood' 14
Cowen, Joseph 118–19
cricket 244–6
Cromwell, Oliver 10–11
Cussins, Manny 238–40, 316, 322

Daiches, Israel Hayim 52, 103, 118, 182
Daiches, Salis and Samuel 103
Davis, Gabriel 28, 37, 267–8
Defoe, Daniel 24
Delius, Frederick 283
DellaPergola, S. 298
Delroy, Ian 255
de-mob clothing 150, 311
Dewhirst, Isaac 270
Diamond, A. S. 52, 59, 121
Diamond, Henrietta 117, 129
diaspora communities 44, 296
Dinur, Ben-Zion 65
discrimination against Jews 13, 113, 133
displaced persons (DPs) 164
Disraeli, Benjamin 14
Donisthorpe and Donisthorpe Hall 194, 321
Dytch, Dressler and Oscar 153

economic migrants 2, 115
Edward VII, King 101
Ellis, John 224
Ellis, Louis 154
emancipation, Jewish 13–14, 65, 284
emigration *see* migration
Endelman, Todd 53, 64

enemy aliens 162–3, 167
entrepreneurial spirit 316, 325
ethnic minorities 4, 297
Etz Chaim Synagogue 196
European Football Championship (2008) 298
evacuation 153, 156–61

family size 325
Fascism and anti-Fascism 122, 137–8, 155, 160–1, 249
Federation of Synagogues 19
Federation Synagogue 188
Feldman, Abraham 272
Feldman, David 64–5
Feldman, Philip 156–7
Fiddler on the Roof 37
Fingret, Peter 268
Fingret, Stanley 251
Finn, Joseph 86–90, 96
First Jewish Bazaar 126
First World War 57–8, 75, 100–10
  legacy for Leeds Jewry 108–10
  memorials of 100–3, 109, 168
football 236–41
Fountain, Frank 120–1
Fox, Joe 134, 247
Frais, Abe 137, 249–50, 271–2, 280
Frais, Jacob 84
Francis Street Synagogue 102, 187
Freedman, Murray 27, 43, 52, 54, 64, 67–8, 72–3, 101–2, 131, 133, 136, 180, 183, 198, 287
Freedman, Samuel 18, 93–6
Friend, Herman 30, 84, 115, 269–70, 317
friendly societies 105, 215–17
Frieze, Neil and Simon 252–3
fundraising in Leeds 137–8, 151, 155, 157, 161–3, 220
furniture manufacture 316

Gasworkers and General Labourers' Union (GGLU) 91–2
ghettos 1, 65, 71, 101, 103, 125, 135, 139, 150, 236
Gildersome Cemetery 100, 182–3, 267–8
Giles, Johnny 243
Gillinson, Basil 194
Glass, Marcus Kenneth 188
Glass, Simon 154
Glucksman, Rhona 253
Godfrey, Louise 317

Godlove, Louis 133
Gold, Gene 67–8
Gold, Sam and Belle 79
Goldberg, Edith Michel and Irmgard 165
Goldberg, Leslie 134, 237
Goldman, Averil 155
Goldsmid, Albert E. W. 73–4
Goldsmid, Isaac 14
golf 249–52
Goodman, Moyshe (Morris) 53, 85
Goodman, Samuel 67–8, 76, 78
Great Reform Act (1832) 27
Great Synagogue, Belgrave Street 16, 37, 102, 135, 175–7, 180, 183, 191–2, 199–200, 219–20, 268, 271
Griffiths, Eldon 250–1
Gryn, Hugo 315

Haig, Lord 108
Hall, Theo and Tilly 166
Hardie, Keir 93–4
Harehills Cemetery 184
Harewood, Countess of 286
Harris, Louis 242, 322
Harrison, Tony 50
Hazlitt, William 26
Hertz, J. H. 16, 19
Hertz, Martin 36–7
Herzl, Theodor 114, 116, 118
Herzl-Moser Hospital 116, 216, 327
Herzl-Moser Institute 119
Herzl-Moser Synagogue 189
Hill Top Cemetery 182–3, 197
Hinchcliffe, G. 158
Hirsch, Paul 218–20, 268–9, 271
Hirschell, Solomon 13
Hobits, Louis 256
Holbeck Moor, Battle of (1936) 137
Holocaust, the 122, 167
Home Guard 152
Honeyman, Katrina 129, 275
housing *see* residential patterns; social housing
Hurwitz, Alter 131, 314, 316–17
Hurwitz, Max 121
Hurwitz, R. H. 221–4
Hurwitz, Tsvi Hirsch 182

identity
  ethnic 64
  Jewish 5–6, 21, 43, 64–6, 114, 139, 294–307, 318, 326

identity (cont.)
   'Leeds Jewish' 50–1, 59–60
   national 294
   religious 127, 298, 300
   social 300
identity politics 297
image of Jewry 294–5
immigration *see* migration
industrial revolution 1, 12, 23–6
integration into society 6, 40, 59, 63, 66–71, 74–7, 105, 108, 126, 129, 136, 139, 150, 221, 286, 295–8, 318, 325
intermarriage 149, 326
internment 163
Israel, State of 21, 41, 122, 161–2, 276, 304–6, 312–13
Israeli sports teams 298–9

Jakobovits, Immanuel 19, 285, 315
The Jewish Chronicle 51, 58–60, 65, 71–2, 104, 115, 120, 127, 132, 156, 163, 178, 187, 216, 249, 321
Jewish communities 1–4, 27–8, 42–4, 50, 55, 59, 63–77, 175–7
   changes seen in 295, 311
   community buildings in Leeds 190–3
   divisions within and between 65–72, 76–7, 91, 102–5, 115–16, 129–30, 163, 294, 313–15, 323–4
   history of 9–11
   leadership of 68
   mutual support in 69, 215–17, 326
   ties and communal life in 74, 308
Jewish Historical Society 106
Jewish Institute 130, 134, 154, 191, 195, 236–7, 240, 254, 280, 327
Jewish Lads Brigade (JLB) 71–5
Jewish National Fund (JNF) 22, 313
Jewish Territorial Society (IZO) 118
The Jewish World 73
Jewish Year Book 38–45, 127, 132
Joseph, Barnett 27
Joseph, Ernest 194
Joseph, Sir Keith 194, 225, 232, 318
Josephy, Henry 268
Joshua, Antony 265
Judean Club 134, 192–3, 236, 254–6
Judeophobia 12

Kingsway Cinema 190
Kramer, Jacob 132, 259, 281–3, 290

Krasner, Gerald 239
Krausz, Ernst 42–3, 323
Kropotkin, Peter 93–4
Kudenko, Irina 50

Labour Party 18, 56, 122, 161
The Lancet 49–59, 86
Lawrence, Johnny 251–2
Leeds
   city of 4–5, 23, 26–30, 36, 42–4, 51–3, 57–9, 63, 73–6, 84, 102, 108, 126–7, 267, 323, 326
   maps of 31–3
   as a reception area in wartime 159
Leeds Central High School 158–9, 283
Leeds City Council / Corporation 26, 28–9, 180–1, 192, 317
Leeds Express (newspaper) 89
Leeds Hebrew Literary Society 116
Leeds Intelligencer (newspaper) 26–7
Leeds Jewish Board of Guardians 51, 155, 217–27, 269, 271, 280, 311, 326
   offices 230
Leeds Jewish Housing Association (LJHA) 225–6, 321
Leeds Jewish Representative Council (LJRC) 108, 216, 280, 308, 314–15, 321–2, 327
Leeds Jewish Welfare Board 226–7, 311, 319–22
Leeds Jewish Workers' Burial and Trading Society 51, 104, 183, 187–8
Leeds Jewish Young Men's Association 236, 254, 268
   see also Jewish Institute
Leeds Maccabi Football Club 241
Leeds Mercury (newspaper) 26–7, 217
Leeds Parish Church 241, 319
Leeds Piano Competition 258, 285–7
Leeds Talmud Torah education board 192–3, 216, 255, 277
Leeds Trades Council 92–4
Leeds United Football Club 50, 134, 237–40, 287
Leigh, Mike 160
leisure activities 254–6
Lestchinsky, Jacob 17–18
Lester, Bernard 243
Lester, Philippa 154
Levine, Abraham 161
Levy, D. 105

Leylands district 49–53, 56–9, 67, 71, 76, 86, 100–2, 107, 109, 115, 125–6, 134–5, 138, 149, 175–81, 184, 187, 197, 216, 246–7, 272–3, 286, 312, 324
Liberalism and the Liberal Party 19, 275, 284
Lightman, Harold 271
Lightman, Stanley 217
Lightman, Victor 29, 220, 231, 271–2, 316
Limelight and Young Limelight 257–8, 322
Lipman, Michael 154
Lipman, Vivian 14, 150, 162
living standards 130
Lloyd George, David 19
Lord Mayoral duties 280, 285
Louis Street Synagogue 188
Lovell Road School 159, 237, 240, 283, 322
Lubelski, David 84–6, 90–1
Lubelski, Jack 74
Lyons, Bernard 225–8, 250, 255, 287, 313–15, 322
Lyons, Lewis 96
Lyons, Rudolph 317
Lyons, Samuel H. 217

Macaulay, Thomas Babington 27
McKenzie, Alistair and Charles 250
Macmillan, Harold 311
Maguire, Tom 56, 90–1
Manchester 4, 76, 295
Manning, Henry Edward 17
Manning, Irving 256
Manning, Joe 101
Mariempoler Synagogue 179, 184, 190
Marks, Michael 270–2
Marks, Minnie 144–6
Marshall, John and John junior 24, 27, 37
Mason, Harry 134, 247
Mass Observation 161
Matthay, Tobias 286
May, Fiona 253
May, Phil 283
MAZ Centre 193, 258, 319, 321
Mellor, Kay 258
Members of Parliament 13
Merrion Centre 319
middle-class Jewry 109, 130–1, 138, 162, 268, 296, 311, 325
Middlesbrough 23
migration
    Jewish 1–3, 12, 15–20, 29–30, 37–8, 42, 50–3, 56, 63–72, 76–7, 92, 101–3, 134, 176, 312–13, 323

'push' and 'pull' factors in 2–3
'voluntary' and 'forced' 2
mikvaot 180–2, 196, 202
military service 106–8, 152–4, 274, 312
mobility *see* migration; social mobility
Montefiore, Claude 119
Montefiore, Sir Francis 116, 118
Montefiore, Moses 13–14
Moor Allerton Golf Club 4, 133, 137, 192, 217, 236, 252, 280, 321
Moor Allerton Sports and Social Centre 256
Moortown 5, 150, 159, 190, 193–4, 324
Morris, Albert 226, 238
Morris, Hyman 132–3, 137, 216, 220–1, 224, 229, 279–81, 288–9, 325
Morris, William 18
Moser, Jacob 116–17
Mosley, Oswald 137–8, 162
Mountbatten, Countess 255
multiculturalism 297, 300

national citizenship 296, 299, 307
National Jewish Community Survey (2013) 302
National Union of Tailors and Garment Workers 95, 97, 191
nationalism 114
Nazism 164, 269, 278
    see also Fascism
New Briggate Synagogue 177–9, 184
New Central Synagogue 188, 190
New Farnley Cemetery 183–4
New Synagogue, Chapeltown Road 5, 179, 184–5, 195, 204, 324
'new unionism' 91–2, 95
Newtown Picture Palace 104

O'Brien, Rosalind 64–8, 76, 115
Ognall, Sir Harry 317
Orientalism 178, 180, 184
Orthodox Judaism 19, 304–5, 314–15, 324–5
'otherness' 64–5
outdoor relief 218–19
Oxley, Bernard 243–4

Palestine 41, 113–21, 161–2
Park Estate 26
Parliamentary representation 27
patriotism 75, 164–5
Paylor, Tom 90–1

Pepys, Samuel 11
philanthropy 215, 227–8, 320, 326–7
Picture Post 151–2
piecework system 94
Pinsker, Leon 114
pogroms 113–14
Policoff, David 18
Polish Synagogue 187–8
political engagement 132, 161–2, 317–18
Poor Law 217–19, 222
population estimates 6, 15–16, 21, 23–5, 28, 35–45, 51, 58, 102, 115, 127, 149–50, 197, 312, 325
  prospects for 44
  sources of 35–6, 40, 323
poverty 14–15, 69, 130, 215, 219–22
Poylisher Yidl (newspaper) 54–5
pride in being Jewish 307
'private Jewishness' 296
professional careers for Jews 131–2, 139, 316–17
proletarian background and culture 16, 88–9, 129, 311, 325
Proscenium Players 257, 322
prostitution 105
Puritanism 10–11

Queenshill Estate 193–4, 225–6, 233

racism 296, 306
rationing 151–2
Reform Judaism 13–14, 164, 193, 303, 315, 324
refugees 2, 10, 15, 40–2, 115, 138–9, 151, 155, 162–8, 177, 323
Reginald Terrace Synagogue 189
religious education 150, 154
religious life in Leeds 103–4, 304–6
religious minorities 43–4
Relwysko, George de and George junior 248–9
residential patterns 4–5, 101–2, 115, 126, 136, 175, 179, 184, 302–3, 312, 324, 328
Revie, Don 238
rioting, anti-Jewish (1917) 100–1, 107–8, 126, 272, 314, 326
Rosenberg, Eugene 195
Rosenberg, L. 106–7, 132–3, 317–18
Rosenberg, Wilf 242, 260–1
Rosenthal, Erich 65
Rosenthal, Hirsch 249–50

Rosenthal, Jonathan 253–4
Rothschild, Anthony de 278
Rothschild, Lionel de 13–14
Rothschild, Walter 315–16
'Round Church', Bradford 195
Roundhay Park 30, 252, 319
Ruby, Paula 132
Ruby, Thelma 258
rugby league 241–4
Russia and the Russian Empire 3, 15, 29–30, 36–9, 58, 65, 69, 77, 85, 101, 106, 113–16, 177, 268, 277, 283, 324

Sadler, Sir Michael 27, 132, 277, 281–2
Saffer, Abe 156
Saffer, David 242
Saffer, Laurence 308
Saipe, Louis 59, 121, 187
Samuels, David 279–80
scholarships 130–1
schools 19, 64, 67, 127, 130, 150, 156–9, 191–2, 196–8, 321–2
Sclare, Moses 55–6, 83, 87, 92–5, 318
Seaton, Bernard ('Seggy') 245–6
second- and third-generation residents 64, 125, 149, 190, 216, 322–3
Second World War 41, 149–69, 197
  on the home front 151–5
  home life in 160
sectarianism 115–16, 138
secularisation 155, 197, 300, 305, 312
self-help tradition 126, 215, 220, 326
Sephardic Jews 11–12, 188
Shechita Board 127, 324
Sheinblum family 135, 284
Shooman, Bernard 244, 262
Silman, Julius 131–2, 134–5
Silver, Bernard 63, 150, 279
Silver, Leslie 122, 238–9, 287, 319, 322
Silverman, Julius 130, 318
Simon, Ernst and Kurt 166
Simon, Sydney 238
Sinai Reform Synagogue 315, 324
Singers Hill Synagogue 4
slum clearance 135, 138, 184, 197, 225
Smith, Issy 133
Smith, Stephen Ernest 176
social capital 303, 327
social cohesion *see* community cohesion
social control 16, 134
social housing 225

social mobility 3–5, 74, 130, 296, 311, 316, 322, 325
social solidarity 326
socialising 134, 149, 254
socialism 17–18, 89–91, 104, 285
Socialist League 95
socio-cultural attributes of Jewish identity 302–3
Sokolow, Nahum 119–21
Spencer, Thomas and Simon 270
spirituality 305
sporting activities 133–4, 235–54
  traditional Jewish view of 236, 240
stereotyping of Jews 137, 139, 160
Sterne, Ernest 119, 121, 131–2, 187
strike action 89–96, 122, 275
subcontracting of work 84
subdivisional production system 84–9
suburbanisation 149, 175, 197–8, 297
Sumrie, Charles 224–6
Sumrie, Esther 69–70
Sunlight, Joe 185
sweated labour 88, 149, 191
Sweeney, James 56, 87, 90–1
Sykes, Sir Mark 120
synagogues 2, 19, 28, 37, 70, 77, 116, 149–50, 175–80, 183–6, 195–8, 321
  attendance at 52
  see also individual institutions

Tagger, Harry 144–5
Tagger, Jenny 143
tailoring *see* clothing industry
teachers 152–6
  training of 105
Tebbit, Norman 298
Teeman, Louis 56–7, 132–3, 136, 159, 281
Teeman, Ronnie 243
tennis 252–3
tolerant attitudes in society 13
trade unionism 3–4, 17–18, 55–9, 83–5, 88–96
Trades Union Congress (TUC) 18, 56, 87, 93

Uganda 118
Umanski, Augusta 131, 317
Umanski, Moses ('Jack') 116–17
Umanski, Rebecca 117, 119
Union of Orthodox Hebrew Congregations 19

United Garment Workers Trade Union (UGWTU) 56, 83, 95, 191
United Hebrew Congregation (UHC) 100–1, 109, 127, 175, 177, 183–6, 190, 195, 201, 205, 313–14
United Ladies' Tailors' Trade Union (ULTTU) 96–7
United Synagogue 19–20
university education 130–1

Vaughan, Frankie 320
victimisation 90
Victoria, Queen 29, 101
Villiers, Cyril 241, 254
Villiers, Joan 254
Dos Volk (newspaper) 117

Waldenberg, Shlomo ('Sam') 316
Waldenberg Brothers (company) 330
Walsh, Brian 244, 317
Walsh, Joshua ('Jos') 117, 119, 136, 275, 283–5
war memorials 100–3, 109–10, 168
Waterman, Fanny 258–9, 285–7
Waterman, S. 39, 322
Webb, Sidney and Beatrice 88, 222
Weizmann, Chaim 118–19, 274
'whistle blowers' 223
White, Arnold 56
white slaving 105
Wilson, Sir Charles 121
Winchevsky, Morris 54–5, 85–6
Wolfe, (Rachel) Ada 285
women's rights 306
women's work 129, 152
workhouses 218–19
working-class Jewry 53–4, 76, 120, 122, 150
working conditions 86–91, 129–30, 274–5
workshops in tailoring 54, 83–7, 90–1, 95–6, 115
World Zionist Congress (Basle, 1897) 114–15
wrestling 248–9

xenophobia 12, 74–5

Yiddish language 127, 149, 197, 269
Yorkshire Evening Post 125–6, 133
Yorkshire Factory Times 94
The Yorkshire Post 117, 155, 249
Yorkshire pride 50, 56, 59

Yorkshire regiments in the First World War 107

Zangwill, Israel 20, 118
zero hours contracts 274
Ziff, Arnold 238, 287, 311, 318–22
Ziff, Fanny 129
Ziff, Max 224, 318
Ziff, Michael 318
Ziff community centre *see* MAZ Centre
Zionism 21, 113–22, 125–6, 155, 162, 274–9, 284, 298, 300, 303–4, 313
  origins of the movement 116–17
  'practical' and 'political' 114, 118
Zionist organisations 117–22, 138, 189
'the Zone' (youth club) 193, 255–6, 321
Zossenheim, Maximillian 37